RESISTING PUNITIVENESS IN EUROPE?

This volume provides an important and exciting contribution to the knowledge on punishment across Europe.

Over the past decade, punitiveness has been studied through analyses of 'increased' or 'new' forms of punishment in western countries. Comparative studies, on the other hand, have illustrated important differences in levels of punitiveness between these countries and tried to explain these differences by looking at risk and protective factors. Covering both quantitative and qualitative dimensions, this book focuses on mechanisms interacting with levels of punitiveness that seem to allow room for less punitive (political) choices, especially within a European context: social policies, human rights and a balanced approach to victims' rights and public opinion in constitutional democracies.

The book is split into three sections:

1. *Punishment and Welfare.* Chapters look into possible lessons to be learned from characteristics and developments in Scandinavian and some Continental European countries.
2. *Punishment and Human Rights.* Contributions analyze how human rights in Europe can and do act as a shield against – but sometimes also as a possible motor for – criminalization and penalization.
3. *Punishment and Democracy.* The increased political attention to victims' rights and interests and to public opinion surveys in European democracies is discussed as a possible risk for enhanced levels of punitiveness in penal policies and evaluated against the background of research evidence about the wishes and expectations of victims of crime and the ambivalence and 'polycentric consistency' of public opinion formations about crime and punishments.

This book will be a valuable addition to the literature in this field and will be of interest to students, scholars and policy officials across Europe and elsewhere.

Sonja Snacken is Professor of Criminology, Penology and Sociology of Law at the Vrije Universiteit Brussel and Research Fellow at the Straus Institute for the Advanced Study of Law and Justice at the New York University School of Law. She is a member of the Editorial board of *Punishment and Society* and *Déviance et Société*, and President of the Council for Penological Cooperation of the Council of Europe.

Els Dumortier is Professor in Youth Criminology and Constitutional Criminal Law at the Vrije Universiteit Brussel. Her research focuses on questions concerning (the effectiveness of) children's rights in the domain of juvenile justice, both in contemporary times and in the past (twentieth century).

RESISTING PUNITIVENESS IN EUROPE?

Welfare, human rights and democracy

Edited by Sonja Snacken and Els Dumortier

Routledge
Taylor & Francis Group

LONDON AND NEW YORK

First published 2012
by Routledge
2 Park Square, Milton Park, Abingdon, Oxon, OX14 4RN

Simultaneously published in the USA and Canada
by Routledge
711 Third Avenue, New York, NY 10017

Routledge is an imprint of the Taylor & Francis Group, an informa business

British Library Cataloguing in Publication Data
A catalogue record for this book is available from the British Library

Library of Congress Cataloguing in Publication Data
Resisting punitiveness in Europe : welfare, human rights, and democracy/
edited by Sonja Snacken and Els Dumortier.
p. cm.
1. Punishment--Europe. 2. Public welfare--Europe. 3. Human rights--Europe.
4. Democracy--Europe. I. Snacken, Sonja. II. Dumortier, Els.
HV7342.A62011 R47 2011
364.6094--dc22
2011006343

ISBN 978-0-415-67892-6 (hbk)
ISBN 978-0-415-67893-3 (pbk)
ISBN 978-0-203-80665-4 (ebk)

Typeset in Bembo
by GCS, Leighton Buzzard, Bedfordshire

MIX
Paper from
responsible sources
FSC
www.fsc.org   FSC® C004839

Printed and bound in Great Britain by
TJ International Ltd, Padstow, Cornwall

CONTENTS

FIGURES

TABLES

CONTRIBUTORS

Milena Abbiati is a PhD psychologist. The theme underlying her research focus, which deals primarily with identity, violence, coping and social regulation, is the interest in the intersection of emotion and cognition as well as social behaviors. She worked at the Law Faculty in Geneva for the 'Law and Emotions' project. She investigated how lay support and experience of the criminal justice system relate to the emotions and coping of victims of interpersonal violence. In particular, she studied to what extent these to factors could help victim's recovery with the purpose to constitute a set of guiding rules concerning how best to interact with and support different kinds of victim, with a particular focus on violence against women. She is Chief of Research at the Sex Crime Unit at the Psychiatric State Lausanne Hospital, Switzerland.

Ivo Aertsen is Professor of Criminology at the KU Leuven (Belgium). He holds degrees of psychology and law from the same university. His main fields of research and teaching are Victimology, Penology and Restorative Justice. Within the Leuven Institute of Criminology, he coordinates the Research Line on Restorative Justice. Dr Aertsen has been chair of the European Forum for Restorative Justice from 2000 to 2004, and has coordinated COST Action A21 on Restorative Justice research in Europe from 2002 to 2006. He is an editorial board member of several journals and is involved in various practice- and policy-oriented partnerships, at both national and international level.

Paul De Hert is an international human rights expert. The bulk of his work is devoted, but not limited, to criminal law and technology and privacy law. He is Professor at the Vrije Univesiteit Brussel, where he teaches and has taught several courses in the area of Criminal Law, International and European Criminal Law, Human Rights, Legal Theory and Constitutional Criminal Law. He is Director of the VUB Research Group on Fundamental Rights and Constitutionalism (FRC), Director of the Department of Interdisciplinary Studies of Law (Metajuridics) and core member of the research group Law, Science, Technology and Society (LSTS). He is an associate professor at Tilburg University where he teaches 'Privacy and Data Protection'. He is a member of the editorial boards of several national and international scientific journals such as the *Inter-American and European Human Rights Journal* (Intersentia), *Criminal Law and Philosophy* (Springer) and *The Computer Law and Security Review* (Elsevier). He is co-editor in chief of the *Supranational Criminal Law Series* (Intersentia) and the *New Journal of European Criminal Law* (Intersentia).

David Downes is Professor Emeritus of Social Policy at the London School of Economics and a founder member of the Mannheim Centre for Criminology and Criminal Justice. His books include *The Delinquent Solution* (1966), *Gambling, Work and Leisure* (main author) (1976), (with Paul Rock) *Understanding Deviance* (1982; 5th edn, rev. 2007), *Contrasts in Tolerance: Postwar Penal Policy in The Netherlands and England and Wales* (1988) and (co-ed.) *Crime, Deviance and Social Control: From Moral Panics to States of Denial – Essays in Honour of Stanley Cohen* (2007). He is currently working jointly with Tim Newburn and Paul Rock on the official history of criminal justice policy in England and Wales from 1965 to 1997.

Els Dumortier has a Master's degree in Law and Criminology and a PhD in Criminology. She is full-time Professor in Youth Criminology and Constitutional Criminal Law at the Faculty of Law and Criminology at the Vrije Universiteit Brussel, Belgium. Her research focuses on questions concerning (the effectiveness of) children's rights in the domain of youth justice and on the (punitive) practices of the youth court both in contemporary times and in the past (twentieth century). Currently, Els Dumortier is particularly interested in judicial trajectories of young delinquents and in children as victims of institutional violence. She participates in several national and international scientific networks in the domain of juvenile justice (Dutch, English and French speaking), both contemporarily focused and historical.

Serge Gutwirth is Professor of Human Rights, Legal Theory, Comparative Law and Legal Research at the Faculty of Law and Criminology of the Vrije Universiteit Brussel (VUB), where he studied law and criminology and also obtained a postgraduate degree in technology and science studies. Serge Gutwirth founded and still chairs the VUB Research Group Law, Science Technology and Society. He publishes widely in Dutch, French and English. Among his recent co-edited publications are *Privacy and the Criminal Law* (Intersentia 2006), *Safeguards in a World of Ambient Intelligence* (Springer, 2008), *Profiling the European Citizen* (Springer 2008), *Reinventing Data Protection?* (Springer 2009), *Data Protection in a Profiled World* (Springer 2010) and *Computers, Privacy and Data Protection: An Element of Choice* (Springer 2011). Currently, Serge Gutwirth is particularly interested both in technical legal issues raised by technology (particularly in the field of surveillance, data protection and privacy) and in more generic issues related to the articulation of law, sciences, technologies and societies.

Dan Kaminski holds an MA in Law, an MA in Criminology and a PhD in Criminology. He is Full Professor of Criminology at the School of Criminology of the University of Louvain-la-Neuve (UCL) and director of the CRID&P (Interdisciplinary Research Centre on Deviance and Penality). He is a member of the editorial board of *Déviance et société* and *Revue de droit pénal et de criminologie*. His major publications include: co-editor *L'institution du droit pénitentiaire. Enjeux de la reconnaissance des droits des détenus* (2002); editor *L'usage pénal des drogues* (2003); author *Entre criminologie et droit pénal. Un siècle de publications en Europe et aux Etats-Unis* (1995) and *Pénalité, management, innovation* (2010).

Stein Kuhnle has been Professor of Comparative Politics, University of Bergen, since 1982, and Professor of Comparative Social Policy at the Hertie School of Governance, Berlin, since 2006. He has also been an Adjunct Professor at the Centre for Welfare State Research, University of Southern Denmark, Odense, since 2005. Among his recent books are: *The Nordic Welfare State* (in Chinese) (Shanghai: Fudan University Press 2010), edited with Chen Yinzhang, Klaus Petersen and Pauli Kettunen; *Normative Foundations of the Welfare State: The Nordic Experience*, ed. with Nanna Kildal (London: Routledge 2005); *Survival of the European Welfare State* (ed.) (London: Routledge 2000).

Noëlle Languin is a sociologist and has worked as a researcher at CETEL (Centre d'étude, de technique et d'évaluation législatives) at the Faculty of Law, University of Geneva. She has directed and published several research topics in the field of Sociology of Law. Her work has essentially focused on liability law, respresentations of the penal sanction and the place of the victim in the penal process.

Tapio Lappi-Seppälä has been the Director of the National Research Institute of Legal Policy since 1995 and a member of the Finnish Academy of Sciences. Alongside his current position he has been acting as a part-time Professor in Criminology and Sociology of Law at the University of Helsinki. His long career as a senior legislative adviser in criminal law in the Ministry of Justice includes the membership and chair of several law reform committees. He has actively taken part in international cooperation in criminal justice issues in the Scandinavian Research Council for Criminology, Council of Europe, in the International Penal and Penitentiary Foundation (Vice President 2005–9) and in the European Society of Criminology (Member of the Board 2008–10). His publications of around 200 titles include books, research reports and articles in criminology, penal policy, sentencing and the system of sanctions.

Miklós Lévay is Professor of Criminology and Criminal Law and head of the Department of Criminology at Eötvös Loránd University (ELTE), Budapest, Hungary. He is also a judge of the Constitutional Court of Hungary. Between 1981 and 2006 he worked for the Faculty of Law, University of Miskolc. He is a member of the Directory Board of the Hungarian Society of Criminology, a member of the Scientific Committee of the International Society of Criminology and a member of the editorial board of the *European Journal of Criminology*. He is the president of the European Society of Criminology. His research interests primarily include penal law and criminological issues related to drugs and drug policies, juvenile justice, relations between social change and crime and the constitutional limits of criminalization. Some of his most important publications available in English, include: '"Social exclusion": a thriving concept in contemporary criminology: social exclusion and crime in Central and Eastern Europe', *Penal Policy, Justice Reform, and Social Exclusion*, ed. Kauko Aromaa. Helsinki: HEUNI, No. 48 (2007): 7–26; 'Criminology, crime and criminal justice in Hungary' (with Klára Kerezsi), *European Journal of Criminology*, 5(2) 2008: 239–60.

Philippe Mary holds a Master's degree in Sociology and a PhD in Criminology. He is Full Professor of Criminology, Penology and Criminal Policy at the School of Criminology of the Université Libre de Bruxelles (ULB). He is an Associated Researcher to the International Centre for Comparative Criminology (Montreal). He is a member of the editorial board of *Déviance et société*, *Champ pénal/Penal field* and *Revue de droit pénal et de criminologie*. He is the author of *Révolte carcérale. Changements et logique pérenne de la prison* (Story Scientia 1988), *Délinquant, délinquance et insécurité: un demi siècle de traitement en Belgique (1944–1997)* (Bruylant 1998) and *Insécurité et pénalisation du social* (Labor 2003).

Jacky Nagels has been Professor in Political Economy at the Université Libre de Bruxelles since the 1980s and Professor Emeritus since 2002. As a full-time professor he lectured on several courses on political economy in general, on the transition from a planned economy to a free market economy and on the history of economic thinking. He has written six books as a single author, including *Eléments d'économie politique, critique de la pensée unique* (1997). In addition he has also directed several readers such as *Contre-projet pour l'Europe*, edited by the Groupe d'Economie Marxiste over which he presided. Between 1967 and 2006 he also published more than 60 articles and contributions at scientific conferences.

Mina Rauschenbach holds a PhD in Social Sciences from the Faculty of Social and Political Sciences of the University of Lausanne as well as a Master's (MSc) Degree in Forensic Psychology from Glasgow Caledonian University and a Master's Degree (DEAAPS) in Social Psychology from the University of Geneva. Her doctoral thesis concerned the role of legal and moral dimensions in the attribution of criminal responsibility for fatal road traffic offences. She previously took part in interdisciplinary research on the influence of emotions on the increasing importance given to the victim in the legal system and the social scene. She was also a teaching assistant for the Criminology course at the Faculty of Law of the University of Geneva. She has also worked on research into the social representation of discrimination in the framework of the European Court for Human Rights judgments concerning this issue. Curently, Mina Rauschenbach is working as a Research Fellow at the Geneva Academy of International Humanitarian Law and Human Rights on an interdisciplinary research project about the perspective of the accused of the International Criminal Tribunal for the former Yugoslavia. Her main research areas concern justice perceptions and social representations, inter-group processes in international conflicts and attributions of responsibility in the legal context, as well as the issues of victims and their experience of justice and restorative justice.

Christian-Nils Robert has been Ordinary Professor of Criminal Law and Criminology (Faculté de droit, Université de Genève, 1974–2008), Visiting Professor at the Université de Fribourg (1987–9) and the Université de Lausanne (1988) and Expert for the Federal Office of Justice (Berne, 1986–90), and is Expert for the CPT (Conseil de l'Europe, since 1991), a member of the editorial board of *Déviance et Société* (since 1977), the Chairman of the Directory Board of the Centre for Teaching and Research in Humanitarian Action (CERAH, since 2007), and Emeritus Professor and Lawyer in a law firm (Geneva, since 2009).

Sonja Snacken is Professor of Criminology, Penology and Sociology of Law at the Vrije Universiteit Brussel (Belgium), where she now holds a 'Research Fellowship' (2006–16). She is currently Research Fellow at the Straus Institute for the Advanced Study of Law and Justice at the New York University School of Law (2010–11). Her research focuses on the place, choices and consequences of punishment in Belgium and Europe. She is a member of the editorial board of *Punishment and Society* and *Déviance et Société*. She was president of the European Society of Criminology (2004–5) and has been a member since 2001 (and President since 2006) of the Council for Penological Cooperation of the Council of Europe. Recent international publications include: D. van Zyl Smit and S. Snacken, *Principles of European Prison Law and Policy* (Oxford: Oxford University Press 2009); 'Penal policy and practice in Belgium', in M. Tonry (ed.), *Crime, Punishment and Politics in Comparative Perspective*, in *Crime and Justice: A Review of Research*, Vol. 36 (Chicago: Chicago University Press 2007: 127–216); 'A reductionist penal policy and European human rights standards', *European Journal of Criminal Policy and Research*, 12, 2006: 143–64.

Françoise Tulkens has a doctorate in law, a degree in criminology and a higher education teaching certificate (*agrégation*) in law. She was a professor at the University of Louvain (Belgium) and has taught in Belgium as well as abroad – as a visiting professor at the Universities of Geneva, Ottawa, Paris I, Rennes, Strasbourg and Louisiana State University – in the fields of general criminal law, comparative and European criminal law, juvenile justice and human rights protection systems. She has authored many publications in the areas of human rights and criminal law and, recently, two reference books: *Introduction au droit pénal. Aspects juridiques et criminologiques* (with M. van de Kerchove), 9th edn (2010) and *Droit de la jeunesse. Aide, assistance et protection* (with Th. Moreau) (2000). She is doctor *honoris causa* of the Universities of Ottawa, Geneva and Limoges. Françoise Tulkens has been a Judge of the European Court of Human Rights since 1 November 1998, Section President since January 2007 and Vice-President of the Court since 1 February 2011.

Kristof Verfaillie has a Master's degree in Criminology (VUB) and in European Criminology and Criminal Justice Systems (UGent). He is a doctoral researcher at the VUB's Department of Criminology, where he is preparing a doctoral study about the relationship between public opinion and legitimate criminal justice. He has published on antisocial behaviour policies, risk assessments and scenario studies in the fields of organized crime control, proactiveness, intelligence-led policing and transnational crime control.

FOREWORD

Michael Tonry*

Resisting Punitiveness in Europe? admirably enriches understanding of why countries adopt particular punishment policies and practices. In three ways it advances the literature. It focuses neither on the world nor on a particular country, but on Europe. This necessitates attention to distinctively European values, such as the legality principle, and institutions, particularly the European Convention on and the European Court of Human Rights and the Torture Convention and Committee. It focuses not on circumstances and processes that conduce to the adoption and use of repressive policies, but on normative and structural impediments to them. This shifts emphasis away from the influence of crime trends, public opinion, political pusillanimity, late modernity and neo-liberalism, which have been discussed *ad nauseum*, and towards fresher topics: human rights protections, substantive criminal law doctrine, and victims' interests and roles. It focuses not on empirical description and grand social theory but on human rights, democratic values and the rule of law.

Knowledge usually advances through the steady accumulation, and repudiation, of insights and hypotheses. Genuine 'Eureka!' moments, when knowledge leaps tall buildings in a single bound, are rare. The search for general explanations of penal policy trends began only in the late 1980s and early 1990s, precipitated partly by recognition that American imprisonment rates tripled between 1973 and 1990 and those rates appeared to be increasing in some other countries, and partly by increased availability of more-or-less standardized national imprisonment data. Before that, there was no general academic literature and lay explanations emphasized rising crime rates, punitive public attitudes and political cynicism. After that, a series of influential publications, exemplified by David Garland's

*Michael Tonry is Bennett Professor of Law and Public Policy and Director, Institute on Crime and Public Policy, University of Minnesota, and a Senior Fellow in the Netherlands Institute for the Study of Crime and Law Enforcement.

magisterial *Culture of Control* (2001), offered general theoretical explanations focusing on heightened insecurities, neo-liberalism, 'penal populism' and various 'conditions of late modernity'.

Although a literature of general explanation continues to accumulate, general theoretical explanations at most illuminate common background conditions. They offer little insight into why particular countries' policies and practices take particular forms. This can be seen by looking at the radically different experiences of broadly similar and contiguous countries such as the United States and Canada and Finland and Sweden. All are wealthy countries affected by globalization, rapid social change, major economic dislocations and increasing population diversity. All experienced steeply rising crime rates from the early 1970s to the 1990s, and falling crime rates since. Against those common background conditions, America's imprisonment rate has quintupled since 1973 while Canada's has oscillated in a narrow band around 100 per 100,000. America in many ways starkly increased the severity of its sentencing laws; Canada did not. In Scandinavia, Finland's imprisonment rate declined by two-thirds between 1970 and 1995, a period when crime rates tripled; Sweden's also tripled, but the imprisonment rate was essentially flat.

The explanations for why countries have particular penal policies and practices are general and particular. They are general in the sense that some structural features of government and society such as income inequality, welfare expenditure, trust, legitimacy and consensual political systems seem to be associated with particular kinds of crime control policies and punishment practices. They are particular in the sense that the details of national history and culture powerfully affect both those structural features and their effects. Every developed country experienced wrenching social and economic changes in the last third of the twentieth century, for example, but only in a few did penal policies become markedly more severe.

Cultural and political values are not serendipitous. They evolve over time and are shaped by history and experience. In the United States, three factors – Evangelical Protestant fundamentalism, a conflictual political system and the history of race relations – go a long way to explain why penal policies evolved as they did in the final quarter of the twentieth century. In Eastern and Central Europe, the lingering effects of Communist rule, in concert with longer-term features of the distinctive histories and traditional cultures of individual countries, are important backdrops to contemporary policies and practices.

Research agendas in coming years should focus on this level of explanation, as do the essays in *Resisting Punitiveness in Europe?* The central questions will be different in different countries, and better questions will enrich understanding of why countries respond to crimes and criminals in the ways they do. In France, for example, why is it that French men and women have for centuries accepted the legitimacy of broadly based amnesties and pardons of offenders and prisoners? In Italy, a mass commutation in 2006 reduced the prison population by 40 per cent. There were no mass outcries. Similar policy decisions in the United States, England or the Netherlands would produce firestorms of public and political indignation. Something in Scandinavian and German history and culture resulted in the adoption of restrained penal policies for at least half a century. Explanations can be offered in the terms provided above – consensus political systems, high levels of legitimacy and trust, and so on – but they beg the question. What in the (very different) histories and cultures of those countries produced those characteristics?

Winston Churchill a century ago, when British Home Secretary, observed:

> The mood and temper of the public in regard to the treatment of crime and criminals is one of the most unfailing tests of any country. A calm, dispassionate recognition of the rights of the accused and even of the convicted criminal; ... tireless efforts towards the discovery of curative and re-generative processes; unfailing faith that there is a treasure, if you can only find it, in the heart of every man. These are the symbols which, in the treatment of crime and the criminal, mark and measure the stored-up strength of a nation, and are the sign and proof of the living virtue within it.

Resisting Punitiveness in Europe? constitutes a major step forward. Learning from and building on it, we may come better to understand why countries' policies differ so much. Maybe the fruits of that learning will enable those countries with excessively severe and inhumane policies – the United States, England and Wales, many in Eastern and Central Europe – better to mark their stored up strength and prove their living virtue.

Reference

Garland, D. (2001) *The Culture of Control: Crime and Social Order in Contemporary Society.* Oxford: Oxford University Press.

ACKNOWLEDGMENTS

First and foremost we would like to thank the participating authors of this book who remained committed to this project despite several delays. The book results from the seminar 'Factors of Criminalization – A European Comparative Approach' that was organized within the CRIMPREV Coordinated Action, financed by the European Union under the 6th Framework Programme from 2006 to 2009. The seminar was organized in April 2007 at the start of the project and aimed to look into factors enhancing or restraining primary and secondary criminalization in Europe. Most of the texts in this book are based on contributions during that seminar.

Taking into account the importance of the CRIMPREV project and seminar for the further development of this book, we would like to thank the European Union, the CRIMPREV Research Consortium and its coordinators, Dr René Lévy and Daniel Ventre, respectively Director and Secretary General of GERN (Groupe Européen de Recherches sur les Normativités, Paris) for their invaluable support throughout the CRIMPREV project. Furthermore, we would like to thank the Research Council of the Vrije Universiteit Brussel for their funding of the interdisciplinary research project 'Legitimate Criminal Justice in Times of Insecurity' (2005–9), which formed the scientific framework for this seminar and for some of the chapters in this book.

In addition we would like to thank Ms Betty Jackson of Iris Traductions (Brussels) for her excellent translations of the French contributions into English. She translated the texts without delay and with special attention to judicial jargon. Thanks also to Ms Bessie Leconte from CESDIP (Paris) for her editorial support in one of the originally French chapters.

Finally thanks to Brian Willan at Willan Publishing and to Julia Willan at Routledge, who remained confident in the end result of this book and who guided us swiftly through its publishing process.

Sonja Snacken and Els Dumortier

ABBREVIATIONS

CME	coordinated market economy
CPT	Committee for the Prevention of Torture
ECHR	European Convention on Human Rights
ECPT	European Convention for the Prevention of Torture and Inhuman and Degrading Treatment or Punishment
ECtHR	European Court of Human Rights
ESF	European Social Fund
ESS	European Social Survey
EU ICS	EU Crime and Safety Survey
EUSI	EU Studies Institute
GDP	gross domestic product
GNP	gross national product
ICPS	International Centre for Prison Studies
ICVS	International Crime Victims Survey
LIS	Luxembourg Income Study
LME	liberal market economy
NAVS	National Association of Crime Victims and Surviving Families (Japan)
NICC	National Institute of Criminalistics and Criminology (Belgium)
OECD	Organization for Economic Cooperation and Development
PDI	personal disposable income
PPP	purchasing power parity
UNCRC	UN Convention on the Rights of the Child
UNRISD	UN Research Institute for Social Development.
WVS	World Values Survey

1

RESISTING PUNITIVENESS IN EUROPE? AN INTRODUCTION

Sonja Snacken and Els Dumortier

1.1 Introduction

This book is both an end and a beginning. It is an end result of CRIMPREV, a Coordinated Action financed by the European Union under the 6th Framework Programme from 2006 to 2009, in which we organized a comparative seminar looking into factors enhancing or restraining primary and secondary criminalization in Europe. The seminar was organized in April 2007 at the start of the project. The authors of the different chapters in this book were also the original contributors to the seminar. Since that date, the field we were discussing has known significant developments. As such, this book participates in a broader movement which has developed over the last years aiming at understanding punitiveness and the mechanisms behind it by analysing both similarities (e.g. Garland 2001; Wacquant 2006) and national differences in punishment trends between countries (e.g. Tonry 2001, 2007; Whitman 2003; Cavadino and Dignan, 2006; Lacey 2008). The emphasis on 'resistance', however, indicates that this book wants to look at factors in those mechanisms that allow for *choices* to be made, primarily at the political and judicial levels. It attempts to do so within a 'European' context, in which 'Europe' is understood both in a comparative sense, looking at differences between European states, and in an institutional sense, looking at European institutions such as the Council of Europe or the European Union. We therefore do not claim to deal in this book with all the 'risk and protective factors' (Tonry 2007: 13-38) known to influence levels of punitiveness in different countries. This book wants to discuss a selection of what could be perceived as protective factors in a more horizontal, transnational way, trying to understand how these may – or may not or only partly – contribute to the aim of achieving more 'penal moderation' (Loader 2010) in Europe.

Hence the importance of the question mark in the title of the book. We do not claim that 'Europe' overall *is* resisting increased punitiveness, and there are many worrying developments to the contrary. We would rather argue that levels of punitiveness are related to such core values in European societies (and beyond) – social equality, human rights, democracy – that we should resist increasing punitiveness. This means, however, that we first have to explain *what* we understand by punitiveness and why we think it *could* be resisted at all.

1.2 The concept of punitiveness

'Punitiveness' is a complex, not always clearly defined concept. The ambivalence is already apparent in daily language. In the Oxford English Dictionary the adjective 'punitive' is explained both neutrally as 'inflicted or intended as punishment' ('punitive measures') and more quantitatively as 'extremely high' ('punitive interest rates'). The same double meaning can be found in criminological literature. 'Punitiveness' refers in general to 'attitudes towards punishment' but is mostly understood as referring to 'harsh' (cf. Whitman's *Harsh Justice*, 2003) versus 'lenient' or (better) 'moderate' attitudes to punishment (Loader 2010). The complexity doesn't end here though. The concept of punitiveness refers to a wide *variety of actors*: to 'popular' attitudes towards punishment in the so called 'public opinion' or in the media, to political discourse, to primary criminalization by legislators, to decisions taken by practitioners within the criminal justice system (police, prosecution, sentencing, implementation of sentences, release procedures, etc.), or to attitudes of revenge or forgiveness of victims of crime.

'Punitiveness' also has a *quantitative* and a *qualitative dimension*. In the criminological literature of the last decennium, 'punitiveness' has mainly been studied with reference to forms of 'increased' or 'new' punitiveness in Western countries over the last 20 or 30 years (Garland 2001; Wacquant 2004; Pratt *et al.* 2005; Kury 2008; Muncie 2008). Comparisons of levels of 'punitiveness' between countries or of historical developments in one particular country are often based on (trends in) the use of imprisonment. The most commonly used indicator is prisoner rates, i.e. the average number of prisoners per 100,000 inhabitants (i.e. 'stock'). This is but an imperfect criterion, as it results from a combination of the incarceration rate (how many persons are incarcerated over a year: flow) and the length of stay in the prison, leaving the question unanswered whether countries who incarcerate less people but for longer sentences are more or less punitive than countries incarcerating more people but for much shorter sentences. Moreover, prison rates depend on what national authorities themselves define as 'prison'. Juvenile custodial(-like) institutions, psychiatric units in prisons, asylums, etc. are not always taken into account. Pitts and Kuula (2005) have estimated that Finland via its youth welfare system may remove from home and institutionalize more children pro rata than do England and Wales. Such research reinforces concerns whether the concept of 'punitiveness' should only be measured with reference to rates of *penal* custody (Muncie 2008: 116). But 'increased' punitiveness also refers more qualitatively to a decline of rehabilitative ideals, harsher prison conditions, more emotional and expressive forms of punishment emphasizing shaming and degradation (e.g. chain gangs) or increased attention to victim's rights as opposed to rights of offenders, etc. (Garland 2001). Examples of 'new' punitiveness are found in new forms of penal power which constitute a radical departure from previous trends in punishment, such as sexual predator laws which introduce civil commitment statutes, sex offender registration and notification schemes and mass incarceration (Brown 2005: 282–6) or the 'adulteration' of youth justice (Goldson and Muncie 2006: 199).

These increased or new forms of punitiveness do not tell the whole story though. The overall picture of punishment, more particularly in Europe, is much more *diverse*. Over the same period, the death penalty has been abolished on the whole European continent.[1] Prison rates vary greatly, both in western and in eastern European countries (see Table 1.1). They have increased in several European countries, but have remained fairly stable (Scandinavian countries, Germany, Switzerland) or decreased in others (especially eastern European countries). Prisoners' rights have been reinforced through the case law of the European Court of Human Rights (ECtHR) and the European Committee for the Prevention of Torture and Inhuman or Degrading Treatment or Punishment (CPT) standards (van Zyl Smit and Snacken 2009). Restorative justice has gained political legitimacy in some countries as a valuable alternative to tackle victims' rights and interests, even in the wake of horrendous crimes (Snacken 2007). All eastern European countries have now introduced non-custodial sanctions and measures (van Kalmthout and Durnescu 2008) and treatment programmes for offenders are (re-)introduced by 'what works' evidence-based penal policies in many western and eastern European countries (Canton 2009; Bauwens and Snacken 2010). In many continental European countries the traditional 'welfare' approach to juvenile offenders remains strong and is still reflected in legislation emphasizing 'protection measures' (Junger-Tas 2006: 515; Dünkel *et al.* 2010).

TABLE 1.1 National differences: prison population rates USA and Europe 2000–2005–2008

USA	700	738	760	Russian Fed.	635	611	628
Portugal	130	121	104	Latvia	353	292	288
UK (E&W)	125	148	151	Slovakia	297	172	151
Spain	115	145	163	Lithuania	240	240	234
Italy	95	104	97	Romania	221	175	126
Germany	95	95	88	Czech Rep.	219	185	206
Netherlands	85	128	100	FYROM	75	99	107
Belgium	84	91	93	Serbia	76	104	143
France	80	85	96	Croatia	59	81	93
Denmark	61	77	63	Slovenia	57	65	65
Norway	59	66	69				
Finland	52	75	64				

Source: World Prison Brief (ICPS 2010).

Furthermore, how should we assess the level of punitiveness of *all forms of penal interventions*? Indeed, non-custodial sanctions, restorative justice or treatment programmes can also be 'punitive', measured by their interference in the fundamental rights and freedoms of offenders. For an illustration, see Barbara Hudson's (2006) analysis of the latter two forms of penal interventions into the privacy and the 'secrets of the self' of offenders. Or see the criticisms on an unfettered welfare (Van de Kerchove 1977: 246) or restorative justice (Eliaerts and Dumortier 2002; Dumortier 2003) approach to juvenile delinquents, which may mask punitive practices while downplaying due process guarantees. Non-custodial sanctions vary in the number of obligations imposed, the level of control and surveillance involved and the stigma resulting from the imposition or implementation. 'Intermediate sanctions' have been introduced in many countries with the explicit aim of being more controlling and punitive than normal probation but less so than prison (Byrne *et al.* 1992). Or to be 'more burdensome and restrictive', as described by Tonry and Hamilton (1995: 15). If their application results in pure net-widening, the level of punitiveness increases. If they really replace imprisonment, the level of punitiveness could be said to decrease, at least if they impose less restrictions and control than imprisonment.[2]

It is impossible to deal with all these complexities in this book. We do cover, however, both quantitative and qualitative dimensions of punitiveness. Prisoner rates are used in Chapters 2 and 3 as the basis for comparisons between different countries and the search for possible explanations. Quantitative and qualitative dimensions of punitiveness are illustrated in Chapters 6 to 8 with reference to the impact of human rights standards on (limits to) criminalization and on the (qualitative) treatment of prisoners and in Chapters 9 to 12 on the possible impact of the increased attention to victims of crime and 'public opinion'. We also look at different actors involved in determining levels of punitiveness and their interactions: policy-makers, judiciary, victims, members of the public.

1.3 Explaining trends in punitiveness – possibilities for resistance?

1.3.1 Global trends versus national differences

Recent studies into explanations of trends in punitiveness reflect diverging approaches. One approach emphasizes social and political changes common to all western societies which are described as influencing their criminal justice systems in similar more punitive directions. Garland's (2001) analysis of the US and the UK as two late-modern, high-crime societies, in which an angry and anxious public has led politicians to resort to punitive policies of exclusion, or Wacquant's (2004, 2006) study of the neo-liberal transformation of western welfare states into penal states, are illustrations of this approach. Another approach stresses and attempts to explain different developments in individual jurisdictions (Tonry 2001; Cavadino and Dignan 2006). A third approach looks at both convergences and diversity emerging from such comparisons and analyses not only risk but also protective factors for increased punitiveness (Goldson and Muncie 2006; Tonry 2007; Lappi-Seppälä 2007, 2008; Lacey 2008).

Whatever the approach, the question of possibilities of resistance against increased punitiveness is dependent on two conditions: first, that the factors explaining trends in punitiveness within one country or between different countries leave some possibilities of (political) choices; second, that these possibilities of choices are not linked to 'ontological' or historical characteristics of the nations concerned which make them not transferable to other jurisdictions. Both aspects have been the subject of quite some debate.

1.3.2 The (relative) importance of political decision-making

Garland's (2001) analysis of the emergence of a new 'culture of control' in the UK and the US has sparked interesting debates on this issue. His emphasis on the totality of the *field* of crime control rather than on 'penality' alone allowed him to focus on and to explain the increased importance of non-state reactions to crime and insecurity: 'the biggest change had been the shifting place of crime in our daily lives, our built environment, and our cultural imagination [...], the emerging tendency towards the breakup of the state's supposed monopoly of crime control [...], the shift from law enforcement to security management' (Garland 2004: 170). The result, however, has been criticized for creating a 'bleak' or 'dystopian' outlook (Zedner 2002) or a 'criminology of catastrophe' in which politics seems 'epiphenomenal' (Loader and Sparks 2004: 15–16). Garland refutes these arguments, but also warns against focusing too much on politicians as 'the usual suspects' (Garland 2004: 185). At the end of *Culture of Control*, he stresses that the current configuration of crime control and criminal justice in the UK and the US 'is the [...] outcome of political and cultural and policy choices – choices that could have been different and that can still be rethought and reversed' (Garland 2001: 201). He also acknowledges that 'while in the UK and the US political decisions have stressed exclusion and punitive measures, other countries may choose differently' (Garland 2001: 202). The possibilities of choices may even be enhanced now, as 'a field in transition makes it more open than usual to external forces and political pressures. Hence this is a historical moment that invites transformative action [...] precisely because it has a greater than usual probability of having an impact' (Garland 2001: 25). On the other hand, he qualifies the possibility of political choices, contending that they must resonate with political, popular and professional cultures emerging in the same period:

> But it is possible to overestimate the scope for political action, and to overestimate the degree of choice that is realistically available to governmental and non-governmental actors. And it is all too easy to forget the extent to which political actors are, in their turn, acted upon. (Garland 2004: 181)

> I do not consider politics to be merely epiphenomenal [...] The political is
> clearly a crucial level with its own dynamics, contingencies and dispositive
> effects. But nor do I consider it to be an unconditioned domain. Indeed
> a primary concern of the Culture of Control is to identify the social,
> economic, cultural and criminological circumstances that constrain and
> enable political action. (Ibid.: 187)

As far as these criminological circumstances are concerned, he acknowledges
that his focus on the shifts in 'official criminology', showing 'the emergence of
new criminological rationales that came to dominate governmental practices and
the reasons why these were preferred to the social welfare criminologies that
previously prevailed', tends 'to misrepresent the real nature of the field' and to
disregard the continued 'cultural capital and prestige' of critical and sociological
criminology, even if it has lost political power (in the UK and the US). It is
precisely 'the continuing force of these competing actors and discourses' that
gives 'sociological substance' to the claim that choices can still be rethought and
reversed (Garland 2004: 167-8).

   This is exactly what this book aims for. Other case studies of penal policies
and their ensuing 'scales of imprisonment' have demonstrated that, although they
result from a complex interaction of different factors, they are – or can be – at
least partly influenced by political decision-making (Rutherford 1984; Zimring
and Hawkins 1991; Snacken et al. 1995; Snacken 2007; Goldson 2010). Some
of these factors lie outside the criminal justice system ('external factors'), such
as demographic changes (age structure, immigration) and economic trends.
Others refer to attitudes and decisions made within the criminal justice system
('internal factors') or to factors at least partly influenced by the criminal justice
system ('criminality' as defined and tackled by the system). A third category
('intermediate factors') refers to the interaction between penal policies and public
opinion, the media and the political reactions to both (Snacken et al. 1995) (see
Figure 1.1). Although these interactions are contingent and not deterministic
(Zimring and Hawkins 1991), this analysis has led to our earlier conclusion that
an increasing prison population is not a 'fate' that has to be suffered passively but
is at least partly influenced by political decision-making (Snacken et al. 1995).
Rutherford's description of penal policies as 'expansionist', 'reductionist' or 'stand-
still' policies and his analysis of the reductionist policies developed by England
(1908–38), the Netherlands (1950–75) and Japan (1950–75) equally illustrate this
point (Rutherford 1984). His arguments have since been reinforced by the much
analysed and debated decline of the Finnish prison population over the last 40
years, which has been explained as resulting from a coherent set of 'reductionist'
penal policy initiatives. These initiatives originated in expert-led political
decision-making, but were expressly and purposely developed in such a way as
to encompass and convince legislators, prosecutors and judges, the media and the
public (Tornudd 1993; Lappi-Seppälä 2001, 2007; Chapter 3 this volume). The
abolition of the death penalty in Europe is another instance 'where governments

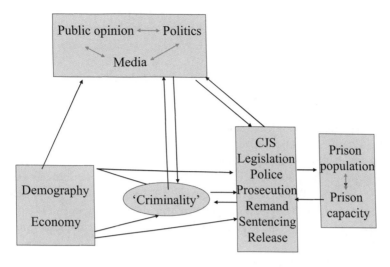

FIGURE 1.1   Factors explaining changes in penal policies and prison populations
Source: Snacken, Beyens, Tubex (1995).

lead by example' (Girling 2006: 72; see also Chapter 6 this volume). Political leadership is not incompatible with democracy, although some Americans have equated the European abolition of the death penalty independently from public support as illustrating political cultures which may be 'morally superior, but less democratic' than the US (Marshall 2000: 12). As one of us has argued elsewhere (Snacken 2010), such criticism is based on an interpretation of 'democracy' as 'populism' rather than as a form of government aiming at the general interest, which includes the fundamental rights and interests of unpopular minorities such as offenders and prisoners. But such tensions between democracy and populism certainly also exist in Europe and deserve further scrutiny (see Chapter 12 this volume).

1.3.3 Factors influencing political decision-making

If political decision-making is still important in at least partly understanding and shaping penal policies, the next question is then what factors influence this political decision-making? And can European countries learn from one anothers' experiences or are these factors linked to national characteristics that make them unfit for policy transfer? Or can some of these factors be considered to be pan-European and to reflect common fundamental values which could reinforce attempts at penal moderation in Europe?

Over previous years, an increasing number of comparative studies have led to a better understanding of which factors are particularly important in explaining the different levels of punitiveness in the penal policies of western countries. The most important factors to date seem to be as follows:

- *Welfare and political economy.* Investments in social policies and levels of social equality are inversely correlated with prison rates (Becket and Western 2001; Downes and Hansen 2006; Cavadino and Dignan 2006; Lacey 2008; Lappi-Seppälä 2007, 2008; Pratt 2008).
- *Human rights.* Human rights traditionally act as a bulwark against criminalization and over-penalization by state authorities. The balance between crime control and human rights is important in understanding the different punishment levels and trends in the US and Europe (Tonry 2001; Kurki 2001; Morgan 2001; Whitman 2003; Muncie 2008).
- *Political culture and populist punitiveness.* Majoritarian democracies are more prone to populist punitive penal policies than consensual democracies (Green 2007; Tonry 2007), where expert opinion still has legitimacy (Lappi-Seppälä 2007; Snacken 2007). This is also reflected in the media (Green 2007, 2008; Snacken 2007) and in policies towards victims' rights and interests (Snacken 2007, 2010).
- *Judicial structure and independence.* Elected judges and prosecutors are more prone to populist punitiveness than non-partisan judges and prosecutors (Tonry 2007).

Ian Loader concedes that these findings about the 'socio-economic, political and cultural prerequisites of relatively mild penal systems' seem to point to 'those features of a society that are most difficult to change' (Loader 2010: 359). However, he also emphasizes that 'those societies which have effected reductions in the use of prison and/or sustained relatively mild penal systems have done so through acts of political will', while 'in England and Wales as in the USA, the neo-liberal political project has *opted* for penal over social regulation' (ibid.). We probably can't expect countries to change the fundaments of their political or judicial structures purely on the basis of the expected outcomes in levels of punitiveness. On the other hand, the first three domains mentioned in the list are certainly *not static.* The attack on the welfare system by Margaret Thatcher in the UK and Ronald Reagan in the US were political moves (Wacquant 2004, 2009) and so is Barack Obama's attempt to reform the healthcare system in the US. Due process and human rights for offenders and prisoners were better protected in the 1960s–70s by the Supreme Court in the US than by the European Court of Human Rights (ECtHR) in Europe, while the reverse is true now (Morgan 2001; Kurki 2001; van Zyl Smit and Snacken 2009). Interrogation techniques which in Europe would amount to torture were defended by politicians in the US as necessary in the 'war on terror' (see Chapter 6 this volume). But the European Union has also been criticized for prioritizing crime control over civil liberties in its elaboration of 'An Area of Freedom, Justice and Security', though not in a manner fitting into the 'new punitiveness' mould (Baker and Roberts 2005: 128). And political parties sometimes make fundamental U-turns in penal policies and discourse, as with the wish of the US Democrats or the UK's New Labour no longer to be

seen as 'soft on crime' in the 1990s (Wacquant 2004), or the recent (30 June 2010) reversal in the UK of former Conservative Secretary of State Michael Howard's slogan 'prison works' into 'prison does not work' by current Conservative Justice Secretary Ken Clarke and his reference to 'intelligent sentencing' as imposing more community sanctions.

The question of policy travel is a complex one (Dolowitz and Marsh 2000; Newburn and Sparks 2004) and has mostly been described with regard to the travelling of penal policies from the US to other Anglo-Saxon countries, more particularly to the UK (see, for example, Jones and Newburn 2002). Tonry (2001) emphasizes that penal policies travel mostly within legal cultures but seldom between common law and continental European legal cultures. On the other hand, Karstedt (2002) argues that, despite the dominance of the US on convergence of policy transfer, a number of jurisdictions are also looking to Western Europe for 'models'. The question we have to deal with is, however, not limited to penal policies, but encompasses findings about welfare and social policies, human rights, the importance of public opinion in democracies, etc. For European countries to learn from one another in these respects then probably requires some basic common values which allow them to surpass the peculiar or idiosyncratic characteristics that differentiate them. In order to find such values, policies developed at the European political level by the Council of Europe and the European Union can be helpful, as can the surveys of Eurobarometer concerning values held by European citizens. The three topics that we have chosen for this book fulfil this condition: 'welfare' – or maybe better 'social equality', 'human rights' and 'democracy' (see Figure 1.2). Despite national variations in interpretations and means to achieve these aims each of these topics is considered to be part of the fundamental values in the construction of a 'European' identity and is widely supported by European citizens (Snacken 2010). We will come back to this issue in the conclusion.

The aim of this book is hence to focus in more detail on these three areas, which have been recognized as of major importance for explaining levels of punitiveness, in which political choices seem possible and which rely on fundamental values that could constitute levers through which increasing levels of punitiveness could be resisted in Europe:

1. Punishment and Welfare
2. Punishment and Human Rights
3. Punishment and Democracy, with special emphasis on the role of victims and public opinion.

1.4 Structure of the book

The book is divided into three parts, each devoted to one of the aforementioned topics.

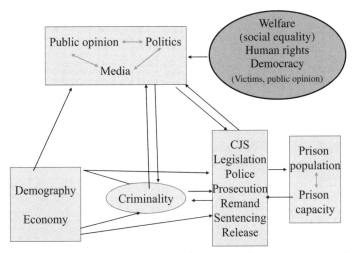

FIGURE 1.2 Selected values interacting with levels of punitiveness: welfare/social equality, human rights, democracy
Source: Snacken (2010).

Part 1: Punishment and Welfare – From Correlations to Interactions?

Esping-Anderson (1990) distinguishes different welfare models in the western world: the Scandinavian, the Anglo-Saxon and the continental European models. These welfare models are known to be correlated with different criminal and penal policies. Becket and Western's (2001) conclusion for 32 states in the US that investments in welfare are inversely related to prison populations has since been confirmed for Europe (Downes and Hansen 2006; Cavadino and Dignan 2006; Lacey 2008).

David Downes in Chapter 2 gives an overview of the recent comparative studies that have illustrated this inverse correlation between investments in welfare capital and penal capital, both in the US and in Europe. This relates not only to prison rates but also, for example, to the age of criminal responsibility or prison privatization. Must the vast differences between prison rates in the US and in Europe be understood as illustrating a form of American 'exceptionalism' due to the peculiarities explaining mass incarceration in the US? Or is the US merely 'a harbinger of future penal trends in Europe or indeed the world at large'? Referring to Nicky Lacey's (2008) distinction between coordinated and liberal market economies, and looking with more detail into incarceration rates for foreign prisoners in both forms of political economies, he concludes that 'there are real grounds for optimism that dystopian analyses have been overplayed'. But he also argues that 'a substantial welfare state is increasingly a principal, if not the main protection against the resort to mass imprisonment in the era of globalization'.

But how does this correlation between punishment and welfare work? How can it be explained? In Chapter 3, Tapio Lappi-Seppälä aims to explain the Scandinavian 'exceptionalism' of low prison rates on the basis of a large cross-comparative study covering 25 countries, including central and eastern European countries and Baltic states. Looking into the correlations between prison rates and several social and political characteristics of the countries studied, he finds that Scandinavian countries not only have less income inequality, but also enjoy the highest level of trust and legitimacy, both vertically (political legitimacy) and horizontally (social trust), while this is lowest in the most punitive countries such as England and Wales and Eastern European countries. He argues that welfarist social policies reduce social distances and enhance the development of social (and economic) capital, hence creating more social equality and social bonds that support inclusion and leniency. He hypothesizes that these are not only based on feelings of solidarity (which could also result in empathetic identification with the victim – see Part 3 of this book) but also on broad concepts of social and collective responsibility. The higher level of political trust resulting from more generous welfare systems reduces the need for 'political posturing and expressive gestures ... in order to defend the positions of power'. The direct and indirect connections between political economy and punitiveness demonstrate and explain why consensus democracies are more welfare friendly and less populist than majoritarian democracies. The legislative drafting process in Scandinavia is a good illustration of this. His warning that the decision-making process within the European Union could hamper this tradition of careful deliberation and bears a risk of increased politicization of criminal policy should certainly be taken seriously.

In Chapter 4, Stein Kuhnle explains in more detail how the Scandinavian welfare model has developed over time and what differentiates it from other European welfare models. He argues that the Scandinavian welfare state seems not only to make up a distinct type of welfare state, but also can and actually sometimes does serve as a positive model for reforms and developments in other countries. The fact that it can serve as a model is related to the fact that 'the outcomes of the various welfare state institutions seem to be successful in terms of values and objectives highly regarded by many: limited poverty; relatively high degree of income equality; social stability – and – relatively less crime of various kinds (although there are variations within the Nordic area), which again is conducive to less expenditure in other chapters of government budgets.' And even where crime rates are higher (the EU ICS 2005 Survey describes Sweden and Finland as relatively low-crime countries and Denmark as a 'high-crime country'), respondents report lower feelings of insecurity than in other European countries. These are benefits that, according to Kuhnle, 'can be assessed independent of specific historical prerequisites'. Of course, many commentators and researchers have argued that 'if the welfare system grows too large, it risks perverting incentive structures in both working life and society in general'. However, the universal, citizenship-based social rights approach to welfare in Scandinavia after the Second World War has also been work-friendly, has led to unprecedented economic growth and has effectively countered the risk of increasing dualisation of society after the economic recession in the 1990s. Although the universal, social rights approach sets the Scandinavian model apart from other welfare states, Kuhnle reminds us of the fact that the principle of universalism was also part of the Beveridgean post-Second World War development in Britain, which inspired at least partly Scandinavian postwar developments. Whether the Scandinavian model will survive the more intensive globalization since the 1980s in terms of communications, migration, economics, politics and culture (see warnings in this respect by Pratt 2008) should be further closely monitored through comparative research at both macro and micro levels.

In Chapter 5, Philippe Mary and Jacky Nagels acknowledge the increasingly clear connection between the globalization process of the last 20-odd years and the weakening of the social state in western countries. Universalist integration policies switch over to individual inclusion policies that develop specific treatments for populations with problems. Penal policies, presented as being integrated and comprehensive, intervene in a growing number of social sectors and contribute to the development of penal treatment of the social question. However, they suggest that the term *social and security* state (*Etat social-sécuritaire*) is more appropriate than 'penal state' to account not only for the changes under way, but also for the preservation, if only in a defensive mode, of a certain level of social protection that many traditionally social-democrat countries in Europe have maintained under the heading of the 'Third Way' or the 'active social state'. By studying the evolution with regard to pensions, poverty and healthcare in four countries belonging to Cavadino and Dignan's conservative corporatist category (Germany, Belgium, France and the Netherlands) they show that the social state is being maintained in those countries but affects different population groups in different ways due to the ageing of the population and the explosion in healthcare costs. As a result, the risk of poverty is highest for the unemployed (and for elderly women) and both the poverty rate and the unemployment rate are highest for the immigrant population and primarily for non-EU nationals. These are exactly the populations that have been described as the most vulnerable not only from a societal point of view, but also in terms of interventions by the criminal justice system. These insights show us that global comparisons of welfare investments and prison rates do not tell the whole story, and that more attention should be paid to the different target groups within the different forms of social interventions.

Part 2: Punishment and Human Rights – Shield or Sword?

Human rights are traditionally seen as a bulwark against criminalization and over-penalization, as the punitive system of criminal law cuts deep into the freedom of the citizens. Criminal law should therefore be minimal and marginal and must meet a number of severe constitutional and human rights related conditions and standards. National constitutional courts and international human rights courts, such as the European Court of Human Rights (ECtHR), play an essential role in setting these conditions and standards. But criminal law and punishment are also defended as instruments of crime control and enhanced security. The balance between crime control and due process has therefore been described as important in understanding punishment levels and trends (Tonry 2001: 519). Several authors have argued that the emphasis on human rights for offenders and prisoners is now much stronger in Europe than in the US, thanks to the case law of the ECtHR (Tonry 2001; Kurki 2001; Morgan 2001; van Zyl Smit and Snacken 2009). There has also been an explicit political emphasis on the protection of human rights as an essential characteristic of a 'European' identity by the Council of Europe and the European Union, especially with regard to the death penalty and to the accession of the former communist countries to the European institutions (Girling 2006; Snacken 2006). There is, however, a more recent tendency, even within the ECtHR, in which criminalisation is seen as a necessary instrument for the protection of the human rights of victims of crime by their fellow citizens or by the state. This Part hence looks in more detail into the judicial and political protection of human rights in Europe as a possible shield against or sword for increased punitiveness. Taking into account the political importance of the accession of the former communist countries to the institutional 'Europe', this Part also includes an illustration from Hungary.

In Chapter 6 the authors (Dumortier *et al.*) analyse what human rights can do about the rise of the penal state in Europe. By means of some particularly illustrative judgments of the ECtHR they show how the Court limits the competence of the 47 member states of the Council of Europe to impose penal sentences as well as to incriminate behaviour. One of the most obvious differences between the USA and Europe is the abolition of the death penalty, which is clearly followed in the Court's case law. The protection of prisoners and the prohibition of illegitimate detention equally illustrate how human rights can function as a bulwark against punitiveness. In the same line, the authors present case law through which the ECtHR imposes limits on member states' competence to incriminate behaviour, such as the Court's opposition to the concept of 'shared criminal liability' and to the overzealous incrimination of European citizens' sexual practices. However, the authors also question this at first sight optimistic view of human rights as a shield against increased punitiveness. First, the attitude of the Court remains ambivalent towards interfering in certain national penal policies resulting, in the authors' view, in an insufficient protection against disproportionate penalisation. Second, in some cases the Court even obliges member states to have recourse to criminal law, especially when the physical integrity of victims is at stake. This tendency seems to invert the 'right to punish' of member states into a 'duty to punish' and to be myopic to criminological knowledge showing the limited effectiveness of criminal remedies and deterrence. To counterbalance this vulnerability and ambivalence of the Court's case law the authors suggest the implementation of a coherent human rights framework that proclaims 'new' human rights against punitiveness (e.g. a ban on life sentences without parole) and hence 'constitutionalises' the principles of a moderate penal law. Such principles should, however, also be based on a more coherent and critical criminological and penological framework.

In Chapter 7 Miklós Lévay illustrates how the Hungarian Constitutional Court has acted as a bulwark against punitiveness by abolishing the death penalty and by restricting the incrimination of 'incitement against the community'. However, at the same time, the Constitutional Court did not act against the imposition of stricter rules in cases of recidivism, nor against the incrimination of drug use. On the contrary, in the latter case the Court even annulled regulations that depenalized the handing over of small amounts of drugs in case of 'shared drug consumption'. As a consequence, Miklós Lévay concludes that human rights can act as a bulwark against, but also as a motor for, criminalization. He also analyses the influence of penal policy and human rights on sentencing practices in Hungary. Before 1989-90, when Hungary had an authoritarian one-party system governed by 'the socialist rule of law', imprisonment was the core element of penal policy with high imprisonment rates as a logical consequence. During and after the political changes, the growing importance of human rights led to a reductionist penal policy and a decrease in the use of imprisonment. However, in 1998 the opposition party coming to government kept its electoral promises of strict measures against the growing rate of criminality. As a consequence of this expansionist policy the rate of unconditional prison sentences grew again. The Hungarian experiences clearly illustrate the influence of political decision-making and human rights on levels of punitiveness.

In Chapter 8, Françoise Tulkens, judge at the ECtHR, analyses both the offensive and defensive role of human rights in penal policies. Concerning the offensive role, she observes that the Court only obliges member states to have recourse to criminal law in extreme and exceptional situations relating to the right to life or the prohibition of torture and inhuman or degrading treatment or punishment. Contrary to the criticisms on over-criminalization by the Court, she hence wonders whether the Court is not actually preserving the criminal law as a real 'final remedy'. At the same time, however, she acknowledges 'the idealized image of criminal law held by some of the Court's judges, coming from other horizons, who often attach a great deal of importance to the symbolic aspect of criminal law.' Constant vigilance is hence needed to avoid the offensive role of human rights spreading out to other situations that are less straightforward. According to the author, the Court's tireless further development of the defensive role of human rights is an important factor in this respect. She illustrates this through some promising evolutions she observes in the Court's case law, such as its growing tendency to apply the Convention's guarantees also to the implementation phase (instead of merely to the phase of sentencing). Judge Tulkens concludes by wondering whether the proposition of the authors in Chapter 6 to 'constitutionalize' the principles of a moderate and humane criminal law might not be counterproductive because further evolution can be frozen: 'More flexible case law, more attached to individual situations, is perhaps capable of going further.'

Part 3: Punishment and Democracy – Which Role for Victims and Public Opinion?

Increased levels of punitiveness in the US and the UK (and other Anglo-Saxon countries) have been linked to two aspects which raise important questions with regard to the very concept of 'democracy': the 'return of the victim' and an increased 'penal populism' (Garland 2001). Part 3 of this book analyses these phenomena in more detail.

Garland (2001) describes how in the US victims' rights are explicitly referred to as justification for harsher law and order politics, while in the UK victims appear at rallies of political parties. The relation between measures for victims and for offenders is seen as a 'zero sum policy': every measure 'in favour' of offenders is seen as 'to the disadvantage' of victims, and being 'for' victims automatically means being 'tough on offenders'. This is, however, not necessarily in accordance with the needs and wishes of the individual victims or the victim movements themselves and this political (ab)use of the suffering of victims has been described as 'tertiary victimization' (Sessar 1990). Which place do and should victims' rights and interests receive in European penal systems? Some authors have described the solidarity with victims as the only remaining morality and basis for solidarity in our postmodern western cultures (Boutellier 2008). But does that mean that the penal system is the most appropriate and adequate institution to care for their needs and to express this solidarity?

In Chapter 9, Noëlle Languin *et al.* point to the dangers of a 'society of victims' and the fostering of the criminal justice system as 'the most effective means at our disposal for sanctifying the victim, sacrificing the offender and obtaining compensation for losses of all kinds'. Their empirical research into the experiences and expectations of (violent) crime victims with the criminal justice system in Switzerland illustrates the many disappointments that respondents feel about the penal reaction to their victimization. Many of those disillusioned refer to a lack of 'procedural justice', such as the absence of clear explanations, the lack of follow-up or more in-depth handling of the case, and the lack of consideration for the victim showed by the penal actors. Others, however, illustrate a more fundamental frustration with the core principles of a criminal trial, such as the presumption of innocence for the offender or the greater attention paid to the accused than to the victim during the trial, an inequality experienced as a renewed injustice. The authors warn, together with others (Salas 2005; Cesoni and Rechtman 2005), that 'criminal justice is credited with cognitive and reparatory expectations that far exceed its capacities'. This can only lead to secondary victimization and to an increased 'emotionalization' of the criminal law, which 'exacerbate exclusively punitive expectations'.

Dan Kaminski in Chapter 10 continues the arguments against a 'victimist' society, expressing his indignation with the political treatment of the question of victims of crime and the contemporary 'victimological (com)passion'. He emphasizes the divisive nature of this compassion, renewing and reinforcing the ideal-type image of the innocent and vulnerable victim as a counterpoint to the ideal-type image of the strong and evil offender. It 'forces a polarisation between offenders and victims to the point of leaving offenders outside of any possible comprehension'. The influence of victims of crime on increased punitiveness takes on many forms: through 'grouped', 'threatening' and 'rhetorical' victims. But consequently, the victim also 'must be irreproachable, "a proper victim", failing which he will lose the anticipated empathy'. These victimist concerns lead to a remoralization of penality 'which shields penality from its contemporary deficit of legitimacy'. As traditional penality has a limited capacity to meet victims' needs or expectations, this must either lead to increased punitiveness (Languin *et al.* in Chapter 9), or to a more procedural, civilized and communicative justice (Aertsen in Chapter 11). He argues that the first hypothesis is more close to reality. The criminal justice system raises expectations for victims that it cannot fulfil, thus enhancing the risk of secondary victimization and disappointment (like 'taking your broken car to a pizzeria'). This can only lead to them falling back on the result of the trial and the measurement of the inflicted punishment and hence structurally induces punitive outbidding.

In Chapter 11, Ivo Aertsen emphasizes the differences between the actual victims of crime, the 'virtual' or prototypal conceptions of victimhood in society, and the variations in political use that is made of them. Expectations of actual victims towards the criminal justice system as they emerge from years of empirical research appear to be in the procedural sphere rather than in the field of the (punitive) outcome. In general, the punitive attitudes of victims do not assume extreme proportions but individual differences and differences between types of crime play an important part. The punishment needs of individual victims must be understood within the broader framework of psychological coping, which takes place within a permanent interaction with the victim's informal and institutional environments. The International Crime Victim Survey indicates rather moderate punitive attitudes among the general public in most western industrialized countries, with the exception of the US and the UK. Victim movements equally show a large variation in 'victimagogic' ideologies, with more emphasis on a rights perspective in North America and on assistance and services to victims in Europe, thus possibly contributing in the latter to a more moderate punitive approach. However, a new generation of 'single-issue' victim movements seems to be emerging which expressly advocates more punitive policies. The possible impact of such movements must be assessed within the bigger social and political entity, including the citizens' confidence in the authorities and the continuation of an expert culture (see Lappi-Seppälä in Chapter 3 this volume). The European Union's Framework Decision of 15 March 2001 enhances the victims' standing and rights in criminal proceedings. The most important advantage of victim impact statements in common law countries and the Netherlands (where civil party procedures do not exist) is to improve the feeling of recognition and participation in the procedure. Ivo Aertsen therefore concludes that the development of a 'communicative model' of victim participation would be much more significant than implementing an 'impact model'.

In Chapter 12, Kristof Verfaillie continues the discussion on punitive feelings in the general public and the increased punitiveness witnessed in several countries resulting from 'penal populist' policies. 'Penal populism' is characterized by a 'politics of simplicity' based on references to 'the' public opinion and simplistic 'common-sense' answers to complex problems. It reduces public debate and policy-making to dualisms and political essentialism, rephrasing these complex problems in polarizing, unequivocal and uncompromising terms. Political references to 'public opinion' can be merely rhetorical or based on a variety of sources. Certain quantitative opinion polls are of a high methodological standard and offer a wealth of knowledge about how opinions are distributed in society. They consistently show paradoxes and ambivalence in the public's attitudes towards punishment and criminal justice but cannot explain them. Through his ethnographic approach Kristof Verfaillie shows the complexity of opinion formation, the different sources of authority used (personal experiences, media reports) and the 'polycentric consistency' of the opinions expressed. He concludes that the importance of contextualization in understanding the apparent paradoxes emerging from the individual answers makes 'public opinion' unfit as a basis for populist punitive policies.

The analyses in this book convince us that both 'Europe' as an institutional structure and the separate European countries are currently facing fundamental choices as to the kind of society they want to build for the future. In the conclusion, we will therefore turn the *empirical findings* about the correlations or interactions between these three areas and levels of punitiveness into *normative arguments* for 'resisting punitiveness' in a Europe based on social equality and social inclusion, protection of human rights for every person and a democracy aiming at the general interest.

Notes

1. With the exception of Belarus, the only European country which is not a member of the Council of Europe.
2. The dimensions of punitiveness of non-custodial sanctions are just beginning to be studied (see, for example, Durnescu 2010; May and Wood 2010), but are not covered in this book.

References

Baker, E. and Roberts, J. (2005) 'Globalization and the new punitiveness', in J. Pratt, D. Brown, M. Brown, S. Hallsworth and W. Morrison (eds), *New Punitiveness: Trends, Theories, Perspectives*. Cullompton: Willan, pp. 121–38.

Bauwens, A. and Snacken, S. (2010) '"Modèles de guidance judiciaire": sur la voie d'un modèle intégré?', in *Sécurité avant tout? Chances et dangers du risk assessment dans les domaines de l'exécution des sanctions et de la probation*. Bern: Stämpfli Verlag, Vol. 1, pp. 93–107.

Becket, K. and Western, B. (2001) 'Governing social marginality. Welfare, incarceration and the transformation of state policy', *Punishment and Society*, 1: 43–59.

Boutellier, H. (2008) *Solidariteit en slachtofferschap. De morele betekenis van slachtofferschap in een postmoderne cultuur.* Amsterdam: Amsterdam University Press.

Brown, D. (2005) 'Continuity, rupture or more of the "volatile and contradictory"? Glimpses of New South Wales' penal practice behind and through the discursive', in J. Pratt, D. Brown, M. Brown, S. Hallsworth and W. Morrison, *The New Punitiveness. Trends, Theories, Perspectives.* Cullompton: Willan, pp. 27–46.

Byrne, J. M., Lurigio, A. J. and Petersilia, J. (1992) *Smart Sentencing. The Emergence of Intermediate Sanctions.* Thousand Oaks, CA and London: Sage.

Canton, R. (2009) 'Taking probation abroad', *European Journal of Probation*, 1(1): 66–78.

Cavadino, M. and Dignan, J. (2006) *Penal Systems. A Comparative Approach.* London: Sage.

Cesoni, M. L. and Rechtman, R. (2005) 'La réparation "psychologique" de la victime: une nouvelle fonction de la peine?', *Revue de droit pénal et de criminologie*, 85(2): 158–78.

Dolowitz, D. and Marsh, D. (2000) 'Learning from abroad: the role of policy transfer in contemporary policy making', *Governance*, 13, (1): 5–24.

Downes, D. and Hansen, K. (2006) 'Welfare and punishment in comparative perspective', in S. Armstrong and L. McAra (eds), *Perspectives on Punishment. The Contours of Control.* Oxford: Oxford University Press, pp. 133–54.

Dumortier, E. (2003) 'Legal rules and safeguards within Belgian mediation practices for juveniles', in E. Weitekamp and H.-J. Kerner (eds), *Restorative Justice in Context. International Practice and Directions.* Cullompton: Willan, pp. 197–207.

Dünkel, F., Grzywa, J., Horsfield, P. and Pruin, I. (eds) (2010) *Juvenile Justice Systems in Europe – Current Situation and Reform Developments.* Mönchengladbach: Forum Verlag Godesberg, Vols 1–4.

Durnescu, I. (2010) 'Pains of probation: effective practice and human rights', *International Journal of Offender Therapy and Comparative Criminology.* Online publ: May 2010 doi 10.1177/0306624X10369489

Eliaerts, C. and Dumortier, E. (2002) 'Restorative justice for children: in need of procedural safeguards and standards', in E. Weitekamp and H.-J. Kerner (eds), *Restorative Justice. Theoretical Foundations.* Cullompton: Willan, pp. 204–23.

Esping-Anderson, G. (1990) *The Three Worlds of Welfare Capitalism.* Princeton, NJ: Princeton University Press.

Garland, D. (2001) *The Culture of Control. Crime and Social Order in Contemporary Society.* Oxford: Oxford University Press.

Garland, D. (2004) 'Beyond the culture of control', *Critical Review of International Social and Political Philosophy*, 7(2) (Special issue on Garland's *The Culture of Control*): 160–89.

Girling, E. (2006) 'European identity, penal sensibilities and communities of sentiment', in S. Armstrong and L. McAra (eds), *Perspectives on Punishment. The Contours of Control.* Oxford: Oxford University Press, pp. 69–81.

Goldson, B. (2010) 'The sleep of (criminological) reason: knowledge-policy rupture and New Labour's youth's justice legacy', *Criminology and Criminal Justice*, 10: 137–54.

Goldson, B. and Muncie, J. (eds) (2006) *Comparative Youth Justice: Critical Issues.* London: Sage.

Green, D. (2007) 'Comparing penal cultures: child-on-child homicide in England and Norway', in M. Tonry (ed.), *Crime, Punishment and Politics in Comparative Perspective*, in *Crime and Justice: A Review of Research*, Vol. 36. Chicago: University of Chicago Press, pp. 591–636.

Green, D. (2008) *When Children Kill Children: Penal Populism and Political Culture.* Oxford: Oxford University Press.

Hudson, B. (2006) 'Secrets of the self: punishment and the right to privacy', in E. Claes, A. Duff and S. Gutwirth (eds), *Privacy and the Criminal Law.* Antwerp and Oxford: Intersentia, pp. 137–62.

Jones, J. and Newburn, T. (2002) 'Policy convergence and crime control in the USA and the UK', *Criminal Justice*, 2(2): 173–203.

Junger-Tas, J. (2006) 'Trends in international juvenile justice: what conclusions can be drawn?', in J. Junger-Tas and S. Decker (eds), *International Handbook of Juvenile Justice.* New York: Springer, pp. 505–32.

Karstedt, S. (2002) 'Durkheim, Tarde and beyond: the global travel of crime policies', *Criminology and Criminal Justice,* 2(2): 111–23.

Kurki, L. (2001) 'International standards and limits on sentencing and punishment', in M. Tonry and R. Frase, *Sentencing and Sanctions in Western Countries.* New York: Oxford University Press, pp. 331–78.

Kury, H. (ed.) (2008) *Fear of Crime – Punitivity. New Developments in Theory and Research,* Crime and Crime Policy, Vol. 3. Bochum: Universitätsverlag Brockmeyer.

Lacey, N. (2008) *The Prisoners' Dilemma: Political Economy and Punishment in Contemporary Democracies* (The Hamlyn Lectures 2007). Cambridge: Cambridge University Press.

Lappi-Seppälä, T. (2001) 'Sentencing and punishment in Finland: the decline of the repressive ideal', in M. Tonry and R. Frase (eds), *Punishment and Penal Systems in Western Countries.* New York: Oxford University Press, pp. 92–150.

Lappi-Seppälä, T. (2007) 'Penal policy in Scandinavia', in M. Tonry (ed.), *Crime, Punishment and Politics in Comparative Perspective,* in *Crime and Justice: A Review of Research,* Vol. 36. Chicago: University of Chicago Press, pp. 217–96.

Lappi-Seppälä, T. (2008) 'Trust, welfare, and political culture: explaining difference in national penal policies', in M. Tonry (ed.), *Crime and Justice: A Review of Research,* Vol. 37. Chicago: University of Chicago Press, pp. 313–87.

Loader, I. (2010) 'For penal moderation: notes towards a public philosophy of punishment', *Theoretical Criminology,* 14: 349–67.

Loader, I. and Sparks, R. (2004) 'For an historical sociology of crime policy in England and Wales since 1968', *Critical Review of International Social and Political Philosophy,* 7(2) (Special issue on Garland's *The Culture of Control*): 5–32.

Marshall, J. M. (2000) 'Europe's death penalty elitism. Death in Venice', *New Republic,* 223(5): 12–14.

May, D. C. and Wood, P. B. (2010) *Ranking Correctional Punishments: Views from Offenders, Practitioners and the Public.* Durham, NC: Carolina Academic Press.

Morgan, R. (2001) 'International controls on sentencing and punishment', in M. Tonry and R. Frase (eds), *Sentencing and Sanctions in Western Countries.* New York: Oxford University Press.

Muncie, J. (2008) 'The "punitive turn" in juvenile justice: cultures of control and rights compliance in Western Europe and the USA', *Youth Justice,* 8: 107–21.

Newburn, T. and Sparks, R. (eds) (2004) *Criminal Justice and Political Cultures. National and International Dimensions of Crime Control.* Cullompton: Willan.

Pitts, J. and Kuula, T. (2005) 'Incarcerating children and young people: an Anglo-Finnish comparison, *Youth Justice,* 5(3): 147–64.

Pratt, J. (2008) 'Scandinavian exceptionalism in an era of penal excess, Part I: The nature and roots of Scandinavian exceptionalism, 'Part II: Does Scandinavian exceptionalism have a future?', *British Journal of Criminology,* 48: 119–37; 275–92.

Pratt, J., Brown, D., Brown, M., Hallsworth, S. and Morrison, W. (eds) (2005) *The New Punitiveness. Trends, Theories, Perspectives.* Cullompton: Willan.

Rutherford, A. (1984) *Prisons and the Process of Justice: The Reductionist Challenge.* London: Heinemann.

Salas, D. (2005) *La volonté de punir. Essai sur le populisme pénal.* Paris: Hachette.

Sessar, K. (1990) 'Tertiary victimization: a case of the politically abused crime victim', in B. Galaway and J. Hudson (eds), *Criminal Justice, Restitution, and Reconciliation.* Monsey, NY: Willow Tree Press, pp. 37–45.

Snacken, S. (2006) 'A reductionist penal policy and European human rights standards', *European Journal of Criminal Policy and Research,* 12: 143–64.

Snacken, S. (2007) 'Penal policy and practice in Belgium', in M. Tonry (ed.), *Crime, Punishment and Politics in Comparative Perspective, Crime and Justice: A Review of Research,* Vol. 36. Chicago: University of Chicago Press, pp. 127–216.

Snacken, S. (2010) 'Resisting punitiveness in Europe?', *Theoretical Criminology,* 14: 273–92.

Snacken, S., Beyens, K. and Tubex, H. (1995) 'Changing prison populations in western countries: fate or policy?', *European Journal of Crime, Criminal Law and Criminal Justice*, 1: 18–53.

Tonry, M. (2001) 'Symbol, substance and severity in western penal policies', *Punishment and Society*, 4: 517–36.

Tonry, M. (ed.) (2007) *Crime, Punishment and Politics in Comparative Perspective*, in *Crime and Justice: A Review of Research*, Vol. 36. Chicago: Chicago University Press.

Tonry, M. and Hamilton, K. (eds) (1995) *Intermediate Sanctions in Overcrowded Times*. Boston: Northeastern University Press.

Tornudd, P. (1993) *Fifteen Years of Decreasing Prisoner Rates in Finland*. Helsinki: National Research Institute of Legal Policy.

Van de Kerchove, M. (1977) 'Des mesures répressives aux mesures de sûreté et de protection. Réflexions sur le pouvoir mystificateur du langage', *Revue de Droit Pénal et de Criminologie*, 4: 245–79.

Van Kalmthout, A. and Durnescu, I. (eds) (2008) *Probation in Europe*. Nijmegen: Wolf Legal Publishers.

van Zyl Smit, D. and Snacken, S. (2009) *Principles of European Prison Law and Policy. Penology and Human Rights*. Oxford: Oxford University Press.

Wacquant, L. (2004) *Punir les pauvres. Le nouveau gouvernement de l'insécurité sociale*. Paris: Editions Dupuytren.

Wacquant, L. (2006) 'Penalization, depolitization and racialization: on the overincarceration of immigrants in the European Union', in S. Armstrong and L. McAra (eds), *Perspectives on Punishment. The Contours of Control*. Oxford: Oxford University Press, pp. 83–100.

Wacquant, L. (2009) *Punishing the Poor. The Neoliberal Government of Social Insecurity*. Durham, NC: Duke University Press.

Whitman, J. Q. (2003) *Harsh Justice. Criminal Punishment and the Widening Divide between America and Europe*. Oxford: Oxford University Press.

Zedner, L. (2002) 'Dangers of dystopia in penal theory', *Oxford Journal of Legal Studies*, 22: 341–61.

Zimring, F. E. and Hawkins, G. (1991) *The Scale of Imprisonment, Studies in Crime and Justice*. Chicago: University of Chicago Press.

Zimring, F. E. and Johnson, D. T. (2006) 'Public opinion and the governance of punishment in democratic political systems', in S. Karstedt and G. LaFree (eds), *Democracy, Crime and Justice: The Annals of the American Academy of Political and Social Sciences*. Thousand Oaks, CA: Sage, pp. 266–80.

PART 1

Punishment and Welfare – From Correlations to Interactions?

2

POLITICAL ECONOMY, WELFARE AND PUNISHMENT IN COMPARATIVE PERSPECTIVE

David Downes

2.1 Introduction

Work on the social analysis of punishment during the past three decades has arguably neglected the impact of a commitment to welfare on the scale of imprisonment. For the first seven decades of the past century, the principal hope of criminologists, penal reformers and most politicians was that welfare, the 'welfare state' and allied forms of social provision for human needs would lead to a reduction in both crime and the need for punishment. However, the apparently remorseless rise in crime rates from the mid-1950s until, in most countries, the mid-1990s eroded that confidence. Moreover, the watershed of the late 1960s and early 1970s, when researchers threw doubt on the efficacy of treatment programmes, saw those hopes dashed and their assumptions fundamentally challenged. As a result, the past 30 years have seen a dramatic decline in optimism about welfare in relation to crime and punishment. Despite continued growth in welfare investment and provision, it is viewed as lacking any real purchase on the character of crime and punishment. The era of 'penal welfarism' is seen as ceding ground to the era of the 'culture of control' (Garland 1985, 2001), with welfare an increasingly marginal variable in criminal justice policy and practice.

Investment in welfare as distinct from penal capital is now under more severe threat than at any point since 1945. Welfare entitlements are increasingly seen by politicians as a burden on social democratic economies that render them uncompetitive with neo-liberal states in a globalized world market. In punishment terms, over the past two decades, the contrast between the competing political economies of Europe and the United States has become, if anything, even sharper. The '*macho* penal economy' (Downes 2001) of the USA has grown to surpass the mark of two million prisoners held daily – some two per cent of the male labour force. For over two decades, the trend towards mass imprisonment has been accompanied by ever tighter restrictions on welfare rights for the poorest families.

Trends in the United Kingdom and some other European countries are emulating these tendencies, both in terms of penal expansion and welfare contraction. Yet the relationship between these factors remains largely unexplored.

What follows is a résumé of four studies of that relationship, using different methods and bases of comparison, yet coming to essentially the same conclusion: that investments in welfare capital and penal capital are increasingly inversely related. These findings are of substantial importance from a policy perspective, as they indicate that a country that increases the amount of its GDP spent on welfare sees a relatively lower rate of increase or a greater decline in its imprisonment rate than in the past.

2.2 The United States: social marginality and penal exclusion

In the most systematic study of the welfare/punishment links to date, Beckett and Western (2001) view social and penal policy as inextricably linked, with policy responding to social marginality. They argue that welfare regimes (US states in their case) vary according to their commitment to including or excluding marginal groups. Inclusive regimes emphasize the social causes of marginality and aim to integrate the socially marginalized through generous welfare programmes. These regimes have less harsh views on crime and are likely to have lower imprisonment rates. By contrast, exclusionary regimes lay responsibility for social problems in the hands of the socially marginalized. Thus the unemployed are seen as work-shy, deviancy is unjustifiable and deviants are non-reformable. Such regimes provide less generous welfare, take a harsher stance on crime and are more likely to favour imprisonment.

Beckett and Western test this approach using data from 32 US states for 1975, 1985 and 1995. After controlling for several factors such as crime rates, they find that as welfare spending increases, rates of imprisonment increase less sharply or are relatively lower. They also find a clearly positive relationship between imprisonment in a state and the proportion of black and other ethnic minority groups, the poverty rate and Republican representation in that state. Poor states with high poverty rates and large numbers of ethnic minority groups that have Republican-dominated legislatures tend to have higher incarceration rates. Most of these relationships are stronger in 1995 than in earlier periods. This leads them to suggest that social and penal policy are especially closely tied at specific times 'when efforts are made to alter prevailing approaches to social marginality' (2001: 46), as was the case with the Reagan administration. Not only did states with less generous welfare spending have higher imprisonment rates in the 1990s, but this later period also saw states with a higher proportion of blacks, other ethnic minorities and greater poverty having higher imprisonment rates. Thus they argue: 'The more exclusionary approaches to social marginality are especially likely to be adopted by states which house more of those defined in contemporary political discourse as "trouble makers"' (2001: 46).

In his *Punishment and Inequality in America* (2006), Bruce Western analyses how, over time, the zero-sum relationship between welfare and penal capital has developed into a corrosive concealment and deepening of inequality along racial lines:

> The calculations were simple, but the results were startling. Among black male high school dropouts aged twenty to thirty-five, we estimated that 36 percent were in prison or jail in 1996. The US Census Bureau's labor force survey ... estimated that 46 percent of young black male dropouts were employed, but this number dropped to 29 percent once prison and jail inmates were included in the population ... Among black male dropouts born in the late 1960s, 60 percent had prison records by their early thirties.
> (p. xii)

African-Americans are now eight times more likely to be incarcerated than whites. In 2004, over 12 per cent of black men aged 25–29 were behind bars. Great damage has been inflicted on the life course of a greatly increased proportion of this group in particular. Former inmates suffer damage to job prospects and family life. Few couples survive a term of imprisonment. 'By 2000, over one million black children – 9 percent of those under 18 – had a father in prison or jail ... Although the normal life course is integrative, incarceration is disintegrative, diverting young men from the life stages that mark a man's gradual inclusion in society' (p. 5). The 'war on crime' and the 'war on drugs' have coalesced into a war on an entire class and ethnic group.

Nor do the effects stop there. The core of the prison system has crystallized into the inhumanities of the Super Maximum Security prisons, holding over 20,000 inmates under conditions amounting to being buried alive (Shalev 2008), yet somehow escaping indictment as 'cruel and unusual punishment' under the US constitution. In many states, the sheer scale of felon disenfranchisement among largely Democrat-voting ethnic minorities, resulting in the main from mass imprisonment, had a pivotal effect on the 2000 presidential election, which turned on the slender majority of George W. Bush over Al Gore in Florida. In sum, it all adds up to 'a profound social exclusion that significantly rolls back the gains to citizenship hard won by the civil rights movement' (Western 2006: 6).

2.3 Cross-national analysis of the punishment and welfare thesis

The United States is not the only country where welfare policies are becoming tougher. Policies in European countries where welfare has traditionally been more encompassing than in the USA are increasingly incorporating aspects of the American market-driven approach to welfare (Gilbert 2002), largely as a response to globalization. Despite these trends, huge national differences remain in the generosity of welfare provision. Despite recent changes, for example, the Nordic countries largely continue to provide a generous universal welfare state with, for the most part, high labour market security and a low incidence of poverty.

By contrast, neo-liberal market approaches, typified by the United States, attach strict conditions to time-limited welfare, are less concerned with redistribution or equity across classes and associate welfare spending with creating a culture of dependency. Unsurprisingly, as a result, inequality among citizens is great, as are its costs. A major comparative study found that economic inequality and low welfare provision are strongly related to high rates of lethal violence. 'Overall levels of homicide will be lower in capitalist societies that have decommodified labor by reducing dependence on the market for personal well-being' (Messner and Rosenfeld 1997: 1407).

While these differences do not translate into lower rates of crime in general for more generous welfare states, they do link such provision with less exposure to the most feared types of crime and to a more restrained use of imprisonment. The underlying reasons arguably have much to do with the greater social cohesion and stability that flow from perceptions of fairness and investment in social capital. Despite having had for almost a decade a daily prison population of over two million, between five and ten times the rate of Canada and most Western European countries, the US homicide rate remains at least three times their level.

In testing this hypothesis using comparative data from 18 OECD countries, results matched the findings of Beckett and Western using US state-level data: that is, states that spent more on welfare had lower imprisonment rates (see Table 2.1). Downes and Hansen (2006) employed regression analysis to explore the relationship between daily rates of imprisonment per 100,000 and the proportion of GDP spent on welfare in 1988 and 1998. Figure 2.1 plots two graphs which show that the regression slope between welfare expenditure and imprisonment is more negative in 1998 than in 1988, i.e. expenditure on welfare had a greater impact on imprisonment rates in 1998 than it did a decade before. In fact, while the earlier period produces a negative relationship between the two variables, the results remain statistically insignificant. These differences remain even after controlling for unemployment and lagged crime rates. This is true with or without including the USA and Japan, outliers at the top and bottom of the imprisonment rate distribution but sharing low welfare expenditure.

Analysis of the data for all the years between 1987 and 1998 confirm that this appears to be a trend rather than two random findings: the association between imprisonment rates and welfare spending becomes more sensitive as we move towards 1998. This echoes the analysis of data for the USA, where Beckett and Western found that while the relationship was not strong in the 1980s, it was very evident by the late 1990s. Moreover, by looking at changes within countries through time using 'fixed effects models', it is possible to estimate how changes in welfare spending are associated with changes in imprisonment rates. That association becomes greater as the sample progresses over time, indicating that a country that increases the amount of GDP spent on welfare sees a lower rate of growth or a greater decline in its imprisonment rate than in the past. Approaching the relationship in a different way, one can ask, for example: what would the prison population have looked like in England and Wales in 1998 if welfare expenditure

TABLE 2.1 Descriptive statistics on imprisonment, GDP and welfare across countries*

Country	Imprisonment ranking	Imprisonment rate (per 100,000 of the population aged 15+)**	Percentage of GDP spent on welfare	Welfare score
USA	1	666	14.6	−8.2
Portugal	2	146	18.2	−4.6
New Zealand	3	144	21.0	−1.8
UK	4	124	20.8	−2.0
Canada	5	115	18.0	−4.8
Spain	6	112	19.7	−3.1
Australia	7	106	17.8	−5.0
Germany	8	95	26.0	3.2
France	9	92	28.8	6.0
Luxemburg	10	92	22.1	−0.7
Italy	11	86	25.1	2.3
Netherlands	12	85	24.5	1.7
Switzerland	13	79	28.1	5.3
Belgium	14	77	24.5	1.7
Denmark	15	63	29.8	7.0
Sweden	16	60	31.0	8.2
Finland	17	54	26.5	3.7
Japan	18	42	14.7	−8.1

* Data are from 1998.

**These are the number of prisoners held either as remand prisoners or those convicted and sentenced per 100,000 of the population aged 15 and over. These numbers are slightly different from those published in the World Prison Population list, which gives the imprisonment rate per 100,000 of the entire population. We have excluded young children here as they are excluded from the imprisoned population.

had stayed at its 1987 level? The analysis shows that there would have been an additional four prisoners per 100,000. That may not appear much of a difference, but it amounts to one-fifth of the rise in the prison population between 1987 and 1998, i.e. the rise in imprisonment 1987–98 would have been 20 per cent greater if welfare expenditure had not risen but remained at its 1987 level.[1]

2.4 Penal systems and political economy

Welfare is but one component, albeit a major strand, of political economy. In the most wide-ranging survey to date of the relationship between types of political economy and the character of punishment, Cavadino and Dignan (2006) analyse the penal systems of twelve societies. Basing their typology on Esping-Anderson's landmark study of welfare in late-modern capitalist societies (1990), they distinguish between four types of political economy and their penal tendencies as follows (Cavadino and Dignan 2006: 15):

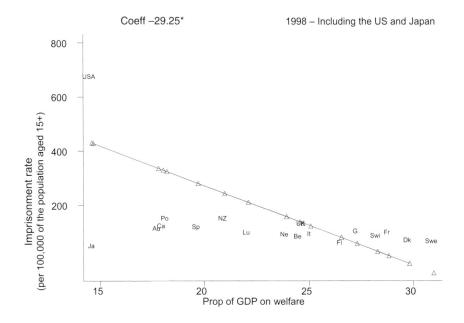

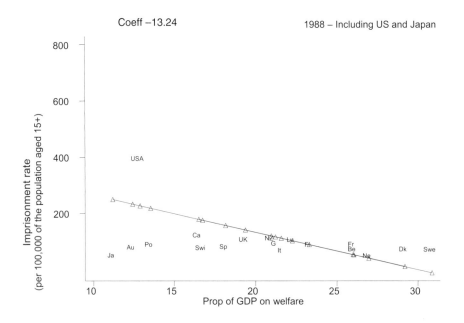

FIGURE 2.1 Imprisonment and welfare, 1998 and 1988

- *Neo-liberalism*: free market, low welfare provision, extreme inequality, limited social rights, right-wing politically, highly exclusionary both socially and penally, high imprisonment rate: archetype the USA, but also England and Wales, Australia, New Zealand and South Africa.
- *Conservative corporatism*: moderately mixed economy and welfare state, pronounced inequality, qualified social rights, centrist politically, penally rehabilitative, medium imprisonment rate: archetype Germany, but also France, Italy and The Netherlands.
- *Social democratic corporatism*: universalistic, generous welfare state, limited inequality, relatively unconditional social rights, left-wing politically, rights-based penally, low imprisonment rate: archetype Sweden, but also Finland (and, logically, Norway and Denmark).
- *Oriental corporatism*: private sector welfare system, very limited inequality, quasi-feudal inclusiveness, politically centre-right, inclusionary penalties, low imprisonment rate: archetype Japan.

All typologies entail a certain Procrustean severity, and many English, Australian and New Zealand commentators would baulk at being clumped together with the USA as offering only 'minimalist' or 'residual' welfare provision; and it is far from easy to find a bedfellow for Japanese 'oriental corporatism'. There are also societies, notably Canada, which would logically be placed in the 'neo-liberal' category, yet whose political economy has proved notably resistant to penal expansionism. Nevertheless, the categories do correspond broadly with actual differences in imprisonment rates per 100,000 which, in 2002–3, were 'true to type' (Cavadino and Dignan 2006: 22):

- *Neo-liberal*: USA 701; South Africa 402; New Zealand 155; England and Wales 141; Australia 115.
- *Conservative corporatist*: Italy 100; The Netherlands 100; Germany 98; France 93.
- *Social democracies*: Sweden 73; Norway 70.
- *Oriental corporatist*: Japan 53.

Moreover, even more recently, trends have confirmed the tendency for neo-liberal countries to move rapidly closer to the US level, New Zealand's rate now being 186 per 100,000 and England and Wales 148 (Walmsley 2007). As Reiner has commented, 'although the groupings show considerable variation between the countries comprising them, there is no overlap between the types in terms of imprisonment rates' (2007a and b, note 41), though recent increases in the Dutch prison population may have pushed them higher than the Australian. The differences also hold broadly for variations in the age of criminal responsibility and for the extent to which the private sector has been enabled to acquire a stake in prison management. In both the USA and England and Wales, the age threshold for criminal prosecution is as low as 10. By contrast, in the Nordic social democracies, it is 15. The market sector has made its greatest inroads into prison management in the USA, England and Wales, Australia and South Africa. By contrast, in the Nordic countries, it has no stake whatsoever (see Cavadino and Dignan 2006: Chapters 14 and 15).

The main point, therefore, is not to become too fixated on particular levels of difference at specific points of time but to examine the fundamental components of the broad correspondence between political economy and penal system variables. This is borne out by the detailed examination of each country's specific characteristics, written in collaboration with criminological experts in each country.

2.5 Penal trends and political economy

In her *The Prisoners' Dilemma: Political Economy and Punishment in Contemporary Democracies* (2008), Nicola Lacey brings more recent developments in political science to bear on these issues in comparative criminology. She sets out to distil from the growing body of work in both fields 'the institutional preconditions for a tolerant criminal justice system' (p. xvii). Setting out from the exclusionary and punitive turn in some, but not all, western democracies, she examines how far existing theories adequately account for the huge variation in criminal justice policies. In particular, she queries the utility of the emphasis, in the work of David Garland (2001) in particular, on 'late modernity' as the crucible of penal populism. Late modernity takes diverse forms in different types of political economy. Though the trend towards marketization and individualism is a common denominator, the more coordinated market economies have shielded certain core institutional components against their permeation more effectively than the neo-liberal market economies of the USA and Britain. Cavadino and Dignan have established the links between types of political economy and penal policy, but ultimately focus on correlation rather than cause in relation to the key role played by institutional variables.

To answer the question as to why the variations in punishment take the form they do, Lacey combines the model of political economy of Cavadino and Dignan with the contrast between 'coordinated' and 'liberal' market economies proposed by Hall and Soskice (2001). 'Coordinated' market economies (CME) (a term embracing Cavadino and Dignan's 'corporatist' and 'social democratic' types) are linked not only to inclusionary criminal justice policies, more egalitarian social policies, high commitment to welfare and a relatively low crime rate, but also to electoral systems based on proportional representation and frequent coalition government. 'Liberal' market economies (LME) ('neo-liberal' to Cavadino and Dignan) are more prone to exclusionary criminal justice policies, high inequality, less commitment to welfare and relatively high crime rates and are based on first-past-the-post majoritarian electoral systems (see also Green 2007 and Lappi-Seppälä, Chapter 3 this volume). A key inference is that the erosion of party bases of support in majoritarian countries leaves them more vulnerable to single issue, median, floating voters, among whom crime and punishment figure as highly contentious issues, leading to hyperactive government responses on this front. Such governments are also more likely to disparage experts and bureaucratic structures, encourage presidential-style politics and over-rely on a stream of consultants and advisers whose expensiveness is matched only by their lack of expertise. A 'new politics of law and order' has emerged from this matrix in both Britain and the USA, based on the appeal to penal populism and bitter partisan rivalry on which party can be 'toughest on crime'.

Other key differences are the much higher investment in education, training and poverty reduction and stronger 'anti-degradation' criminal justice policies (Whitman 2003) in CMEs by comparison with LMEs. Of particular significance are investments in highly specific skill training as favouring generous and inclusive unemployment benefits. The autonomous selection, training and tenure of judges render a highly trained professional judiciary less vulnerable to popular opinion than is otherwise the case. The election of judges in the USA, and lay magistrates in Britain, mean they are more exposed to populist pressures.

The vast differences that still obtain between mass imprisonment in the USA and rates of imprisonment among western democracies in general should give grounds for optimism that the USA is an 'exceptionalist' outlier, not a harbinger of future penal trends in Europe or indeed the world at large (the world still at large, so to speak). The difference between a prison population per 100,000 rate of 725 and the European average of 135 is little changed over the past decade. The peculiarities that have proved a recipe for mass imprisonment in the American case – *inter alia* an extreme exemplification of the LME political economy, plus deindustrialization, plus the politics of race, plus the war on drugs, plus the collapse of the rehabilitative idea – have not combined to produce the same effect in Europe, Britain included (Tonry 2007). But could they over time?

The arguments that the USA is ahead of the trend rather than uniquely punitive in relation to crime among democracies are twofold:

1. The political economies of Europe are moving away from the CME towards the LME model, under the pressure of globalised neo-liberalism.
2. The politics of immigration both from within and from without Europe is becoming the equivalent of the politics of race in the USA (see especially Wacquant 2001).

Against the first point, Lacey argues that the apparent success of the USA as an economic force wedded to neo-liberal precepts is, at least in part, a mirage, with an unemployment rate heavily masked by the sheer size of the prison population (Downes 2001; Western 2006) and unduly dependent on inherently unproductive 'guard labor' (Bowles and Jayadev 2006). Moreover, other economic successes in both the LME and CME groups of countries, such as Canada, Australia and Germany (despite the strains of reunification), have accomplished their achievements without a grotesquely inflated prison-industrial complex. CME countries also show a resistance to the flexibilization of labour markets that runs counter to neo-liberal dogma. In sum, it is far too premature to write off the resilience of social democratic CMEs that have evolved for over a century as a genuine Third Way between the extremes of capitalist laissez-faire and communist bloc authoritarianism.

On the second point, it has to be acknowledged that far higher rates of custody are seen in CMEs for foreign nationals, foreign-born indigenous and other ethnic minority groups of colour than can be explained by their proportionate share of the national populations of Europe. The very integrative qualities that lend CMEs their social cohesion can militate against their incorporation of outsiders and second-generation insiders who reject, or are seen as rejecting, key aspects of national cultures. There are, however, some key variations that suggest reasons for the differences within continental Europe lie within the institutional domain rather than amounting to a blanket 'othering' of all immigrants and minorities as 'aliens' at risk of perpetrating lethal terrorist violence, high levels of street crime and threats to hard-won liberal freedoms from censorship and normal forms of sexual deviance. There are differences between Germany and the Netherlands, for example, in relation to industrial skills and trade unionism that may help account for the much greater over-representation of foreign nationals in Dutch than in German prisons. Counter-intuitively, migrant workers may have fared better via the German system of sectoral bargaining than the Dutch reliance on inter-elite negotiations (see Lacey 2008: 156–64 in particular, drawing on unpublished work by Leo Halepli). There is also the fact that it is difficult to ascertain population bases for making such comparisons. For example, once age and socio-economic status are controlled for, the over-representation of foreign nationals in Danish prisons falls from 49 to 8 per cent! In sum, though the integration of greatly increased numbers of immigrants exerts real strain on integrative institutions, there are real grounds for optimism that dystopian analyses have been overplayed.

It is worth noting that the contrast between European levels of imprisonment and those of the United States is bound to convince some European commentators that even the expansion of prison numbers in most European countries over the past two decades is nothing to worry about. However, given that crime rates have levelled off or fallen in general, the increase in prison populations in Europe remains significant. The current recession, which threatens to be longer and deeper than any since the 1930s, is all too likely to drive crime rates upwards and prison numbers even further as a consequence. In England and Wales in particular, the projected rate of prison population by 2014 is nearing 200 per 100,000, the lower slopes of mass imprisonment, despite the greatly increased expenditure on welfare over the past decade. The relation between welfare expenditure and rates of imprisonment is by no means automatic, however. It is also possible, as the section on cross-national analysis of the punishment and welfare thesis above indicates, that imprisonment levels could have been even worse had welfare expenditure shown lower growth.

Conclusion

All four studies show a significant and growing relationship between the nature of political economy and the commitment to welfare, on the one hand, and the scale and punitiveness of penal systems, on the other. It is difficult to believe that the consistent finding of an inverse relationship between the commitment to welfare and the scale of imprisonment, both cross-nationally and across the United States, is simply accidental or coincidental, especially when such variations cannot be accounted for by crime rates.

Moreover, these findings indicate that the principal criterion of social democracy, the willingness to intervene in the market for social and welfare ends, remains as, if not more, important as in the past, just when the welfare principle is under sustained threat from pressures to offload the costs of welfare provision onto individuals themselves or the market, via privatization, contracting-out and/ or the voluntary sector. Above all, these studies imply that a substantial welfare state is increasingly a principal, if not the main, protection against the resort to mass imprisonment in the era of globalization, and what John Gray (1998) has termed the delusions of global capitalism in its neo-liberal form. Now that those delusions have been so starkly exposed, the case for retaining and strengthening the bases of social democratic political economy should be all too evident.

Note

1. This interpretation differs from that in Downes and Hansen (2006: 152) where the effect is overstated as a 20 per cent greater impact on the size of the prison population as a whole.

References

Beckett, K. and Western, B. (2001) 'Governing social marginality', in D. Garland (ed.), *Mass Imprisonment: Social Causes and Consequences*. London: Sage, pp. 35–50.

Bowles, S. and Jayadev, A. (2006) 'Guard labor', *Journal of Development Economics*, 79(2): 328–48.

Cavadino, M. and Dignan, J. (2006) *Penal Systems: A Comparative Approach*. London: Sage.

Downes, D. (2001) 'The *macho* penal economy: mass incarceration in the US – a European perspective', in D. Garland (ed.), *Mass Imprisonment: Social Causes and Consequences*. London: Sage, pp. 51–69.

Downes, D. and Hansen, K. (2006) 'Welfare and punishment in comparative perspective', in S. Armstrong and L. McAra (eds), *Perspectives on Punishment: The Contours of Control*. Oxford: Oxford University Press, pp. 133–54.

Esping-Anderson, G. (1990) *The Three Worlds of Welfare Capitalism*. Princeton, NJ: Princeton University Press.

Garland, D. (1985) *Punishment and Welfare: A History of Penal Strategies*. Aldershot: Gower.

Garland, D. (2001) The Culture of Control. Oxford: Oxford University Press.

Gilbert, N. (2002) *Transformation of the Welfare State: The Silent Surrender of Public Responsibility*. Oxford: Oxford University Press.

Gray, J. (1998) *False Dawn: The Delusions of Global Capitalism*. Cambridge: Granta.

Green, D. A. (2007) 'Comparing penal cultures: two responses to child-on-child homicide', *Crime and Justice – A Review of Research*, 36: 591–643.

Hall, P. A. and Soskice, D. (2001) 'An introduction to the varieties of capitalism', in P. A. Hall and D. Soskice (eds), *Varieties of Capitalism*. Oxford: Oxford University Press, pp. 1–68.

Lacey, N. (2008) *The Prisoners' Dilemma: Political Economy and Punishment in Contemporary Democracies*, The Hamlyn Lectures 2007. Cambridge: Cambridge University Press.

Messner, S. E. and Rosenfeld, R. (1997) 'Political constraint of the market and levels of criminal homicide: a cross-national application of institutional-anomie theory', *Social Forces*, 75(4): 1393–416.

Reiner, R. (2007a) 'Political economy, crime and criminal justice', in M. Maguire, R. Morgan and R. Reiner (eds), *The Oxford Handbook of Criminology*, 4th edn revised. Oxford: Oxford University Press, pp. 341–80.

Reiner, R. (2007b) *Law and Order: An Honest Citizen's Guide to Crime and Control*. Oxford: Polity Press.

Shalev, S. (2008) *A Sourcebook on Solitary Confinement*. London: Mannheim Centre for Criminology, London School of Economics.

Tonry, M. (2007) 'Determinants of penal policies', in M. Tonry (ed.), *Crime, Punishment, and Politics in Comparative Perspective, in Crime and Justice: A Review of Research*, Vol. 36. Chicago: University of Chicago Press, pp. 1–48.

Wacquant, L. (2001) 'Deadly symbiosis: when ghetto and prison meet and mesh', in D. Garland (ed.), *Mass Imprisonment: Social Causes and Consequences*. London: Sage, pp. 82–120.

Walmsley, R. (2007) *World Prison Population* List, 8th edn. London: International Centre for Prison Studies, King's College London.

Western, B. (2006) *Punishment and Inequality in America*. New York: Russell Sage.

Whitman, J. Q. (2003) *Harsh Justice: Criminal Punishment and the Widening Divide between America and Europe*. New York: Oxford University Press.

3

EXPLAINING NATIONAL DIFFERENCES IN THE USE OF IMPRISONMENT

Tapio Lappi-Seppälä

3.1 Introduction

Unprecedented expansions of penal control have occurred in recent decades in different parts of the world. American imprisonment rates have increased nearly fivefold and Dutch rates sixfold since the early 1970s. Substantial changes of differing magnitudes may be observed in many countries. This increase in states' willingness to use penal power has provoked criminological and sociological explanations, most from writers in North America and English-speaking countries. An unspoken assumption that developments in the United States and England and Wales occurred elsewhere has influenced efforts to formulate general explanations of changes taking place under general conditions of late modern society. However, things have not happened in the same way everywhere. Alongside general growth in cultures of control, there are divergent trends and country-specific deviations. The Scandinavian countries with their more restrained penal policies serve as one important counter-example, but there are others. To overlook these differences may lead to overgeneralized and simplified pictures of the dynamics of penal change. This essay explores explanations for differences in penal severity in industrialized countries. The focus is not restricted to the Anglophonic world but also encompasses the Scandinavian countries, Western and Eastern continental Europe and the Baltic countries.[1]

3.2 Trends and differences in prisoner rates

3.2.1 Trends

Since the mid-1970s prisoner rates in the US have increased by well over 300 per cent from around 170 to around 750 per 100, 000 pop. (see Table 3.1) The US seems to have a strong model-effect in the English-speaking world. Similar

– albeit smaller – changes have also taken place in Australia, New Zealand and the UK Among the Anglo-Saxon countries Canada has a deviant role. During the last 15–20 years the prisoner rates have been more or less stable.

TABLE 3.1 Prisoner rates in selected Anglo-Saxon countries 1970-2007 (per 100,000 pop.)

	1970	1980	1990	2000	2005	2007/8	Change 1970– 2007 %	Change 1990– 2007 %
USA	166	221	461	684	738	756	+355	+64
New Zealand	83	88	114	151	186	185	+123	+62
UK	71	85	90	125	144	152	+114	+69
Australia		59	84	113	125	129		+54
'Deviants'								
Canada	88	98	113	101	107	116	+32	+3

Source: National Statistics, ICPS.

Trends in continental Europe are diverse (see Table 3.2). Some Western European countries have fairly stable prisoner rates at the level of 80–90 per 100,000 (Germany, Austria and Switzerland). Some have reached this level after a fairly steep increase from the 1970s onwards (France and Belgium). But there are also notable exceptions. Between 1970 and 2005 the Netherlands had increased their prisoner rate more than six fold from the low of 20 to 130 per 100,000. Spain had more than tripled its rates from 40 to 140 per 100,000. The latest figures indicate different trends in these two countries. Between 2005 and 2008 the Dutch figures decreased by over 20 per cent[2], while the Spanish figures still keep climbing. Had we also included countries from Eastern Europe, we would have found figures which are about double those in Western Europe. Including the Baltic countries would raise figures even higher.

The Scandinavian countries differ from many other European as well as non-European countries both in terms of stability and leniency of penal policy. For almost half a century the prisoner rates in Denmark, Norway and Sweden have stayed between the narrow limits of 40–60 prisoners (see Table 3.3).

However, Finland has followed its own path. At the beginning of the 1950s, the prisoner rate in Finland was four times higher than in the other Nordic countries. Finland had some 200 prisoners per 100,000 inhabitants, while the figures in Sweden, Denmark and Norway were around 50. Even during the 1970s, Finland's prisoner rate continued to be among the highest in Western Europe. However, the steady decrease that started soon after the Second World War continued, and during the 1970s and 1980s, when most European countries experienced rising prison populations, the Finnish rates kept on going down. By

TABLE 3.2 Prisoner rates in selected Western European countries 1970-2007 (per 100,000 pop.)

	1970	1980	1990	2000	2005	2007/8	Change 1970– 2007 %	Change 1990– 2007 %
France	55	66	77	82	88	96	75	25
Belgium	61	58	66	86	93	93	52	41
Germany	86	92	82	97	97	89	3	9
Switzerland		62	77	79	83	76		−1
Austria		107	83	85	108	95		14
'Deviants'								
Spain	38	85	113	145	160			88
Netherlands	21	23	43	84	127	100	376	133

Source: National Statistics, ICPS.

TABLE 3.3 Prisoner rates in selected Scandinavian countries 1950-2008 (per 100,000 pop.)

	1950	1960	1970	1980	1990	2000	2005	2008	Change 1970– 2008 %	Change 1990– 2008 %
Norway	51	44	44	44	56	57	68	73	+54	+21
Denmark	88	71	70	63	67	67	78	68	+11	+16
Sweden	35	63	65	55	58	60	78	74	+20	+34
'Deviants'										
Finland	187	154	113	106	69	55	74	67	−35	+7

the beginning of the 1990s, Finland had reached the Nordic level of around 60 prisoners. From 1980 to 2005 Norway, Denmark and Sweden also experienced a period of increased prisoner rates. In Finland this took place in 2000 to 2005. Most recent figures show versatile trends (increase in Norway, stable in Sweden, and declining in Denmark and Finland).[3]

Diverging long-term trends in the US and the Scandinavian countries are highlighted in Figure 3.1. During the last 60 years things have certainly gone differently in Finland and in the US What applies to the US does not evidently fit to Finland.

3.2.2 Status and differences

Prisoner rates by regions in 2007/2008 are represented in Figure 3.2. In a global context Scandinavia as a region has among the lowest level of prisoners in Europe

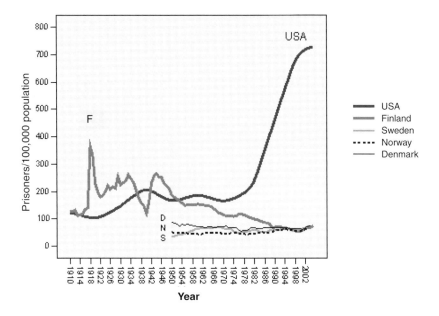

FIGURE 3.1 Long-term prisoner rates in Scandinavia and US
Source: Falck *et al.* (2003) updated, US Department of Justice.

(with Ireland, Switzerland and Slovenia roughly on the same level). At the moment the Scandinavian figures vary between 45 and 75 with an average of 67. The corresponding figures for other Western European countries are between 65 and 160 (average 103), in Eastern Europe between 148 and 222 (175), in the Baltic countries between 234 and 288 (260), in Russia 629 and in the US 756.

These figures raise several questions:

- What explains the steep increase in especially the US and several European countries?
- What explains the diametrically opposed development in Finland (and some other countries, too)?
- What are the reasons behind the overall leniency in Scandinavian countries?

A majority of research has tried to explain the 'American exceptionalism' and the rise of prisoner rates in the Anglophone world (for example, Garland 2001 and Tonry 2004). This paper looks at the opposite view and seeks to explain the differences among (mostly) Western European countries. A major focus will be in explaining the 'Scandinavian exceptionalism': why Scandinavia, as a whole, has been able to maintain a (comparatively) low level of penal repression for such a long time. The article presents the main results of a large cross-comparative study covering 25 countries.[4] This abridged version concentrates on macro-level indicators related to social/economical circumstances, social/moral values and

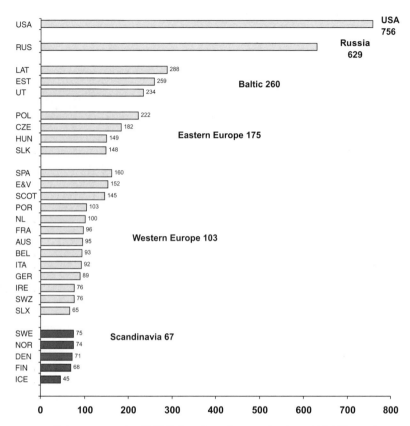

FIGURE 3.2 Prisoner rates in 2007/8 in selected countries (per 100,000 pop.)

Source: ICPS; for Scandinavia Kristoffersen (2010) updated.

political economy/political culture, using imprisonment rates (per capita) as the major indicator for the levels of punitiveness and penal severity.[5]

3.3 Crime rates and prisoner rates

It is natural to assume that the differences in prisoner rates reflect differences in the level of crime. The influence of crime rates on prison rates may be either direct (high crime rates indicate high conviction rates) or indirectly (high crime rates create pressures for harsher policies). This section aims to find out how prisoner rates and crime rates relate in cross-sectional and time series analyses.

3.3.1. Cross-sectional comparisons on crime and prisoner rates

Figure 3.3 compares prisoner rates, victimization and an index of reported crime based on four basic offences (homicide + robberies + theft + assault / 100,000).

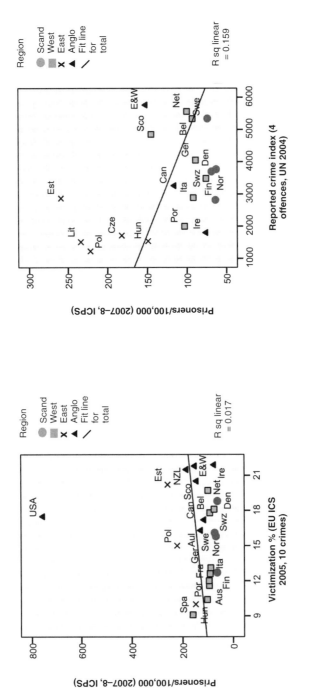

FIGURE 3.3 Prisoner rates 2007–8, victimization and reported crime (basic sample)

Lower incarceration rates can hardly be explained by lower victimization rates as the correlation remains close to zero. The association between reported crime and prisoner rates is, in fact, negative: the higher the crime rates, the fewer prisoners. However, some caveats are needed. First, victimization surveys are concentrated on minor property offences. In most Western European countries these crimes have a quite limited relevance for prisoner rates. Secondly, differences in reported crime are highly dependent on recording practices and legal definitions. There are evident differences between developing and developed countries, as well as between western and eastern countries (see van Dijk *et al.* 2007: 105ff.).[6] Lethal violence provides an opportunity for more reliable comparisons. Overall, homicide and prisoner rates are positively correlated.[7] However, it also turned out that these associations vary in different regions (see Figure 3.4).

Homicide and prisoner rates correlate positively in Eastern Europe but negatively in the Latin American and Caribbean region. Prisoner rates in western democracies (US excluded) seem to be fairly independent of the level of lethal violence, or, if there is a positive association, there are important outliers such as England and Wales and Finland at the opposite ends of the scale. Overall, evidence from reported and actual crime hardly justifies a conclusion of any notable positive correlation between prisoner rates and the level of crime. This impression gets stronger once we look at changes over time.

3.3.2 Trends in prisoner rates and reported crime 1980–2005

Trend analyses provide another possibility for testing these associations. Figure 3.5 compares trends in prisoner rates and reported crime in Finland, Canada and the USA in 1980–2005 (1980 = 100).

These three countries provide an example of diverging trends. In Finland prisoner rates fell as crime rates were increasing (1980–90). Canada kept its prisoner rates stable while crime was either stable (1980–90) or falling (1990–2000). The USA has an almost identical crime profile as Canada, but shows a sharply increasing prisoner profile. It is hard to conclude from all this that there should be any systematic association between these series.

3.3.3 Crime rate and prisoner rates in Scandinavia 1950–2005

The fall of prisoner rates in Finland was not associated with falling crime levels – on the contrary. Crime was going up when prisoner rates were going down. This leaves us with the awkward question: can rising crime rates be explained by decreasing prisoner rates? To answer this from the Finnish point of view, we need to include the other Nordic countries in the analyses. These countries share strong social and structural similarities but they have very different penal histories. This provides an excellent opportunity to test how drastic changes in penal practices in one country (Finland) have been reflected in the crime rates, compared with countries with similar social and cultural conditions but which have kept their

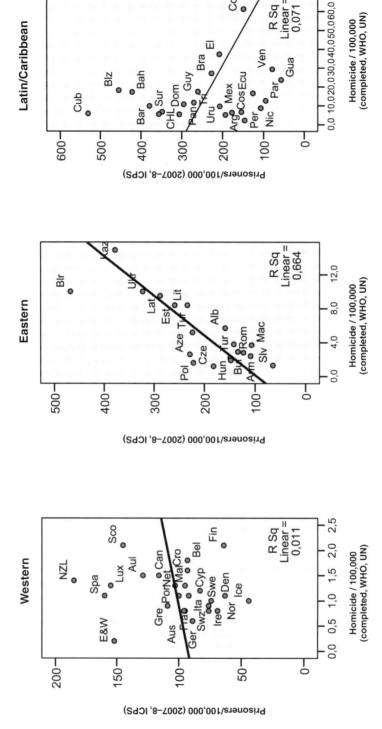

FIGURE 3.4 Reported homicide and assault in 2003 (per 100,000, global sample, US excluded)

Source: ICPS, WHO, UN.

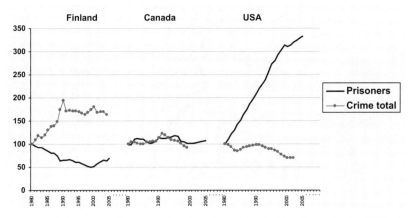

FIGURE 3.5 Prisoners and reported crime in Finland, Canada and the USA (per 100,000, 1980 = 100)

Source: Sourcebook 2006 complemented.

penal systems much more stable. Figure 3.6 shows prisoner rates and reported crime rates in Finland, Sweden, Denmark and Norway from 1950 to 2010.

There is a striking difference in the use of imprisonment and a striking similarity in trends of recorded crime. That Finland has substantially reduced its prisoner rate has not disturbed the symmetry of the Nordic crime rates. These figures, once again, support the general criminological conclusion that crime and incarceration rates are fairly independent of one another; each rises and falls according to its own laws and dynamics.

Prisoner rates are largely unrelated to victimization rates as well as to reported crime. The development of prisoner rates in 1980–2005 showed no consistent patterns with total recorded crime. In different times different countries showed different patterns. These results fit well with the conclusion from prior literature that differences in the use of imprisonment cannot be explained by the level and trends in criminality (see, for example, Greenberg 1999; von Hofer 2003, Sutton 2004; Ruddell 2005). Crime is not the explanation, either for differences or for trends. The rest of this paper searches for explanations from other sources.

3.4 Welfare and social equality

There is an evident connection between welfare orientation and penal culture. A straightforward way of defining the relationship between welfare and incarceration is to draw a straight line between these two: 'Locking people up or giving them money might be considered alternative ways of handling marginal, poor populations – repressive in one case, generous in the other' (Greenberg 2001: 70). A 'war on poverty' leads to a different penal policy than a 'war on crime'. The association between the emergence of punitive policies and the scaling down of the welfare state in the US and in the UK has been noted by several commentators.[8] The

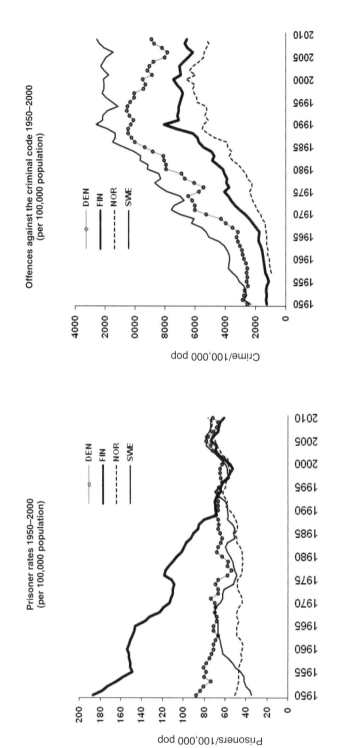

FIGURE 3.6 Prison rates and crime rates 1950–2010

Source: Falck *et al.* (2003) and Kristofferssen (2010) updated

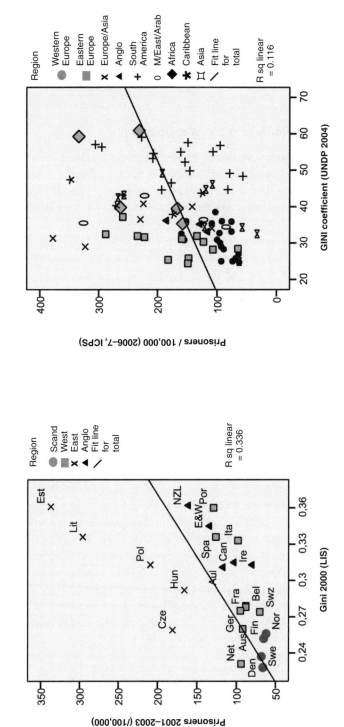

FIGURE 3.7 Gini index and prisoner rates in basic sample (left) and global sample (right)

Source: Sourcebook 2006 complemented, ICPS, LIS, UN.

connection between the level of repression and welfare receives support also from the Finnish story, as the period of penal liberalization in Finland started at the time when Finland 'joined the Nordic welfare family'. This all indicates that factors such as a high level of social and economic security, equality in welfare resources and generous welfare provision should contribute to lower levels of punitivity and repression.

3.4.1 Income inequality and social expenditures

There is a strong positive correlation between income inequality[9] and prisoner rates among western countries (left panel, Figure 3.7). Eastern countries also follow a similar pattern (but on a higher level in prisoner rates). Expanding the analyses to other regions maintains the association, but in a weaker form (right panel).

Figure 3.8 compares investments in welfare and the scale of imprisonment. The extent of welfare provision is measured both in relative (left) and absolute (right) terms (as percentage of GDP and as €/per capita).

There is a clear inverse relation between the commitment to welfare and the scale of imprisonment. In the lower right corner are countries with strong proportional and absolute investments in welfare and low imprisonment rates, with Sweden and Denmark in the lead. In the upper left corner we find the Eastern countries and from Western Europe, England and Wales, Portugal and Spain.

3.4.2 Regional patterns and penal regimes?

In closer analysis it also turns out that countries cluster in terms of their penal policy into 'penal regimes', closely related to the regimes developed in comparative welfare theory. In his classical *The Three Worlds of Welfare Capitalism*, Esping-Andersen (1990) detected a pattern among western (capitalist) welfare states. With regard to the extent and structure of welfare provision, the values and principles aimed at and expressed in welfare policies, countries in Esping-Andersen's study clustered fairly neatly in three welfare regimes: the social-democratic (Scandinavian) regime, the Christian democratic (Conservative/European regime) and the liberal (Anglo-Saxon) regime. These regimes bunch particular values together with particular programmes and policies. Different regimes pursue different policies and for different reasons. Esping-Andersen's findings haven't been contested, although his original classification has subsequently been refined, *inter alia*, by introducing a separate Southern cluster.[10] Including the former socialist countries in the analysis would require additional revisions.[11]

The relevance of welfare-classifications for this analysis is simple: if welfare policies matter for penal policies (as it seems), then differences between welfare regimes should find a comparable reflection in differences in penal policies. To test the hypothesis, we have clustered the countries in five regions. The clustering

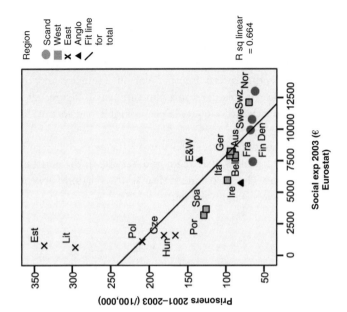

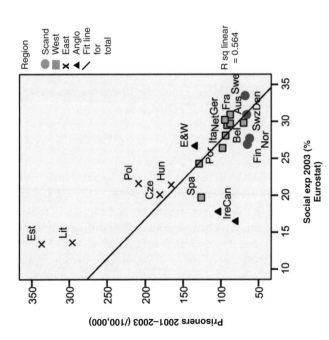

FIGURE 3.8 Social expenditure and prisoner rates (basic sample)

Source: Sourcebook 2006 complemented, ICPS, Eurostat.

follows the original classification of Esping-Andersen but adds three clusters: the Mediterranean countries, the former traditional socialist countries and the Baltic countries. This leaves us with six regions (excluding the US): Scandinavia (Finland, Denmark, Sweden, Norway), Western Europe (Austria, Belgium, France, Germany, the Netherlands, Switzerland), Mediterranean Europe (Spain, Italy, Portugal), Anglo-Saxon countries (UK, Ireland, and outside Europe Australia, Canada and New Zealand), Eastern Europe (Poland, Hungary and the Czech Republic) and the Baltic countries (Estonia and Lithuania). Figure 3.9 illustrates the association between prisoner rates, welfare provision and income inequality in these six regions.

The relative position of different regimes mirrors the general pattern emerging from welfare analyses. Different welfare regimes differ also in the penal policy and in the use of penal power. This is strikingly clear in the relation between welfare provision and prisoner rates (Figure 3.9 left).

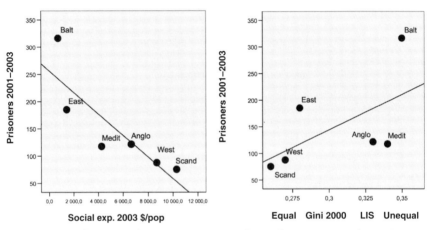

FIGURE 3.9 Welfare expenditures, income inequality and prisoner rates by regions
Source: Sourcebook 2006 complemented, OECD, LIS.

3.4.3 Why welfare?

The connection between commitments to social welfare and prison rates is explicit in the old slogan 'Good social policy is the best criminal policy'. This was just another way of saying that society will do better by investing more money in schools, social work and families than in prisons. Welfarist penal policy is, almost by definition, less repressive. No wonder, the general scaling down of welfare states especially in Anglo-Saxon countries during recent decades coincides with the simultaneous growth of penal control. But this is not to *explain* the association between social policy orientation and penal severity. We still need to ask, why does welfare affect penal severity? Several propositions can be put forward.

Welfarist social policy reduces social distances and welfare differences. It also creates and fortifies social bonds and enhances the development of social (as well as economic) capital.[12] Distance feeds exclusion and severity while equality and social bonds support inclusion and leniency. But why? Following the Durkheimian tradition, one could emphasize the feelings of social solidarity. In David Greenberg's words, the comparative leniency and low degree of economic inequality may be seen 'as manifestations of a high degree of empathic identification and concern for the well-being of others' (Greenberg 1999: 297).

But why shouldn't feelings of solidarity also have an opposite effect through an empathic identification with the position of the *victim*? One answer for this could be that penal policies in welfare society are shaped not only by the feelings of solidarity but also by broad concepts of social and collective responsibility. In the end what matters are the society's views on the sources of risk and allocation of blame: whether risks originate from individuals who are to be blamed or whether the sources of social problems are given a wider interpretation. Shared risk is a mirror image of shared responsibility. Societies with a strong sense of shared and collective responsibility are less eager to attribute social problems to individuals.[13] Thus not only the social sentiments of solidarity but also the prevailing view of the origins and causes of social risks (in this case crime) are of importance. If the roots of the problem lie outside the individual offender then that's also where the actions should be targeted.[14] However, as in Barbara Hudson's phrase, penal cultures in the late-modern risk society are marked by 'atomistic and aggressive individualism'. The balancing of the rights of different parties has gone, while the only rights that matter for most are the safety rights of selves (there is only one human right – the right not to be victimized). Also the sense of shared risk and shared responsibility is gone, as we now cope with the risks by a constant scanning of all whom we come into contact with, in order to see whether or not they pose a threat to our security, ending up in exclusionary policies targeting individuals instead of social conditions (see Hudson 2003: 74).

Behind a less repressive inclusive social policy orientation one finds feelings of solidarity and a broad, less individualistic understanding of the origins of social risks. But a welfare society which organizes its social life from these starting points has also triggered other mechanisms which may contribute to a less repressive direction. Taking into account material resources and economic security of an affluent welfare state, it may be easier to express tolerance and empathy when one's own position is secured.[15] Empathy and feelings of togetherness are also easier to achieve among equals. And as already pointed out, growing social divisions breed suspicions, fears and feelings of otherness.

Finally, strong welfare states may also contribute to lower levels of repression by producing less stressing crime problems by granting safeguards against social marginalization. And furthermore, as a functional community corrections system demands resources and a proper infrastructure, other and better alternatives to imprisonment are usually at hand in a generous welfare state.

3.5 Trust and legitimacy

3.5.1 Between Durkheim and Weber

Alongside the Durkheimian tradition, which links together the level of repression with feelings of social solidarity, there is a Weberian tradition that seeks to explain the level of penal repression in terms of power concentration and the need to defend political authority (see, for example, Killias 1986). The rise of harsh and expressive policies in the US and in the UK has also been explained by reference to the loss of public confidence, a legitimacy crisis and the state's need to use expressive punishments as a demonstration of sovereignty. David Garland refers on various occasions to the state's failure to handle the crime problem and the resulting 'denial and acting out': unable to admit that the situation had escaped from the government's control and in order to show to the public that at least 'something' was being done with the crime problem, the government resorted to expressive gestures and punitive responses (Garland 2001: 103ff.). It has also been pointed out that in the US since the 1960s, the scope of federal government activity and responsibility has expanded into fields like healthcare, education, consumer protection, discrimination, etc but has led to a spiral of political failures. This in turn has led to the collapse of public confidence. Subsequent expressive and punitive actions against crime were, in part, meant to save the government's credibility (see Tonry 2004: 41–4 with references). The loss of public confidence in the political system has also been seen as one of the major causes behind the rise of punitive populism and the subsequent ascendancy of penal severity in New Zealand (see Pratt and Clark 2005).

3.5.2 Social and institutional trust

Empirical testing needs operationalization. In the following analysis, political legitimacy is measured with social survey data on citizens' confidence and trust in political institutions. The analysis extends from political legitimacy (Weber) to social trust (Durkheim), as the surveys cover both dimensions. The European Social Survey (ESS) contains several questions measuring trust in people (horizontal, generalized or social trust) and trust in different social institutions (vertical or institutional trust). The World Values Surveys (WVS), conducted in a larger number of countries, contain similar questions measuring citizens' confidence both in one another and in social and political institutions. Results for Europe (ESS 1st round) are in the left-hand panels of Figure 3.10 and results from World Values Surveys (WVS round 2005 or latest) are in the right-hand panels.

Figure 3.10 shows a strong inverse association between the levels of repression, legitimacy and social trust. The legitimacy of social and political institutions remains the highest in Scandinavia and Switzerland. These countries also tend to have the lowest prisoner rates. Close to these rankings in trust come Austria and the Netherlands. In the opposite corner one typically finds the Eastern European countries and England and Wales.[16] Extending the analyses outside

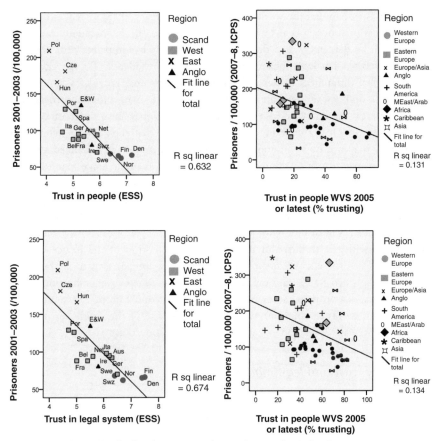

FIGURE 3.10 Trust in the legal system and trust in people and prisoner rates
Source: Sourcebook 2006 complemented, ICPS, ESS and WVS..

Europe weakens the associations. However, the general trend remains the same. A closer look at the results indicates that the associations between forms of trust and prisoner rates remain highest in the developed countries, while in the developing and transitional countries correlations are much weaker.

The correlations (WVS) in the OECD countries (n = 27, US excluded) were the following: trust in people −0.53★★, in police −0.61★★, in justice −0.63★★, in parliament −0.47★, and in government −0.28. All correlations, except trust in government (n = 20), were statistically significant. However, including the US in the analyses weakens the correlations significantly. Outside the OECD region the corresponding figures were: people −0.11 (n = 39), police −0.28 (n = 35), justice −0.13 (n = 37), parliament −0.18 (n = 36) and government −0.15 (n = 32). Different rules seem to apply to developed and less developed countries. And among the developed countries the US seems to follow its own path. This pattern repeats itself also with economic and political indicators. In poorer countries economic wealth and prisoner rates correlate positively (GDP per capita <4,000 $

r = −0.46★★), but among the wealthier countries (GDP >4000 $) increase in wealth produces less prisoners (−0.56★★ US excluded and −0.18 US included). A similar pattern will be detected when the level of democracy is compared with prisoner rates (see Table 3.4 below). This curvilinearity places challenges for the efforts to explain global differences in penal severity. There remains the risk of comparing apples with oranges, as the countries in comparisons may differ due to factors unreachable by the analyses. Also the indicators used may have different content and meaning in grossly differing societies.[17] Factors that seem to be relevant in one setting may not be so in another. What fits to Europe and advanced affluent democracies may not fit to the rest of the world. For example, since extensive use of imprisonment requires money, the lack of resources may keep prisoner rates down, even in the presence of the political will to incarcerate many more people. In some developing countries high imprisonment rates are heavily affected by practical problems in dealing with pre-trial and remand prisoners, which have very little to do with the punitive or non-punitive orientation of the justice system. These types of problems do not render global cross-comparisons futile, but they underline the need to be cautious with global single-factor generalizations. And once the analyses on penal severity are extended beyond Europe, more attention must be paid to other sanctions, most notably the use of the death penalty (see also Lappi-Seppälä 2008a: 331–2 and 373 and Johnson 2008).

3.5.3 Why trust and legitimacy?

Evidently, trust and the level of repression are interconnected. For Fukuyama high prisoner rates constitute 'a direct tax imposed by the breakdown of trust in society' (Fukuyama 1995: 11). Again we are faced with the question, why do trust and legitimacy bring leniency and distrust produces severity? Trust in institutions (vertical, institutional trust) and trust in people (horizontal, personalized trust) are essential for the functioning of social institutions, for norm-compliance and for political responses to law-breaking, and this in different ways and for various reasons.

A decline in legitimacy and trust in institutions calls for political action. In a system with a high level of confidence and trust there is also less need for political posturing and expressive gestures: 'punitive outbursts and demonizing rhetoric have featured much more prominently in weak political regimes than in strong ones' (Garland 1996: 462). Thus a low legitimacy may call for tough measures for political reasons in order to defend the positions of power.

Trust also has social dimensions. Trust in people, fears and punitive demands are interrelated. The decline in trust, reported in many western countries since the 1960s (see LaFree 1998), has been associated with the weakening of community ties, the rise of individualism and the growth of the 'culture of fear' (Furedi 2002). In a world of weakening solidarity ties, other people start looking like strangers rather than friends. We do not know whom to trust. This, together with the increased feelings of insecurity caused by new risks which are beyond individual control, provides a fertile ground for fear of crime. Crime is an apt object of fears and actions for anyone surrounded by growing anxieties and abstract threats. Crime and punishment are tangible and comprehensible targets: we 'know' what causes crime and we 'know' how to deal with the problem (especially when the media and the politicians do such a good job in teaching us to look for simplistic answers). Declining trust and increased fears go a long way together. Fears, in turn, correlate strongly with prisoner rates (Figure 3.11), as well as with trust (Figure 3.11).[18]

Trust is relevant also for social cohesion and (informal) social control. Generalized trust and trust in people is an indicator of social bonds and social solidarity. Decreasing trust indicates a weakening solidarity and declining togetherness. And declining solidarity implies readiness for tougher actions.

On the other hand, communities equipped with trust are better protected against disruptive social behaviour. They are 'collectively more effective' in their efforts to exercise social control.[19] This ability may also be gathered under the broad label 'social capital', including the existence of those social networks and shared values that inhibit law-breaking and support norm compliance. There is a link from trust, solidarity and social cohesion to effective informal social control.

Finally, trust in institutions and legitimacy is also conducive to norm compliance and behaviour. Both later theories of procedural justice (see Tyler 2003) and traditional Scandinavian penal theories of the norm creating and enforcing effect of the criminal law (see Andenaes 1974) stress the idea that in a well ordered society norm compliance is based on internalized (normative) motives – not on fear. And the crucial condition for this to happen is that people perceive the system as fair and legitimate. A system which seeks to uphold norm compliance through trust and legitimacy, rather than fear and deterrence should be able to manage with less severe sanctions, as the results also indicate.

To sum up: the association between trust and the level of repression is the function of several coexisting relations. The lack of institutional trust creates political pressures towards more repressive means in order to maintain political authority. The lack of personal trust associated with fear results in ascending punitive demands and increases these pressures. Trust may also be beneficial for the construction of bureaucratic controls between public demands and the delivery of penalties. Political and institutional mistrust may, in turn, discourage the delegation of penal powers and favour mandatory penalties and rigid guidelines.[20] On the other hand, increased personal trust, community cohesion and social capital strengthen informal social control. Associated with norm-compliance based on legitimacy, this decreases the need to resort to formal social control and to the penal system. But what are the structures upholding and enhancing trust (and welfare)? This brings political culture and political economy into the spotlight.

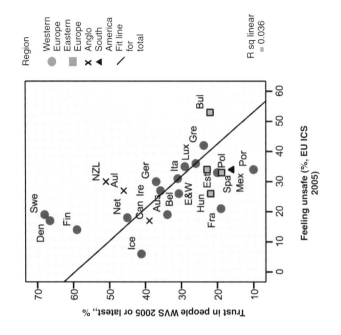

FIGURE 3.11 Trust, fear and prisoner rates
Source: ICPS, EU ICS and WVS..

3.6 Democracy and political economy

3.6.1 Does democracy matter?

All the above-mentioned elements also have a political side. Socio-economic factors, public sentiments or the feeling of trust do not just develop by themselves into penal practices. In the end, prison rates (and social policy) are an outcome of policy choices and political actions, taken within a given political culture. Comparative historical evidence indicates clearly that imprisonment rates are lower in democracies than in countries with other political systems (see Greenberg 2002: 246 and Sung 2006: 312, both with references). Also cross-sectional analyses confirm that the level of democracy and the number of prisoners correlate inversely: the higher the level of democracy, the fewer prisoners. However, there are obvious outliers (such as the US), and there are also differences in the use of imprisonment among countries at the top of the conventional democracy rankings.

The standard democracy indicators from the Polity IV project and Freedom House (see for an overview Inglehart and Welzel 2005: 173ff.) correlate inversely, albeit fairly weakly, with prisoner rates (Freedom House civil and political rights $r = -0.14$ ($n = 98$) and Polity IV $r = -0.16$ ($n = 85$); correspondingly $r = -0.20\star$ and $-0.23\star$ US excluded). However, the results are again sensitive to the countries involved (for example, Sung 2006 found a stronger correlation of -0.37 between the Freedom House democracy index and incarceration in 77 countries). Furthermore, the association follows the curvilinear model, detected also (see Lappi-Seppälä 2011c p. 52) between economic resources and imprisonment rates. In countries at the low end of the democracy scale the level of democracy was either unrelated or associated positively with prisoner rates (= higher democracy, more prisoners). In more advanced countries the association was clearly negative (higher democracy, fewer prisoners, with the US as an exception). This takes us back to the hypotheses already discussed above. In the least developed countries the rise in the level of democracy may coincide with the simultaneous construction of infrastructure necessary for the routine use of imprisonment. This may mean that the prisoner rates in countries at the lowest end of the democracy scale are 'artificially' low or, at least, constrained by factors less relevant for other countries (see also Johnson 2008: 51).

The level of democracy matters, but much depends also on how democracy is conceptualized and measured. The extent of political and civil rights and the dimensions of constitutional and liberal democracies are important, but equal attention should be directed to the actual substantiation of these rights ('effective' or 'substantive' democracy, see, for example, Welzel and Klingemann 2008). Qualitative aspects, easily neglected by formal indicators, may also be of importance. The penal changes in the US, to take an example, have been explained with reference to the bi-polar structure of the political system and to the struggle to win swing-voters (see Caplow and Simon 1999 and Tonry 2004: 38ff.). The Scandinavian leniency, in turn, has been explained with reference to the corporatist and consensual model of political decision-making (for example, Kyvsgaard 2004; Bondeson 2005; Cavadino and Dignan 2006: 149 ff; Green 2007 and 2008; and more recently Lacey 2008). The following adds some comments and empirical data to this discussion.

3.6.2 Typologies of political economy

3.6.2.1 Consensual and majoritarian democracies

In political theory, the differences between democratic political systems have been characterized with the distinction between 'consensus and majoritarian democracies' (Lijphart 1999). The terms themselves express the main differences. In relation to the 'basic democratic principle', majoritarian democracy stresses the majority principle: it is the will of the majority that dictates the choices between alternatives. Consensus democracy wishes to go a little further and tries to maximize political participation over mere majorities. The majority principle means that the winner takes all; consensus means that as many views as possible are taken into account. Majority-driven politics are usually based on two-party competition and confrontation whereas consensus driven policy seeks compromises. Instead of concentrating power in the hands of the majority, the consensus model tries to share, disperse and restrain power in various ways, i.e. by allowing all or most of the important parties to share executive power in broad coalitions and by granting widespread interest group participation (see Lijphart 1999: 34ff.).

Several institutional arrangements separate these two systems. Consensus democracies typically have a larger number of political parties, a proportional electoral system and either minority governments or widely based coalition governments. Political decision-making processes are characterized by consensus-seeking negotiations, with well coordinated and centralized interest groups actively cooperating.

3.6.2.2 Corporatism and neo-corporatism

Bringing interest group participation into the analysis extends the perspective into broader political processes and the relations between the state, corporations, workers, employers and trade unions. The concept of (neo-)corporatism aims to capture essential features in these processes. The term refers to tripartite processes of bargaining between labour unions, the private sector and government, taking place typically in small and open economies. Such bargaining is oriented toward dividing the productivity gains created in the economy fairly among the social partners and gaining wage restraint in recessionary or inflationary periods. Neo-corporatist arrangements usually require highly organized and centralized labour unions which bargain on behalf of all workers. Examples of modern neo-corporatism include the collective agreement arrangements of the Scandinavian countries, the Dutch 'Poldermodel' system of consensus and the Republic of Ireland's system of social partnership.

There is an obvious link between these two aspects. Consensus democracies and corporatism usually go hand in hand. Scandinavian countries are typical examples of consensual – or corporatist – (social) democracies. Switzerland, also, is classified as a paradigmatic example of a highly corporatist (Christian) democracy. To this group belong also Austria, Belgium, France, Germany, Italy and the Netherlands. Majoritarian (and usually also less corporatist) democracies include Australia, Canada, Ireland, New Zealand, the UK and the US.[21]

3.6.3 The relevance of political economy: Initial remarks

In Lijphart's own analysis, consensus democracies outperformed the majoritarian democracies with regard to the quality of democracy and democratic representation and the 'kindness and gentleness of their public policy orientation' (Lijphart 1999: 301). Consensual democracies were also characterized by better political and economic equality and enhanced electoral participation. Moreover, Lijphart found that (in 1992 and in 1995) consensual democracies put fewer people in prison and held much more restrictive views on the use of death penalty (286, 297–8). Table 3.4 compares trends in prisoner rates in consensual and majoritarian democracies in 1980–2007.

Consensual democracies are associated with a more lenient penal policy. However, in 1980 the prisoner rates in the eleven consensus democracies and four majoritarian democracies were almost even. During the following 25 years the majoritarian democracies increased their prisoner-rates by 76 per cent and the consensus democracies by 26 per cent. If the US had been included in the latter group (as it should have been), these differences would have become even greater.

TABLE 3.4 Prisoner rates (per 100,000) in consensus and majoritarian democracies 1980–2007

	1980	1990	2000	2007	Increase 1980–2007
Consensus 11	66	67	76	83	26%
Majoritarian 4	83	100	123	146	76%
USA	221	461	684	756	242%

Consensus 11: Austria, Belgium, Denmark, Finland, France, Germany, Italy, Netherlands, Norway, Sweden, Switzerland.
Majoritarian 4: Australia, Canada, New Zealand and England and Wales.

3.6.4 *Measuring political economy*

More detailed empirical testing requires operationalization. Lijphart measured the 'consensus – majoritarian quality' of democracies with a set of indexes concerning the extent of interest group participation and centralization, the number of political parties, the balance of power between governments and parliaments, the type of electoral system, etc. Lijphart's summary index 'Executives-parties' (or 'joint-power') index offers a possibility for quantitative measurements between prisoner rates and the type of democracy as well as the degree of corporatism. The other major indicator available comes from the Luxembourg income study. This 11-component neo-corporatism index measures, *inter alia* the wage-bargaining processes, the role of the unions and the degree of centralization in interest group participation (see in more detail Huber *et al.* 2004). Figure 3.12 illustrates the association between Lijphart's general index (measuring first and foremost the extent of power sharing, interest participation and the degree of corporatism) and the Luxembourg Income Study (LIS) index of neo-corporatism.

Consensual democracies and neo-corporatism are associated with a more lenient penal policy. The R^2 indicates that among Western European countries about 50 per cent of prisoner-rates variation could be explained by the type of democracy and the degree of corporatism.

3.6.5 *Explaining the relevance of political economy*

Why, then, do consensus democracy and corporatism bring leniency and conflict democracy severity? This is an issue that has received much less attention in criminological theory.[22]

The type of democracy and the level of repression seem to have *both indirect and direct connections.* First, it looks as if welfare states survive better in consensual and corporatist surroundings. Consensual democracies are more 'welfare friendly'. This may partly be the result of the more flexible negotiation procedures which enable different kinds of 'trade-offs'. In contrast to the 'winner takes all' systems, consensual structures where 'everyone is involved' offer better chances that everyone (or at least most) will get (at least) something. Thus consensual democracies produce more welfare and display lower social and economic disparities.

There are, in addition, more direct links between penal policies and the established political traditions and structures. They flow from the basic characteristics of political discourse. While the consensus model is based on bargaining and compromise, majoritarian democracies are based on competition and confrontation. The latter sharpens the distinctions, heightens the controversies and encourages conflicts. This all has its effect on the stability and content of the policies and on the legitimacy of the system.

In a consensus democracy there always remains the need to maintain good relations with your opponent. You will probably also need them after the election. As expressed in Scandinavian politics: 'There are no knock-out winnings in

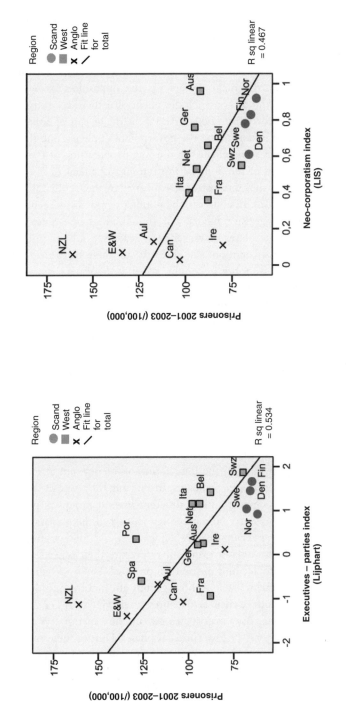

FIGURE 3.12 Political culture (Lijphart index), neo-corporatism (LIS) and prisoner rates

Source: Sourcebook 2006 complemented, Lijphart, LIS..

politics, only winnings by scores'. In consensus democracy there is less to win and more to lose in criticizing the previous government's achievements. There is also less criticism and less discontent, due to the fact that policies and reforms have been prepared together by incorporating as many parties as possible in the process.

There is also less 'crisis talk'. In majoritarian democracies and under a competitive party system, the main project for the opposition is to highlight societal or political crisis and to convince the public that there is an urgent need to remove the governing party from power. And if the major part of political work is based on attacking and undermining the government's policies, one should not be surprised if this also has some effects on the way people think of the contents of these policies, as well as of the political institutions in general.

The lower level of trust may thus partly be explained by the fact that the conflict model invites more criticism. In addition, the conflict democracies seem often to be burdened by more aggressive media. For this, there is one quite plausible explanation: conflicts create better news. Very few readers would be interested in reading about agreement of opinion. But this may also help to explain why the majoritarian democracies are more susceptible to episodes of penal populism and why the consensus democracies tend to have lower incarceration rates.

Consensus seems to bring also both *stability and deliberation*. The Social Democrats have been in power in Denmark, Sweden and Norway from the 1930s till the late 1990s with only minor interruptions. This hegemony, combined with a consensual political culture under a minority government (when you have to negotiate with the opposition) or under a coalition government (when you have to negotiate with your cabinet partners), has produced unprecedented stability. New governments rarely have had the need to raise their profile by making spectacular turnovers.

One aspect of this stability is that changes do not happen every day. And when they do, they usually do not turn the situation upside down. Consensual criminal policy puts extra value in the long-term consistency and in incremental change, instead of rapid, overnight turnovers. In Finland, the work of drafting the law tries to gain as wide support among different interest groups as possible. To achieve this, different groups may be represented already in the preparatory phase as members of the drafting committees. A remission round follows after the first proposal, during which the interest groups may prepare their official statements. This feedback is taken into account in the final proposal. The final handling takes place in parliamentary hearings where those groups affected by and interested in the reform have, once more, a chance to express their views. In general, reform work therefore takes time. Any major changes in the sanction systems occur usually only after several years of experimental phases. During these preparations different groups have a chance to express their views on several occasions, which evidently increases the degree of their commitment to the final outcome.

This description of the Finnish law-drafting process also applies more or less to other Scandinavian countries. There are, certainly, some differences. From the

Finnish point of view, it seems that the Swedish legislator is more willing to act quickly and to pass 'single-problem solutions'. There may be also other differences between the Scandinavian countries. The closer you look the more differences you find.[23] But in a picture that covers not only the Scandinavian countries but also the UK, these differences look small. And if one wishes to incorporate the US in the same picture, the Nordic countries look more or less identical.

However, some caveats must be added, especially when we move to the present-day law-drafting work. Many routines have been turned upside down by the EU. The implementation of the framework decisions and the harmonization of national codes in accordance with the demands of different EU instruments allow very little scope for reasoned deliberation – or national discretion for that matter. Long-lasting committees and careful preparations have been reduced to two-day trips to Brussels. Arguments in principle and evidence-based assessments on different options have been replaced by political arguments and symbolic messages. This all bears an evident risk of politicization of criminal policy, also in Scandinavia.

3.7 The drivers of penal policy – an overview

Comparative analysis indicates that differences in prisoner rates cannot be explained by differences in crime. Instead, penal severity seems to be closely associated with the extent of welfare provision, differences in income equality, trust and political and legal cultures. The analysis supports the view that the Scandinavian penal model has its roots in a consensual and corporatist political culture, in high levels of social trust and political legitimacy, as well as in a strong welfare state. These different factors have both indirect and direct influences on the contents of penal policy.

The link between penal leniency and welfare state is almost conceptual. A welfare state is a state of solidarity and social equality. A society of equals, showing concern for the well-being of others, is less willing to impose heavy penalties upon its co-members compared with a society with great social distances where punishments apply only to 'others' and to the underclass. Increasing social distances increase readiness for tougher actions; equality has the opposite effect. In more concrete forms, welfare states sustain less repressive policies by providing workable alternatives to imprisonment. Extensive and generous social service networks often function also, per se, as effective crime prevention measures, even if that is not or only a partial motivation for these practices (such as encompassing day-care, parental training, a public schooling system based on equal opportunities for all, etc.).

Indirect effects take place through enhanced social and economic security, lesser fears, lower punitive projections and, especially, via high social trust and political legitimacy, both supported and sustained by the welfare state. The type of welfare regime may also be of importance. Need-based selective social policy concerns 'other people', those who are marginalized and those who are culpable for their own position. This feeds suspicion and distrust. Universalistic social policy that assigns benefits to everyone, grants social equality and makes no distinctions between persons has a different moral logic (see Kuhnle in Chapter 4 this volume). Social policy then concerns us all. Debates on social policy are efforts to solve our common problems. This all gives strong support for social trust. In addition to all this, the social and economic security granted by the welfare state as well as the feelings of social trust it promotes sustain tolerance, lower level of fears and less punitive projections.

Liberal penal policies and low prisoner rates are also by-products of consensual, corporatist and negotiating political cultures. These cultures are, for one thing, more 'welfare friendly', as compared with many majoritarian democracies. The direct links between penal policies and political cultures flow from the basic characteristics of political discourse. Consensus brings *stability and deliberation.* Political changes are gradual, not total as in majoritarian systems where the whole crew is changed. In consensus democracies, new governments rarely have the need to raise their profile by making spectacular turnovers. Consensual criminal policy puts extra value on long-term consistency and incremental change instead of rapid, overnight turnovers. While the consensus model is based on bargaining and compromise, majoritarian democracies are based on competition and confrontation. The latter sharpens the distinctions, heightens the controversies and encourages conflicts. This affects the stability and content of the policies, as well as the legitimacy of the political system as a whole. There is more crisis talk, more criticism, more short-term solutions and more direct appeals to public demands. In short: consensual politics lessen controversies, produce less crisis talk, inhibit dramatic turnovers and sustain long-term consistent policies. In other words, consensual democracies are less susceptible to political populism.

The interplay between the different factors influencing the contents of penal policy is illustrated in Figure 3.13.

In addition to these three basic factors – welfare, trust and political economy – there are several other elements requiring our attention. These would include structural factors such as demographics. Population homogeneity may ease the pursuit of liberal penal policies but is no guarantee for success (nor has multiculturalism led to harsher regimes).[24] Sometimes geography may also matter, as was the case when Finland motivated decarceration policies with reference to Nordic cooperation (see in more detail Lappi-Seppälä 2007: 241–4; see also Christie 2000).

One factor certainly deserving more attention is the *role of the media and of media culture.* Public opinion and public sentiments are shaped in a reciprocal interaction with political decision-makers and special interest groups. In short, consensual politics lessen controversies, produce less crisis talk, inhibit dramatic turnovers and sustain long-term consistent policies. Consequently, consensual democracies are less susceptible to political populism and the news media (on this, see Roberts et al., 2003: 86–7). Public opinion is affected by both media representations and political decisions. Sensationalist media feed public fears

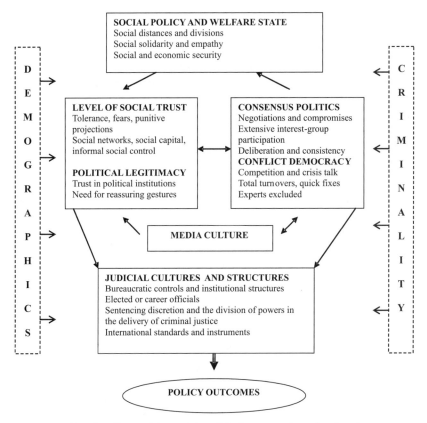

FIGURE 3.13 Penal policy and its social, political, economic and cultural contexts

and distrust. They reinforce the pressures from the punitive public. At the same time, the media express their own preferences for the political system. There are differences in the way policy-makers pay attention to public demands as well as in the way these sentiments are conveyed to policy-makers. If the political system chooses to take a responsive and adaptive role, the media shape and influence the policy outcomes both directly and indirectly (though invoking public demands).

Also *judicial structures and legal cultures* play an important part, especially in explaining the role of the differences between continental and common-law countries. The inheritance of the Enlightenment and the division of state powers have shielded the continental and Scandinavian courts from political interventions. The US legal system, to take an example from the other extreme, with politically elected criminal justice officials (prosecutors, judges, sheriffs and governors) is much more vulnerable to short-term populist influences on everyday sentencing practices and local policy choices (see Zimring *et al.* 2001 and Tonry 2007). The need to measure one's popularity among the people ensures that the judiciary is much more closely attuned to public opinion and organized interest groups. These differences are further reinforced by different techniques in structuring sentencing discretion. The Scandinavian and continental sentencing structures where the legislature decides only in broad terms on the scope, and the rest is at the discretion of independent judges, seems to be less vulnerable to short-sighted and ill-founded political interventions as compared with politically elected bodies with the powers to give detailed instructions on sentencing (see in more detail Lappi-Seppälä 2001).

In addition, numerous details in the criminal justice proceedings may have an impact on sentencing policies. Widespread victim impact statements, unknown in this form to most continental legal systems, may have but one effect in sentencing. In the Scandinavian criminal process, the victim's rights are associated, not with the right to exercise a personal vendetta in the court, but with the victim's possibilities of getting his/her damages and losses compensated.[25] Compensatory claims of the victim are always dealt with in the same process together with the criminal case. These claims are taken care of by the prosecutor on behalf of the victim. Taking proper care of the compensatory claims may well have a mitigating impact on the demands related to punishment (see Chapters 8 and 9 in this volume).

Legal training, judicial expertise and professional skills matter as well. Judges and prosecutors may differ in their criminological knowledge, both individually and in different jurisdictions. Countries with trained professional judges and with criminology included in the curriculum of law faculties may expect to have judges and prosecutors with a broader and deeper understanding of issues such as crime and criminal policy. This expertise may be enhanced by professional training programmes and by organizing seminars and meetings for judges etc. Evidently the receptiveness of the judiciary for this kind of activity and the exchange of information vary between different jurisdictions. Effective networking between the research community and the judiciary is essential if one wishes to increase the impact of criminological knowledge in sentencing and penal practices (on this see Snacken 2007: 201ff. and Downes and Swaaningen 2007: 39ff.).

Finally, one should also leave room for 'country-specific exceptionalism'. While a good many penal practices can be explained by reference to these general social, political, economic and cultural factors, their impact is difficult to condense in terms of a simple statistical model. These factors occur in different combinations in different places and at different points in time. The associations detected are neither atomistic nor mechanical. The effects are context-related and countries may experience unique changes. Also, individuals and elites matter. Penal policies may occasionally be heavily influenced by individual experts, opinion leaders or politicians (see Chapter 11 in this volume). This kind of personal and professional influence by individuals may be easier to achieve in a small country like Finland.

So, where does this all leave us? Have we been able to construct a clear-cut explanation for national differences in the use of imprisonment? Obviously not, had the aim been a simple statistical causal model applicable around the world. But we have been able to detect a number of central factors (risk factors and protective factors) contributing to the shapes of national penal policies in (mostly developed western) democracies. Most of these factors (such as welfare, equality, trust, political culture, fears) are interconnected in a manner that makes it difficult to establish each one's own 'independent' weight and relevance. But that wasn't the goal either. More important was to sketch a preliminary general structure of the interplay of these structural and cultural factors and the way they *together* contribute to the final outcome.

As often pointed out, the outcome of the analyses is heavily dependent on the countries included. In this case the strongest patterns were found among the OECD countries and in Western Europe. As indicated, patterns that apply to developed western democracies may not hold with developing countries from Asia, Africa and South America. This does not render the detected patterns irrelevant but it may well suggest that policies in developing and transitional countries may be influenced by other factors (such as bureaucratic inefficiency, lack of judges and prosecutors, absence of legal aid, high corruption, ongoing political crises, overwhelming drug problems, general lack of material resources, etc.).[26] One can hardly assume a complex social institution like criminal punishment to be explainable by a simple causal model, even within Western Europe (and most certainly not worldwide). Still, one should be able to say something of the roles and internal relations of those socio-economic, cultural and political factors that contribute to the huge variations in penal policies to be found even among the developed democracies.

These findings may be of some value for those interested in the dynamics of penal change, but what is the message for those who wish to bring change about? If the use of imprisonment is determined by structural and cultural factors, doesn't this rule out the role of human action? Obviously not. Macro-level structural factors do not determine the outcome, they merely increase the *probability* of some type of policies (and they may make other policies less probable). Still, they never dictate the end result. Structure is not determination (Lacey: 2008: 205), and there always remains room for choice. A simple example of this is provided by those countries (above and below the regression lines) which have not followed the general patterns. Finding 'deviant countries' which do not 'fit in the model' does not render the model inadequate. On the contrary, studying these countries may give added information on the specific local conditions that have influenced or guided the policy choices.[27]

3.8 Postcript

Nordic penal policy has been an example of a pragmatic and non-moralistic approach, with a clear social policy orientation. It reflects the values of the Nordic welfare-state ideal and emphasizes that measures against social marginalization and inequality work also as measures against crime. It stresses the view that crime control and criminal policy are still a part of social justice, not just an issue of controlling dangerous individuals. These liberal penal policies are to a large extent also a by-product of an affluent welfare state and of consensual and corporatist political cultures. These structural conditions have enabled and sustained tolerant policies, made it possible to develop workable alternatives to imprisonment and promoted trust and legitimacy. This all has relieved the political system's stress on symbolic actions and it also has enabled norm compliance based on legitimacy and acceptance instead of fear and deterrence. Further factors explaining the Scandinavian leniency included strong expert influences, (fairly) sensible media and demographic homogeneity.

Whether this state of affairs will continue into the future goes beyond the scope of this paper. Critical remarks have already been put forward by a number of Nordic commentators during the 1990s.[28] However, were we to view the Nordic countries from a broader comparative perspective, there may still be room for some optimism. Overall, prisoner rates are still low. Nor is the path taken by many other penal systems an inevitable one. Very few of those social, political, economic and cultural background conditions which explain the rise of mass imprisonment in the US and UK apply to any of the Scandinavian countries as such. The social and economic security granted by the Nordic welfare state may still function as a social backup system for a tolerant crime policy. The judges and the prosecutors are, and will, remain career officials with a professional touch to these matters. Political culture still encourages negotiations and appreciates expert opinions – at least that is something one may hope for.

Luckily enough, this is not only a matter of hope. In a political culture which, in general, values rational, pragmatic and responsible argumentation, there is a lot that can be done (on this, see especially Roberts *et al.* 2003: 160ff.). We must improve the pre-conditions of rational policy-making over populist posturing by producing more and better information for the politicians, practitioners and the public. We should also apply the normal rules of political accountability in penal discourse. Nowhere else in political life can plans and proposals be presented without estimations of costs, benefits and possible alternatives. Why should this be allowed in criminal policy, where decisions infringe legally protected basic rights and are hugely expensive? And we should take advantage of the fact that, in politics in general, there prevails a distaste of populism and political cynical score-hitting – if exposed. Exposing populism and showing the attitudinal oversimplifications, false premises and the dubious value-commitments of populist proposals, provide important weapons in the hands of political opponents of any penal populist.

And for those societies which in other respects claim to defend policies based on social equality, full citizenship, solidarity and respect for reason and humanity remains the crucial question: why should we, then, choose to carry out criminal policy which shows so little appreciation of these very same values and principles? Preventing crime would not be the answer, as there are notably better, cheaper, more effective and more humane ways of protecting the public from the threats of crime.

Notes

1. This is an abridged version of a study published in Lappi-Seppälä (2008a and 2010).
2. This recent decrease in the Netherlands has been mainly due to an increased use of community service. In reading the Dutch figures one must also take into account that these figures also include a high number of mental patients, juveniles and foreigners detained on the basis of aliens legislation. This causes an artificial increase of around 30 per cent to the Dutch prisoner rates, which should be taken into account in international comparisons. On the comparability of the prisoner figures and different adjustment methods, see Lappi-Seppälä (2008a: 320–32) and Aebi and Stadnic (2009), both with examples of 'adjusted' prisoner rates. Other alternative indicators for punitivity are analyzed in Lappi-Seppälä (2011a).
3. Scandinavian countries are discussed in more detail in Lappi-Seppälä (2007 and 2010) and Pratt (2008). Most recent trends in Finland are commented on in Lappi-Seppälä (2011b).
4. The original sample included 16 Western European countries, 3 Eastern European countries (the Czech Republic, Hungary and Poland), 2 Baltic countries (Estonia and Lithuania) and 4 Anglo-Saxon countries outside Europe (US, Canada, New Zealand and Australia). Information on prisoner rates is taken from ICPS, Council of Europe Prison Information Bulletins, Sourcebooks 1995, 2000 and 2006, SPACE I, national statistics and various research reports. The main factors explaining prisoner rates include fears, punitivity and trust (measured by survey data from ICVS, EU ICS, ESS and WVS), income inequality and social welfare expenditures (data from LIS, Eurostat, UN, EUSI and OECD) and political culture and corporatism (on political indicators see Lijphart 1999 and Huber *et al.* 2004). The sources are described in more detail in Lappi-Seppälä (2008a and 2009). The selection of the countries in the basic sample was much influenced by the availability of data from four main sources: ESS round 1, LIS database, ICVS and OECD databases. Since then the analyses have been extended to cover 99 countries around the world. The US has been left out of most graphic illustrations due to the differences in the scale of imprisonment (see also Figure 3.3). However, correlations are usually reported separately with the US both included and excluded from the samples.
5. Other possible measures for penal severity have been discussed in more detail in Lappi-Seppälä (2008a and 2011a) and Harrendorf and Smit (2010). Despite their limitations, imprisonment rates remain in wider cross-comparative analyses 'an excellent proxy for many other measures or societies' responses to acts defined as crimes' (Wilkins 1991: 13). Including other sanctions, for example fines and community alternatives, could well change the picture. But in doing so we should be clear what we are measuring: penal severity or something else?
6. To overcome some of these difficulties recorded crime figures were adjusted by taking into account differences in reporting. This, however, had only a small effect on the results.
7. Correlation in the global sample was 0.25 (n = 82) and in the basic sample 0.68★★ (n = 24). Van Dijk (2008: 269) reports an even higher correlation between prisoner rates and homicide (r = 0.48), however with ranked values.
8. Most notably by Garland (2001); see also the discussions in Cavadino and Dignan (2006: 00ff.) and Downes (Chapter 2 this volume).
9. The 'fairness' of income distribution is measured by this Gini index. This index expresses to what extent the real income distribution differs from the 'ideal' and fair distribution (0 = total fairness, 1 = total unfairness). On the associations between income inequality and imprisonment, see also Killias (1986) and Tham (2005).
10. Vogel (2003) distinguishes the Northern European cluster (Scandinavia), which exhibits 'high levels of social expenditure and labour market participation and weak family ties, relatively low levels of class and income inequality, low poverty rates but a high level of inequality between younger and older generations'. The Southern European cluster

(Greece, Italy, Portugal and Spain) has a much lower welfare state provision, lower rates of employment, strong family ties, higher levels of class and income equality and poverty but low levels of inter-generational inequality. The Western European cluster (Austria, Belgium, France, Germany, Ireland, Luxembourg, the Netherlands and the UK) occupy the middle position. However, the UK borders on the southern cluster in terms of income equality, poverty and class inequality (see Vogel 2003 and Falck *et al.* 2003). Castles (2004: 2ff.) follows a similar classification but treats Switzerland as a special case.

11. In terms of the extent of welfare provision they all place themselves quite low, but in terms of income equality differences would emerge. Traditional socialist countries have maintained fairly even income distribution, while the Baltic countries are approaching western neo-liberal states in their income and economic policies.

12. On the relationship between social policy and economic developments, see Kangas and Palme (2005).

13. As described in cultural-anthropological studies, in individualistic cultures risk-posing is attributed to specific individuals and, as a rule, the weak are going to be held to blame for the ills that befall them (see Hudson 2003: 51–2 with references).

14. From this point of view rehabilitative penal policies express themselves as procedures of risk-balancing between different parties (the offender, victim and society). As pointed out by Jonathan Simon, institutions such as parole, probation and juvenile justice all reflected a willingness to take a risk with offenders and to reduce the risk that adult imprisonment would do them more harm (see Simon 2007: 23). This balancing of risks was manifestly expressed in the general policy aim of 'fair distribution' in Finnish criminological theory in the 1970s (see Lappi-Seppälä 2001).

15. There is a link between prosperity and tolerance. David Garland (quoting Mary Douglas) writes how the 'no fault' approach to crime – which is what penal welfarism implicitly tends towards – depends upon an extensive network of insurance and gift-giving. Cultures which rely on restitution instead of blame-allocation are typically the ones where restitution can reasonably be expected and relied upon. The 'non-fault' approach requires material background and mutual trust (see Garland 2001: 47–8). In other words, only under certain conditions 'can one afford to be tolerant'.

16. A separately conducted regional analysis produces similar results to those above: the Scandinavians have higher social trust as well as trust in their political and legal institutions. The Eastern cluster occupies the opposite position in both measurements. Continental western countries are close to Scandinavia in political trust and at the same level as the Anglo-Saxon countries in social trust (see Lappi-Seppälä 2008a).

17. On the differences between individual-level determinants of social and institutional trust in western and eastern countries, see Kaasa and Parts (2008).

18. The data for trust is from the WVS and for fears from the EU ICS (see van Dijk *et al.* 2007). The countries in the sample are determined by the EU ICS.

19. Sampson *et al.* (1997) refer to 'collective efficacy', defined as 'social cohesion among neighbours combined with their willingness to intervene on behalf of the common good'.

20. On the link between trust and structural arrangements in the delivery of justice see in more detail Zimring *et al.* (2001: 73ff.) and Zimring and Johnson (2006). As the authors point out, direct democratic control over concrete levels of punishment goes together with increased severity, while the creation of bureaucratic controls between public participation and case-by-case individual decisions (for example in the form of wide and independent judicial discretion) leads to penal moderation. Trust becomes relevant in this setting once we ask: 'Why would voters tolerate these exercises of punishment powers so far removed from direct democratic control?' And the authors answer: 'mainly because citizens trust government to behave responsibly, and this trust encourages leniency by permitting structural arrangements (such as delegated discretion) that permit judges to individualize sentencing decisions' (Zimring and Johnson 2006: 274).

21. The role of political culture and political economy in shaping penal policies is discussed in several essays in Volume 36 of the Crime and Justice series (see the introduction by Tonry 2007 and also Green 2008). Lacey (2008), in turn, employs the distinction cooperative (social-democratic) market economies and (individualistic, uncoordinated) liberal-market economies.
22. However, see Green (2007 and 2008) and note 24.
23. Trends and differences between the Scandinavian countries are discussed in more detail in Lappi-Seppälä (2007) and Pratt (2008). For an exhaustive analysis and comparison between Norway and England and Wales, see Green (2008).
24. The role of demographic factors, as well as a number of other factors (including fears and punitive emotions), are discussed in more detail in Lappi-Seppälä (2008a).
25. And if not by the offender, from state funds. No doubt, the fact that compensation is always ordered together with the punishment also gives the public a more realistic view of the overall consequences of the crime (in contrast to systems which hide the compensation in another process which the victims may not even be able to carry out).
26. There are differences even within European countries. As will be demonstrated in Lappi-Seppälä (2011a) the 'southern block' seems to follow partly a different pattern in an intra-European comparison.
27. For example, a single-country case study from Finland (see Lappi-Seppälä 2011b) may illustrate how it has been possible to swim against the tide in times when other countries were moving in the opposite direction.
28. See Victor (1995: 71–2), Jareborg (1995), Tham (2001) and Balvig (2004), and for the discussions Lappi-Seppälä (2007: 285–90).

References

Aebi, M. and Stadnic N. (2007/2009) *Council of Europe SPACE 1: 2005/2007 Survey on Prison Populations*, Document PC-CP (2007) 2 / (2009) 1. Strasbourg: Council of Europe.

Aebi, M., Aromaa, K., Aubusson de Cavarlay, B., Barclay, G., Gruszczyñska, B., von Hofer, H., Hysi, V., Jehle, J.-M., Killias, M., Smit, P. and Tavares, C. (2006) *The European Sourcebook of Crime and Criminal Justice Statistics – 2006.* The Hague: Boom Juridische uitgevers.

Andenaes, J. (1974) *Punishment and Deterrence.* Ann Arbor, MI: University of Michigan Press.

Balvig, F. (2004) 'When law and order came to Denmark', *Journal of Scandinavian Studies in Criminology and Crime Prevention*, 5: 167–87.

Beckett, K. and Western, B. (2001) 'Governing social marginality: welfare, incarceration, and the transformation of state policy', in D. Garland (ed.), *Mass Imprisonment: Social Causes and Consequences.* London: Sage, pp. 35–50.

Bondeson, U. (2005) 'Levels of punitiveness in Scandinavia: description and explanations', in J. Pratt, M. Brown, S. Hallsworth and W. Morrison (eds), *The New Punitiveness: Trends, Theories, Perspectives.* Cullompton: Willan.

Caplow, T. and Simon, J. (1999) 'Understanding prison policy and population trends', in M. Tonry (ed.), *Prisons*, in *Crime and Justice: A Review of Research*, Vol. 26, ed. M. Tonry. Chicago: University of Chicago Press, pp. 63–120.

Castles, F. (2004) *The Future of the Welfare State. Crisis Myths and Crises Realities.* Oxford: Oxford University Press.

Cavadino, M. and Dignan, J. (2006) *Penal Systems: A Comparative Approach.* London: Sage.

Christie, N. (2000) *Crime Control as Industry: Towards Gulags Western Style*, 3rd edn. London: Routledge.

Downes, D. and Hansen, K. (2006) 'Welfare and punishment in comparative perspective', in S. Armstrong and L. McAra (eds), *Perspectives on Punishment: The Contours of Control.* Oxford: Oxford University Press, pp. 133–54.

Downes, D. and Swaaningen, R. (2007) 'The road to dystopia? Changes in the penal climate of the Netherlands', in M. Tonry (ed.), *Crime and Justice: A Review of Research*, Vol. 35. Chicago: University of Chicago Press, pp. 31–72.

Esping-Andersen, G. (1990) *The Three Worlds of Welfare Capitalism*. Cambridge: Polity Press.

European Sourcebook of Crime and Criminal Justice Statistics – 2003. Boom distributiecentrum, The Netherlands.

Falck, S., von Hofer, H. and Storgaard, A. (2003) *Nordic Criminal Statistics 1950–2000*, Report 2003:3. Department of Criminology, Stockholm University.

Fukuyama, F. (1995) *Trust: The Social Virtues and the Creation of Prosperity*. New York: Free Press Paperback.

Furedi, F. (2002) *Culture of Fear: Risk-Taking and the Morality of Low Expectation*, rev. edn. London: Continuum.

Garland, D. (1996) 'The limits of the sovereign state: strategies of crime control in contemporary society', *British Journal of Criminology*, 36(4): 445–71.

Garland, D. (2001) *The Culture of Control: Crime and Social Order in Contemporary Society*. Chicago: University of Chicago Press.

Garland, D. (2005) 'Capital punishment and American culture', *Punishment and Society: The International Journal of Penology*, 7(4): 347–76.

Green, D. (2007) 'Comparing penal cultures: child-on-child homicide in England and Norway', in M. Tonry (ed.), *Crime and Justice: A Review of Research*, Vol. 36. Chicago: University of Chicago Press, pp. 591–636.

Green, D. (2008) *When Children Kill Children: Penal Populism and Political Culture*. Oxford: Oxford University Press.

Greenberg, D. (1999) 'Punishment, division of labor, and social solidarity', in W. S. Laufer and F. Adler (eds), *The Criminology of Criminal Law, Advances in Criminological Theory*, Vol. 8. New Brunswick, N.J.: Transaction Press, pp. 283–361.

Greenberg, D. (2001) 'Novos ordo saeclorum? A commentary on Downes, and on Beckett and Western', in D. Garland (ed.), *Mass Imprisonment: Social Causes and Consequences*. London: Sage, pp. 70–81.

Greenburg, D. (2002) 'Striking out in democracy', *Punishment & Society: The International Journal of Penology*, 4 (2): 237–252.

Greve, V. (1995) 'European criminal policy: towards universal laws?', in N. Jareborg (ed.), *Towards Universal Laws: Trends in National, European and International Lawmaking*. Uppsala: Iustus, pp. 91–116.

Harrendorf, S. and Smit, P. (2010) 'Attributes of criminal justice systems – resources, performance and punitivity', in S. Harrendorf, M. Heiskanen and P. Smit (eds), *International Statistics on Crime and Justice*. Helsinki: Heuni publications 64/2010.

Huber, E., Ragin, C., Stephens, J., Brady, D. and Beckfield, J. (2004) *Comparative Welfare States Data Set*. Northwestern University, University of North Carolina, Duke University and Indiana University.

Hudson, B. (2003) *Justice in the Risk Society*. London: Sage.

Inglehart, R. and Welzel, C. (2005) *Modernization, Cultural Change, and Democracy: The Human Development Sequence*. Cambridge: Cambridge University Press.

Jareborg, N. (1995) 'What kind of criminal law do we want?', in A. Snare (ed.), *Beware of Punishment: On the Utility and Futility of Criminal Law*, Scandinavian Studies in Criminology, Vol. 14. Oslo: Pax Forlag, pp. 17–26.

Jareborg, N. (1998) 'Corpus Juris', *Nordisk Tidskrift for Kriminalvidenskab*. Vol. 85 (3–4): 255–270.

Johnson, D. (2008) 'Japanese punishment in comparative perspective', *Japanese Journal of Sociological Criminology*, 33: 46–6.

Kaasa, A. and Parts, E. (2008) 'Individual-level determinants of social capital in Europe: differences between country groups', *Acta Sociologica*, 145–68.

Kangas, O. and Palme, J. (2005) *Social Policy and Economic Development in the Nordic Countries*. Basingstoke: Palgrave Macmillan.

Killias, M. (1986) 'Power concentration, legitimation crisis and penal severity: a comparative perspective', *International Annals of Criminology*, 24: 181–211.

Kristofferssen, R. (2010) *Correctional Statistics of Denmark, Finland, Iceland, Norway and Sweden 2004–2008*. Correctional Service of Norway Staff Academy Oslo, May 2010.

Kyvsgaard, B. (2004) 'Youth justice in Denmark', in M. Tonry (ed.), *Crime and Justice: A Review of Research*, Vol. 31. Chicago: University of Chicago Press, pp. 349–90.

Lacey, N. (2008) *The Prisoners' Dilemma. Political Economy and Punishment in Contemporary Democracies*, The Hamlyn Lectures 2007. Cambridge: Cambridge University Press.

LaFree, G. (1998) *Losing Legitimacy: Street Crime and the Decline of Social Institutions in America*. Oxford: Westview.

Lappi-Seppälä, T. (2001) 'Sentencing and punishment in Finland: the decline of the repressive ideal', M. Tonry and R. Frase (eds), *Punishment and Penal Systems in Western Countries*. New York: Oxford University Press, pp. 92–150.

Lappi-Seppälä, T. (2007) 'Penal policy in Scandinavia', in M. Tonry (ed.), *Crime and Justice: A Review of Research*, Vol. 36. Chicago: University of Chicago Press, pp. 217–96.

Lappi-Seppälä, T. (2008a) 'Trust, welfare, and political culture: explaining difference in national penal policies', in M. Tonry (ed.), *Crime and Justice: A Review of Research*, Vol. 37. Chicago: University of Chicago Press, pp. 313–87.

Lappi-Seppälä, T. (2008b) 'Politics or policy – fluctuations in the Finnish penal policy', in *Ikke kun straf ... Festskrift til Vagn Greve*. Copenhagen: Juris- og Ökonomiforbundets Forlag, pp. 333–57.

Lappi-Seppälä, T. (2010) 'Explaining variations in the use of imprisonment in developed democracies', in B. Lemann Kristiansen and A. Storgaard (eds), *Nordisk retsociologi. Status – aktuelle udföringer – visioner*. Copenhagen: Jurist- og Okonomiforbundets Forlag.

Lappi-Seppälä, T. (2011a) 'Explaining imprisonment in Europe', *European Journal of Criminology* (forthcoming).

Lappi-Seppälä, T. (2011b) 'Changes in penal policy in Finland', in H. Kury and E. Shea (eds), *Punitivity: International Developments Vol. 1: Punitiveness: A Global Phenomenon*. Bochum: Universitätsverlag Dr. N. Brockmeyer.

Lappi-Seppälä, T. (2011c) *Causes of Prison Overcrowding?* In a report of the Workshop Strategies and Best Practices Against Overcrowding in Correctional Facilities. Tokyo: United Nations Asia and Far East Institution for the Prevention of Crime and the Treatment of Offenders (UNAFEI). March.

Lijphart, A. (1999) *Patterns of Democracy. Government Forms and Performance in Thirty-six Countries*. New Haven, CT and London: Yale University Press.

Mayhew, P. and van Kesteren, J. (2002) 'Cross-national attitudes to punishment', in J. V. Roberts and M. Hough (eds), *Changing Attitudes to Punishment: Public Opinion, Crime and Justice*. Cullompton: Willan, pp. 63–92.

Nuotio, K. (2003) 'Reason for maintaining the diversity', in M. Delmas-Marty, G. Giucidelli-Delage and É. Lambert-Abdelgavad (eds), *L'Harmonisation des Sanctions Pénales en Europe*. Paris: Société de Legislation Compare, pp. 465–71.

Pratt, J. (2008) 'Scandinavian exceptionalism in an era of penal excess. Part I: The nature and roots of Scandinavian exceptionalism', *British Journal of Criminology*, 48: 119–37.

Pratt, J. and Clark, M. (2005) 'Penal populism in New Zealand', *Punishment and Society: The International Journal of Penology*, 7(3): 303–22.

Roberts, J. (2004) *The Virtual Prison. Community Custody and the Evolution of Imprisonment*, Cambridge Studies in Criminology. Cambridge: Cambridge University Press.

Roberts, J., Stalans, L., Indermaur, D. and Hough, M. (2003) *Penal Populism and Public Opinion: Lessons from Five Countries*. Oxford: Oxford University Press.

Ruddell, R. (2005) 'Social disruption, state priorities, and minority threat: a cross-national study of imprisonment', in *Punishment and Society: The International Journal of Penology*, 7(1): 7–28.

Ryan, M. (2003) *Penal Policy and Political Culture in England and Wales: Four Essays on Policy and Process*. Winchester: Waterside Press.

Sampson, R., Stephen, R., and Felton, E. (1997) 'Neighborhoods and violent crime: a multilevel study of collective efficacy', *Science*, 277: 918–24.

Simon, J. (2007) *Governing Through Crime. How the War on Crime Transformed American Democracy and Created a Culture of Fear*. Oxford: Oxford University Press.

Snacken, S. (2007) 'Penal policy and practice in Belgium', in M. Tonry (ed.), *Crime and Justice: A Review of Research*, Vol. 36. Chicago: University of Chicago Press, pp. 127–216.

Sung, H.-E. (2006) 'Democracy, and criminal justice in cross-national perspective: from crime control to due process', *Annals of the American Academy of Political and Social Science*, 605: 311–37.

Sutton, J. (2004) 'The political economy of imprisonment in affluent western democracies 1960–1990', *American Sociological Review*, 69: 170–89.

Tham, H. (2001) 'Law and order as a leftist project?', *Punishment and Society. The International Journal of Penology*, 3(3): 409–26.

Tham, H. (2005) *Imprisonment and Inequality*, Stockholm University, Department of Criminology. Working paper prepared for the 5th Annual Conference of the European Society of Criminology, Kraków, 31 August – 3 September.

Tonry, M. (2004) *Thinking about Crime: Sense and Sensibilities in American Penal Culture*. Oxford: Oxford University Press.

Tonry, M. (2007) 'Determinants of penal policies', in M. Tonry (ed.), *Crime and Justice: A Review of Research*, Vol. 36. Chicago: University of Chicago Press, pp. 1–48.

Träskman, P.-O. (1999) 'A good criminal policy is more than just new law', in V. Heiskanen and K. Kulovesi (eds), *Function and Future of European Law*. Forum Juris, Faculty of Law, Unversity of Helsinki.

Tyler, T. (2003) 'Procedural justice, legitimacy, and the effective rule of law', in M. Tonry (ed.), *Crime and Justice: A Review of Research*, Vol. 30. Chicago: University of Chicago Press, pp. 283–357.

van Dijk J., van Kesteren, J. and Smit, P. (2007) *Criminal Victimisation in International Perspective. Key Findings from the 2004–2005 ICVS and EU ICS*, WODC 257/2007.

van Kesteren, J., Mayhew, P. and Nieuwbeerta, P. (2000) *Criminal Victimisation in Seventeen Industrialised Countries*, WODC 187/2000.

Victor, D. (1995) 'Politics and the penal system – a drama in progress', in A. Snare (ed.), *Beware of Punishment: On the Utility and Futility of Criminal Law*, Scandinavian Studies in Criminology, Vol. 14. Oslo: Pax Forlag, pp. 68–88.

Vogel, T. (2003) *European Welfare Production: Institutional Configuration and Distributional Outcome*. Dordrecht: Kluwer.

von Hofer, H. (2003) 'Prison populations as political constructs: the case of Finland, Holland and Sweden', *Journal of Scandinavian Studies in Criminology and Crime Prevention*, 4: 21–38.

Welzel, C. and Klingemann, H.-D. (2008) *Democratic Congruence Rediscovered: A Focus on 'Substantive' Democracy*, World Values Research Papers, Vol. 1, No. 3.

Wilkins, L. (1991) *Punishment, Crime and Market Forces*. Aldershot: Dartmouth.

Zimring, F. and Johnson, D. (2006) 'Public opinion and the governance of punishment in democratic political systems', *Annals of the American Academy of Political and Social Science*, 605: 266–80.

Zimring, F., Hawkins, G. and Kamin, S. (2001) *Punishment and Democracy: Three Strikes and You're Out in California*. Oxford: Oxford University Press.

4

THE SCANDINAVIAN PATH TO WELFARE

Stein Kuhnle

4.1 Introduction

The modern welfare state is a European invention which can trace its institutional roots, if not its concept and conception, to the last two decades of the nineteenth century. Comprehensive national social insurance, originating in Bismarck's Germany in 1883, spread all over Europe before 1920. The German social insurance of the 1880s inspired initiatives for social insurance legislation in the Nordic countries (Kuhnle 1981). In the interwar period, the European ideal of social security spread all over the world. Towards the end of the twentieth century core elements of the welfare state have been established and consolidated in the democratizing East Asian miracle economies such as South Korea and Taiwan. Ever since the inception of state-backed social insurance and healthcare, voices of anxiety about the cost and size of public social responsibility have been raised. In Germany, the allegedly excessive economic burden imposed by Bismarck's social legislation had already been debated in the beginning of the 1900s at a time when government expenditure for social insurance amounted to a tiny fraction of gross domestic product (GDP). In 1952, *The Times* in Britain inaugurated the first of many debates ever since on the 'crisis'. In that year, 15.6 per cent of the British GDP was spent on social security and services. Fifty years later, Britain spent much more, and European countries in general spend between 20 and 32 per cent of their GDP on welfare state purposes. In 1994, the newspaper *The European* (28 January 1994) wrote: 'The welfare state is at a breaking point.' Assessments of this kind have been ample throughout European welfare state history, but welfare states have survived, although under more or less constant small-scale reconstruction in recent decades (Kuhnle 2000).

The comprehensive Scandinavian welfare states have also from time to time been the objects of criticism and incredulity, not least from the Organization for Economic Cooperation and Development (OECD), for being too generous, but have in recent years won renewed praise and admiration from a variety of sources. The Scandinavian welfare states seem not only to make up a distinct type of welfare state, but appear indeed sometimes also to serve as a positive model for reforms and developments in other countries. Why is it a model? Basically, I would claim, because the outcomes of the various welfare state institutions seem to be successful in terms of values and objectives highly regarded by many: limited poverty, a relatively high degree of income equality, social stability and relatively less crime of various kinds (although there are variations within the Nordic area), which again is conducive to less expenditure in other chapters of government budgets. Both the process through which social and welfare policies and institutions are made, most often with broad political consensus, and the outcome of policies enjoy high legitimacy in the population. Scandinavian countries enjoy a high degree of 'double legitimacy', i.e. procedural legitimacy (how decisions are made) and outcome legitimacy (results of decisions and implementation). And Scandinavian countries have at the same time on the whole been economically successful. The association between welfare state designs and criminality is a field which deserves more research attention. It makes sense to hypothesize that institutional designs have an impact upon attitudes, norms, perceptions, needs and social and political behaviour. What are the features which seem to make this model interesting far beyond Scandinavia and the rest of Europe?

Due to the intertwined history of the Nordic geographical area and the subsequent common cultural patterns the concept of Scandinavia is often used in a broad sense to include Norway, Sweden, Denmark, Finland and Iceland. The area constitutes almost one-third of the total area of Western Europe, but only five per cent of its population. The Scandinavian countries, with their small populations and relatively scarce resources, have developed many institutions and cultural patterns of their own, and in many studies of current societies they are considered distinct examples of developed welfare states. I shall use 'Scandinavian' and 'Nordic' interchangeably when referring to all Nordic countries, although the adjective 'Scandinavian' normally refers only to Denmark, Norway and Sweden.

I shall in the following give an interpretation of the concept of the welfare state, trace the steps in the development of the Scandinavian welfare states and highlight some of their major characteristics which relate to the underlying values of the Scandinavian welfare state construct. It is also possible to draw some general lessons as to the political, social and economic effects of welfare state institutions. Finally, I propose that it would be of interest to develop research on the relationship between the types or 'models' of welfare state and the scope and kind of criminality in society, and also research on to what extent increased mobility and communications of any kind in a globalizing world, and the consequent growth of more heterogeneous populations, will affect patterns of criminality and punishment.

4.2 The concept and meaning of the welfare state

The concept of the welfare state denotes a form of government in which the state through legislation takes on the responsibility of protecting and promoting the basic well-being of all its members. Essential elements include legislation which guarantees income maintenance and other kinds of support for individuals and families in cases of occupational accidents and diseases, sickness, old age, unemployment and childbirth.

The ideology of the welfare state grew out of the experience of the Second World War. Sir William Beveridge's plan (1942) for a 'social service state' and the Philadelphia resolutions of the International Labour Organization (1944) became basic reference documents for the legitimation and the practical build-up of welfare state institutions and programmes after the war. Britain in the 1940s and 1950s has been perceived as exceptional in the history of European welfare state development. Academic social scientists made an important impact on the development of social policy. In addition to Beveridge, the influence of T. H. Marshall and Richard Titmuss was significant. All three were affiliated to the London School of Economics and Political Science. Many of their concepts and conceptions have played a major role in social policy debates in West European countries since 1950, and in recent decades also far beyond Europe, not least because of further inspiration provided by the book *The Three Worlds of Welfare Capitalism* (Esping-Andersen 1990), where the conception of different welfare regimes is elaborated. The idea and practice of universal social security schemes, i.e. schemes that cover the entire population or population categories, are typical postwar constructs in European welfare states. The principle of universality, signifying a crucial value basis, was first carried farthest in Britain and the Scandinavian (Nordic) countries, and the latter are currently seen as prime examples of comprehensive, encompassing, universalistic welfare states.

The growth of the welfare state has been understood in a number of ways. It can broadly speaking be seen as a response to two fundamental developments: that of the formation of national states and their transformation into mass democracies, and that of the growth of capitalism after the Industrial Revolution (Flora and Heidenheimer 1981; Alber 1982). The welfare state can be interpreted as a response to the demand both for socio-economic equality and for socio-economic security, or – in a broader meaning – as a response to the demand and/or political will for promoting social justice.

The welfare state implies a transformation of the state itself, of its structure, functions and legitimacy. It has alleviated social cleavages and may have created new ones. It is commonly assumed that the welfare state in Europe has contributed to social security, social harmony and political stability; that it has weakened the appeal of orthodox socialism; that it has stabilized the economy; and that it has contributed to the equalization of living conditions and life chances between social classes and groups.

4.3 The developmental welfare state in Scandinavia

In a century-long perspective, a strong social and democratic state has not been antithetical to modern values underpinning the security and well-being of the market: personal freedoms, private initiative and individual property rights, thus fostering private entrepreneurship and rapid industrialization (Kuhnle *et al.* 2003; Hort and Kuhnle 2000).

Throughout the twentieth century, the scope of social planning in Scandinavia continuously expanded with the aim of achieving a balanced economic and social development, i.e. economic growth as well as social justice. Thus fighting poverty went hand in hand with state institution-building for social and economic growth as well as political democracy, pioneered by broad-based popular social movements (Olsson 1993). New, tax-financed social programmes were always launched with a strong emphasis on their impact on macro-economic efficiency and individual work incentives. For instance, the breakthrough of social policy during the late nineteenth and early twentieth centuries had a competitive edge directed against the emigration of skilled labour to North America, while the housing and population policies of the 1930s had a 'productivist' emphasis on the upbringing and maintenance of the future and current labour force respectively (Myrdal and Myrdal 1934). However, it was not until the emergence of the full employment or active labour market policy of the 1950s and 1960s and the expansion of the public sector – comprehensive state education as well as public health – that a coherent developmental perspective on economic prosperity and social change became part and parcel of welfare state philosophy. Thus, at least since the last quarter of the twentieth century, this has characterized welfare state theory and practice in general: from child to disability policy – 'from the cradle to the grave', as the saying goes about the universal Scandinavian welfare model. Moreover, during the rather painful reconstruction of the welfare state during the last decades of the twentieth century, the relationship between economic growth and social development has been a hot topic on the public agenda throughout Scandinavia, but so far the policy balance and conflict between efficiency and equality has in most cases been resolved and maintained in the five Nordic countries.

It can be argued that there is such a thing as a Scandinavian or Nordic type of welfare state, the core of which has been characterized as lying in 'broad public participation in various areas of economic and social life, the purpose of which is to promote economic efficiency, to improve the ability of society to master its problems, and to enrich and equalize the living conditions of individuals and families. In social policy, the cornerstone of the model is universalism' (Erikson *et al.* 1987). By universalism is meant that the Scandinavian countries have set out to develop a welfare state that includes the entire population.

Although the Swedish case since the mid-1930s has been identified as the empirical embodiment of the Scandinavian type of welfare state, in fact all five Nordic countries took off in the same developmental direction during the 1930s. All of the Nordic countries got their crisis compromises in that decade, leading to institutional solutions for mediation between the interests of organized labour and employers and to lesser tensions between agricultural and industrial interests. This is the Nordic *Sonderweg*: crucial steps were taken, unique in Europe, I believe, towards building a broad political consensus on a platform of a state-regulated, socially modified capitalism before the Second World War (Kildal and Kuhnle 2005).

A number of components of welfare systems, when taken together, set Scandinavian/Nordic countries (with partial exceptions – Iceland having a smaller public sector) apart from other welfare states (Kuhnle 1990). Among these are the relative size of governmental welfare provision, the size of welfare employment (broadly speaking, i.e. employment in social services, institutional care, social insurance administration, health services and education), public employment as a proportion of total employment; redistribution; high legitimacy for state and public welfare provision; and universal, citizenship-based social rights. 'Their universal embrace has anchored the Scandinavian welfare states' claim to a special status' (Baldwin 1990: 51–2), but the principle of universalism is also part of the Beveridgean post-Second World War development in Britain. And indeed, Scandinavian postwar developments are partly inspired by, or were accelerated by, Beveridge (1942) and the introduction of National Health Insurance in the UK in 1948.

The hallmark of the contemporary Scandinavian institutional welfare state is expressed in terms of three essential features: social policy is comprehensive; the social entitlement principle has been institutionalized (social rights); and social legislation has a solidaristic and universalist nature.

Is there a 'Scandinavian' route to contemporary societies with democratic regimes, affluent economies and comprehensive welfare states? Even if the historical experience of any country or region cannot be repeated, are there any lessons to be drawn from the experiences of the Scandinavian countries as to how a coherent development of democratic governance, a productive economy and universal welfare provision and income security can occur with relative success? How have comprehensive welfare states been justified in economic, political and moral terms? Is the Scandinavian welfare state construction robust in the era of increasing economic globalization? These are questions which can only be briefly dealt with in the following (see also Kuhnle and Hort 2004).

The beginning of the modern Scandinavian welfare states can most meaningfully be traced to the last decades of the nineteenth century, as elsewhere in Europe. Quite remarkably, the first major social insurance laws were passed at about the same time, in the course of three years (1891-4), in Denmark, Norway and Sweden.

The shift in the concept of poor law relief to the idea of social insurance was a dramatic and significant change in terms of attitudes to public responsibility for certain types of risks or individual misfortunes. Scandinavian debates, and to some extent social policy developments, were influenced by German legislation (Kuhnle 1996), but decisions varied as to the priority of insurance needs, the form of organization, the extent of population or worker coverage and whether insurance should be voluntary or compulsory.

The 'social question' had been on the agenda for some time; associations for economists were created in all three countries in the 1870s and 1880s, and the idea of an active role for the state was generally accepted among elite groups from different sectors of the society. Economics of a positive or normative kind became firmly established as a university discipline. Forums for informed scientific and public political debate were created. Parallel to, and interlinked with, this development of a positive social science was the expansion of a state apparatus for the registration of social problems and collection of new social statistics. The capacity to collect and the actual collection of relevant data for social legislation, e.g. data on the scope and activities of voluntary associations, were factors explaining the variations in the priorities of the first laws enacted across the Scandinavian countries.

During the whole of the nineteenth century the Scandinavian countries remained predominantly agrarian. Even in the 1920s and early 1930s agriculture was the most important source of employment in all of the Scandinavian countries. There were important differences between the Scandinavian countries with regard to the development of the industrial and service sectors of the economy (Alestalo and Kuhnle 1987: 12–18), but it is worth noting some commonalities which set the region apart from the experience in the rest of Europe. Combined with the agrarian surroundings of the industry, the arrival of the industrial revolution had different social effects from those in European centres. The bulk of social problems existed in rural areas and the Scandinavian cities avoided the most destructive dysfunctions of industrial capitalism. The cities were never overcrowded with slums and the exploitation of the industrial labour force never reached the magnitude of the capitalist cities (Pollard 1981: 233). During the interwar years, the Scandinavian countries remained highly dependent on the British market. The decline of the British economy turned the greater flow of exports to Germany, and from the smaller Scandinavian countries to Sweden. During the late 1930s the share of exports to Great Britain and Germany was 75 per cent of Denmark's exports, over 50 per cent of Finland's and 40 per cent of Norway's and Sweden's (Jörberg and Krantz 1976: 400–4; Wallensteen *et al.* 1973: 31–40). All four countries experienced diversification of their production, export and import structures during the period of rapid economic growth after the Second World War, but this trend was almost universal among highly developed countries in this period. The level of economic development, as measured by GDP per capita, was considerably lower in all Scandinavian countries compared with the USA and the United Kingdom throughout the nineteenth century. But by the middle of the twentieth century during the 'golden age of capitalism', i.e. in the 1950s and 1960s (Maddison 1977: 103–4; 1980: 247), the Scandinavian countries grew to be among the richest countries in the world at about the same time as the 'mature' universalistic welfare state was institutionalized. Economic growth evidently did not take place at the cost of welfare state growth or vice versa.

The universal character of the Nordic welfare states is a rather recent phenomenon, a typical construct of the early post-Second World War decades. The postwar construction of the welfare state went through two phases: the first was characterized by the general acceptance and establishment of universal population coverage (or relevant category of population) with a flat-rate benefit system; the second phase from the 1960s is marked by the introduction of earnings-related and adequate benefits, and thus also maintenance of the status (and to a larger extent income) achieved in gainful employment. Since the 1960s social care services have been greatly expanded at the local government level all over Scandinavia, e.g. institutional or home-help care for the elderly, and kindergartens. Since the 1970s, also paid parental leave schemes have also been established and greatly extended into the most generous schemes in the world.

Two characteristics of the Scandinavian type of welfare state are of prime importance and were visible from early on: public responsibility for welfare provision and the principle of universal coverage based on the idea of social rights. Arguments in favour of universalism (cf. Kildal and Kuhnle 2005) can have power independent of context, and once universalistic institutions have been implemented, the worth or benefit of the principle of universalism can be assessed independently of specific historical prerequisites. Ideas and institutions can be diffused and planted in new political contexts. The question to be asked then is: Does the principle of universalism serve certain desirable social values and political goals? It can be argued that universalism has been conducive to equality and security. And if the values of relatively egalitarian income distributions, little poverty, high levels of employment, political stability and steady economic growth or development are set high on the agenda, the Scandinavian welfare states have been successful, comparatively speaking. But one may ask: have comprehensive welfare states evolved at the price of weak economic development? Are Scandinavian welfare states – and the historically important principles they build on – at the present time seriously challenged?

During the early postwar period there was all over Western Europe considerable consensus – among organized interests on the labour market, among political parties of various colours and not least in the profession of economists – regarding the role of state involvement in the economy. The Keynesian welfare state actively intervened in the workings of the markets, in particular the labour market, and heavily regulated certain sectors of the economy (the health system, education, etc.).

In the social policy debate of the 1980s and 1990s, the deeper moral aspects of welfare policy came under scrutiny once again. Many commentators and researchers argue that, if the welfare system grows too large, it risks perverting incentive structures in both working life and society in general. Welfare breeds a dependent underclass. Scholars have pointed to what they consider to be excessively generous sickness benefits and to the manifold opportunities for drawing disability pensions, and they claim that this excessive generosity has resulted in various forms of over-utilization (OECD 2006; *Swedish Economy* 2003).

Overall, a universal welfare state can be seen as an experiment in solidarity behaviour on a massive scale. If benefits are widely and systematically abused, this solidarity comes under severe stress. Thus, the solidarity necessary for the system's preservation is not absolute but conditional (Rothstein 1998).

The welfare state can be described historically and currently to serve a number of functions, and an evaluation of its achievements and degree of success can only be measured against considerations of specific values and political and social goals (fairness, justice, cohesion, stability, material and physical security, well-being, economic growth, etc.). Among the many characteristics which can be ascribed to the Scandinavian type of welfare state is its 'work-friendliness': the persistent efforts to develop social security and labour market policies which promote competitiveness as well as 'full employment' and which have helped put the Scandinavian countries on top of the list of employment ratios of OECD countries. Being among the most comprehensive welfare states, providing income transfers and services on a more universal basis than elsewhere in Europe, it is interesting to note that all of the Nordic countries showed increasing labour productivity in the 1990s compared with the previous decade, and that the level was everywhere higher than for the USA and for the EU average (Kuhnle *et al.* 2003). Among European welfare states, the Scandinavian countries were also the most 'family-friendly', i.e. in terms of having developed policies conducive to labour force participation by both women and men in families with children and/or other care responsibilities – which may be another way of looking at the degree of 'work-friendliness' of welfare states. The Scandinavian countries have for long had the most extensive provision of (local) government welfare and care services for children and the elderly among American/European welfare states (Kohl 1981; Kautto *et al.* 1999). Parental leave schemes, the most generous paid parental leave schemes in the world, were consolidated and expanded (in particular in Norway) during the 1990s. Pragmatic and operational lessons from the Scandinavian experience may be drawn by other nations. A judgment of 'work-friendliness' can also indicate the degree of 'business-friendly environment' (Hort 2001).

Politics and welfare state construction are to my mind fundamentally about equalization of life chances, social justice, social security, social cohesion and stability, all of which are also in various ways related not only to economic growth and the dynamics of economic development, climate of investments, etc., but also to political preferences, ideologies, interests and values. Thus what kinds of welfare state policies are possible is also at all times a question of what is considered desirable by governments and voters, and what is considered desirable – what the state *can* and *ought to* do (Rothstein 1994) – is a question of political and cultural context (norms, expectations, value structures) as much as a question of the level of economic development and theories and knowledge of prerequisites for economic growth and efficiency.

4.4 Possible lessons from the Scandinavian welfare political experience

One lesson to be drawn from the early social insurance legislation in Scandinavia is that without data, without a statistical basis, legislation was not likely and that state capacity in terms of the ability to provide statistics was important for legislative efforts (Kuhnle 1996). Another historical lesson is that social insurance programmes were originally modest and limited and were gradually extended.

The uniqueness of the Scandinavian historical experience does not rule out an assessment of the implications of developing governmental capacity and institutions for promoting welfare, and for the possible positive implications of the principle of universal policies for the general level of welfare.

The scope of social planning, including establishing and developing social security, health and educational systems during the first half of the twentieth century, was clearly a result of democratic political processes aimed at balancing demands for and goals of economic growth and social justice. Scandinavian history has shown that 'welfare' can be 'productive'. The early institutional solutions chosen may have had an effect on the later expansion and development of social programmes, e.g. programmes first introduced based on the principle of economic means-testing may have been more conducive to develop into universal programmes than those programmes first established for defined groups of the economically active population.

Early Scandinavian focus on general education and universal health services may have proved of great importance for subsequent successful economic development and 'national wealth'. State and public responsibility for a healthy population was from early on argued for in the context of creating national wealth and strength.

Social security and welfare state arrangements can serve many purposes, income security in cases of unemployment, old age, sickness, etc. being one such. Another core aspect of a social security system lies in how to organize it in such a way that it provides incentives to work, which seems an important goal of most governments. One possible effect of an unemployment insurance system is that it facilitates the process of restructuring in industry and business. Economic security may reduce workers' and employees' resistance to change.

Recent Scandinavian (and European) experience indicates that there is no obvious clear link between the scope of the welfare state, taxation levels, employment rates, labour productivity and economic growth. The examples of Sweden and, especially, Finland during the 1990s show that comprehensive, democratic welfare states are fully capable of making policy adjustments to stimulate new economic growth when 'hit' by a serious economic recession or backlash (Kuhnle *et al.* 2003). Social security represents a shock absorber. Democratic institutions have been shown to be responsive to economic and social challenges. Another lesson for other countries may be that in the era of globalization, meaning greater economic integration in the world, the need for a consolidated, national social security system is 'objectively' greater than before.

In a more globalized world, we may expect more rapid changes in labour markets, more mobility, more flexible work and more career shifts during the period of labour market participation. This may induce reforms, e.g. Sweden reformed its pension system in 1999 in a way which may offer other countries a lesson, because it combines the manifest 'work-friendly' aspect with a universal guarantee of income security in old age. This means that even if a citizen or resident has never been gainfully employed and contributed to a pension (insurance) scheme, he or she is entitled to a minimum old age pension (but one must have resided 40 years in the country to receive a *full* minimum pension). Thus the system as a whole is one where maintenance of status is combined with poverty prevention.

Another aspect of Scandinavian welfare states, their emphasis on (public) social services for children, the old and sick, may offer another lesson, but perhaps one more controversial in other cultural contexts. In one way, such government schemes may be considered both 'work-friendly', 'family-friendly' and 'business-friendly'. If families are relieved of part of their role as caregivers (for their young, old and sick family members) their labour market activity and labour mobility can increase, and thus also positively affect economic productivity and growth. Government social policies can provide the basis for flexible solutions for families, for workers/employees and for firms. Globalization also has a cultural dimension, and the idea, demand and expectations of greater gender equality in all spheres of society may spread worldwide. It may thus well be that in the future 'global world', welfare states with social policies which are relatively more 'gender sensitive' will be most successful in terms of both economic development and social peace and harmony.

4.5 Future research: institutions, trust and criminal behaviour

David Downes refers in this volume (Chapter 2) to the fact that generous welfare states do not necessarily have lower overall crime rates, but that research indicates that 'economic inequality and low welfare provision are strongly related to high rates of lethal violence'. The EU ICS 2005 Survey indicates that Sweden and Finland are relatively low-crime countries (e.g. burglaries), while Denmark is described as a 'high-crime country' (e.g. burglaries, car theft, hate crimes). However, respondents in all three countries report lower feelings of insecurity than in other European countries (van Dijk *et al.* 2007). Fundamental reasons for these facts and observations may be many and diverse, and not always easily measurable, e.g. relatively egalitarian social structures in the pre-industrial and pre-welfare state eras; relatively small and ethnically and culturally homogenous populations; short distances between citizens and decision-making authorities; historical strength of local governments and communities; strong sense of local and, later on, national identity conducive to social cohesion. The kind of welfare model that has been developed and constructed after industrialization and democratization

– comprehensive and universalistic with relatively extensive state responsibility for citizen welfare – may also be related to these overall historical characteristics of Nordic societies. And thus, we may also entertain the hypothesis that the kind of welfare model – the kind of institutional design – affects norms, trust, perceptions and behaviour. In all international comparative studies of trust – either trust in political institutions or trust in 'others' – the Nordic countries come out on top (Halpern 2005; Listhaug and Ringdal 2007; see also Lappi-Seppälä in Chapter 3 this volume). It is likely that variations of trust are a fundamental characteristic and measure of social cohesion in a society, and one which is conducive to variations in social and asocial (criminal) behaviour – both property-related, 'economic' crimes and violent crimes. Alber (2001) has also suggested that there is an association between social integration via the welfare state and criminality – the more integration, the less crime – but cautions that macro-patterns hinge very much upon the USA. Relationships are not easily researched with macro-data – such studies warrant further investigations into the relationships between the design of welfare institutions and policies and the extent of various kinds of crime.

One would of course also have to take into account how the overall context of welfare models changes over time. More intensive globalization since the 1980s – in terms of communications, migration, economics, politics and culture – also creates new challenges and opportunities for Scandinavian societies and their citizens, which may affect both their welfare models and patterns of crime and punishment. Social changes occur more rapidly than before, populations are becoming more heterogeneous and established patterns of social stability, cohesion and trust may come under pressure, which subsequently affects norms, attitudes, actions and behaviour (see Pratt 2008). Thus a topic for research at both macro and micro levels would be to study such relationships between changes in welfare institutional and societal characteristics and patterns of criminality and punishment in historical and comparative perspectives, controlling for the kind or level of exposure to various indicators of globalization.

References

Alber, J. (1982) *Vom Armenhaus zum wohlfahrtstaat. Analysen zur Entwicklung der Sozialversicherung in West Europa*. Frankfurt: Campus.

Alber, J. (2001) 'Hat sich der Wohlfahrtstaat als soziale Ordnung bewährt?', in K. U. Mayer (ed.), *Die Beste aller Welten? Marktliberalismus versus Wohlfahrtsstaat*. Frankfurt: Campus, pp. 59–111.

Alestalo, M. and Kuhnle, S. (1987) 'The Scandinavian route: economic, social and political developments in Denmark, Finland, Norway, and Sweden', in R. Erikson, E. J. Hansen, S. Ringen and H. Uusitalo (eds), *The Scandinavian Model: Welfare States and Welfare Research*. London and Armonk, NY: M. E. Sharpe, pp. 3–38.

Baldwin, P. (1990) *The Politics of Social Solidarity: Class Bases of the European Welfare States 1875–1975*. Cambridge: Cambridge University Press.

Beveridge, W. H. (1942) *Social Insurance and Allied Services*. London: HMSO.

Erikson, R., Hansen, E. J., Ringen, S. and Uusitalo, H. (eds) (1987) *The Scandinavian Model: Welfare States and Welfare Research*. London and Armonk, NY: M. E. Sharpe.

Esping-Andersen, G. (1990) *The Three Worlds of Welfare Capitalism.* Cambridge: Polity Press.

Flora, P. and Heidenheimer, A. J. (eds) (1981) *The Development of Welfare States in Europe and America.* New Brunswick, NJ and London: Transaction Books.

Halpern, D. (2005) *Social Capital.* Cambridge: Polity Press.

Hort, S. E. O. (2001) 'Sweden – still a civilized version of Workfare?', in N. Gilbert (ed.), *Activating the Unemployed: A Comparative Appraisal of Work-Oriented Policies.* New Brunswick, NJ: Transaction Books, pp. 243–66.

Hort, S. E. O. and Kuhnle, S. (2000) 'The coming of the East and South-east Asian welfare state', *Journal of European Social Policy*, 10(2): 162–84.

Jörberg, L. and Krantz, O. (1976) 'Scandinavia, 1914–1970', in C. M. Cipolla (ed.), *The Fontana Economic History of Europe*, Vol. VI (2). London and Glasgow: Collins/Fontana.

Kautto, M., Heikkilä, M., Hvinden, B., Marklund, S. and Ploug, N. (eds) (1999) *Nordic Social Policy. Changing Welfare States.* London and New York: Routledge.

Kildal, N. and Kuhnle, S. (2005) 'The Nordic welfare model and the idea of universalism', in N. Kildal and S. Kuhnle (eds), *Normative Foundations of the Welfare State: The Nordic Experience.* London: Routledge, pp. 13–33.

Kohl, J. (1981) 'Trends and problems in postwar public expenditure development in Western Europe and North America', in P. Flora and A. J. Heidenheimer (eds), *The Development of Welfare States in Europe and America.* New Brunswick, NJ and London: Transaction Books, pp. 307–44.

Kuhnle, S. (1981) 'The growth of social insurance programs in Scandinavia: outside influences and internal forces', in P. Flora and A. J. Heidenheimer (eds), *The Development of Welfare States in Europe and America.* New Brunswick, NJ and London: Transaction Books, pp. 125–50.

Kuhnle, S. (1990) 'Den skandinaviske velferdsmodellen – skandinavisk? Velferd? Model?', in A. R. Hovdum, S. Kuhnle and L. Stokke (eds), *Visjoner om velferdssamfunnet.* Bergen: Alma Mater, pp. 12–26.

Kuhnle, S. (1996) 'International modeling, states and statistics: Scandinavian social security solutions in the 1890s', in D. Rueschemeyer and T. Skocpol (eds), *States, Social Knowledge, and the Origins of Modern Social Policies.* Princeton, NJ: Princeton University Press, pp. 233–63.

Kuhnle, S. (ed.) (2000) *Survival of the European Welfare State.* London: Routledge.

Kuhnle, S. and Hort, S. E. O. (2004) *The Developmental Welfare State in Scandinavia: Lessons for the Developing World, Social Policy and Development*, Paper No. 17. Geneva: United Nations Research Institute for Social Development (UNRISD).

Kuhnle, S., Hatland, A. and Hort, S. E. O. (2003) 'A work-friendly welfare state: lessons from Europe', in K. Marshall and O. Butzbach (eds), *New Social Policy Agendas for Europe and America. Challenges, Experience, and Lessons.* Washington, DC: World Bank, pp. 325–48.

Listhaug, O. and Ringdal, K. (2007) *Trust in Political Institutions: The Nordic Countries Compared with Europe.* Paper prepared for the Norwegian Political Science Meeting, NTNU, Trondheim, 3–5 January.

Maddison, A. (1977) 'Phases of capitalist development', *Banca Nazionale del Lavoro, Quarterly Review*, 121: 103–37.

Maddison, A. (1980) 'Western economic performance in the 1970s: a perspective and assessment', *Banca Nazionale del Lavoro, Quarterly Review*, 134: 246–89.

Myrdal, A. and Myrdal, G. (1934) *Kris i befolkningsfrågan.* Stockholm: Bonniers.

OECD (2006) *Sickness, Disability and Work: Breaking the Barriers – Norway, Poland, and Switzerland*, Report published 7 November. Paris: OECD.

Olsson, S. E. O. (1993) *Social Policy and Welfare State in Sweden.* Lund: Arkiv.

Pollard, S. (1981) *Peaceful Conquest. The Industrialization of Europe, 1760–1970.* Oxford: Oxford University Press.

Pratt, J. (2008) 'Scandinavian exceptionalism in an era of penal excess, Part. I: The nature and roots of Scandinavian exceptionalism'; Part II: Does Scandinavian exceptionalism have a future?', *British Journal of Criminology*, 48: 119–37; 275–92.

Rothstein, B. (1994) *Vad bör staten göra?* Stockholm: SNS-förlag.

Rothstein, B. (1998) *Just Institutions Matters – The Moral and Political Logic of the Universal Welfare State.* Cambridge: Cambridge University Press.

Swedish Economy, The (2003) 'Over a million persons receiving social benefits', 1 December. Stockholm: National Institute of Economic Research (Konjunkturinstitutet).

van Dijk, J., Manchin, R., van Kesteren, J., Nevala, S. and Hideg, G. (2007) *The Burden of Crime in the EU: A Comparative Analysis of the European Crime and Safety Survey (EU ICS) 2005.* Brussels: Gallup Europe, UNICRI, Max Planck Institute, January.

Wallensteen, P., Vesa, U. and Väyrynen, R. (eds) (1973) *The Nordic Structure and Change, 1920–1970,* Research Report No. 6. Tampere Peace Research Institute.

5

PENALIZATION AND SOCIAL POLICIES

Philippe Mary and Jacky Nagels

5.1 Introduction

The question of the relationship between social and penal policies is relatively complex because it implies more fundamentally an analysis of the state and thus the adoption of both an historical and a macro-sociological approach. A methodological problem arises given the numerous and diverse empirical indicators that necessitate choices which may then orientate the interpretations of the changes at work. What is more, there is also the difficulty of comparative analysis, even when it is limited to western societies presenting numerous similarities. Although such limits make analysis hazardous and should be kept in mind when drawing up contributions to the debate, they should not paralyse us.

In this paper on the relationship between penalization and social policies, we will proceed in two stages. First, we will return to the analysis of what we have referred to as 'penalization of the social sphere' (Mary 1997, 1998) and contemporary changes in the state. In general, we will discuss the relationship between the particular entity known as the social state and the imposition of punishment, and criticisms of the hypothesis of a recomposition of the state focused on security and punishment. Second, based on the observation that the social state is being maintained in various forms and stands in the way of exacerbated penalization, we will examine certain social protection arrangements in four European Union countries (Germany, Belgium, France and the Netherlands): on the one hand, pensions and poverty, and on the other healthcare, with a view to understanding which logic results in minimalizing pensions and maximizing the efficiency of healthcare. The hypothesis here is that although the social state is being maintained, it is also being recomposed and its interventions no longer affect different population groups in the same way.

5.2 Relationship between the social and penal spheres in the framework of the social state

Addressed by a growing number of criminologists and sociologists, the hypothesis of the penalization of the social sphere may briefly (and for the time being) be summed up as follows: for around the last 20 years in western societies, a growing number of social problems that used to be addressed by other social institutions (family, school, associate sector, world of work, etc.) have come to be handled through the penal system – directly or in terms of intervention logic – and social control has consequently been expanded and reinforced, in particular for 'high-risk' groups. Basically the issue is not new, but it appears to be taking on an exceptional dimension within the framework of neo-liberal policies that are leading to the gradual dismantling of the welfare state in its different forms in these western societies. Analysis of the hypothesis implies at the very least that we first examine if only briefly two historical moments: the advent of the welfare state in the nineteenth century and its crisis beginning in the 1970s. We will then review the debates surrounding it, in particular with regard to the comparison between the United States and (Western) Europe.

5.2.1 The advent of the welfare state and penality

Two reference works make it possible to zero in on the question of the relationship between the social and penal spheres within the framework of the advent of the welfare state: Ewald's work (1986) on the birth of the welfare state and Garland's work (1985) on modern penal strategies.

Ewald's starting point is the problem of occupational accidents towards the end of the nineteenth century as a result of industrialization. He presents an analysis of the transformations of liberal law through the transition from sanctioning individual fault to prevention and correction of social risks. Since society's production of goods appeared to be inevitably linked to the production of individual evils (occupational accidents), 'justice could not mean sanctioning activities, conduct or behaviours on which the good of all depended, but instead placing on all the burden of the individual evils, the necessary ransom of collective advantages' (Ewald 1986: 19).[1] Justice thus becomes social justice, correcting imbalances, reducing inequalities, compensating for what the author calls the 'social evil'. The fact that this social evil no longer originates in an individual fault but in relations between individuals in the normal course of the activities of different individuals makes society itself the source of these relations and consequently obliges it to modify them to reduce this evil. Thus emerged the welfare state, an 'insurance society' with unlimited power, enabling it to match every right to which its members are entitled with an equal number of positive obligations merging into a social morality that assures risk prevention. Within this framework, insurance is more than simply one state institution among others: it becomes a principle, a rationality that structures social policies – and therefore regulation policies – implemented by the state.

Garland (1985) analyses the way in which modern penal institutions step into the shoes of the other social institutions with regard to individuals who wish to escape their grasp or have already done so. First, they strengthen the standards of conduct that determine access to social benefits, doing so in a negative way by sanctioning individuals who do not submit to them, in other words where normal socialization processes are not enough. New laws, e.g. on children or habitual offenders, have supplemented the guilt criterion by taking into account elements such as behaviour or lifestyle as indicators of a failure or an incapacity to assume one's social obligations, while responsibility runs up against a growing number of exceptions based on empirical investigations. We thus witness a shift from the law (legality, guilt, responsibility, etc.) to the 'norm', which gives precedence to expert opinions in order to take the individual's characteristics into account. An auxiliary of socialization institutions, penality will therefore no longer be limited to intimidation, but will place such individuals in the hands of a number of institutions before sending them back into society or excluding them once and for all.

Garland develops a typology of these institutions, which he ranks in a continuum ranging from normalization to segregation, including correction. Normalization is the sector closest to socialization institutions. Together with probation or post-penitentiary assistance, it is possibly the innovation which has the greatest repercussions by allowing for the extension of judicial power and the exercise of a less punitive and more discrete control than prison, appearing to be a means of reforming offenders that increases well-being rather than reducing it. Similarly, correction, including for instance school-prisons, extends penal control and strengthens its effectiveness, but in the institutional mode in this case, while also giving it a positive image through its reforming action. Lastly, segregation, the final stage destined for those who reject or are incapable of submitting to the dominant social order, will be the *ultima ratio* of penality, just as the latter is to the social sphere. Interactions exist among these three sectors: intimidation by means of segregation supports normalizing interventions, the more severe sectors serve as an intermediary so that the others are not obliged to use force or, conversely, the possibility of a return to less severe sectors. Penality thus strengthens the positive representation of the state, the latter developing productive forces while the former builds the personality. Over the longer term, the social reforms of the start of the twentieth century will determine the balance of political forces and the orientation of social policies for decades to come, and penal reforms will do the same with regard to penal discourse and official practices, the whole of which has been weakened only recently.

One of the consequences highlighted by the author, which we consider fundamental, is the depoliticization of the question of crime (Garland 1985: 168–70). The political challenge that crime represents in state regulation mechanisms is masked due to the predominance of individualizing concepts in the sphere of punishment and in social work: social reform issues were separated from the task of individual reform and 'of course the more social reform occurred in the 1940s and 1950s, the more this separation ensured that the problem of deviance became increasingly seen as one of individual pathology and responsibility' (Garland 1985: 254).

The social and penal spheres thus developed in both complementary and contrasting ways. This development was complementary because, from prevention (of risks) to segregation (of those beyond redemption), a continuum of social control was deployed to protect the order of expanding industrial societies. It was contrasting because the intervention logics and terms of each of these two sectors took significantly different directions: the former focused on the integration of populations, where the social question was politicized under the aegis of solidarity and equality; the latter dealt in correction of individuals, where the question of crime was depoliticized under cover of individual responsibility or dangerousness.

5.2.2 The crisis of the social state

Turning to the crisis that hit the social state starting in the 1970s, we should first recall the pioneering work of Rosanvallon and his thesis that the question at the heart of the crisis is not so much that of the financial impasse in which the state finds itself but rather that of the 'sociological limits' of its development and the 'degree of redistribution that its financing involves', i.e. a questioning of 'equality as a social aim' (Rosanvallon 1981: 31). Unlimited equality would be called into question, first by higher demands for security owing to urban insecurity, major technological risks and international instability, which would qualify the demand for equality, or by social 'corporatization' due to the fact that the state is no longer the only means of social protection, resulting in a crisis of solidarity. This would mean a return to the classic liberal state having the tasks of producing security and reducing uncertainty with a view to protecting the right to life and property. It is useful to complement these views with those of Balibar, who explains, although in another theoretical register, that capitalist globalization is leading to the state's reduction to its punitive functions and its return to a combination of security and humanitarian practices:

> Such a combination seems to take us back to a 'primitive' stage of the constitution of the public space in bourgeois societies. It can sometimes claim to be more efficient than the institutional machinery of the social state in crisis. In any case, however, it finds expression in a disqualification of the idea of solidarity *policy* as the means and purpose of 'citizenship' (Balibar 1995: 193)[2].

An increasingly clear connection is thus being established between this crisis and the globalization process which has been swept across the planet for the last 20-odd years by the neo-liberal tidal wave. With the help of privatization and deregulation, this process has contributed appreciably to the weakening of the social state with the scrapping of full employment policies, the reduction of social benefits or the decrease in resources allocated to fighting poverty. On top of these changes has come the increase in supranational constraints, principally European, which go as far as encroaching on governing powers such as foreign policy or currency. The reduction of the role played by the state in the economy and the weakening of the social state are therefore two key elements in the current changes, which encourage the reduction of the state to its authority and security roles, i.e. the transition from a social state to a 'security state',[3] to the extent that 'the more the state withdraws by deregulating social and economic management to allow market forces to come into play, the more it effectively expands the role of the penal dimension in social control, in classic disputes over the protection of goods and violence, finding therein an expression of its legitimation' (Houchon 1996: 82).[4] There is also 'generally a tendency to reduce the complex question of existential uncertainty, a consequence of the globalization process, to a simple problem of "maintaining law and order"'. It emerges, for instance, that 'security' preoccupations, which are most often reduced to concerns about bodily protection and protection of goods, are on the contrary 'overdetermined': they receive the full brunt of the angst produced by one of the fundamental aspects of present-day existence – uncertainty (Bauman 1999: 12–13).

In such a context, attention has been drawn to the switchover from universalist integration policies to individual inclusion policies that develop specific treatments for populations with problems (Castel 1995), as well as to the transformation of policies acting on distribution structures into policies of simple correction of the effects of unequal distribution of economic and cultural resources:

> Along with the weakening of trade unionism and of bodies capable of building support, the new forms of the state's action thus contribute to the transformation of the *people* (potentially) mobilised into a heterogeneous aggregate of fragmented *poor*, of the 'excluded', as they are known in official discourse, discussed above all (if not exclusively) when they 'create problems' or to remind the 'affluent' of the privilege a steady job represents. (Bourdieu 1993: 223)[5]

These new policies are also characterized by the delegation to the local authorities of certain social and law enforcement policies, in which contractualization has become a central element. Such a movement cannot but reinforce the individualized treatment of social problems because the local level, i.e. the city, the neighbourhood or even the building, will be perceived as a total social phenomenon sufficient unto itself, masking generally decisive supra-local parameters. Local policies thus emerge as ersatz global policies that have failed and whose failure they mask (Castel 1995).

Presented as being integrated and comprehensive, penal policies intervene in a growing number of social sectors, transformed by a logic of social control and focused on petty crime that is primarily the work of those populations that increasingly form a sub-proletariat owing to the dismantling of the social state. They tackle the effects more than the causes of this crisis and contribute to the development of penal treatment of the social question. Penality is thus used increasingly as an institution of management and regulation in societies where other integrating processes no longer play their role, resulting in a toughening of state interventionism in compensation for the state's powerlessness to halt socio-economic insecurity and offering it a new source of legitimacy. Punishment becomes a central figure in state policies to such a point that penalization of the social dimension can be considered an effect of the transformation of the social state and of the management or pragmatic responses to it. In addition, with the end of the Cold War and the hegemony of the neo-liberal ideology, the external enemy has been replaced by an internal one. The need for this enemy to be made visible leads to the definition of new figures of dangerousness among petty criminals and contributes largely to the masking of other forms of unlawful activities such as white-collar crime.

All things considered, the separation between social reforms and individual reform that characterized social and penal policies from the end of the nineteenth century up to the peak of the social state in the 1960s gradually fades, not because individual reform, which is severely criticized, returns to the sphere of social policies, as recommended in the 1970s and 1980s, but on the contrary, because these social policies are increasingly reduced to questions of individual treatment. An important source of state legitimacy, penality reinforces this reduction, at the risk of the social question itself being depoliticized.

5.2.3 What state?

In the above analysis, we mentioned the switchover from the social state to the security state as an effect of socio-economic changes at work today. Others, in much more important analyses, go further, using a more radical term to shed light on the changes in the state or even in contemporary western societies. To mention only two of the most well-known, we will refer to the works of Wacquant and Garland. Wacquant, who analyses US crime policies, in particular their – to say the least – important use of detention, uses the term penal state and foresees its arrival in Europe (Wacquant 1998, 1999). More recently, Garland, starting more or less from the same empirical bases while widening them considerably, supports the thesis of the emergence of a 'culture of control' characterized on the one hand by the orientation of the penal system to risk management and security, to the detriment of reintegration and social policies, and on the other by a cultural attitude focused on control and forming what he calls a *crime complex* (Garland 2001).

Among the most important criticisms of these analyses, we shall point out in particular that of the extrapolation to other contexts of tendencies observed in the United States and for which there is reason to believe that they are specific to that country. For instance, the massive use of imprisonment, which highlights the place given to (selective) neutralization, does not seem to have an equivalent elsewhere in the western world (Zedner 2002: 353–4). The same allegedly holds for other forms of control such as probation or release on parole, for which certain research shows, for Canada (Vacheret *et al.* 1998: 47) or England (Brownlee 1998: 98–101) for example, that while their conception includes a risk-management dimension, their application nevertheless maintains an important rehabilitative dimension attesting more to the continuity of the correctional system than to a break. Some make the same observation for the United States, considering that (liberal) criminologists, professionals and even a part of the public opinion remain attached to the ideal of rehabilitation and resist the new policies of control and neutralization (Body-Gendrot 1999; Cullen *et al.* 1996: 35; Lucken 1998).

Recently, O'Malley (2006) returned to the question to show that countries like Canada and Australia, or even New Zealand or Great Britain, are (more or less) a long way from having reached the 'punitive turning point' described by Garland, and that, in the end, the United States represents an exception, at least compared with Europe and the Commonwealth countries. O'Malley sees therein the influence of the social democrat traditions that characterize these countries and permit the penal system to continue to lean heavily on the social state. We could also point out the important differences between social protection systems, in particular the fact that the US system has never been able to match most European systems. Other contributions to this work (Downes, Lappi-Seppälä, Kuhnle) express exactly the same view. They show that for the Scandinavian countries, the social state (as an institution, but also the conception and representations of social relations) stands in the way of increased punitiveness, or at least of an increase in detention rates understood as indicators of punitiveness.

As the conclusion to a lengthy empirical research project on the socio-penal measures created in Belgium in the 1990s, we, together with Cartuyvels and Rea (2000), suggested the term *social and security* state (*état social-sécuritaire*), which we find more appropriate not only to account for the changes under way, but also for the preservation, if only in a defensive mode, of a certain level of social protection and the important discursive impact of state responses to insecurity. We identified three levels of reality in this research.

First is the discourse defining public security policies in which, over a 20-year period, the shift towards greater security is quite pronounced: until the mid-1980s, the question of insecurity was generally limited to the socio-economic sphere, particularly in the face of the decline in heavy industry and rising unemployment, notably among young people. It later took on another meaning, being reduced first to problems of crime and second to those of urban crime.

Second is the number of measures, which has literally skyrocketed in 20 years. However, based on the results of empirical research, this number seems almost inversely proportional to their effectiveness or, more exactly, to their capacity to meet the objectives assigned to them by political discourse.[6] From this standpoint, it seems that the state's security discourse can sometimes be sufficient unto itself, independently of its practical applications, in that it first serves the state's image and legitimacy, rather than security, and in this sense the policy is increasingly 'for show', seeking to change not the reality but the image individuals have of it (Baratta 1991: 19).

Third is the practices of players, where the situation is growing more complex. On the one hand, as also argued by O'Malley, many agents continue to develop practices that correspond to their representation of the profession and sometimes create a significant counterweight to security and management tendencies. On the other, security rhetoric produces high expectations that influence the feeling of insecurity and relations between social groups in that they literally format social representations and shift the democratic limits of the political agenda. For example, when crime is placed at the centre of policies as a priority target, it becomes increasingly difficult to substantiate the relevance of an intervention that considers the absence of criminal behaviour only as a secondary benefit, a fortiori when the continuity of this intervention depends on state subsidies. At the very least there might emerge the necessity of taking up certain themes of the dominant discourse, at the risk that in the long run the practices themselves may be contaminated. What is more, while the effectiveness of the new measures can be called into question, this must not make us lose sight of the action of the former measures. Although situated at the end of the security chain, prison nevertheless offers a significant example. The Belgian prison population has risen by 85 per cent in 25 years,[7] essentially for three reasons, all related to the practices of agents of the penal system (Snacken 1999; Deltenre 2003): an increase in the number of prisoners and in the length of detention on remand, an increase in the length of penalties (through convictions, possibilities of consecutive sentences, the revocation of probation or early release and the grant of release on parole at a later stage) and the growing proportion of foreign prisoners. Another example is provided by social work in the framework of the judicial system (psychosocial services in prison or supervision of convicted persons in open settings), which today is increasingly reoriented towards supervision and monitoring, against a backdrop of case management, to the detriment of its social assistance dimension. In this regard, recent empirical research highlights the increasing importance of the prospect of risk management in a number of sectors at the crossroads of the judiciary and the social dimensions (de Coninck et al. 2005).

5.3 Poverty, pensions and healthcare in four European Union countries: Germany, Belgium, France and the Netherlands

If we disregard the United States and focus on Europe, it seems quite clear that there is a need to refute the figuration of the penal state or the security state as a contemporary characteristic of state figurations. But this does not imply that the social state remains an unchanged reference of public action. Indeed, many traditionally social-democrat countries have in recent years developed diverse strategies known as the 'Third Way' or the active social state. Although there are several variations on this theme, closely related to Blair's New Labour, it can be summed up as an adaptation of social-democracy to neo-liberalism, from which a number of values are borrowed (responsibility, individualism, free enterprise, minimal state, etc.). It is presented as the European left's response to the need to take into consideration the domination of markets in the framework of globalization, while trying to stem the effects that are most negative for the population's welfare. Among the important elements of this policy, we would mention in particular the determination to break with the 'welfare' social state that simply creates drawing rights and to activate the different benefits granted (in particular concerning unemployment) through the imposition of certain conditions (training, work outside of employee status, etc.) in order to make beneficiaries more responsible.

These changes led to a review of the evolution of the social state's redistribution mechanisms with a view to better identifying the level of protection from which the most vulnerable segments of the population benefit. We selected pensions, poverty and healthcare in four European Union countries that are sufficiently comparable. Pensions and healthcare alone make up approximately two-thirds of social security spending. These two headings have both been rising during the last two decades and this growth will continue until 2050. Poverty concerns 10 to 15 per cent of the total population and is dependent on countless factors, two of which are essential: old age and unemployment. For methodological reasons alone, this is a difficult exercise, particularly in just a few pages, but to its credit, it provides certain information on some of the changes at work.

5.3.1 Pensions and poverty

First, it is important to stress the relative and multifactorial nature of poverty and justify the choice of the four countries. Second, the poverty threshold must be determined and quantified in the different countries. Third, the risk of poverty must be defined and its ensuing evolution reviewed.

5.3.1.1 Relative and multifactorial nature

The risk of poverty is multifactorial. It varies in time and space. It is historically and socially determined. It is not the same at the end of the nineteenth century and the beginning of the twenty-first. Per capita income has exploded in the highly developed countries and the social security system, which was in limbo before the First World War, soared after the Second World War. Social security is dependent on the level of development: we cannot place on the same footing Burundi, with its per capita income of US$622, China with US$6,012 and Germany with US$26,210, i.e. 42 times the income of a country in sub-Saharan Africa.[8] While poverty is determined by the level of development – symbolized here by gross domestic product (GDP) per inhabitant – it also depends on the country's history: although the United States and Japan, like Western Europe, are highly developed countries, their social history is totally different from Europe's.

That is why we only compare European countries that have approximately the same level of development and a similar social history over a lengthy period: Germany, France, the Netherlands and Belgium.[9] Eastern and Southern Europe are separate from this group of four.

5.3.1.2 The poverty threshold

The poverty threshold is a very relative concept. The World Bank places it at one or two dollars a day in most African countries. With this income, an inhabitant of Western Europe would not survive for long. According to the definition commonly accepted in the European Union, the *poverty threshold corresponds to 60 per cent of the median net income.*[10]

Since per capita income in eastern Germany is well below that in western Germany, the country's level fell considerably at the time of reunification. This explains why the poverty threshold in Germany is inferior to that of the other three countries. The other three are neck and neck.

5.3.1.3. The risk of poverty

The risk of poverty – i.e. the risk of having an income below the poverty threshold as defined in Table 5.1 – strikes two social groups more severely: the jobless and the elderly.

While the risk of poverty for the population as a whole ranges between 10 and 15 per cent (cf. Table 5.2) in the four countries considered, it is two to three times higher for the unemployed, i.e. 27 per cent in the Netherlands, 29 per cent in France, 31 per cent in Belgium and 42 per cent in Germany. In three of the four countries (the Netherlands, Belgium and Germany) the risk is similar for men and women. France alone is the exception: 34 per cent for men and 25 per cent for women. To sum up, between one quarter and one third of the jobless – or even more in Germany (42 per cent) – can be considered to be poor.

The national averages do not reflect strongly contrasting regional realities. For instance, although the unemployment rate is around 10 per cent in Belgium, it is

TABLE 5.1 Poverty threshold in the four countries in 2005 (in €)

	Annual	*Monthly*	*Rank*
Germany	9,270	781	4
France	9,712	809	3
Netherlands	10,356	863	1
Belgium	10,316	860	2
(EU-15)	(9,256)	(771)	

Source: Committee for the Study of Ageing (2008: 7).

TABLE 5.2 Risk of poverty by age groups (%)

Risk of poverty	Germany	France	Neth.	Belgium	EU-15
For the total population	13	13	10	15	16
For the over-65 male population	12	18	7	22	17
For the over-65 female population	14	18	6	25	22
Rank	2	3	1	4	

Source: Committee for the Study of Ageing (2008).

over 12 per cent in Wallonia and less than half that rate in Flanders: 5.4 per cent. The poverty rate is similar to the unemployment rate in the two main regions of the country (European Commission 2007: 167). The same holds for Germany: the risk of poverty is 17.3 per cent in eastern Germany and 12 per cent in western Germany (European Commission, 2007: 201). In the Netherlands, '… there is a strong ethnic dimension in poverty risk: ethnic minorities account for 23.4 per cent of the total number of minimum-income households, whereas the remaining population makes up only 6.2 per cent of such households' (European Commission 2007: 248). The same phenomenon is seen in France, where both the unemployment rate and the poverty rate are above the national average for the immigrant population and primarily for non-EU nationals (European Commission 2007: 248).

Among the elderly, lone women are the most affected, for three main reasons. First, women work considerably fewer years than men because women make up the bulk of part-time workers (labour market, family responsibilities, etc.). In addition, women's average salary is less than men's. Since the size of the pension depends essentially on the number of years worked and the salary level, the result is that women are penalized. Lastly, their life expectancy at birth is more or less five years longer than men's (in Belgium, around 83.3 years for women and 77.5 for men). The same configuration holds for the other three countries. The very elderly (age 85 and higher) face the greatest risk of poverty. Since life expectancy at age 75 is eight years for women and three years for men, it stands to reason that very elderly women are more vulnerable than men.

France and Germany present similar indicators.

> In the Netherlands, the general law on old age [*Algemene Ouderdomswet*] establishes the payment of a flat-rate legal pension to all inhabitants of the country aged 65 and older. All persons living in the Netherlands are insured between 15 and 65 years of age and thus accumulate pension rights. This system makes no distinction based on gender or on whether the person is employed or not. (European Commission 2006)

The Netherlands ranks first because this legislation is quite generous, while Belgium ranks last. Access to property (housing) of the elderly is higher there, which partially offsets the low level of old-age pensions.

5.3.1.4. Evolution of the risk of poverty

During the last decade, the risk of poverty among persons over 65 years of age evolved little in the four countries concerned. It is again in Belgium that the risk is highest (24 per cent in 2006) and that the evolution between 1995 and 2006 is the smallest: −1 per cent compared with −2 per cent to −3 per cent in the other countries (see Table 5.3).

TABLE 5.3 Evolution of the risk of poverty from 1995 to 2006 (%)

	1995		2006	
	%	Rank	%	Rank
Germany	15	2	13	2
France	19	3	16	3
Netherlands	8	1	6	1
Belgium	25	4	24	4
EU-15	21		20	

Source: Committee for the Study of Ageing (2008).

This risk of poverty among the elderly is somewhat eased by the fact that they are homeowners. The French and Belgians invest in housing, with 80 per cent of those over age 65 owning their home. This rate is 57 per cent in Germany and 46 per cent in the Netherlands. This element does not come into play in calculating disposable income because the imputed income of home ownership is not taken into account. Where the risk of poverty is highest – Belgium and France to a lesser extent – home ownership is the highest. So one might say that there is a certain 'compensation': those who own their homes are obviously not obliged to pay rent. Consequently, although their disposable income is lower, they are able to buy as much or even more consumer goods and services.

Nuance should be given to this 'compensation' considering the high percentage of elderly (over 65) who live in housing where one of the three basic comfort factors is lacking: hot running water, bathtub or shower, and toilet. This percentage is again the highest in Belgium: 32 per cent, followed by 19 per cent in the Netherlands, 18 per cent in France and nearly 12 per cent in Germany. The impact of unemployment on poverty is therefore manifest. The average unemployment rate for 1995–2006 is around 10 per cent in France, Germany and Belgium. It is half that rate in the Netherlands (4.7 per cent). The unemployment rate is calculated on the labour force, which includes working people and the unemployed, or around 50 per cent to 60 per cent of the total population. The poverty rate is calculated not on the *labour force* but on the *total population*. Consequently, a 10 per cent unemployment rate concerns only around 5 per cent of the total population, whereas a 10 per cent poverty rate concerns 10 per cent of the population.

5.3.2 Healthcare costs

We will first review the evolution of healthcare costs over a long period, then the causes of the increase in costs, and lastly the special problem of public healthcare versus private healthcare.

5.3.2.1 The evolution of healthcare costs

In all the developed countries – Organization for Economic Cooperation and Development (OECD) zone – the cost of healthcare is rising faster than GDP. Its relative share is therefore increasing: from more or less 5 per cent of GDP in 1970 to 10 per cent in 2005 (Belgium: 9.3 per cent; Netherlands: 9.8 per cent; France: 10 per cent; Germany: 10.9 per cent) (European Commission 2007). According to the OECD's forecasts, this tendency will continue until 2050.

As a general rule, growth in the cost of healthcare was faster than economic growth during the three and a half decades from 1970 to 2005, but the reasons for this growth differ from one sub-period to the next. In the 1970s, the increase in the costs of all care stemmed primarily from two factors: increasing population coverage and rising public healthcare expenditure. In the 1980s and 1990s, growth resulted from higher per capita income which allowed for wider access to care. At the start of the 1990s, the trend of stagnation in healthcare prevailed, in particular due to cost-containment policies: certain therapies and certain groups of medicines were either no longer reimbursed or so at lower rates. At the end of the 1990–2000 decade and during the first decade of the twenty-first century, healthcare expenditure started to rise again as a result of the ageing of the population and the sophistication of medicine (European Commission 2007: 94ff). The evolution of the ageing of the population is accelerating. The over-65 age bracket represented just over 15 per cent in 2007 and, according to OECD forecasts, will account for 25 per cent in 2050. The sophistication of medicine translates into higher prices for healthcare, which rose twice as fast as those of all goods and services during the period 1997 to 2005, 4.1 per cent for healthcare and 2.1 per cent for the consumer price index, respectively.

5.3.2.2 Causes of growth in medical costs

Countless elements contribute to growing medical costs: lifestyle, education, family context, the practice of sports, the unemployment level, the poverty of certain segments of the population, membership of certain ethnic groups (immigrants), the use of alcohol and/or drugs and many other factors. The following can be considered three fundamental elements of causality.

First, there is an *income effect*. When there is an increase in households' disposable income,[11] they devote a larger part of their income to medical expenses in the broad sense. A 'comfort' element can come into play. In case of hospitalization, for instance, the high-income segments of the population choose a private room rather than a room with four beds. In the four countries, the income effect, which could act as a brake on care, is of little consequence since expenses are covered by a highly developed insurance system. The percentage of the population not covered is extremely low: less than 1 per cent (e.g. 0.1 per cent in France).

Second, a *supply-side effect* comes into play on both quantities and prices. A scan costs more than an X-ray but it also provides more information and consequently allows more efficient care. The prices of medicines, which represent 10 to 20 per cent of healthcare in the four countries concerned, are rising faster than consumer goods prices. The growing specialization of doctors also has an impact on the prices of consultations …

A third element, which may be described as a *demand effect*, is primarily due to the ageing of the population. If medical consumption is limited to one unit during an individual's lifetime, it is far less from age 2 to 55 years, then surges from age 65 and reaches two units for the 70 to 75 age bracket, while 'over age 75, the multiplier is 4.1' (Esping-Andersen 2008: 110). Expenses soar when the individual is close to death.

5.3.2.3 Public healthcare and private healthcare

The process of privatization that has characterized the evolution of capitalism since the 1980s also affects medicine. The evolution is most pronounced in the Netherlands: from 33 per cent in 1980 to 39 per cent in 2004 (European Commission 2007: 86). This is also the country whose system is closest to the Anglo-Saxon model. During the same period (1980–2004), Germany experienced a slight increase, from 19 per cent to 22 per cent, while France kept to a level of 23 per cent and Belgium 30 per cent.[12]

Private healthcare in itself does not constitute an obstacle to quality and reasonably priced medicine, provided of course that low-income patients have access, in other establishments for example, to quality care. A survey on this subject was carried out in Belgium in 193 hospitals and clinics at the end of the 1990s. Using the results collected, a comparison was made for the cost of a seven-day hospitalization for a fractured tibia with care provided by a radiologist, orthopaedist, anaesthesiologist, physical therapist, etc. The same surgery under the same medical conditions can cost the patient €364.73 in a four-bed room in a university hospital where 'fund'[13] doctors practise and €5,661.19 in a private room in a private clinic working with non-fund doctors, i.e. 15 times as much. Since this is not more costly for society – the direct-settlement system[14] is identical in both cases – and since high-quality healthcare coverage is generalized, this difference has no harmful social consequences.

There is nevertheless a danger. If privatization accelerates and the public sector, for lack of resources, no longer has the capacity to offer the full range of treatments at a socially acceptable price, patients' financial inequality will lead to a regression in access to care for the most vulnerable social groups. This eventuality is unfortunately not unrealistic. This danger emerges in particular for certain types of care such as dental and ophthalmological treatments or the treatment of hearing problems, which are the most widespread among the elderly. Insurance covers these types of treatment only very partially because some are considered luxury expenditure.

5.4 Conclusion

In his theory of societal vulnerability, Walgrave (1992) explains that this vulnerability stems from the fact that institutions provide goods to citizens through society, in exchange for which society demands their conformity with its rules and introduces a monitoring system to enforce its conditions of adaptation and solidarity. The social institutions are therefore situated in a continuum ranging from control, such as that exercised by penal justice through constraint, to supply of services, such as those offered by private centres intervening at the request of users, and a mix of supply of services and control, such as schools, which provide learning subject to control through discipline, or social security, whose benefits depend on respect for strict conditions. Through coherence between the functions of these institutions, a balance between supply of services and control is established, social ties are built and conformity takes hold. However, just as success in one institution will increase the chances of success in the next, failure will weaken them, so that from failure to failure

> parts of the population find themselves confronted with a mass of controls, discriminations and sanctions, without being able to profit from the services that social institutions provide. In this type of imbalance, there is no longer any reason to maintain conformity. Punitive control is the only way to extort it. It is this situation that we refer to as societal vulnerability. (Walgrave 1992: 90)

This analysis nevertheless omits a case (Mary 1998: 460-6), already mentioned by Merton (1938): society's supply of public goods can weaken independently of citizens' conformity, not only in one of the social institutions, but above all in the entire continuum that they form. This situation can lead the citizen to turn to other institutions, private institutions capable of providing the same or comparable goods (see the example of private medical care above). In this case, the supply is also subject to conditions, but they are no longer those of 'adaptation and solidarity' mentioned by Walgrave with respect to society's offer: based on profit, the private sector will make its services conditional more simply, but also much more strictly, on the financial resources available to the interested party or the stability of his employment.[15] However, this privatization is again different for the different target groups: the affluent elderly may take out private insurance policies to be sure of having a pension or healthcare, while the young jobless cannot insure themselves against unemployment and poverty. So there remains the part of the population that is not only confronted with the decline in society's services, but is also increasingly unable to respond to the conditions of private-sector services. In this case, if we follow Walgrave's analysis, for want of incentives to conform, society will have to reinforce or even count exclusively on its control mechanisms to ensure conformity. And that is where penalization mechanisms come into action.

Notes

1. Translator's note: unofficial translation.
2. Translator's note: unofficial translation.
3. Interestingly, according to the *Petit Robert*, in French the concept of 'sécuritaire' dates back to 1983.
4. Translator's note: unofficial translation.
5. Translator's note: unofficial translation.
6. To take but a few examples: security contracts that have never succeeded in putting into place the integrated (police and social) prevention policy of which they were the symbol, penal mediation that is struggling to be maintained on the fringe of the judicial system, an immediate summary trial procedure that was virtually stillborn, electronic surveillance that is struggling to get on its feet, etc.
7. It has not remained stable at all, as Zedner maintains (2002: 354).
8. These are amounts relative to per capita gross national product (GNP) (2005) in constant US$ and taking account of purchasing power parity (PPP). From 2005 to 2009, the relative position of the three countries remained unchanged (International Labour Office 2008).
9. In 1995, per capita GNP totalled US$26,210 in Germany, US$29,078 in the Netherlands, US$27,033 in France and US$28,575 in Belgium.
10. Net income or disposable income is equal to gross income, plus net social security contributions, minus direct personal income taxes. If we rank 100 pensioners by growing order of pensions, the *median* income is that of the 50th pensioner.
11. PDI: Personal Disposable Income or net household income, i.e. gross income less direct income taxes paid by households and to which social security interventions are added.
12. The countries most affected by this evolution are the former socialist countries where private medicine was virtually non-existent and where its share now matches or exceeds that of the Europe of Six (Poland: 30 per cent; Hungary: 28.2 per cent).
13. 'Fund' doctors are those who sign an agreement between the medical profession and health insurance funds, which places a ceiling on their remuneration.
14. A 'direct settlement system' provides payment out of a pool financed by workers' contributions and employers' contributions to the social security system.
15. In the case of intervention by the employer, as often occurs in matters of complementary insurance.

References

Balibar, É. (1995) 'Sûreté, sécurité, sécuritaire', *Cahiers marxistes*, 200: 185–99.
Baratta, A. (1991) 'Les fonctions instrumentales et les fonctions symboliques du droit pénal', *Déviance et société*, 15(1): 1–25.

Bauman, Z. (1999) *Le coût humain de la mondialisation*. Paris: Hachette Littératures.

Body-Gendrot, S. (1999) 'La politisation du thème de la criminalité aux Etats-Unis', *Déviance et société*, 23(1): 75–89.

Bourdieu, P. (1993) 'La démission de l'Etat', in P. Bourdieu (ed.), *La misère du monde*. Paris: Seuil.

Brownlee, I. (1998) *Community Punishment: A Critical Introduction*. London and New York: Longman.

Cartuyvels, Y., Mary, P. and Rea, A. (2000) 'L'État social sécuritaire', in L. Van Campenhoudt *et al.* (eds), *Réponses à l'insécurité. Des discours aux pratiques*. Brussels: Labor, pp. 407–29.

Castel, R. (1995) *Les métamorphoses de la question sociale: Une chronique du salariat*. Paris: Fayard.

Comité d'étude sur le vieillissement du Conseil supérieur des Finances (Belgium) (2008) *Rapport annuel*, June.

Cullen, F. T., Van Voorhis, P. and Sundt, J. L. (1996) 'Prisons in crisis: the American experience', in R. Matthews and P. Francis (eds), *Prisons 2000: An International Perspective on the Current State and Future of Imprisonment*. London: Macmillan, pp. 21–52.

de Coninck, Fr., Cartuyvels, Y., Franssen, A., Kaminski, D., Mary, P., Rea, A. and Van Campenhoudt, L. (with Toro, F., Hubert, G., Hubert, H.-O. AND Schaut, Ch.) (2005) *Aux frontières de la justice, aux marges de la société. Une analyse en groupes d'acteurs et de chercheurs*. Ghent: Academia Press – Politique scientifique fédérale.

Deltenre, S. (2003) 'De l'impact du prononcé de peines privatives de liberté sur l'évolution de la population pénitentiaire belge entre 1994 et 1998', *Revue de droit pénal et de criminologie*, 2: 168–205.

Esping-Andersen, G. (2008) *Trois leçons sur l'Etat-Providence*. Paris: Seuil.

European Commission (2006) *Adequate and Sustainable Pensions*, Synthesis Report. Brussels.

European Commission (2007) *Joint Report on Social Protection and Social Inclusion*. Brussels.

Ewald, F. (1986) *L'État providence*. Paris: Grasset.

Feeley, M. and Simon, J. (1992) 'The New Penology: notes on the emerging strategy of corrections and its implications', *Criminology*, 30(4): 449–74.

Feeley, M. and Simon, J. (1994) 'Actuarial justice: the emerging new criminal law', in D. Nelken (ed.), *The Futures of Criminology*. London: Sage, pp. 173–201.

Garland, D. (1985) *Punishment and Welfare: A History of Penal Strategies*. Aldershot: Gower.

Garland, D. (2001) *The Culture of Control: Crime and Social Order in Contemporary Society*. Oxford: Oxford University Press.

Houchon, G. (1996) 'Propos optimistes d'un abolitionniste morose', in Fr. Tulkens, H.-D. Bosly (eds), *La justice pénale et l'Europe*. Brussels: Bruylant, pp. 75–101.

International Labour Office (2008) *Key Indicators of the Labour Market (KILM)*, 5th edn. Geneva.

Lucken, K. (1998) 'Contemporary penal trends: modern or postmodern?', *British Journal of Criminology*, 38(1): 106–23.

Mary, P. (1997) 'Le travail d'intérêt général et la médiation pénale face à la crise de l'État social: dépolitisation de la question criminelle et pénalisation du social', in P. Mary (ed.), *Travail d'intérêt général et médiation pénale: socialisation du pénal ou pénalisation du social?* Brussels: Bruylant, pp. 325–47.

Mary, P. (1998) *Délinquant, délinquance et insécurité. Un demi-siècle de traitement en Belgique (1944–1997)*. Brussels: Bruylant.

Merton, R. K. (1938) 'Social structure and anomie', *American Sociological Review*, 3(5): 672–82.

O'Malley, P. (2006) '"Mondialisation" et justice criminelle: du défaitisme à l'optimisme', *Déviance et société*, 30(3): 323–38.

Rosanvallon, P. (1981) *La crise de l'État providence*. Paris: Seuil.

Snacken, S. (1999) 'Analyse des mécanismes de la surpopulation pénitentiaire', in P. Mary and T. Papatheodorou (eds), *La surpopulation pénitentiaire en Europe. De la détention avant jugement à la libération conditionnelle*. Brussels: Bruylant, pp. 9–31.

Vacheret, M., Dozois, J. and Lemire, G. (1998) 'Le système correctionnel canadien et la nouvelle pénologie: la notion de risque', *Déviance et société*, 22(1): 37–50.

Wacquant, L. (1998) 'L'ascension de l'État pénal en Amérique', *Actes de la recherche en sciences sociales*, 124: 7–26.

Wacquant, L. (1999) *Les prisons de la misère*. Paris: Raison d'agir.

Walgrave, L. (1992) *Délinquance systématisée des jeunes et vulnérabilité sociétale. Essai de construction d'une théorie intégrative*. Geneva: Médecine et Hygiène – Méridiens Klincksieck.

Zedner, L. (2002) 'Dangers of dystopias in penal theory', *Oxford Journal of Legal Studies*, 22(2): 341–66.

PART 2

Punishment and Human Rights – Shield or Sword?

6

THE RISE OF THE PENAL STATE: WHAT CAN HUMAN RIGHTS DO ABOUT IT?

Els Dumortier, Serge Gutwirth, Sonja Snacken and Paul De Hert[1]

> Our global society is transforming, yet few are noticing. We are blind to these dynamics. And increasingly few have the capacity to do anything about it.
>
> But comparative studies help. [...] While Governments insist on copying bad laws and outdoing one another with greater powers, they are not so eager to learn from what has been tried and failed elsewhere. Instead they endeavour to minimize debate and discussion, ignoring all input and the diversity of views. It is almost as though they believe that in order to save the Open Society, its principles must be trodden upon. These are precarious times for such a cavalier attitude particularly when there is so much at stake.
> (Gus Hosein, 2005: 46–7)

6.1 Introduction

In this contribution, we take a look at the impact of human rights on substantive criminal law, i.e. on the definition of offences as well as on the legislator's choice of penalties and the court's choice of sentences. We consider this analysis important in the light of the rise of the 'penal state' in Europe. After a brief description of Garland's, Wacquant's and our own views on the rising penal state in Europe, our analysis will show that European human rights, as applied by the European Court of Human Rights (ECtHR), have a restraining impact on several important chapters of substantive criminal law. However, this analysis also reveals the ambivalence of the Court and the limits of human rights' ascendancy over the growing punitive tendencies of national legislators and criminal courts. This raises the question whether the basic principles of a humanist criminal law based on penal moderation should not be more clearly anchored in legally binding European instruments.

6.2. The rise of the penal state in Europe

6.2.1 The rise of the penal state in the United States and Great Britain

David Garland demonstrates in his now classic work *The Culture of Control* (2001) that, since the 1970s, a 'new culture of control' has taken root and expanded in the United States and in Great Britain. This culture of control is characterized by punitive policies of exclusion, stimulated by what he calls 'an angry and anxious public'. He identifies a number of signs and developments such as: the decline of the ideal of rehabilitation; the increasingly retributive and draconian[2] punishments; the return of the victim in penal discourse as a justification for more severe and harsher responses to crime; the re-emergence of the prison as an effective measure of retribution and incapacitation[3] ('prison works'); an increasingly proactive and preventive police action; the prevalence of public protection from crime in terms of security, crime reduction and risk management over the aim of protection from the state in terms of human rights and rule of law; the politicization of penal and security policies by a new populism; the expansion of crime prevention and community security infrastructures; the involvement of civil society and the privatization/marketing of crime control; and lastly, the escalation of security and crime reduction policies.[4]

Garland also suggests that, globally speaking, the European countries seem to be heading down the same path as the United States under the pressure of similar populist and exclusionist penal policies. A closer look shows that there is no lack of factors contributing to acceptance of this thesis and it is easy to comprehend: the deployment of a penal state is related to *transnational* phenomena such as economic deregulation, neo-liberalism, the decline of the welfare state, and correlatively, the rise in insecurity and uncertainty as passionate political issues (Mary 2003). Deregulation is therefore alleged to have the effect of reducing the state to its repressive functions. In this way, the politicization of insecurity appears less a problem than a solution (Van Campenhoudt 1999). Many researchers consider that the emergence of the 'penal state' or 'law-and-order state' results from this reorientation in terms of a new legitimacy (Garapon and Salas 1996; Brants *et al.* 2001).

6.2.2 Penalization is related to neo-liberalism and continental Europe is not spared

Europe is also affected by the phenomenon of the rise of the penal state. Loïc Wacquant (2006a) thus describes the global expansion of the transnational neo-liberal revolution, in which the market is presented as the optimal means of regulating human actions, not only in terms of the economy and work, but also health and education. Accordingly, the state finds itself subject to market mechanisms, which implies a significant conversion of the welfare state: while everyone can claim certain socio-economic rights in the welfare state, the new state will have to endeavour to reintegrate into the market as quickly as possible every individual who has received socio-economic aid. Wacquant notes a transition from *welfare* to *workfare*: the welfare state does not shrink but adopts a new philosophy. The collective right to aid or assistance is replaced by an individual relationship to the welfare state in the form of a contract (Wacquant and Heijne 2006). Henceforth, it is the individual who must assume his responsibilities on the labour market, in education and in health and social security. If unsuccessful, poverty, marginality and exclusion are the direct and rapid result. In other words, the welfare state in which individuals could still claim rights is being dismantled and supplanted by systems for the distribution of public goods based on market principles. Wacquant, however, in contrast with the neo-liberal creed, argues that all this adds up not to less state, but to more: more state to control this mass of 'losers', 'poor' and others who fail to adapt to market forces. The welfare state is consequently being *transformed* into a penal state, whose power and competences constantly expand in matters of punitive action, police, security and control.

While this process is quite obvious in the United States, according to Wacquant, it is also identifiable in Europe. Four 'broad trends' can be observed in Europe: a sharp increase in incarceration rates in most European Union countries; a massive carceral over-representation of what Wacquant calls 'labour market cast-offs' (such as and especially post-colonial immigrants or blacks), prison overcrowding, and a toughening of criminal policies that tend to neutralize convicted persons rather than rehabilitate them (Wacquant 2006a: 285–6). Wacquant expressly adds that the carceral over-representation of post-colonial immigrants in Europe is comparable with and sometimes even greater than that of African-American inmates in the United States (Wacquant 2006b). He argues that this over-representation of non-white and foreign inmates demonstrates that 'with the onset of neo-liberal hegemony, penal segmentation has become a key modality of the drawing and enforcing of salient social boundaries in the Old World as in the New World' (Wacquant 2006b: 88). In addition, post-colonial immigrants in Europe are specially targeted by police forces and judicial authorities, a de facto situation that fully confirms that Europe is headed down the same path as the United States in terms of the penalization of urban poverty and marginality (ibid.: 100), and more generally society as a whole. In short, notes Wacquant, in terms of the toughening up of the penal and punitive climate, there is not a clear distinction between continental Europe and the United States or Great Britain.

6.2.3 Counter-terrorism as 'turbo-penalization': Europe is not faring any better than the United States

Against this backdrop has come a proliferation, in the wake of the attacks of 11 September 2001, of counter-terrorism measures on both sides of the Atlantic, measures which can without a doubt be said to have provided a 'turbo' to the penalization engine. Indeed, the United States and Great Britain were not the only countries, in response to the rallying cry of the war on terrorism, to bolster their arsenal of control, inquisition and punitive measures. It is clear that the war on terrorism has resulted in a significant escalation of penal measures and the punitive climate and that it has contributed to direct violations of a number of fundamental rights which the Western world customarily sees as part of its identity: the ban on arbitrary arrest and deprivation of liberty, the prohibition of torture, the right to a fair trial, freedom of expression, the right to privacy and the right for a prisoner not to be subject to extradition to a country where he faces the risk of torture.[5]

Even though in continental Europe we tend to believe that 'American' measures like the Patriot Act, the preventive screening of civil aviation passengers, the Guantanamo prison camps, the calls in favour of 'legitimate torture', etc. have not been taken in Europe and certainly not in the same proportions, one might wonder whether this attitude is justified. We need only read the report by Gus Hosein – *Threatening the Open Society: Comparing Anti-Terror Policies in the US and Europe* (2005) – to have our confidence shaken. His comparison of anti-terror policies in Europe and the United States shows that the measures taken in Europe often go even further than US measures,[6] particularly because many of the American measures only concern foreign nationals, whereas their European equivalents also apply to all European citizens themselves. To say the least, these controversial measures spark vigorous political and public debate in the United States, whereas in the European Union, decision-making processes are not very open to opposition by parliament and civil society. On the contrary, European measures are often adopted in intergovernmental sanctums (EU Framework Decisions) and are presented nationally as inevitable measures the states must implement by virtue of their European Union obligations. In short: 'If there is one remarkable difference between the two, it is that when the U.S. goes too far on a policy and controversy arises, eventually public discussion and the democratic process tend to restrain the powers of Government. There is no similar policy deliberation process in Europe' (Hosein 2005: 41).

6.2.4 A brief illustration: the 'nieuwe gestrengheid' ('the new severity') in the Netherlands

What has been briefly described above demonstrates quite well that the rise of the penal state (since the 1980s) is a phenomenon that concerns Europe as well as the United States. The ascendancy of the executive over the police and judicial system has increased and strengthened on both shores of the Atlantic Ocean. This movement is vindicated through law-and-order thinking that develops at the expense of respect for individuals' fundamental rights, the system of checks and balances and democratic debate.[7] It is clear that the huge mobilization against terrorism has amplified this movement on both sides of the Atlantic.

Even in the Netherlands, a country that used to be renowned for its openness, tolerance and moderate penal policy based on rehabilitation, events have taken the same turn. In recent decades, the increase in the incarceration rate has even been higher than in the United States. Of course, the United States had a substantial lead, but the fact remains that, since 1973, the number of prisoners in the US has grown fivefold, whereas it has grown sevenfold in the Netherlands. Along with England and Portugal, the Netherlands heads the group of countries with a high incarceration rate (Wacquant 2006b: 89), although it has gone down again over the last five years (Van Swaaningen 2010). According to Ybo Buruma (2005), a reputable commentator in the Netherlands, in 2005 the public prosecutor was prosecuting more cases and the courts were punishing with increasing severity: they were ordering more (even short- term) custodial sentences and work penalties (*taakstraffen*). Stricter penal laws were being developed which, over and above the measures taken in the framework of counter-terrorism (Van Gunsteren, 2004),[8] increased maximum sentences, concentrated law enforcement on certain forms of crime and refined the directives issued to the public prosecutor.

These developments have inspired the former president of the College of Public Prosecutors of the Netherlands, J. L. de Wijkerslooth (2005), to observe that a new penal paradigm was emerging in the Netherlands, which he named *nieuwe gestrengheid* ('the new severity'). Under this new paradigm, any offence involving a victim must absolutely be elucidated and prosecuted, which represents a form of zero tolerance. Sentences must be made harsher because society no longer accepts arguments in support of moderate or alternative sentences. In the 'new severity', penal policy must concentrate on crime that is directly perceptible, such as violence and urban nuisances. The individualization of measures against criminals must make room for 'actuarial' categories ('recidivists') and tariff measures. De Wijkerslooth added that the impact of the *nieuwe gestrengheid* has not been purely advantageous for the public prosecutor (increase in resources, support for reorganization, wider powers, clarification of the legal framework of operation, etc.), but has also brought with it a number of major disadvantages, in particular a greater political interest in the public prosecutor's office, resulting in a loss of autonomy and increasingly frequent government intervention (the government making promises that only the prosecutor can keep).

6.2.5 However, there are differences between the New World and the Old

Although the penal state seems to be developing in parts of Europe and 'penal populism' has met with a great deal of success in the Old World, many will raise the objection of its equivalence or comparison with the American penal state. In his essay on the rise and effects of penal populism in France, Europe and the United States, Denis Salas (2005)[9] endeavours to demonstrate that even if there is unquestionably a sharp increase in 'punitivity' – the 'will to punish' – in France and in Europe, the situation there is quite different from that in the United States.[10] In Europe, we are not confronted with 'cowboy-like practices' such as the CIA's secret flights, secret prisons, the open return to the use of torture, the artificial creation of an area of non-law where prisoners assumed to be Taliban and terrorists could be mistreated and humiliated. Furthermore, in criminal matters,

Europe does not have the death penalty, death rows, justice as a 'live show' as in the trial of O. J. Simpson, chain gangs, etc.

Consequently, there are indeed differences. How can they be understood and explained? For example, while similar socio-economic movements can be identified on both sides of the Atlantic, this does not go as far as likening American ghettoes to French urban fringe areas.[11] Michael Tonry (2001) rightly points out that the penal policies of most European countries differ substantially in spite of similar economic transformations and similar trends in public opinion. American penal innovations seem to be successful only in common law systems, as in Australia and England, whereas the traditions of European continental law do not find favour in the United States and Great Britain. Although systematic and thorough comparative research on penal practices is still limited, there are good reasons to give nuances to the thesis of isomorphic penal policies in the western world.

The origin of the differences could be rooted in the relative autonomy of the criminal justice systems from changing socio-economic factors. Judicial institutions do not exclusively pursue a general aim of crime control. They also pursue intrinsic objectives (such as fair trials and respect for human rights) and organizational aims (management of human and financial resources) (Denkers, 1976; Foqué and 't Hart, 1990).

Tonry (2001: 530) also refers to cultural and anthropological differences between countries to explain differences between their penal policies. This perspective takes us, for example, to Salas who shows that in (American) Protestantism man must answer for his acts on his own, in his moral conscience. There is no mediating body, as in continental Catholicism, in the form of a church whose task is to help, absolve and 'rehabilitate' the lost sheep. In a Protestant perspective of imprisonment and confinement, 'if prison is useful, it is with the aim of restoring moral conscience' (Salas 2005: 105).

One might also refer to the different concepts of 'state' to explain differences between the old and the New World. The finding that the French *Declaration of the Rights of Man and of the Citizen* gives the accused few procedural rights in comparison with the American Bill of Rights suggests that another anthropology is at work there. The *Declaration* does not seem to have needed to create an elaborate range of procedural rights against the 'state'. According to Edelman (1995: 101–2) this is related to the concept of republican liberty that underpins it. This concept of liberty, rooted in the thinking of Rousseau and Kant, is fundamentally different from the American concept of individual liberty in the 'state' as elaborated by Hobbes and Locke.

The procedural consequences of this approach are well known. The inquisitorial judicial traditions within the continental system differ quite sensibly from the Anglo-Saxon adversarial traditions. Of course, where the two penal law systems meet, there have been transfers and some degree of osmosis has occurred.[12] However, the observation that the Anglo-Saxon countries continue to prefer the adversarial procedure while the continental countries opt for the (mitigated) inquisitorial system is still relevant.

The existence of different concepts of state and different legal, procedural and penal traditions (Damaska 1986; Garapon and Papadopoulos 2003; Gutwirth and De Hert 2001; Whitman 2003) may hence have contributed to the development of divergent penal policies.

6.2.6 The impact of the protection of human rights?

The analysis presented so far would not be complete without a reference to human rights and their development during the latter half of the twentieth century. It is unquestionable that human rights, in particular those written into the 1950 European Convention on Human Rights (ECHR), have contributed to the convergence between distinct legal families. In reaction to the atrocities and abuse of European dictatorships and the signature by European countries of the Universal Declaration of Human Rights (1948) and the European Convention for the Protection of Human Rights (1950) after the Second World War, elements of American constitutionalism were seen to penetrate the constitutional and penal law of continental European legal systems (Tulkens 1992).

Salas (2006) maintains that the ECHR and the procedures it has introduced provide a major explanation for the remaining differences between the United States and Europe in terms of the imposition of punishment. The humanism of penal policy and the moderation of sentences in Europe can be understood, he argues, through the European cultural heritage, strongly revitalized after the horrors of the Second World War, in which the right to punish is by definition limited and controlled. In the United States, on the other hand, a culture of violence and war is alleged to have gained the upper hand, under the hold of penal populism and counter-terrorism policy. Therefore, in the United States, protection of human rights by the Supreme Court is said to be different from that provided by the Strasbourg-based European Court of Human Rights (ECtHR): 'The human rights perimeter is transnational in Europe, whereas it is tied to a very national narrative, recounted tirelessly by the judges of the Supreme Court, in the United States. The identity proposed by this interpretative community is not in the least comparable to the European peoples' aspiration to a common law' (Salas 2006: 128). In other words, the role of acceptance of the international oversight of the ECtHR appears to be, for Salas, a decisive element in explaining the more humanist and moderate turn taken by penal policies in Europe (2006: 124–40).

Along the same lines, Van den Wyngaert (2006) and Snacken (2006) highlight the opportunities for developing an individualized and moderate penal law offered by the ECHR and the Court's interpretations thereof. That is precisely the aim of the remainder of this contribution. What is the role that European human rights have played and could play in the face of the rise of the penal state in Europe? What is the impact of the European system of human rights protection on the development of the penal or law-and-order State in Europe?

To answer these questions we have analysed the ECtHR's case law. Following on from the analysis by Van Den Wyngaert, we will address here the impact of human rights on criminal incriminations and on penal sentences. Our analysis thus specifically focuses on the impact of human rights on 'substantive criminal law', which refers to, on the one hand, criminal incriminations determined by the legislator and, on the other hand, penal sentences defined by the legislator and imposed by all the judicial and administrative actors involved in the sentencing process.

The ECHR's important provisions concerning this *substantive criminal law* are: the right to life (Article 2), the prohibition of torture and inhuman or degrading treatment or punishment (Article 3), the right to a fair trial and the presumption of innocence (Article 6), the principle of the legality of incriminations and sentences (Article 7), the right to a private and family life (Article 8) and the right to freedom of expression (Article 10).

The central questions guiding the remainder of this contribution can be summarized as follows: Does the ECtHR limit (or not) the powers of European States to incriminate behaviour and impose penal sentences and, if so, in what way? How does the Court legitimize these restrictions?

6.3 Keeping 'punitiveness' in check: what does Strasbourg do?

Our analysis of the ECtHR case law shows that the Court limits both penal sentences and incriminations. The following sections, however, do not pretend to be exhaustive and complete. The case law is too broad, diverse and complex to be captured in a few pages. As a consequence we have opted to select some particularly illustrative examples.

6.3.1 Limiting penal sentences

6.3.1.1 The abolition of death penalty

One of the most obvious differences between the USA and Europe is the abolition of the death penalty. This abolition occurred despite the fact that Article 2 of the ECHR of 1950 (only five years after the horrors of the Second World War) which protects the right to life, made an exception for the death penalty for crimes: 'Everyone's right to life shall be protected by law. No one shall be deprived of his life intentionally save in the execution of a sentence of a court following his conviction of a crime for which this penalty is provided by law.' The legislator thus has the duty to protect the right to life 'by law' and one could presume that this should be done by making it a crime to take someone's life. The legislator must also ensure that 'no one is deprived of his life intentionally', but an exception is made for the death penalty, without any indication of the type of crime that can be punished by this penalty, thus giving the national legislator tremendous freedom. Europe has nevertheless undergone an important political evolution in relation to capital punishment. Thirty years after the ECHR, Protocol 6 (1980) proposed the abolition of the death penalty in times of peace. In 2002, Protocol 13 proposed its total abolition.

The Court's case law has followed this evolution. A first step was taken in *Soering* v. *United Kingdom*, of 7 July 1989: extradition to the United States was rejected because the situation in death rows was considered inhuman and degrading treatment and thus in breach of Article 3. In *Öcalan* v. *Turkey* (12 March 2003), the Court observed the general abolition of the death penalty in Europe and concluded that this penalty, even though it is still foreseen under Article 2, is now considered unacceptable, inhuman and degrading and thus runs counter to Article 3. This constitutes an illustration of the interactions between the Court and other human rights instruments or policies. As from 1994, the countries of Central and Eastern Europe that wished to become members of the Council of Europe were obliged to ratify Protocol 6, to immediately halt all executions and to abolish the death penalty within two years. The Council of Europe and the EU have for many years now pursued an explicit policy in this connection, not only within the European borders but also *inter alia* in relation to the United States. This is illustrated, for example, by the *amicus curiae* sent by the EU and the Council of Europe during the debates before the Supreme Court that led to the abolition of the death penalty for minors (*Roper* v. *Simmons*, 1 March 2005). With the United States having observer status in the Council of Europe since 1995, a difficult discussion has developed over the death penalty. For the United States, the death penalty is not a human rights problem and its legitimacy resides in its high level of support in American public opinion. For the Council of Europe and the European Union, the death penalty is contrary to human dignity and therefore essentially a human rights problem 'that should never depend on a changing public opinion' (Council of Europe 2001: 12–13; see also EU Charter of Fundamental Rights, where the prohibition of the death penalty (Article II-2) falls under Title 1 'Human dignity').

6.3.1.2 Protecting prisoners

Article 3 also plays a considerable and growing role in the protection of prisoners and the relative humanization of prison conditions. Increasingly aware of the need to protect citizens against the danger of serious ill-treatment during police custody or deprivation of liberty, the Court has *strengthened* protection under Article 3 in *Selmouni* v. *France* (28 July 1999) by reinterpreting forms of ill-treatment that were previously considered to be inhuman or degrading such as torture, i.e. the most severe form of ill-treatment. This strengthening is in line with the findings since 1989 by the European Committee for the Prevention of Torture (CPT) that there is a high risk of serious physical or psychological ill-treatment of offenders during arrest and detention by the police in many European countries (12th General Report, CPT/Inf (2002)15: §§32–39).

The influence of the CPT on the ECtHR is even more obvious where prison conditions are concerned. There has been, for instance, a major reversal in the

Court's case law in relation to prison overcrowding. Up until 2001, the Court held that while overcrowding was not desirable, it did not constitute in itself a breach of Article 3 since there was no deliberate will to impose a humiliating penalty. In the wake of *Dougoz* v. *Greece* (6 March 2001), however, overcrowding in itself can constitute a breach of Article 3 and the absence of intention to humiliate no longer rules out such infringement. CPT reports and standards exerted a considerable influence on this about-face in case law (van Zyl Smit and Snacken 2009). Since prison overcrowding is often a consequence of increased penalization (Snacken *et al.* 1995), we can consider that the Court provides here a shield against one aspect of increased punitiveness.

More generally, we are seeing an increase in the number of proceedings instituted by prisoners which meet with success, not only on the basis of Article 3 (e.g. *Van der Ven* v. *Netherlands* of 4 February 2003 concerning daily strip-searching in a maximum security institution, considered unjustified and degrading), but also of Article 8 (e.g. *Messina* v. *Italy (No. 2)*, 28 September 2000, concerning the right to family visits) and Article 10 (e.g. *Yankov* v. *Bulgaria*, 11 December 2003, concerning freedom of expression for prisoners, including the right to criticize the prison system and its staff) (see for a more thorough analysis van Zyl Smit and Snacken, 2009). This strengthening of the protection of prisoners' fundamental rights against overpenalization or excessive security in prisons also indicates that, even if the Court has always accepted the humiliating nature inherent in all penalties, it would reject some type of penalties applied in the United States, such as chain gangs or supermax prisons (see, for example, *Messina* v. *Italy*, 28 September 2000, or *Ramirez Sanchez* v. *France*, 4 July 2006, on its refusal of total isolation in maximum security conditions).

6.3.1.3 Prohibition of illegitimate detention

Besides the already mentioned Articles 2 and 3, Article 5 of the ECHR also helps to limit the legislator and penal actors in their sanctioning competence. Article 5 states that 'No one shall be deprived of his liberty save in the following cases [listed under 5§1] and in accordance with a procedure prescribed by law': the deprivation of liberty must be in conformity with the substantive and procedural provisions of such laws. However, since the right to liberty is the norm, restrictions must be exceptional and respect the principles of legality, legitimacy and proportionality. Thus detention becomes illegitimate when there is no connection between the aim of the detention and its setting or regime. In *Bouamar* v. *Belgium* (29 February 1988), the Court found the nine consecutive detentions of a minor in a remand prison to violate Article 5§1d as these detentions were never meant or used as 'a preliminary to a regime of supervised education'. In *Aerts* v. *Belgium* (30 July 1998) the Court held unanimously that in order to be legitimate, deprivation of liberty of a mentally disturbed offender must be effected in a hospital or other appropriate institution. The absence of adequate psychiatric treatment in a prison during nine months for a delinquent presenting serious mental disorders and detained for an indeterminate period makes such detention illegitimate.

The frequency or duration of detention can be a factor of the Court's assessment: the 119 days of detention in nine consecutive court orders for *Bouamar*, and the nine months of detention without adequate treatment for *Aerts* also came into play, but in interaction with the conditions of detention.

In general, however, the Court finds that Article 5§1 does not allow it to review the appropriateness of a penalty imposed by the sentencing court (*Weeks* v. *United Kingdom*, 2 March 1987, §50). The duration of a sentence in itself is rarely the subject of a Court decision. However, in *Stafford* v. *United Kingdom* (28 May 2002, §64) the Court explains that it is not enough to review the lawfulness of the detention under national legislation. In this case, an inmate sentenced to life imprisonment for murder was released on parole then re-incarcerated for fraud. The Home Secretary refused to release him at the end of the sentence served for fraud in 1997, referring to the 1967 life sentence for murder. The Court held that a life sentence, even mandatory, does not necessarily mean imprisonment for life. The lack of causal connection between the risk of new non-violent offences and the earlier conviction for murder was found to breach Article 5§1, which emphasizes protection against arbitrary decisions.

Within the context of the rising penal state and growing 'populist punitiveness', it is also interesting to see in *Stafford* v. *United Kingdom* (28 May 2002, §82) that the ECtHR refuses to admit public opinion as a factor that can legitimize a refusal to grant early release to an inmate who has served the required proportion of his sentence and does not constitute a danger to society. This brings to mind the *Bulger* case (*T.* v. *United Kingdom*, *V.* v. *United Kingdom*, 16 December 1999), in which the Court held that taking account of a public opinion demanding severe sentences in a specific case would run counter to Article 6 and the court's independence. On the other hand, on pre-trial detention, the Court seems to focus more on the presence of procedural guarantees such as the right to judicial appeal against the deprivation of liberty than on the lawfulness (*Erdem* v. *Germany*, 5 July 2001) or the absolute necessity of the detention (*Bouchet* v. *France*, 20 March 2001).

6.3.2 Limiting penal incriminations

The case law also illustrates efforts by the ECtHR to impose limits on the European states' competence to incriminate behaviour. The ECtHR clearly refuses to give a 'wild card' to European states to incriminate as they please. We illustrate this through the Court's refusal of the principle of 'shared criminal liability' and its objections to incriminations that infringe in an unnecessary or disproportionate way the right to privacy or the freedom of religion and expression.

6.3.2.1 Against 'shared criminal liability'

Article 6.1 protects the right to a fair criminal trial within a reasonable time by an independent and impartial tribunal established by law. This also implies access to a tribunal and, in criminal matters, the right to a presumption of innocence (Article 6.2) and the right of the defence (Article 6.3). This article seemingly has little importance for substantive criminal law due to its focus on criminal procedural law. The ruling in *Goktepe* v. *Belgium* (2 June 2005) nevertheless shows that procedural guarantees may in some cases influence substantive criminal law. In this judgment, the Court objects to the theory of 'shared criminal liability' (*emprunt matériel de criminalité*), consisting of automatically holding all participants in a criminal offence liable for the aggravating circumstances that accompanied it. In this case, Goktepe was found guilty not only of the main offence of theft – which he did not contest – but also of assault and homicide against the victim, aggravating circumstances that accompanied the theft but in which the accused denied his personal participation. After finding that, in spite of the applicant's objections, the questions submitted to the jury of the Assize Court as to the existence of objective aggravating circumstances made no distinction between the defendants, the Court declared that 'for a court not to take into account arguments on a vital issue that entailed such severe consequences must be seen as incompatible with adversarial process that lies at the heart of the concept of a fair trial guaranteed by Article 6 of the Convention'.

Goktepe v. *Belgium* teaches us that a system of automatic imputability of objective aggravating circumstances runs counter to the requirements of a fair trial. For responsibility and sentencing to be in conformity with the ECHR, they must therefore be individualized and based on the acts as they may be imputed to their perpetrator.

6.3.2.2 Right to private (sexual) life

Concerning Article 8 and the right to private life, the ECtHR has restricted the substantive criminal law of the member states that were overzealous in incriminating their citizens' sexual practices. In *Norris* v. *Ireland* (26 October 1988) where the 'homosexual' applicant considered himself a victim of Irish laws criminalizing homosexual acts between consenting men, the Court held that 'the maintenance in force of the impugned legislation constitutes a continuing interference with the applicant's right to respect for his private life [...] within the meaning of Article 8 par. 1.' (§38). Furthermore, the Court considered it impossible to maintain that a 'pressing social need' in Ireland justifies making such acts criminal offences. With regard more specifically to proportionality, the Court stated that justifications 'for retaining the law in force un-amended are outweighed by the detrimental effects which the very existence of the legislative provisions in question can have on the life of a person of homosexual orientation like the applicant'. Consequently, the reasons put forward to justify the interference found are not sufficient to satisfy the requirements of paragraph 2 of Article 8. There was accordingly breach of that article (§§46–47).

On the other hand, in *K.A. and A.D.* v. *Belgium* (17 February 2005) where two applicants were criminally prosecuted and convicted for sadomasochistic acts, the Court held that there was no breach of Article 8. The Court nevertheless declared that criminal law may not, in principle, be applied in the case of consensual sexual practices, which are a matter of individual free will. There must consequently be 'particularly serious reasons' for interference by the public authorities in matters of sexuality to be justified for the purposes of Article 8.2 (§84). In this case, the Court held that these particularly serious reasons existed, considering the victim's injuries, the continuation of the sadomasochistic acts when the victim used words which had been agreed would be used as a signal for the activity to cease and the applicants' lack of control of their sadomasochistic acts due to their consumption of large quantities of alcohol.

6.3.2.3 Freedom of expression

The right to freedom of thought, conscience and religion (Article 9) and freedom of expression (Article 10), like the right to the protection of private life (Article 8), has nothing to do as such with criminal law provided the legislator does not create incriminations that restrict these rights. The ECtHR is opposed to incriminations that give disproportionate weight to freedom of religion (*Manoussakis et al.* v. *Greece*, 26 September 1996). Within the scope of Article 10 ECHR and the freedom of expression, the Court found in *Muller* v. *Switzerland* (24 May 1988) that a confiscation of a work of art is in breach of the right guaranteed by Article 10. Reference can also be made to well known cases such as *Open Door and Dublin Well Woman* v. *Ireland* (29 October 1992). In this case, the Court held that Article 10 had been breached by the prohibition to communicate information on abortion.

In another contribution (De Hert and Gutwirth 2005a), two of us demonstrated the importance the Court attaches to freedom of expression, which it recognizes as a foundation of democratic society. The Court's case law on the application of Article 10 of the Convention in conflicts over legal procedures is an excellent illustration of the humanist criminal law that we defend. In *Du Roy and Malaurie* v. *France* (3 October 2000, §35), for example, where the domestic courts had convicted a journalist and editor of a weekly for publishing information on applying to join criminal proceedings as a civil party, the Court concluded that there was breach of Article 10.1. Although this offence was foreseen and punished by French law to protect the presumption of innocence of those being prosecuted but not yet convicted on a complaint accompanied by a civil-party application, the Court refused to accept that such a 'general and absolute prohibition of the publication of any type of information' was necessary in a democratic society. In *Weber* v. *Switzerland* (22 May 1990) the Court ruled that imposing a fine on a journalist who breached the confidentiality of a preliminary investigation was not consistent with the principle of proportionality. In *Saday* v. *Turkey* (30 March 2006), the applicant alleged breach on several scores of Article 10 of the Convention. He was prosecuted by virtue of Article 146, para. 1 of the

Criminal Code for having attempted to endanger the constitutional regime of the Republic of Turkey. The applicant did not deny his connections with an illegal organization, but essentially defended the legitimacy of his political convictions. Part of his pleadings concerned the Turkish judicial system and in particular the existence and practice of state security courts. The Turkish court ruled his remarks 'improper' and convicted him for contempt of court. The ECtHR agreed that the applicant had made particularly acerbic remarks in his arguments and accepted the court's imposition of a penalty. It nevertheless ruled that the severity and length of the sentence, namely two months' solitary confinement, constituted a breach of Article 10 ECHR. This sentence appeared disproportionate to the aims pursued and therefore not 'necessary in a democratic society' (§37).

We see here that the Court does not restrict its role to analysing the nature of the penalties imposed, but also assesses their severity when measuring the proportionality of the interference (§36).

6.4 The vulnerability of the Court's case law

Although the above mentioned examples are particularly illustrative for the efforts of the ECtHR to limit certain forms of 'punitiveness', two comments give nuances to this at first sight optimistic conclusion on human rights acting as the 'bad conscience' of criminal law to guard against excessive incriminations or penalties.

First, there is the ambivalent attitude of the Court concerning interfering in national penal policies, which does not attest to a perfectly coherent 'shield' approach. Second, in some cases the Court does not hesitate to cite human rights protection to promote a penal approach: are human rights becoming the 'good conscience' of criminal law?

6.4.1   The court's ambivalence

Two cases are illustrative of the Court's hesitation to interfere in national penal policies, resulting in our view (and, interestingly, also in the view of some of the judges of the ECtHR) in an insufficient protection against disproportionate penalization.

6.4.1.1 Young children's full penal responsibility?

When introducing Article 3 above, we wrote that excessive penalties or incriminations may be at odds with Article 3. Why 'may'? The difficulty lies not only with the legislator (national and international), but also within the ECtHR, as the Court does not seem to have adopted a clear and uniform line of conduct. As described above, several judgments demonstrate a heightened sensitivity to Article 3 of the Convention. In its ruling in *Selmouni* v. *France* (28 July 1999, §101), the Court stated that 'the increasingly high standard being required in the area of the protection of human rights and fundamental liberties correspondingly and inevitably requires greater firmness in assessing breaches of the fundamental values of democratic societies'. On the other hand, a few months later, in the famous *Bulger* case (*T.* v. *United Kingdom, V.* v. *United Kingdom*, 16 December 1999), in which two 10-year-old boys killed a two-year-old child, the Court showed in our view considerably less 'firmness' on the alleged violation of Article 3. The Court had to review whether the fact of having held the applicant criminally responsible for the acts he had committed at age 10 could in itself constitute a violation of Article 3. Ruling in the negative, the Court held that there is not at this stage any clear common standard among the member states of the Council of Europe as to the minimum age of criminal responsibility (§72). Neither the facts that the 'criminally responsible' applicant had to undergo a public and highly mediatized trial before the Crown Court, in the presence of a fairly hostile public, and that he was sentenced to an indeterminate sentence of detention during Her Majesty's pleasure, nor the circumstance that his name was disclosed following his sentencing, constitute a violation of Article 3. The Court stated that the Convention does not prohibit states from subjecting a child or young offender convicted of a serious crime to an indeterminate sentence allowing for the offender's continued detention where necessary for the protection of the public (§97), although 'a lifelong detention' could possibly raise an issue under Article 3 (§103).

In a joint partly dissenting opinion, Judges Pastor Ridruejo, Ress, Makarczyk, Tulkens and Butkevych objected to this majority's analysis. They considered there to be sufficient evidence that the *combination* of treating children 11 years of age as criminally responsible, prosecuting them in an 'adult' court in the presence of a hostile public and under massive press attention, and subjecting them to an indeterminate sentence resulted in such a substantial level of mental and physical suffering as to constitute inhuman and degrading treatment contrary to Article 3. The dissenting judges also noted that this 'adult' treatment of children did not correspond to a clear European and international trend to apply *relative* criminal responsibility from the age of 13 or 14 – with procedures before special juvenile courts – and full criminal responsibility from the age of 18.

We agree with this dissenting opinion that in considering the age of criminal responsibility in isolation from the trial process, the Court weakens the protection of Article 3, as '(t)he very low age of criminal responsibility has always to be linked with the possibility of adult trial proceedings. That is why the vast majority of Contracting States have eschewed such a very low age of criminal responsibility.' We also agree with their conclusion that 'for us, the public nature of the trial not only contributed to the inhuman but also to the degrading treatment, and the fact that the applicants were tried in accordance with the same criminal procedure as adults and sentenced without sufficient account being taken of the fact that they were children must be qualified as inhuman.' The fact that the Court found the trial to have been a violation of Article 6.1 because it could not guarantee the effective participation of 11-year-old children is indeed a question of a different nature and 'failed sufficiently to address the suffering and humiliation which such a procedure inevitably entails for children'.

We consider that the ECtHR failed to seize the opportunity to proscribe in Europe full criminal responsibility for children 10 years of age. Had it chosen to prohibit such full responsibility on the basis of Article 3, the Court would have given a strong signal against the trend in some European countries to have recourse to criminalization 'as for adults' for acts committed by young children.

6.4.1.2　Right to freedom and the principle of proportionality?

Although the ECtHR ruled in the 1970s and 1980s that infringement of Article 3 could result from unjustified or disproportionate penalties, it has systematically argued that the question of adequate sentencing is largely the domain of national legislation and courts. Accordingly, judicial corporal punishment was considered to run counter to Article 3 (*Tyrer* v. *United Kingdom*, 25 April 1978). However, the Court has stated that the inhuman or degrading nature of a prison sentence should be evaluated in relation to the complainant's age, sex and health, and considers that the length of the penalty in itself would rarely constitute a violation (*Ireland* v. *UK*, 18 January 1978). This depends, however, on the aim pursued by the sentence. A sentence of life imprisonment ordered as retribution for very serious offences is not considered as running counter to Article 3 of the ECHR (*Sawoniuk* v. *United Kingdom*, 29 May 2001). However, in *Weeks* v. *United Kingdom* (2 March 1987), the Court held that sentencing a 17-year-old youth to life imprisonment for armed robbery with an unarmed pistol could have constituted a breach of Article 3 if the sentence had been ordered on a purely punitive basis. In this specific case, it ruled that Article 3 had not been violated because the court had ordered the sentence in reference to the perpetrator's dangerousness to society and because it in fact allowed for earlier release than if a long determinate sentence had been imposed. Defenders of 'just deserts' will doubtless see this as a further argument against the lack of proportionality that results from social protection measures unrelated to the offence committed.

In the *Bulger* case (*T.* v. *United Kingdom, V.* v. *United Kingdom*, 16 December 1999) the Court had to rule on whether an indeterminate deprivation of liberty imposed on a minor for a murder committed when he was 10 years old was in breach of Article 3. The applicant had been detained for six years at the time. The Court agreed that the member states have a duty under the Convention to protect the public against violent crimes. It ruled that, considering all the circumstances of the case, the applicant's age and the detention conditions, a punitive detention period of six years could not be said to amount to inhuman or degrading treatment. Referring to the United Nations Convention on the Rights of the Child (UNCRC) and the Beijing Rules, the Court nevertheless held that a life sentence for a minor with no possibility of early release could pose a problem on the basis of Article 3.

A similar opinion was handed down over a life sentence without the possibility of release for adults (*Kafkaris* v. *Cyprus* [GC], 12 February 2008). However, although the Court has on several occasions recognized the importance of reintegration as an aim of the implementation of prison sentences (see, for example, *Dickson* v. *United Kingdom* [GC], 4 December 2007), it has failed to support conditional release schemes for prisoners sentenced to determinate sentences or to require that such decisions should be taken in accordance with the guarantees of a fair procedure offered by Article 6 (*Ganusauskas* v. *Lithuania*, 7 September 1999; *Zivulinskas* v. *Lithuania*, 12 December 2006). This approach fails to recognize the reality of the effects of parole decisions on the liberty status and civil rights and obligations of prisoners (van Zyl Smit and Snacken 2009: 338–40). As discussed by Judge Costa in his dissenting opinion in *Léger* v. *France* (11 April 2006), it is inappropriate for the ECtHR to construct a theory in which decisions concerning the liberty of a person can be taken arbitrarily and are unreviewable. It also testifies to the absence of a coherent penological framework based on the aim of reintegration for the attribution of prisoners' rights by the ECtHR, compared for example with the German Constitutional Court (Lazarus 2004, 2006), despite improvements in that regard (van Zyl Smit and Snacken 2009: 77–80).

Finally, there remains the question of deprivation of liberty as the ultimate sentence in a penal Europe where all countries have abolished the death penalty and have introduced non-custodial sanctions and measures (van Kalmthout and Durnescu 2008). As mentioned above, Article 5 protects individuals against undue or arbitrary restrictions of their liberty. The right to liberty is the norm, restrictions are the exceptions and must meet strict requirements of legality, legitimacy and proportionality. In *Bouchet* v. *France* (20 March 2001), the Court had to rule on the lawfulness of a 17-month pre-trial detention of an accused suspected of rape, who was subsequently acquitted. The investigating court's decision to release the suspect under judicial supervision after just over two months of detention was set aside on appeal, in spite of the court's arguments that judicial supervision could achieve the same aims as detention and in spite of the expert report by a psychiatrist demonstrating that detention would be harmful to the suspect's psychological health. The Court held that detention was justified due to the seriousness of the offence, the suspect's psychological state and the victim's vulnerability (§48).

As Judges Tulkens, Loucaides and Bratza pointed out in their dissenting opinion[13], the Court's decision in *Bouchet* runs counter to a strict application of the principle of proportionality. Several proportionality criteria can be identified in the Court's practice, ranging from a flexible test where the member states have wide discretion to limit the rights protected by the Convention, to a strict test where such discretion is limited (De Hert 1998, 2005; De Hert and Gutwirth 2005a; De Hert and Nehmelman 2006). As a general rule, the Court applies a flexible test in connection with Article 8 and the right to private life (simple proportionality) and a strict test with regard to Article 10 and the freedom of expression (enhanced proportionality). Objections could be raised to the very existence of different proportionality criteria, since the text of the Convention establishes an almost identical structure for the rights laid down in Articles 8 to 11 (private or family life, freedom of expression, etc.). It seems even less logical for the Court not to apply the stricter test in cases concerning Article 5. This amounts to saying that the right to liberty is less protected by the Court's case law than freedom of expression, which goes against the Convention's very logic. Indeed, the right to liberty has long been recognized as one of the Convention's most fundamental rights. Numerous scientific research results have demonstrated the harmful effects of imprisonment and the influence of the duration of detention on these effects, and the deprivation of liberty leads automatically to certain restrictions on the freedoms guaranteed in Articles 8 to 11. We therefore maintain that any decision on deprivation of liberty (choice of sanction or measure, length, release) should be reviewed on the basis of the strictest test and that only the intervention that is least restrictive for human rights should be considered proportionate and legitimate (for further development of this idea, see Snacken 2005, 2006; van Zyl Smit and Snacken 2009: 359–64).

6.4.2 The court as an amplifier of punitiveness?

In some cases the Court does not hesitate to cite human rights protection to promote a penal approach: human rights as the 'good conscience' of criminal law? This tendency to oblige member states to recourse to criminal law under certain circumstances seems more pronounced when the physical integrity of victims is at issue. Nevertheless, this state's 'duty to punish' – instead of a 'right to punish' – raises two fundamental questions: first, concerning the principle of subsidiarity of the criminal law; second, concerning the concept of 'positive obligations' by states to protect human rights.

6.4.2.1 The state's 'duty to punish'?

An illustrative example of this 'duty to punish' is the *Oneryildiz* v. *Turkey* judgment (30 November 2004). Drawing on Article 2 (the right to life) of the Convention, the applicant maintained that the Turkish authorities were responsible for the death of nine of his family members and the destruction of his property as the result of a methane-gas explosion that occurred on 28 April 1993 in the municipal rubbish tip of Ümraniye (Istanbul). In its ruling, the Court reiterated first that Article 2 also contains the positive obligation for states to take all action necessary to protect the life of persons under their jurisdiction. The Court then held that the Turkish authorities were aware of the imminent dangers of the municipal rubbish tip and neglected to take the necessary measures and to inform the public concerned. There was consequently a violation of the *substantive* aspect of Article 2.

However, the Court went even further. Analysing the *procedural* requirements of Article 2, it first emphasized the need for 'provision for an independent and impartial official investigation procedure'. Sometimes only state agents are in a position to be aware of the exact circumstances in which the death occurred (§§93–

94). Yet in the instant case, the Turkish authorities had opened an investigation which resulted in the identification of possible responsible parties. The Court nevertheless ruled that the 'requirements of Article 2 go beyond the stage of the official investigation, where this has led to the institution of proceedings in the national courts'. In this case, 'the proceedings as a whole, *including the trial stage*, must satisfy the requirements of the positive obligation to protect lives through the law'(§95).

Although it should not be inferred that Article 2 may imply the right for an applicant to seek the prosecution or sentencing of third parties in criminal proceedings, the Court declared, on the other hand, that 'the national courts should not under any circumstances be prepared to allow life-endangering offences to go unpunished'. The judicial punishment of life-endangering offences is vital, argued the Court, both for 'maintaining public confidence and ensuring adherence to the rule of law' and for 'preventing any appearance of tolerance of or collusion in unlawful acts'. The Court's task therefore consists, in its own words, in reviewing whether the courts, in reaching their conclusion, may be deemed to have submitted the case to the careful scrutiny required by Article 2, 'so that the deterrent effect of the judicial system in place and the significance of the role it is required to play in preventing violations of the right to life are not undermined' (§96). In this case, the Court held that the Istanbul criminal court handed down derisory sentences on those responsible (fines of around €9.70 and a suspension), for the sole offence of 'negligence in the performance of their duties', which according to the Court, 'does not in any way relate to life-endangering acts or to the protection of the right to life within the meaning of Article 2'. As a result, the court dealing with the substance of the case left pending all questions related to the possible liability of the authorities in the death of the applicant's nine family members. In short, it must be concluded in this case that the procedural aspect of Article 2 was also violated.

The Court's approach under the procedural aspect of Article 2 gives a dual view of the Court. On the one hand, it asserts the strength of deterrence of the criminal judicial system and uses the principle of proportionality as a 'sword' (more punishment is needed!) to criticize the *lightness* of incrimination. It seems legitimate in this respect to conclude that the ECtHR acts as a 'machine that encourages penal inflation' (De Hert and Gutwirth 2005b: 752). On the other hand, in keeping with the analysis by Judge Françoise Tulkens (2006), we can also see in this ruling an example of the Court's activism to protect the weakest, in the area of housing moreover. In addition, the almost total impunity of the state authorities and agents, which the Court considered as having been established, cannot be reconciled with the principles of the rule of law. Accordingly, the ECtHR could also be presented as the court *that punishes the untouchables*.

Without underestimating the social importance of this type of judgment and the need for the rule of law to avoid the existence of any *untouchable* status, two fundamental questions must be raised.

6.4.2.2 Two fundamental questions

First, is the requirement of penalization not in contradiction with the subsidiarity of criminal law as 'heinous law' (Tulkens and van de Kerchove 2005: 952)? In its judgment in *M.C.* v. *Bulgaria* (4 December 2003), the ECtHR ruled against Bulgaria for undermining the right to a person's physical and psychological integrity (Article 3), and his right to autonomy as a component of the right to a private life (Article 8). In this sensitive case, the Court held that Bulgaria had breached the Convention for failing to prosecute presumed rapists under criminal law on the ground of absence of proof of physical resistance by the victim. The Court found that states have a positive obligation of incrimination and criminal prosecution in matters of sexual violence provided there is lack of consent. The Belgian judge, Françoise Tulkens, shared the Court's view while expressing, rightly in our view, a courageous subtly shaded observation:

> The only point I wish to clarify concerns the use of criminal remedies. [...] The Court considers that 'States have a positive obligation inherent in Articles 3 and 8 of the Convention to enact criminal-law provisions effectively punishing rape [...]'. Admittedly, recourse to the criminal law may be understandable where offences of this kind are concerned. However, it is also important to emphasize on a more general level, [...] that recourse to the criminal law is not necessarily the only answer. I consider that criminal proceedings should remain, both in theory and in practice, a last resort or subsidiary remedy and that their use, even in the context of positive obligations, calls for a certain degree of 'restraint'. As to the assumption that criminal remedies are in any event the most effective in terms of deterrence, the observations set out in the Report on Decriminalization by the European Committee on Crime Problems clearly show that the effectiveness of general deterrence based on the criminal law depends on various factors and that such an approach 'is not the only way of preventing undesirable behaviour'.

Second, by obliging states to make certain infringements of fundamental rights a criminal offence, is not the Court supplanting the national legislator? This tendency by the Court to 'set standards' is closely tied to the growing application of the theory of positive obligations of member states, both 'vertically' (the state relative to the individual) and 'horizontally' (between individuals). One is tempted to ask just how far the Court will go.

The examples of abortion and euthanasia attest to the delicacy of the problems these questions raise. In its judgment in *Vo* v. *France* (8 July 2004), in which medical negligence led to the unintentional killing of an unborn child, the Court stated that, in view of the lack of European consensus on the scientific and legal definition of the beginning of life and the many debates concerning the protection of unborn life in the majority of the Contracting States, 'the issue of when the right to life begins comes within the margin of appreciation which the Court generally considers that States should enjoy in this sphere' (§82). Article 2 requires the state to take appropriate steps to safeguard the lives of those within its jurisdiction (§88), a principle which is also applicable in the public-health sphere (§89). However, this does not necessarily imply criminalization:

> However, if the infringement of the right to life or to physical integrity is not caused intentionally, the positive obligation imposed by Article 2 to set up an effective judicial system does not necessarily require the provision of a criminal-law remedy in every case. In the specific sphere of medical negligence, the obligation may for instance also be satisfied if the legal system affords victims a remedy in the civil courts, either alone or in conjunction with a remedy in the criminal courts, enabling any liability of the doctors concerned to be established and any appropriate civil redress, such as an order for damages and for the publication of the decision, to be obtained. Disciplinary measures may also be envisaged. (§90)

The same questions arise with regard to euthanasia. Does Article 2 oblige contracting states to protect human life against euthanasia? Or, on the contrary, would the ban on euthanasia violate, in some cases, the right to a 'dignified' life? In its ruling in *Pretty* v. *United Kingdom* of 29 April 2002, the Court replied in the negative to a young woman who was left completely disabled as a result of a degenerative illness, who asked that her husband be authorized by the authorities to help her commit 'suicide'. The Court was apparently not convinced that the right guaranteed by Article 2 contains a negative aspect. It consequently ruled that 'Article 2 cannot, without a distortion of language, be interpreted as conferring the diametrically opposite right, namely a right to die' (§39).

However, by intervening this directly in questions of criminal liability in socially sensitive areas, is not the Court at risk of ruling on the political dimensions of law, the legislator's usual preserve especially in continental systems (De Hert and Gutwirth 2005b: 749)?

6.5 Conclusion: towards a coherent framework

We have demonstrated that the ECtHR's case law does indeed set certain restrictions on unlimited penalization. Its rejection of the death penalty, inhuman or degrading penalties, prison overcrowding, disproportionate penalties under Article 3, life without parole and refusal of parole for reasons of pure retribution or public opinion shows that the European Convention on Human Rights can serve as a shield against the penal state. The exercise presented, although not complete,[14] enables us to concur with Van den Wyngaert that the legislator does not have a free hand when it comes to determining incriminations but must take account of human rights and the interpretations made by the ECtHR. As a consequence, we can conclude that human rights influence and can limit substantive criminal law in the broad sense, at the level of incriminations, and the imposition and implementation of sanctions or measures: human rights acting as the 'bad conscience' of criminal law. The exercise, however, has also demonstrated the ambivalence of this case law, as the Court has also cited protection of human rights to promote a penal approach: human rights as the 'good conscience' of criminal law.

The analysis demonstrates in our opinion the vulnerability of this case law as the guarantee of a humanization and moderation of penal policies in Europe. Hence the question arises whether this vulnerability should not be counterbalanced by introducing a coherent and coercive framework that reflects this reductionist and humane penal approach.

The existence of the ECHR and the fact that the Court has indeed laid down certain 'qualitative' restrictions on unlimited criminalization does not mean that things should not go any further. Of course, we acknowledge the influence of other factors on levels of punitiveness, such as the socio-economic (demography, social inequality) and political factors ('populist punitiveness', public opinion, media) dealt with in the other chapters of this book. We still want to argue though for a better codification of the general principles that should guarantee a subsidiary, moderate and proportional criminal law. In our opinion, this requires at least three types of intervention.

First, the legislator must continue to be held in check by proposing rights that protect against criminal law and its penalties. This could be done for the Convention through an additional protocol. Examples to keep in mind include the ban on imprisonment for debt laid down in Protocol No. 4 to the Convention *securing certain rights and freedoms other than those already included in the Convention and in the first Protocol thereto*[15] as well as Protocols Nos. 6 and 13 to the Convention concerning the abolition of the death penalty (see above). Such a protocol could include new rights and prohibitions capable of providing a better framework for a humanist and moderate criminal law. We have in mind, for example, a ban on life sentences or on imprisonment in default, which replaces a fine to the detriment of social justice (see also Van den Wyngaert 2006: 365, 370–1). There are probably numerous other suggestions for this exercise of providing a better framework for the penal power of the democracies that are parties to the Convention.

Second, we must continue the initial project conceived of during the Age of Enlightenment, which had the ambition of constitutionalizing criminal law. This would help make more visible 'the stakes of criminal constitutional law' (Verdussen 1995: 687–787). Another protocol to the Convention could be drawn up, this time laying down the principles that must govern the development and enforcement of criminal laws. If we agree on the subsidiarity of the use of criminal remedies and on a form of restraint in the use of criminal law and penalties, why not write it into a text that gives these principles constitutional strength?

Third, if we seek moderation by all criminal law players and in all cases, i.e. beyond the cases protected by the current system of protection of fundamental rights, we need principles that correspond to this ambition. Article II-109 of the

EU Charter on Fundamental Rights, which became legal through the Treaty of Lisbon on 1 December 2009, thus enumerates the principles of legality, non-retroactivity and proportionality of penalties. This is a good example of 'constitutionalism' and we would like to see it reiterated in a protocol to the Convention. Such principles should, however, also be based on a more coherent criminological and penological framework. These could help solve the current problems raised by the Court's over-reliance on the supposed deterrent effects of the criminal law, its punishments and its ambivalence concerning the implications of the aim of reintegration on prisoners' rights and prison regimes and the importance of non-custodial reactions to delinquency.

Notes

1. This contribution is the result of a collective research project (coordinator Prof. Dr S. Snacken) on Legitimate Justice in Times of Insecurity, conducted by criminologists and legal experts from the Faculty of Law and Criminology, Vrije Universiteit Brussel.
2. The death penalty, chain gangs and corporal punishment become respectable again, as do references to the feelings of the public and of victims towards increasingly expressive punishments.
3. In the United States, penitentiary institutions are the country's fourth largest employer with 2.2 million employees; cf. Wacquant (2006a: 285).
4. Denis Salas (2005: 105–21) presents a similar description of the evolution of American criminal law and penal policy: the meeting of *moral panic* and powerful punitive populism; the return of retributivism (*desert* and *incapacitation*) at the expense of rehabilitationism; the politicization of penal issues; *zero tolerance* and *Prison works!*; and the emergence of a penal market owing to widespread use of *plea bargaining* (in 90 per cent of cases).
5. Cf. FIDH-International Federation for Human Rights, *Counter-Terrorism versus Human Rights: The Key to Compatibility*, Report 429/2, October 2005 (online at: http://www. fidh.org/IMG/pdf/counterterrorism429a.pdf#search=%22%22counter-terrorism%2 0versus%20human%20rights%22%22) and the various contributions to Bribosia and Weyembergh (2002).
6. Council Framework Decision of 13 June 2002 on combating terrorism, the European arrest warrant, The Hague programme on freedom, and security and justice in the European Union, where one can observe a remarkable grouping of the problems of terrorism and serious crime with those of immigration, border controls, collaboration between police forces, SIS I (Schengen Information System) and SIS II, VIS (Visa Information System), the introduction of biometric passports, the retention of communication data, access and interception of communications and so on.
7. Cf. Salas (2005: 12): 'In France, the surge in repression launched by a left-of-centre majority is being carried on by a right-of-centre majority.'
8. The author denounces the tyrannical nature of these perpetual laws and the blindness of the Dutch authorities to rule-of-law principles when they implement anti-terror measures that put tremendous pressure on fundamental rights.
9. Salas links very directly this rise in populism to the victim's political ascension: it is the birth of a 'will to punish' *to satisfy victims*, at the expense of a 'will to punish' to restore social order, that has acted as an initial lever in the transformation of the imposition of punishment in France (Salas 2005: 63–101). See Part 3 of this volume.
10. The fact remains that in France, for example, one finds most of the ingredients of the *culture of control* and the penal or law-and-order state described above. According to Salas, from 1975 to 1980, under the impact of the increase in petty and intermediate-level crimes and victims' discontent, French penal policy developed within a security system that evolved 'from a model of response to an act or treatment of individuals to

the regulation of areas and populations who live in a given area', which goes hand in hand with the development of preventive measures (Salas 2005: 43).

11. Indeed, as Wacquant states on urban marginality, the phenomenon 'is not made of the same fabric in different places: the *generic mechanisms* that produce it, like the *specific forms* it takes, become fully intelligible when one takes the trouble to place them in the historical matrix of relations between classes, the state and the characteristic space of each society at a given time. That means we have to work to develop more complex and differentiated pictures of the "city's damned" if we wish to grasp their social situation correctly and elucidate their collective fate in different national contexts' (Wacquant 2006a: 6).

12. In *Kruslin v. France*, 24 April 1990, the ECtHR places into perspective the difference between the two systems as follows: '[I]t would be wrong to exaggerate the distinction between common-law countries and Continental countries, as the government rightly pointed out. Statute law is, of course, also important in common-law countries. Conversely, case law has traditionally played a major role in Continental countries, to such an extent that whole branches of positive law are largely the outcome of decisions by the courts.'

13. 'We think that the review of the lawfulness of pre-trial detention must take account of all options available to the State, which must choose the measure that is least restrictive to the rights of the accused. The right to liberty and security, guaranteed in a democratic society by Article 5 of the Convention, amounts to admitting only strictly necessary deprivations of liberty.'

14. We could continue our analysis up to the last right mentioned in the Convention or its protocols. On the compatibility of certain confiscations and the right to respect for ownership (first protocol), see Vervaele (1998: 39–56).

15. Protocol No. 4 to the Convention for the Protection of Human Rights and Fundamental Freedoms, *securing certain rights and freedoms other than those already included in the Convention and in the first Protocol thereto*, Strasbourg, 16 September 1963; Article 1: 'No one shall be deprived of liberty merely on the ground of inability to fulfil a contractual obligation.'

References

Brants, C. H., Mevis, P. A. M. and Prakken, E. (2001) *Legitieme strafvordering. Rechten van de mens als inspiratie in de 21ste eeuw*. Anvers-Groningen: Intersentia Rechtswetenschappen.

Bribosia, E. and Weyembergh, A. (2002) *Lutte contre le terrorisme et droits fondamentaux*. Brussels: Bruylant.

Buruma, Y. (2005) 'Kroniek van het strafrecht', *Nederlands Juristenblad*, Afl. 2005/31.

Council of Europe (2001) *La peine de mort hors la loi! Le Conseil de l'Europe et la peine de mort*. Strasbourg: Conseil de l'Europe, Direction Générale des Droits de l'Homme.

Damaska, M. R. (1986) *The Faces of Justice and State Authority: A Comparative Approach to the Legal Process*. New Haven, CT: Yale University Press.

De Hert, P. (1998) *Artikel 8 EVRM en het Belgisch recht. De bescherming van privacy, gezin, woonst en communicatie*. Gent: Mys en Breesch Uitgeverij, pp. 32–3.

De Hert, P. (2005) 'Balancing security and liberty within the European human rights framework', in A. M. Hol and A. E. Vervaele (eds), *Security and Civil Liberties: The Case of Terrorism*. Antwerp and Oxford: Intersentia, pp. 37–76.

De Hert, P. and Gutwirth, S. (2005a) 'Gij zult straffen om de mensenrechten te beschermen! De strafbaarstelling als positieve staatsverplichting', in F. Verbruggen, R. Verstraeten, D. Van Daele and B. Spriet (eds), *Strafrecht als Roeping. Liber Amicorum Lieven Dupont*. Leuven: Universitaire Pers, pp. 729 –55.

De Hert, P. and Gutwirth, S. (2005b) 'Grondrechten: vrijplaatsen voor het strafrecht? Dworkins Amerikaanse trumpmetafoor getoetst aan de hedendaagse Europese mensenrechten', in R. H. Haveman and H. C. Wiersinga (eds), *Langs de randen van het strafrecht*. Nijmegen: Wolf Legal Publishers, pp. 141–75.

De Hert, P. and Nehmelman, R. (2006) 'Privacy versus veiligheid. Een analyse van enkele projecten in de sfeer van de criminaliteitsbestrijding', in W. P. S. Bierens, C. L. C. Richert and P. G. S. Van Schie (eds), *Grondrechten Gewogen. Enkele constitutionele waarden in het actuele politieke debat*. The Hague: Telderstichting, pp. 105–46.

De Wijkerslooth, J. L. (2005) 'De officier van justitie en de nieuwe gestrengheid', *Goed beschouwd*. Den Haag: Voorlichtingsdienst OM, pp. 5–20.

Denkers, F. A. M. C. (1976) *Criminologie en beleid*. Nijmegen: Dekker & van de Vegt.

Edelman, B. (1995) 'What rights for those on trial? Universality and human rights', in M. Delmas-Marty (ed.), *The Criminal Process and Human Rights: Towards a European Consciousness*. Dordrecht: Martinus Nijhoff, pp. 97–108.

Foqué, R. and 't Hart, A. C. (1990) *Instrumentaliteit en rechtsbescherming. Grondslagen van een strafrechtelijke waardendiscussie*. Arnhem and Antwerp: Gouda Quint/Kluwer.

Garapon, A. and Papadopoulos, I. (2003) *Juger en Amérique et en France. Culture juridique et common law*. Paris: Odile Jacob.

Garapon, A. and Salas, D. (1996) *La République Pénalisée*. Paris: Hachette.

Garland, D. (2001) *The Culture of Control: Crime and Social Order in Contemporary Society*. Oxford: Oxford University Press.

Gutwirth, S. and De Hert, P. (2001) 'Een theoretische onderbouw voor een legitiem strafproces. Reflecties over procesculturen, de doelstellingen van de straf, de plaats van het strafrecht en de rol van slachtoffers', *Delikt en Delinkwent*, 31: 1048–87.

Hosein, G. (2005) *Threatening the Open Society: Comparing Anti-Terror Policies in the US and Europe*. London: Privacy International; online at: http://www. privacyinternational.org/issues/terrorism/rpt/comparativeterrorreportdec2005.pdf.

Lazarus, L. (2004) *Contrasting Prisoners' Rights: A Comparative Examination of England and Germany*. Oxford: Oxford University Press.

Lazarus, L. (2006) 'Conceptions of liberty deprivations', *Modern Law Review*, 69: 738–69.

Mary, P. (2003) *Insécurité et pénalisation du social*. Brussels: Labor.

Salas, D. (2005) *La volonté de punir. Essai sur le populisme pénal*. Paris: Hachette.

Snacken, S. (2005) 'Bestraffing, vrijheidsbeneming en mensenrechten', in E. Brems *et al.* (eds), *Vrijheden en vrijheidsbeneming*. Antwerp and Oxford: Intersentia, pp. 323–52.

Snacken, S. (2006) 'A reductionist penal policy and European human rights standards', *European Journal of Criminal Policy and Research*: 143–64.

Snacken, S., Beyens, K. and Tubex, H. (1995) 'Changing prison populations in Western Countries: fate or policy?', *European Journal of Crime, Criminal Law and Criminal Justice*, 1: 18–53.

Tonry, M. (2001) 'Symbol, substance and severity in Western penal policies', *Punishment and Society*, 4: 517–36.

Tulkens, F. (1992) 'La procédure pénale: grandes lignes de comparaison entre systèmes nationaux', in *Procès pénal et droits de l'homme. Vers une conscience européenne*. Paris: Presses Universitaires de France.

Tulkens, F. (2006) *La Convention européenne des droits de l'homme. Les développements récents de la Cour européenne des droits de l'homme*. Inaugural lecture of 10 November. Brussels: VUB Chair 2006–7.

Tulkens, F. and van de Kerchove, M. (2005) 'Les droits de l'homme: bonne ou mauvaise conscience du droit pénal?', in F. Verbruggen, R. Verstraeten, D. Van Daele and B. Spriet (eds), *Strafrecht als roeping: Liber Amicorum Lieven Dupont*. Leuven: Universitaire Pers Leuven, pp. 949–67.

Van Campenhoudt, L. (1999) 'L'insécurité est moins un problème qu'une solution', in Y. Cartuyvels and Ph. Mary (eds), *L'État face à l'insécurité. Dérives politiques des années '90*, Brussels: Labor, pp. 51–68.

Van den Wyngaert, C. (2006) *Strafrecht, strafprocesrecht en internationaal strafrecht in hoofdlijnen*. Antwerpen-Apeldoorn: Maklu.

Van Gunsteren, H. (2004) *Gevaarlijk veilig. Terreurbestrijding in de democratie*. Amsterdam: Van Gennep.

van Kalmthout, A. and Durnescu, I. (eds) (2008) *Probation in Europe*. Nijmegen: Wolf Legal Publishers.

Van Swaaningen, R. (2010) *Bending the Punitive Turn?* Paper presented at the Onati workshop 'European Penology?', organized by T. Daems, S. Snacken and D. van Zyl Smit, 22–23 July. Onati: International Institute for the Sociology of Law.

van Zyl Smit, D. and Snacken, S. (2009) *Principles of European Prison Law and Policy. Penology and Human Rights*. Oxford: Oxford University Press.

Verdussen, R. (1995) *Contours et enjeux du droit constitutionnel pénal*. Brussels: Bruylant.

Vervaele, J. A. E. (1998) 'Les sanctions de confiscation en droit pénal. Une analyse de la jurisprudence de la CEDH et de la signification qu'elle revêt pour le droit (procédural) en droit néerlandais', *Revue de Sciences Criminelles et de Droit Pénal Comparé*: 39–56.

Wacquant, L. (2006a) *Parias urbains: Ghetto – Banlieues – État*. Paris: La Découverte.

Wacquant, L. (2006b) 'Penalization, depoliticization, and racialization: on the overincarceration of immigrants in the European Union', in S. Armstrong and L. McAra (eds), *Perspectives on Punishment: The Contours of Control*. Oxford: Oxford University Press, pp. 83–100.

Wacquant, L. and Heijne, B. (2006) 'Globalisering is geen natuurkracht', *NRC Handelsblad Magazine*, 2 April, pp. 36–7.

Whitman, J. Q. (2003) *Harsh Justice: Criminal Punishment and the Widening Divide between America and Europe*. Oxford: Oxford University Press.

7

HUMAN RIGHTS AND PENALIZATION IN CENTRAL AND EASTERN EUROPE: THE CASE OF HUNGARY

Miklós Lévay

7.1 Introduction

In Hungary, as in many other Central and Eastern European countries, the change in the political system in 1989–90 significantly affected the criminal justice system and penal policy. However, while the structure and institutions of criminal justice continued after 1990 without formal changes, the principles of functioning and the practice, that is the content, changed fundamentally. This change derived from the differences between the political system before 1989–90 and that which followed. Before the change in the system, Hungary had an authoritarian, one-party system. Upon the changes in 1989–90, however, a multi-party, democratic constitutional state came into existence. The changes were especially significant in the field of protection of human rights.

One aim of this paper is to compare the main characteristics of the criminal justice and penal policy before 1989–90 and after, paying special attention to the role of human rights and the development of sentencing practice. The other aim is to describe the developments of the period after 1990. Within this framework the paper deals in particular with the most important decisions of the Hungarian Constitutional Court, established in 1989, in the field of penalization and criminalization.

7.2 Characteristics of the criminal justice system and punishment before 1989–90

7.2.1 Criminal justice system

The political system, which came into existence in Hungary after the defeat of the revolution in 1956 and was named after János Kádár, who ruled the Communist Party (under the name of the Hungarian Socialist Labour Party) till 1988, was initially a totalitarian dictatorship. From the middle of the 1960s, however, it was gradually transformed into an authoritarian one-party system, and till the change in the regime it remained a 'soft dictatorship' (Bihari 2005: 303). As Brunner (2000: 67) writes: 'In comparison with other countries in the Soviet sphere, in the 1960s and 1970s the authoritarian "Kádár system", which already showed elements of the rule of law, distinguished itself with an observable political and economic stability and a certain legitimacy.'

One of the guiding principles of the political consolidation, significant from our topic's perspective, was the so-called socialist form of the rule of law. This principle referred to a break-up and to a difference. It signified a break-up with the Hungary of the 1950s, characterized by a totalitarian dictatorship flouting the law and by the criminal sentencing of innocent people for political reasons. Compliance with the law and its observance, both from the state institutions and the citizens, became an emphatic political goal. The 'socialist' epithet was aimed to express the difference that while in capitalist societies the rule of law only serves the interests of the bourgeoisie, in socialism it serves the interests of both the ruling class, primarily the workpeople, and of the socialist society as a whole.

At the level of legislation, break-up meant that certain institutions of the Hungarian legal traditions before 1945, some solutions of the Western democracies and provisions reflecting the partial fulfilment of the obligations deriving from the country's UN membership were included in the Constitution of 1949, at its modification in 1972 and in the new codexes of criminal justice drawn up in the 1970s. With these, certain elements of the rule of law were present in the socialist criminal justice system.

There were positive consequences of the break-up with the unlawfulness of the 1950s from the point of view of human rights as well as negative consequences resulting from the above mentioned differences. Compared to the rule of law per se, the socialist rule of law meant not more, but less protection than the system of human rights guarantees developed in western societies. This is illustrated by the following solutions and provisions of the 1949 Constitution and the 1978 Penal Code.

The Constitution stated that the 'People's Republic of Hungary' respects human rights (Article 54.1) and contained certain human or, in the previous terminology, citizens' rights. The one-time socialist perception of the protection of human rights is best reflected by Article 54.2 of the text of the Constitution: 'In the People's Republic of Hungary the citizens' rights shall be exercised in accordance with the interests of the socialist society; exercising the rights is inseparable from the fulfilment of citizens' obligations.' The Constitution, however, did not contain guarantees for the protection of citizens' rights. The Constitution itself was a so-called paper or facade constitution that possessed little normative force and did not constrain those who the possessed power (Fleck 2003).

The Constitution, till its modification in 1989, did not contain the rule of law guarantees of the criminal justice (e.g. the principle of *nullum crimen sine lege*, the maxim of fair trial). Parts of these were contained in the Penal Code of 1978 and the Criminal Procedure Code of 1973. Due to the lack of guarantees in the Constitution, and the lack of institutions for the protection of human rights, the principles stated in the codes mentioned above did not ensure the functioning of criminal justice in accordance with the requirements of the rule of law.

Therefore, even though the Penal Code recognized the principles of legality and social dangerousness as an element of crime and as the reason for criminalization, the lack of constitutional limitations turned social dangerousness more into a pretence than into an actual limiting principle to the criminalization of an act. The requirement of proportionality and other human rights considerations did not prevail or only partially prevailed in criminalization. Freedom of speech and the right to privacy were disproportionately restricted by the offence of incitement, an offence against the state. Freedom of movement and the free choice of residence were violated by an offence which criminalized the unlawful crossing of the state frontier, and evasion of regulations of travel and staying abroad. The provisions on offences against the economy partly suspended the principle of equality before the law and partly denied the equal ranking and protection of public and private property. In the socialist era, offences against the economy served to protect only state property and disregarded the private sphere (Tóth 1995: 641). It qualified as a criminal offence if a person did not work for a longer period of time ('unwillingness to work). At the same time, the violations of freedom of religion and the misuse of personal data were not criminalized.

The presence of capital punishment among the punishments of the Penal Code also indicated that the simple declaration of human rights is not a sufficient condition for their emergence. The Constitution stated, though, that 'in the People's Republic of Hungary the citizens have the right to the protection of life, physical integrity and health' (Article 57.1). In the absence of rule of law guarantees of the right to life, however, the question of the constitutionality of capital punishment arose only in 1989.

From the previously mentioned elements, the conclusion may be drawn that in Hungary human rights aspects of criminalization and criminal justice prevailed much more in the period of 'soft dictatorship' than in the 1950s, but still we cannot perceive their real emergence. The socialist political system ensured only the selective possibility of the materialization of human rights (Kulcsár 1988).

7.2.2 Punishment

We must also evaluate the system of punishments and the sentencing practice differently. On the one hand it is true that it was significantly humanized by the Penal Code of 1978 compared with the previous periods. On the other hand, however, it was much stricter and more imprisonment-centred than the European constitutional democracies of the era. Table 7.1 contains the principal penalties before 1989 and in 2008.

TABLE 7.1 Comparative principal penalties of the Hungarian Penal Code in 1985 and 2008

1985	2008
Capital punishment	–
Imprisonment	Imprisonment
For life (eligibility for parole: serving a term at least 20 years)	For life (precluding any eligibility for parole or after serving a term of 20 or at least 30 years)
For a definite term: (i) General minimum: 3 months (ii) General maximum: 15 or 20 years	For a definite term: (i) General minimum: 2 months (ii) General maximum: 15 or 20 years
Reformatory and educative labour (i) Minimum: 6 months (ii) Maximum: 2 or 3 years	Community Service 1 day 50 days
Fine (day fine system) (i) Minimum: 10 days' item (ii) Maximum: 180 or 270 days' item (iii) Minimum of daily amount: 50 HUF (iv) Maximum of daily amount: 1,000 HUF	Fine (day fine system) 30 540 100 HUF (around 0.4 EUR) 20,000 HUF (around 800 EUR)

The theoretical grounds and the most important characteristics of the sanctioning system and sentencing provisions of the repeatedly modified Hungarian Penal Code of 1978 were left essentially unchanged until 2009.[1] These are the following:

- The sanctioning system is a dualist one: it contains penalties and measures. The penalties are divided into principal penalties and secondary ones.
- The Penal Code determines the purpose of penalty as the social interest of general prevention and special prevention (Article 37).
- The sanctioning system is relatively determined. The General Part of the Penal Code contains the general maximum and minimum of all types of penalties and measures. In the Special Part, each criminal offence is given a penalty range with the type of primary penalty or penalties applicable. If the offence is punishable with imprisonment, the penalty range always determines a special maximum, and in many cases a special minimum. Nonetheless, it is for the courts to take these minima and maxima into consideration, to decide on the sanction in a specific case, based upon the circumstances and its own conviction. The elements to be considered can be found in Article 83 'Principles of Infliction of Penalty' of the Penal Code: 'Remaining mindful of

its purpose (Section 37), punishment shall be inflicted within the framework defined by law in such a way that it be commensurate with the dangerousness of the crime and of the perpetrator to society, with the degree of culpability and with other aggravating and attenuating circumstances.'

There is a possibility not to apply the general minimum and maximum laid down in the General Provisions. For example, according to the already mentioned Article 83 of the Penal Code, if the court feels that the minimum sentence would be too rigorous, it may go under the minimum bearing in mind the relevant provisions of the Code. Further circumstances may relate to the level of participation of the offender and the level of completion of the offence. A more rigorous sentence than the special minimum can only be applied in the cases of special and multiple recidivists, organized crime and 'concurrent offences'.

- The Code provides the possibility under certain conditions of suspended and deferred sentencing, and also of conditional release.
- Special provisions apply to juveniles and members of the armed forces. These can be found in the relevant chapters of the Penal Code.

According to the ministerial explanatory notes, one of the substantial aims of establishing the Penal Code of 1978 was 'for the fight against crime … more efficient … tools to be given into the hands of the law enforcement and judicial agencies' (Penal Code 1979: 19). Therefore the main aspect of the establishment of the sanctioning system was expediency i.e. to serve the protection of society, general prevention and individual prevention. Imprisonment remained the core element of the system. The ministerial explanatory notes declared:

> Imprisonment, as the penalty having the strongest preventive effect, is needed. Imprisonment directly serves the protection of society through isolation of the perpetrator. Notwithstanding this security aspect, the correctional educational task of the punishment cannot be carried out without it. (Penal Code 1979: 79)

As a reaction to the contemporary professional criticisms with regard to the harmful effects of prison and the prison maleficence, the ministerial explanatory note stressed that 'the solution, however, is not to put aside the imprisonment from the punishments, but the establishment of such an enforcement system, which eliminates the prison malign influence or minimizes their harmful effects' (Penal Code 1979, 79).

Human rights considerations did not appear among the arguments and reasons with regard to the forming of the sanctioning system. The humanization of the sanctioning system of the Penal Code of 1978 was, however, a pronounced endeavour. Its most important realization was the expression of the exceptional characteristics of capital punishment and the aggravation of the conditions of its application. The lack of human rights approach in connection with punishments, however, is reflected in the following reasoning of the ministerial explanatory note, with regard to capital punishment:

> The justification of maintaining it may be considered primarily whether it is ignorable from the perspective of individual and general prevention. In case of the most severe crimes against life and state, military crimes, and internationally growing dimensions of terrorist acts, the protection of society, at the present, cannot spare the capital punishment. (Penal Code: 1978, 78)

Sentencing practice was also imprisonment-centred. Table 7.2 shows that in the 1980s 50 per cent of adult convicts were sentenced to imprisonment and a quarter were sentenced to unconditional imprisonment. From the perspective of duration, in 1980 almost 50 per cent of the imprisonments imposed was for up to six months, the proportion of imprisonments exceeding 1 year being 16.3 per cent. The proportion of imprisonments exceeding five years was 1.0 per cent. The proportion of the mentioned durations in 1988 were 30.9 per cent, 24.2 per cent and 1.9 per cent (Nagy 2001: 6).

Due to the sentencing practice of the 1980s, the prison population rate for 100,000 inhabitants was very high compared with the Western European countries: between 190 and 200.

In the indicated period we cannot talk about a change of penal policy. The main reason is that, as a result of the one-party system and the lack of free elections, there was no real change of government and hence no change in the penal policy in the period between the coming into force of the Penal Code of 1978 on 1 July 1979 and the change of the political system in 1989–90. Politicians responsible for penal policy, when making statements about sentencing practice, usually criticized the low-scale application of the then Soviet bloc countries' version of community service, Reformatory and Educative Labour. The essence of the punishment was that the convict was obliged to work at the workplace appointed by the court, which could be the workplace where he was in employment. From his wage, 5 per cent to 30 per cent, also determined by the court, had to be withdrawn. As may be seen from the data of Table 7.2, the criticism did not have any particular effect, which at the same time shows that in this period the independence of the judges in the course of sentencing fundamentally prevailed.

7.3 The growing importance of human rights in Hungary during and after the changes of regime

With the change of regime in 1989–90, the politically and culturally relatively closed former regime – which was based upon a one-party system, a planned economic with market economical elements, the hegemony of the Marxist-Leninist ideology, the limitation of human rights and membership in the Council of Mutual Economic Assistance (COMECON) and the Warsaw Pact – started

TABLE 7.2 Sentencing practice in Hungary, 1980–2006 – Adult convicts

Year	Convicts, total		Capital punishment	Imprisonment total*		Of which: suspended imprisonment		Of which: unconditional imprisonment		Community service		Fine		Other penalties and measures	
	Number	%	Number	Number	%	Number	%	Number	%	Number	%	Number	%	Number	%
1980	55,300	100	5	25,066	45.3	11,548	20.9	13,518	24.4	2,591	4.7	26,265	47.5	1,373	2.5
1985	54,851	100	2	26,477	48.3	11,780	21.5	14,697	26.8	2,684	4.9	21,079	38.4	4,608	8.4
1990	42,538	100	–	16,121	37.9	6.005	14.1	10,116	23.8	676	1.6	16,641	43.8	7,094	16.7
1995	77,029	100	–	22,969	29.8	13,682	17.76	9,287	12.05	869	1.1	38,442	49.9	14,749	19.14
2000	87,722	100	–	30,279	34.5	18,537	21.1	11,742	13.4	3,754	3.1	40,220	45.9	14,436	16.5
2003	86,722	100	–	29,744	34.2	18,449	21.1	11,295	13.02	3,794	4.3	39,110	45.9	15,074	16.2
2006	90,324	100	–	27,332	30.3	17,860	19.8	9,472	10.5	5,390	5.96	41,838	46.3	15,762	17.5

Sources: Statistical yearbooks of Hungary. Central Statistical Office, Budapest.
*Capital punishment was abolished in Hungary on 31 October 1990

transforming into a capitalist society based upon parliamentary democracy, a market economy, pluralism, the defence of human rights and membership of the political, economic and military organizations of the 'western countries'.

The amending of the Constitution was the most essential development concerning the transformation of the legal system and the change of regime itself.

In Hungary, the Constitution, originally passed by Act 20 of 1949, was fundamentally amended in 1989–90, taking into consideration joining the Council of Europe, the requirements of the rule of law, the ratification of the European Convention for the Protection of Human Rights and Fundamental Freedoms and certain Hungarian historical traditions.

The modification of the Constitution in 1989 (Act XXXI of 1989) 'declared in the Constitution the principles of parliamentary republic, independent, democratic constitutional state, the division of power, the national sovereignty, the multi-party system, the human rights and the rule of law' (Kukorelli and Takács 2007: 66).

As a tribute to the day of the outbreak of revolution in 1956, the modifying provisions came into force on 23 of October 1989. For our topic, the most important of these are as follows:

> *Art. 2(1)* The Republic of Hungary is an independent and democratic constitutional State under the rule of law.
>
> *Art. 8(1)* The Republic of Hungary recognizes inviolable and inalienable fundamental human rights. The respect and protection of these rights is a primary obligation of the State.
>
> *Art. 54(2)* No one shall be subject to torture or to cruel, inhuman or humiliating treatment or punishment. Under no circumstances shall anyone be subjected to medical or scientific experiments without his prior consent.
>
> *Art. 57(4)* No one shall be declared guilty and subjected to punishment for an offence that was not a criminal offence under Hungarian law at the time such offence was committed.

The democratization of the country, the modification of the Constitution, the establishment and operation of the Constitutional Court and the intention to join the Council of Europe and the European Union had an impact on the development of criminal law and penal policy (Snacken 2006: 148). The determining element of development was the emphasis it placed on the constitutional limitations of human rights and criminal law. It was acknowledged that, in a state governed by the rule of law, the state cannot be allowed unlimited power of punishment, as the authority of the state is itself limited (Szabó 2000: 8). This was expressed by the following provision, which became part of the Constitution in 1990: 'In the Republic of Hungary, the rules respecting fundamental rights and obligations shall be determined by Laws which, however, shall not limit the substantial contents of any fundamental right' (Article 8.2).

As a result of criminal legislation guided by human rights and respecting constitutional limits, the criminal law and especially the criminal procedure of the former regime, which was formed primarily upon social interest and the general defensive function of the state, changed significantly (Kulcsár 1989: 941–2).

Among the factors resulting in changes, joining the Council of Europe and, in its framework, the European Convention for the Protection of Human Rights and Fundamental Freedoms (henceforth referred to as ECHR) must be highlighted. Hungary signed the ECHR on 6 November 1990, which was, together with its eight Protocols, ratified by the Hungarian Parliament and entered into force in Hungary on 15 April 1993 as Act XXXI of 1993.

The ratification of the ECHR had an extremely significant impact on the development of the Hungarian legal system. The intent to conform to the Convention contributed towards transforming our socialist type of legal system into a western one in the areas of legislation, legal practice, law enforcement and legal culture. The most important achievements in the field of criminal justice are to be detected in the widening of the rights of the defendant, securing the guarantees of a fair trial, granting rights to inmates and humanizing prison conditions. Furthermore, imprisonment can only be a judicial decision, and should another authority be entitled on the grounds of special conditions (e.g. military service), the right to a court appeal must be ensured (Bán 1999; Bán and Bárd 1992).

The Hungarian Constitutional Court has also played and continues to play a significant part in the development of criminal justice and penal policy suitable to the requirements of the constitutional state. This will be examined in detail later in this paper.

7.4 Human rights and penal policy after the change of regime

In the almost two decades that passed following the change in the system, criminal justice legislation stressing the constitutional limitations of criminal law and aspects of human rights and the penal policy did not prevail with the same intensity. Like other countries with a multi-party constitutional democracy, the governments elected to power aimed at forming a penal policy in line with their own political considerations (Lévay 2007: 249–52). During this, at a different level for each government, citizens' expectations and public opinion engaged in the fight against crime. Two of the most significant factors in shaping penal policy are the constitutional limitations of criminal law and governments or political parties considerations. The proportion of these two factors considerably shape the overall characteristics of penal policy. In the following we will illustrate this, through evaluating the three most significant modifications of the Penal Code of 1978 since 1989–90.

After the change in regime, the first comprehensive reform of the Penal Code occurred in 1993 (Act XVII of 1993). The Bill, handed in to Parliament by the conservative, centre-right government, was in line with the new approach, which put to the fore human rights considerations and the limitations of the criminal law. The following extract from the Explanatory Notes of Act XVII of 1993 demonstrates this:

> The provisions of the Bill are guided by the principles and propositions of criminal policy that provide a basis for the total transformation of criminal law. Therefore, the Bill approaches to an even greater extent the principle of fair sentencing considering the gravity of offence. The Bill accepts the universally acknowledged theory that the intervention of criminal law must be limited rationally. Therefore, the circle of offences is narrowed down, as it does not wish to persecute those persons already more or less victims. (Criminal legislation 1993: 363–4)

Based on the approach cited, the reforms in 1993, *inter alia*, decriminalized prostitution, made 'treatment instead of punishment' possible for the first time in drug offences of lesser gravity, decreased the general statutory minimum of imprisonment from three months to one day, widened the options to apply alternative sanctions instead of custodial sentences, and abolished the exceptionality of moderation of statutory punishment.

Putting forward human rights in the reforms of 1993 is especially remarkable in light of the contemporary set of criminality. Compared with the period before the change in the system, the number of reported crimes doubled. In 1988, the year prior to the political changes in Hungary, the number of reported crimes was around 185,000, the rate of crime per 100,000 inhabitants was 1,748. After the change of regime in 1992, the number of reported crimes was about 447,000 and thus the rate was 4,326 (Kerezsi and Lévay 2008: 245–8). Following the reform of the Penal Code in 1993, sentencing practice also changed. As may be deduced from Table 7.2, the proportion of unconditional prison sentences dropped by half between 1990 and 1995. Half of the imposed sentences were fines. Against the background of the rise of other punishments and measures stands the more frequent application of release on parole as a non-custodial sanction. The prison population rate also decreased (see Table 7.3).

Based on these facts the reform of the Penal Code in 1993 may be considered, from the perspective of the development of the prison population, as a reductionist penal policy (Snacken 2006).

Reform of the Penal Code in 1998 was significant from an opposite direction. It took place after the parliamentary elections of 1998 and in the electoral campaign, for the first time since the change of the regime, fight against criminality was an issue. The leading party of the opposition promised, should they win, strict measures against the growing rate of criminality and, especially, against organized crime. Coming to government, it kept its promise.

Following the Bill from the newly elected centre-right conservative government, the reform of the Penal Code in 1998 made the sanctioning system more severe (Act LXXXVII of 1998). A life sentence without the possibility of parole was introduced for the first time in Hungarian criminal law. The general statutory minimum of imprisonment was raised to two months and judicial freedom of sentencing was limited. The latter aimed at restricting the imposition of suspended and short-term imprisonments along with the judge's discretion in sentencing.

It may be deduced from the new provisions mentioned that human rights standards with regard to punishments played a smaller role in 1998 than in 1993. The 'imprisonment as last resort' principle prevailed with limitations. It is arguable, moreover, whether life imprisonment without parole is compatible with the prohibition of cruel, inhuman or degrading punishment or not.

As a consequence of this expansionist policy (Snacken 2006), the rate of unconditional prison sentences grew again, while the rate of non-custodial sanctions decreased (see Table 7.2). The prison population and the prison population rate increased (see Table 7.3). While in 1998 the number of inmates was 14,366 and the prison population rate 140, in the year of the next elections, in 2002, it was 17,915 and 178, respectively (Kerezsi and Lévay 2008: 251–3). As a result, the prison occupancy level rose from 140 per cent in 1998/1999 to 160 per cent in 2002 (Kertész 2002: 22).

The governing parties lost the election in 2002. The Bill from the new, social democratic-liberal government for the reform of the Penal Code was approved by the Parliament in 2003 (Act II of 2003). It annulled most of the provisions of the 1998 reforms with regard to the stricter sanctions and the limitation of the judge's discretion in sentencing. The concept of the new reform 'does not agree with the ideas that formed the basis of the amendment of 1998, especially that of expecting the mechanical aggravation of statutory punishments to effectively diminish crime rates' (Explanatory Notes to Act II of 2003). The new provisions aim at decreasing unconditional imprisonment and reducing the prison population. But even the 2003 reform did not abolish actual life imprisonment, nor did it broaden the possibility of applying non-custodial sanctions. In terms of its consequences, the reform of 2003 may be classified as a reductionist policy. Compared with 2003 the prison population (2006: 14,821), the prison population rate (2006: 147) and the occupancy level (2006: 123.7) decreased. In terms of the sentences imposed the rate of unconditional imprisonment decreased while the rate of non-custodial sanctions increased significantly (see Table 7.2).

This review of the penal policy after the change of political regime shows that it is characterized by change, not by relative consistency, which was the peculiarity of the 'soft dictatorship'. One of the most significant explanatory factors of the contents of the changes is how much the shapers of the penal policy took into consideration human rights requirements regarding punishments, as set forth in the Constitution and in international human rights documents. From this perspective the most progressive period of the Hungarian penal policy was the first few years after the change in political system. It must be added, though, that the Hungarian sanctioning system has two characteristics that have remained virtually the same since 1989–90. One of these is that it is extremely imprisonment-centred, while the other is the shortage of non-custodial or alternative sanctions (Kerezsi 2001).

TABLE 7.3 Prison population* rates per 100,000 inhabitants in Hungary

Year	Prison population per 100,000 inhabitants
1988	193
1989	153
1990	122
1991	146
1992	153
1995	121
1998	140
2001	170
2002	178
2004	164
2006	147

*Including pre-trial detainees. Their proportion per year is 25 per cent.
Source: International Centre for Prison Studies (http://www.kcl.ac.uk/depsta/icps accessed 19 July 2008) and National Headquarters of Prison Administration, Budapest.

These two elements can be detected from the Special Part of the Penal Code. The most frequent type of statutory penalty for certain offences is imprisonment. There is no statutory offence in the Penal Code for which the penalty should be community service. Community service as a statutory penalty is always an alternative punishment to imprisonment or a fine. The fine is also primarily an alternative punishment to imprisonment or to community service. The fine can be found as an individual penalty in a small number of statutory offences. On the other hand, legislation and sentencing practice provide certain tools, e.g. diversion and the principle of unconditional imprisonment, as last resort respectively.

7.5 Decisions of the Hungarian Constitutional Court on Penalization and Criminalization

The Hungarian Constitutional Court (thereafter Constitutional Court) had an extremely significant effect on the development of the Hungarian criminal justice policy and the criminal law after the change in regime. As inserted by Article 32/A, the reformed Constitution of 1989 determined the tasks of this body as follows:

> Art. 32/A (1) The Constitutional Court shall review the constitutionality of laws and attend to the duties assigned to its jurisdiction by law.

(2)   The Constitutional Court shall annul any laws and other statutes that it finds to be unconstitutional.

The Constitutional Court started to function on 1 January 1990. Act XXXII of 1989 details the competences of the Constitutional Court consisting of 11 judges. From the aspect of this essay's topic, with regard to these competencies, it is worth emphasizing the posterior and preventive review of the unconstitutionality of statutes. Anyone may file a proposal for posterior review (*actio popularis*), regardless of whether or not the statute challenged concerns or infringes any of his fundamental rights. If in the course of the posterior review the Constitutional Court declares the legal regulation examined to be unconstitutional, it annuls its provisions. The Constitutional Court may not, however, review the Constitution and its modifying Acts. A proposal for preventive review may be filed solely by the President of the Republic, and concerns a review of the constitutionality of Acts already approved by the Parliament but not yet proclaimed. In the case of a declaration of unconstitutionality the Act is returned to the Parliament and the legislature is obliged to eliminate the unconstitutionality.

A permanent aspect of the evaluation of decisions of the Constitutional Court in the field of criminal law is whether or not the statute objected to complies with the requirements of 'constitutional criminal law'. The essence of this is that the criminal law norm, established in line with the principles of *nullum crimen sine lege* and *nulla poena sine lege*, is, in itself, not constitutional. The criminal law norm, established by the legislator, has to comply with the necessity-proportionality test applied by the Constitutional Court with regard to constitutional rights, principles and values.

András Szabó, judge of the Constitutional Court between 1990 and 1998 and specializing in criminal law cases, formulated the essence of 'constitutional criminal law' as follows:

> Deriving from the concept of constitutional criminal law, the principle of *nullum crimen, nulla poena sine lege* shall be reformulated as *nullum crimen, nulla poena sine lege constitutionale*. The Constitutional Court annulled several criminal law provisions due to unconstitutionality, and in the course of these it consistently applied the test of the limitation of fundamental rights, incorporated into the Constitution: criminal law intervention is permitted only in unavoidable cases, in the necessary degree and proportionally. (Szabó 2000: 18–19)

The Constitutional Court, therefore, controls the legislation with regard to criminalization and penalization.

In the following sections we will examine two decisions of the Constitutional Court in connection with criminalization and penalization.[2]

7.5.1 Decision of 23/1990 (X.31) AB on the abolition of the death penalty

The original version of the Penal Code of 1978 contained the death penalty as a punishment in the case of 26 felonies. These felonies included eight political offences, four offences against humanity, two offences against public order, eleven military offences and the offence of the qualified cases of premeditated homicide. However, the death penalty was rarely applied or carried out as a sentence in the 1980s: the highest number of death sentences was five in 1987. At the beginning of the change of regime, in early 1989, lawyers, social scientists, writers, journalists and representatives of several churches established the League against Capital Punishment. The aim of the League was to fight for the abolition of capital punishment with the means at its disposal, primarily through the strength of information and explanation. Soon the League counted more than 600 enthusiastic members, who propagated the aims of the League by means of individual and organized actions in various parts of the country (Horváth 1991: 154).

The steps towards the abolition of the death penalty were the following:

- After the amendment of the Constitution in 1989, the following two provisions were included: 'In the Republic of Hungary, everyone has the inherent right to life and human dignity, of which no one shall be arbitrarily deprived' (Article 54); 'No one shall be subjected to torture, to cruel, inhuman, degrading treatment or punishment ...' (Article 54(2)).
- In the spring of 1990, the leadership of the League decided 'because it seemed impossible for Parliament to deal with the issue of capital punishment at this time, to take the case before the Constitutional Court formed in the meantime, because the League believed capital punishment was irreconcilable with the principle of law expressed in Article 54 of the amended Constitution. Thereafter in April 1990, the League submitted its petition to the Constitutional Court and made a motion that the Constitutional Court declare capital punishment unconstitutional' (Horváth 1991).
- The Constitutional Court of the Republic of Hungary, in its Decision of 23/1990 (X.31), declared capital punishment unconstitutional and repealed all the statutory provisions concerning the infliction and execution of capital punishment.

The Constitutional Court, then counting nine members, decided to abolish capital punishment by a vote of 8 : 1. According to the minority opinion, the decision on the issue did not fall under the competence of the Constitutional Court but should be submitted to Parliament together with a summary of the arguments against capital punishment in order to solve the constitutional controversy. The Court did not base its decision on Article 54(1) of the Constitution already cited, but on Article 8(2). The Constitutional Court held that the provisions of the Penal Code and related regulations on capital punishment were contrary to the prohibition of limiting 'the substantial contents' of the fundamental right to life and human dignity. Namely, the regulations on capital punishment not only limited substantial contents of the right to life and human dignity, but represented its complete and irrecoverable nullification. According to the Constitutional Court the right to human life and human dignity is a fundamental right constituting a unity which is the source and precondition of several other fundamental rights. The rights to human life and human dignity as absolute values represent a limitation against the power of the state to punish.

It can be seen from the above-mentioned Article that the Hungarian solution for the abolition of the death penalty could not have been put through without the 1989–90 amendment of the Constitution. Even though Hungary had been part of international documents before 1989 which provided grounds for the abolition, such as the Universal Declaration of Human Rights and the International Covenant on Civil and Political Rights, due to the lack of elements of the rule of law and the constitutional limits of criminal law, the abolition of capital punishment was not possible based upon internal law. Consequently, the international documents embodying the requirements of the rule of law, even where they are part of internal law, can only serve as catalysts and not as guarantees of the democratic functioning of the state.

The abolition of the death penalty on 31 October 1990 meant that Hungary had fulfilled the requirements of the Sixth Supplementary Protocol to the ECHR concerning the prohibition of the death penalty, even before ratifying the Convention. Thanks to Act No. 3 of 2004, Protocol No. 13 to the ECHR concerning the abolition of the death penalty in all circumstances became part of the Hungarian legal system.

The abolition of the death penalty was attacked harshly by many and is criticized even today by some, justified by the sudden increase in crimes of murder by 50 per cent. Nonetheless, Table 7.4 shows that a decreasing tendency can be detected ever since. Examining the tendency, it can be stated that 'the abolition of capital punishment did not influence the frequency of murder crimes' (Horváth 2004: 123).

7.5.2 Decision of 1214/B/1990 AB on the rules of the Hungarian Penal Code on the special and multiple recidivists

In its decision 1214/B/1990, delivered in 1995, the Constitutional Court rejected proposals for the declaration of unconstitutionality of provisions of the Penal Code, such as rules in connection with the categories of 'recidivist', 'special recidivist' and 'multiple recidivist' (at the time of the Decision: Article 137, subsections 12–14 of the Penal Code), and a sentencing rule with regard to concurrent sentences (Penal Code Article 85, para. 3).

What was the essence of the provisions challenged by the proposal? Certain provisions of the General Part of the Penal Code allow for enforcing stricter rules in certain cases against a perpetrator qualifying as a recidivist. For example,

TABLE 7.4 Number of completed and attempted homicides ('murders') in Hungary, 1990-2006

Year	Completed	Attempted
1990	201	123
1991	307	143
1992	307	136
1993	298	178
1994	313	135
1995	280	120
1996	267	143
1997	281	142
1998	287	164
1999	250	172
2000	205	157
2001	254	157
2002	203	156
2003	228	150
2004	209	153
2005	164	149
2006	174	132

Sources: Horváth 2004: 123, and Yearbooks of Information on Crime 2003, 2004, 2005, 2006

in the case of a misdemeanour, the unconditional imprisonment imposed against a 'first-offender' shall be carried out in the most moderate regime, in jail, while it will be carried out in prison, a stricter regime, against a recidivist. In the case of a so-called special recidivist or multiple recidivist, based on the rules of the General Part of the Penal Code, the upper limit of the statutory penalty range defined for a certain crime in the Special Part increases by half. Therefore, for committing crimes of the same qualification, the judge may apply a longer term of imprisonment to the special recidivist and the multiple recidivist than to the perpetrator not qualifying as such. In the case of cumulative punishment, the General Part of the Code also provides for an increase in the upper limit of the statutory penalty range determined in the Special Part.

The petitioners basically claimed a breach of equality in law and equal treatment (Constitution Article 57, para. 1) in connection with the provisions challenged. In their view, the rules objected to 'reflect the retaliative approach of the perpetrator criminal law perception' (which means that the criminal history of the offender plays a more important role than the seriousness of the given offence) and express that 'people are not, in fact, equal in front of the courts'.

The starting point of the Constitutional Court's decision to dismiss was that the determination of the criminal law rules applicable against recidivists belongs to the competence of criminal policy.

> The Constitutional Court does not have the right to decide with its decision about the justness and reasons of the needs, requirements and goals determined by the penal policy, especially not about their expedience and effectiveness ... The Constitutional Court ... has the right to determine the constitutional limitations of the penal policy, but not to decide about its political content, and in the course of this it shall direct special attention to the constitutional criminal law guarantees of the protection of fundamental rights. (Reasoning: II.2)

During the examination conducted into the aforementioned aspect, the Constitutional Court stated that the solution of the Penal Code, according to which it threatens recidivists with stricter sanctions, is based on constitutional reasons and complies with the constitutional requirements of the criminal law limitations (Reasoning: II.4). In connection with the reasons and criteria, the Constitutional Court declared:

> The criminal law's constitutional guarantees do not exclude, but expressly make necessary the separate evaluation of criminal records in ensuring the legal order; in the normative system of criminal law at the time of determining the upper limit of a punishment the legislator remained in the framework of the proportionate sanctioning; and the normative regulations of sanctioning allow for imposing proportionate, deserved punishment. (Reasoning: II.5.)

In the Reasoning of the Decision, the Constitutional Court also stated that the more severe punishment may not be in conflict with Article 54.2 of the Constitution. 'The liability deepening proportionate punishment shall not be cruel, inhumane or degrading' (Reasoning: II.4.1).

Among the decisions of the Constitutional Court in the field of criminal law much more concerns the relationship of criminalization and human rights than the fundamental law questions of penalization and punishments. In the following we will introduce two of the decisions dealing with the constitutionality of criminalization.

7.5.3 Decision of 30/1992 (V.26) AB on the statutory criminal offence of Incitement against the Community (Art. 269 of the Penal Code)

The decision concerns the constitutional right of freedom of speech and furnishes an answer to where the limits of the freedom of expression may be drawn from a criminal law perspective, and, in a wider range, which are the constitutional requirements for the criminal law limitation of a fundamental right.

The petitioners asked for a declaration of unconstitutionality of the relevant statutory criminal offence of Article 269 of the Penal Code, namely Incitement against a Community. The statutory criminal offence challenged was as follows:

(1)   A person who, in front of a large public gathering, incites hatred
    (a)   against the Hungarian nation or any other nationality.
    (b)   against any people, religion or race, further against certain groups among the population, commits a felony and is to be punished by imprisonment for a period of up to three years.
(2)   Anyone who in front of a large public gathering uses an offensive or denigrating expression against the Hungarian nation, any other nationality, people, religion or race, or commits other similar acts, is to be punished for misdemeanour by imprisonment for up to one year, reformatory and educative labour or a fine.

The petitioners considered the statutory criminal offence unconstitutional basically because it punished behaviour which fell within the scope of the freedom of expression of opinion and freedom of the press under Article 61 of the Constitution and, furthermore, because it 'seems to contradict' Article 8 of the Constitution.

The Constitutional Court dismissed the petitions with regard to Article 269 (1). In the case of paragraph (2), however, it declared the provision unconstitutional and annulled the provision.

During the examination of paragraph (1) the Constitutional Court stated the following:

- To tolerate the exercise of the freedom of expression and freedom of press in a way prohibited under Article 269, paragraph (1) of HPC would contradict the requirements springing from the democratic rule of law.
- According to Article 54, paragraph (1) of the Constitution, everyone has an inherent right to human dignity. Accordingly, human dignity may restrict the freedom of expression.
- The restriction of the freedom of expression and the freedom of press is necessitated and justified by the negative historical experiences connected to raising hatred against certain groups of people, by the protection of constitutional values and by the obligation of the Republic of Hungary to comply with its commitments under international law.
- The first paragraph of Article 269 complies with the requirement of proportionality: it covers only the most dangerous conducts and can be unambiguously applied by the courts (Reasoning: IV).

The Court declared paragraph (2) of Article 269 unconstitutional; its initial approach had been based upon the Acts of Parliament restricting the use of an expression offensive to a national or religious community as generally contrary to the desired peace of society. Thus the statutory definition of a criminal offence amounts to an abstract protection of public order and peace as an end in itself. According to the Constitutional Court, such an abstract threat to public peace is not a sufficient justification for the use of the sanctions of the criminal law to restrict freedom of expression (Reasoning: V).

In connection with the examination of the concrete statutory penalty in this decision, the Constitutional Court set forth its opinion with regard to the social function of criminal law and its last resort nature.

> Criminal law is the last resort in the system of legal responsibility. Its social duty is to be a sanctional closure of the legal system. The criminal law sanction and punishment is to preserve the soundness of moral and legal norms when sanctions of other fields of law are no longer of assistance. It is a contextual requirement derived from constitutional criminal law for legislators not to act arbitrarily when defining the circle of punishable behaviour. When declaring a type of behaviour as punishable, one must employ severe standards: in defence of living conditions, legal and moral norms, the system of measures of criminal law, which must necessarily restrict human rights and liberties, should only be applied when absolutely crucial and proportionate, and the constitutional values and interests of state, society and economy cannot possibly be preserved otherwise. (Point IV.4 of the Reasoning of the Decision 30/1992 (V.26) AB)

7.5.4 Drug use and human rights based on the Decision of 54/2004 (XII. 13.) AB of the Constitutional Court of Hungary

At the end of the 1990s as well as around the year 2000, several petitions were filed at the Constitutional Court in which the petitioners asked for a constitutional review of the HPC's provisions on drug abuse. The Court merged the petitions and issued one decision about them in 2004. The parts of the over 100-page document that will be discussed below concern the criminalization of the use of drugs, the equal treatment with regard to narcotic substances and the depenalization provisions, which were introduced in 2003.

The petitioners, who doubted the constitutionality of the criminalization of the use of drugs and the cultivation and production of a small amount of drugs for personal use, argued that the provisions prohibiting the use of drugs violate the right to human dignity, which is declared in Article 54 of the Constitution and which contains the right to self-determination.

The Constitutional Court dismissed the petitions.

In its reasoning it started from the state's obligation to provide institutional protection, which is declared in Article 8(1) of the Constitution. ('The Republic of Hungary recognizes inviolable and inalienable fundamental human rights. The respect and protection of these rights is a primary obligation of the State.'). According to the opinion of the Court the criminalization of the possession of drugs for personal use is validated by the state's duty to protect human rights. According to the reasoning: 'For the purpose of protecting everyone's personal dignity the state is obliged to avert the dangers threatening its citizens, and to provide at least symptomatic or "palliative" care for those members of the society who cannot do so or who do so only to a limited extent, even if such incapability is the result of their own choice' (Reasoning: IV.2.2.). Henceforth, the Court states:

> The provisions of the HPC on the Abuse of Drugs are aimed at protecting the whole population from the negative effects of drugs, even if such protection involves the restriction of the individual's freedom of action or the potential application of criminal sanctions …. In the scope of special prevention, the restriction of the right to self-determination through means of criminal law cannot be regarded as either unnecessary or disproportionate, taking into account the high level of risks resulting from the uncertainty of the freedom of consumption. (Reasoning: IV. 3.3)

According to the Decision, the unlimited right to be high cannot be derived from Article 54, para. 1, not even indirectly. Based on all of the above, the Constitutional Court did not consider the criminalization of the use of drugs unconstitutional. According to the opinion of the Court, the criminalization of the possession of drugs for personal use enables the realization of the right to the highest possible level of physical and mental health in Article 70/D, Section 1 of the Constitution. (Article 70/D.1: 'Everyone living in the territory of the Republic of Hungary has the right to the highest possible level of physical and mental health.') The protection of human rights is in this case therefore not the limit but the reason for criminalization.

One of the petitions challenging the criminalization of the use of drugs considered a further aspect unconstitutional: namely the discriminative restriction of the right to personal freedom declared in Article 55, para. 1 of the Constitution. (Article 55.1: 'In the Republic of Hungary everyone has the right to freedom and personal security; no one shall be deprived of his freedom except on the grounds and in accordance with the procedure provided for by statute.') According to the petition, the state made an arbitrary decision when, without reasonably selecting among the narcotic substances, it prohibited under criminal law the use of certain substances while tolerating others, regardless of their harmful effects on health. The Constitutional Court dismissed this petition also. In its reasoning the Court argued that Article 70/A of the Constitution prohibits negative discrimination between persons of equal human dignity and not discrimination between various substances suitable for abnormal use. (Article 70/A.1: 'The Republic of Hungary shall ensure the human and civil rights for all persons on its territory without any kind of discrimination, such as on the basis of race, colour, gender, language, religion, political or other opinion, national or social origins, financial situation, birth or any other grounds whatsoever.') According to the Reasoning 'The fact that the rules of the HPC only apply limited consequences to the use of certain substances undoubtedly having harmful effects (e.g. alcohol) does not justify any claim for the liberalization of using other substances suitable for abnormal use' (Reasoning: IV.6.2). In addition, the Court stated that smoking and the consumption of caffeine or alcohol carry lower risks than the use of drugs.

Moreover, argued the Court, the European culture has become used to living together with alcohol, nicotine and coffee (Reasoning: IV. 6.2). Based on this the Court did not consider the selection between narcotic substances discriminative with regard to the right to personal freedom.

During the modification of the Penal Code in 2003 the possibility of 'treatment instead of punishment' was extended to the so-called social supply offences. For instance, the new legislation allowed a person who offers or hands over small amounts of illicit drugs to other people on the occasion of shared drug consumption to choose diversion to the previously mentioned treatment programme.

The new regulation also ensured this possibility in the case of a person not older than 21 who offered or handed over a small amount of drugs to someone, in the case of shared drugs consumption, at a school or in its immediate surroundings. These provisions practically depenalized the social supply offences.

The Constitutional Court followed the petitions challenging the rules broadening this depenalization and annulled them. The basis for this was, on the one hand, that certain wording of the regulations (e.g. 'shared consumption') were ambiguous, therefore violated the requirement of legal certainty, which is a basic criterion of the constitutional state. Accordingly, in the Court's opinion, the provisions concerned violated Article 2 (1) of the Constitution. (Article 2 (1): 'The Republic of Hungary shall be an independent, democratic state under the rule of law.')

A further basis for declaring the unconstitutionality of the depenalization provisions was that the new rules breach Article 16 and Article 7 (1) of the Constitution. Article 16 states the protection of the interests of young generations. (Article 16: 'The Republic of Hungary shall make special efforts to ensure a secure subsistence, education and the raising of the young, and shall protect the interests of the young.') Article 7 (1), in turn, declares that Hungary's legal system complies with the international law obligations undertaken. (Article 7.1: 'The legal system of the Republic of Hungary accepts the generally recognized rules of international law, and shall further ensure the harmony between domestic law and the obligations assumed under international law.') In the view of the Constitutional Court, the fact that the new regulation depenalized cases where a person under 18 is offered or given a small amount of drugs during shared consumption breaches the relevant provisions of the 1989 UN Convention on the Rights of the Child and the 1988 UN Convention Against Illicit Traffic in Narcotic Drugs and Psychotropic Substances. Hungary is a party to these conventions.

The decisions of the Constitutional Court introduced here illustrate that in the course of criminalization, penalization and depenalization the Hungarian Parliament has had to consider the requirements of constitutional criminal law. This includes a consideration of the provisions of the Constitution, of the human rights contained therein, of the international law obligations undertaken by Hungary, and the guarantees found in the criminal law and in criminal procedure law. In most of the respective decisions human rights prevail as constitutional limitations of penal policy. We may further find Constitutional Court decisions (e.g. 54/2004 (XII.13) in which aspects of the protection of society and ensuring the rights of others came to the front in the consideration of criminalization, penalization and depenalization.

7.6 Conclusion

Following this review of the development of criminal policy in Hungary and its relationship to human rights, the most important conclusion is that human rights may only have a real effect on the above mentioned policy and legislation procedures in a democracy, in a constitutional state. In Hungary we may speak of a criminal policy that has consistently taken human rights aspects into consideration since 1989–90. The Hungarian experiences show that human rights are vested with normative force and that the institutions established for their protection (e.g. the Constitutional Court) may be limiting factors to punitiveness. Similar limitations result from international human rights institutions, above all the European Convention of Human Rights and the decisions of the European Court of Human Rights, as well as the activities of the European Committee for the Prevention of Torture and Inhuman or Degrading Treatment or Punishment. At the same time, however, the influence of international documents (e.g. the recommendations of the Committee of Ministers of the Council of Europe) considered to be international 'soft law', urging the application of a rationalist, humanist criminal policy and non-custodial sanctions (Kerezsi 2001), is still low.

It may be seen from the overview of the Hungarian situation that human rights may not only be a bulwark against but also a motor of criminalization. More correctly, the protection of the rights of 'others', of the 'decent people', is frequently refered to in some of the more severe state measures against criminality. The experiences in Hungary of the development of criminality, penal policy and sentencing practice further strengthen the fact there is no correspondence between the trend and level of crime and the level of punitiveness. In Hungary before 1989–90, together with a rather low criminality rate – as in other ex-socialist countries – the imprisonment rate was high; in the first years after the change of regime, on the contrary, in spite of increasing criminality – also as in other regime changing countries (Krajewski 2004; Lévay 2005) – it decreased significantly.

Notes

1. The sanctioning system was reformed in 2009. According to the new rules the principal penalties are imprisonment, community service, fine, suspension of licence, suspension of driving privileges, expulsion. The secondary penalties are deprivation of basic rights, ban. The new rules of the reform came into force on 1 May 2010.
2. Since 21 April 2007 I have been a judge of the Constitutional Court, therefore I do not undertake to evaluate the decisions, only to introduce them.

References

Bán, T. (1999) 'Az Európa Tanács ötven éve: Magyarország tagságának hatása a magyar jogrendszer fejlödésére', *Acta Humana*, 35–6: 8–28.

Bán, T. and Bárd, K. (1992) 'Az Emberi Jogok Európai Egyezménye és a magyar jog', *Acta Humana*, 6–7.

Bárd, K. (2003) 'Az Európai Emberi Jogi Egyezmény szerepe az "európai" büntetöjog alakításában', *Büntetöjogi Kodifikáció*, 2: 3–12.

Bihari, M. (2005) *Magyar politika*. Budapest: Osiris.

Brunner, G. (2000) 'Structure and proceedings of the Hungarian Constitutional Judiciary', in L. Sólyom and G. Brunner, *Constitutional Judiciary in a New Democracy. The Hungarian Constitutional Court*. Ann Arbor, MI: The University of Michigan Press, pp. 65–102.

Büntetö jogszabályok (1993). Budapest: KJK.

Büntetö törvénykönyv (1979). Budapest: KJK.

Explanatory Notes to Act II of 2003 (2003) *Igazságügyi Közlöny*, 2.

Fleck, Z. (2003) *Szociológia jogászoknak*. Budapest: Napvilág.

Horváth, T. (1991) 'A halálbüntetés eltörlése Magyarországon', *Acta Juridica Hungarica*, 3–4: 153–66.

Horváth, T. (2004) 'Tizenhárom év halálbüntetés nélkül', *Belügyi Szemle*, 2–3: 118–32.

Kerezsi, K. (2001) 'Az alternatív szankciók helye és szerepe a büntetöjog szankciórendszerében', *Büntetöjogi Kodifikáció*, 2: 14–24.

Kerezsi, K. and Lévay, M. (2008) 'Criminology, crime and criminal justice in Hungary', *European Journal of Criminology*, 5(2): 239–60.

Kertész, I. (2002) 'Büntetöpolitika – Bönmegelözés', *Büntetöjogi Kodifikáció*, 4: 21–4.

Krajewski, K. (2004) 'Transformation and crime control. Towards exclusive societies Central and Eastern European style?', in K. Gönczöl and M. Lévay (eds). *New Tendencies in Crime, Changes in Criminal Policy in Central and Eastern Europe*. Miskolc: Bibor Kiadó, pp. 19–29.

Kukorelli, I. and Takács, I. (2007) 'A magyar alkotmány története. Az alkotmányos rendszerváltás jellemzöi', in I. Kukorelli (ed.), *Alkotmánytan I*. Budapest: Osiris, pp. 53–77.

Kulcsár, K. (1988) 'Emberi jogok: deklarációk és valóság', in M. S. Katonáné (ed.), *Emberi jogok hazánkban*. Budapest: ELTE JOTOKI Kutató Csoport, pp. 7–20.

Kulcsár, K. (1989) 'A Büntetö Törvénykönyv és a Büntetö eljárás módosításáról', *Magyar Jog*, 11: 941–52.

Lévay, M. (2005) 'Imprisonment patterns in Central and Eastern Europe', *Criminology in Europe*, 4(3): 3, 13–15.

Lévay, M. (2007) 'Changes in the social function of criminal law in Hungary from 1985 to 2005', in A. Jakab, P. Takács and A. Tatham (eds), *The Transformation of the Hungarian Legal Order 1985–2005*. AH Alphen aan den Rijn, Netherlands: Kluwer Law International, pp. 238–52.

Nagy, F. (2001) 'A büntetöjogi szankciórendszer reformja. Büntetések és intézkedések az új büntetö törvénykönyvben', *Büntetöjogi Kodifikáció*, 2: 3–13.

Sólyom, L. and Brunner, G. (2000) *Constitutional Judiciary in a New Democracy. The Hungarian Constitutional Court*. Ann Arbor, MI: University of Michigan Press.

Snacken, S. (2006) 'A reductionist penal policy and European human rights standards', *European Journal of Criminal Policy and Research*, 12: 143–64.

Szabó, A. (2000) *Jogállami forradalom és a büntetöjog alkotmányos legitimitása*. Budapest: Aquinas Alapítvány.

Tóth, M. (1995) 'Piacgazdaság és büntetöjog', *Magyar Jog*, 11: 641–6.

8

HUMAN RIGHTS AS THE GOOD AND THE BAD CONSCIENCE OF CRIMINAL LAW

Françoise Tulkens[1]

8.1 Introduction

The question that runs through the whole problem discussed in the second part of this work, focusing on human rights, is, as far as I am concerned, a truly existential question. What role can fundamental rights, and in particular those laid down in the European Convention on Human Rights, play in the face of the build-up of the 'penal state' we are witnessing today, admittedly with different undertones, on both sides of the Atlantic?

As has already been observed, if we monitor the evolution of the recent case law of the European Court of Human Rights, we clearly perceive the *profound impact* of the extension of positive obligations and the horizontal application of human rights on general human rights theory (Tulkens and Van Drooghenbroeck 2003: 211 and f.). Rights and freedoms, which used to be conceived of solely as acting as a brake on the state's power and the limits of punitive action, can appear today, and in parallel, as the drivers of intervention and justification for the deployment by states of their power of punitive action. Such dialectic can probably appear relatively self-evident because it underpins the doctrine of the social contract. The novelty resides, however, in the fact that these two dimensions of rights and freedoms are today subject to legal obligations on states and may be enforced in court. There is a duality – the obligation to protect v. the obligation to respect human rights – which in my opinion must be stressed. Human rights can constitute both the good conscience and the bad conscience of criminal law, in the sense that they may both *legitimize* criminal law by giving a good conscience to punitive logic and *limit* criminal law by giving a bad conscience to its intervention (Tulkens and van de Kerchove 2005: 950).

8.2 The offensive role of human rights

'Punishment to protect human rights!' This slogan sums up perfectly the growing offensive role of human rights, of which there is no lack of examples (see Chapter 6 this volume). Is it nevertheless possible to maintain, as some suggest, that the European Court, by expanding national obligations to make use of criminal law, has become a 'machine that encourages criminal inflation' (Cartuyvels 2007: 319)? While it is true, as some observe, that the Court sometimes gives in to the questionable charm of more severe criminalization, the reality is more complex. Let's be perfectly clear, however: our aim here is not to defend the way the Court acts or reacts. Instead, we wish to try to understand the reasons that lead it to prefer, in certain cases, criminal-law remedies, and consequently the meaning it gives to that solution. On the one hand, it is important to avoid likening this to a plea for criminal law and over-criminalization. On the other hand, without intending to underestimate the build-up of the penal state being observed also in the Court, in some cases it may consider that the use of criminal law is necessary for other reasons or arguments than a quest for hard-line criminalization.

8.2.1 Significant examples

By analysing certain recent rulings where the Court does not hesitate to use – some might say to exploit – criminal law with a view to reinforcing and guaranteeing more effectively the rights of victims of violations of fundamental rights, we observe that the Court is always confronted with extreme and exceptional situations that make critical arguments on over-criminalization difficult to consider really relevant. This is an obstacle I have often encountered. The situations have so far all come within Article 2 (right to life) or Article 3 (prohibition of torture and inhuman or degrading treatment or punishment) of the Convention. As the report by Professor Lévay demonstrates in Chapter 7 (this volume), the debate on criminalization vs. decriminalization also stems from historic circumstances or social situations.

8.2.2 Positive material obligations

For example, in the field of positive material obligations, i.e. when the Court finds that criminal legislation is necessary to protect fundamental rights, it should be recalled that it was the judgment in *X. and Y.* v. *Netherlands* of 26 March 1985 that first determined that use of criminal law was required to the extent that civil damages were not sufficient relative to the fundamental values involved. The case in point involved the possibility for a *young mentally disabled woman* to pursue at law claims of acts of mistreatment and sexual abuse of which she was victim. In *M.C.* v. *Bulgaria* of 4 December 2003, the Court reacted to the impossibility for *young rape victims* to pursue their complaint at law, particularly due to the requirement of proof of the absence of consent. The case of *Siliadin* v. *France* of

26 July 2005 concerned a 15-year-old Togolese girl who had been employed as a domestic in conditions of *servitude* and whose employers were acquitted in the absence of any legal channels. It is in this context that the Court has made it clear that the states have the positive obligation to adopt criminal legislation making the practices prohibited by Article 4 of the Convention punishable offences.

In the debate that leads the Court to rule in support of the necessity of criminal liability, there often comes into play the idea that criminal law must protect the fundamental rights of the weakest and most vulnerable. It is very difficult in such a context not only to advance but especially to make it understood, in the Court, that criminal law does not necessarily constitute the only solution, that criminal intervention should remain, in theory and in practice, a final remedy – but is that not precisely the case? Above all, the effectiveness, particularly in terms of prevention, attributed to criminal law is a far cry from the reality. In many cases, the 'inhuman' carries a lot of weight and obliges the Court to provide an adequate response.

8.2.3 Positive procedural obligations

In the area of positive procedural obligations, i.e. where the Court establishes a finding of infringement on the absence of criminal proceedings, *exceptional circumstances* obviously also play a crucial role, as seen in the judgment in *Assenov and others* v. *Bulgaria* of 28 October 1998, which was the first to open up this path. This role has grown further in situations of massive violations of fundamental rights. For example, in the *Khashiyev and Akayeva* v. *Russia* judgment of 24 February 2005, which concerns extra-judicial executions in Chechnya, the Court points out that the state's obligations pursuant to Article 2 cannot be met simply by granting compensation; the investigation required by this provision must therefore be 'able to lead to the identification and punishment of those responsible' (para. 153). The same holds for the judgment in *Isayeva* v. *Russia* of the same date, which concerns the firing of missiles in the humanitarian corridor (para. 228). In addition, in these rulings, the Court confirms that 'a civil action is incapable, without the benefit of the conclusions of a criminal investigation, of making any meaningful findings as to the perpetrators of fatal assaults, and still less to establish their responsibility' (*Khashiyev and Akayeva* v. *Russia*, para. 121; *Isayeva* v. *Russia*, para. 157). In other words, criminal proceedings would be the most appropriate, in particular to meet the procedural requirements of Article 2 of the Convention.

The *Öneryıldız* v. *Turkey* judgment of 30 November 2004 is in keeping with this approach. The criterion of the *seriousness of the offence* and of the *damage* caused appears to come into play here. In the case in point, the offence established is that of two mayors who should have known, based on an expert report, that a rubbish tip involved high risks, but who nevertheless failed to take any measures to prevent such an accident. In this context, the Court pointed out that in cases of homicide the interpretation of Article 2 as entailing an obligation to conduct an official investigation is justified not only because any allegations of such an offence normally give rise to criminal liability […], but also because often, in practice, the true circumstances of the death are, or may be, largely confined within the knowledge of state officials or authorities […]. In the Court's view, such considerations are indisputably valid in the context of dangerous activities, when lives have been lost as a result of events occurring under the responsibility of the public authorities, which are often the only entities to have sufficient relevant knowledge to identify and establish the complex phenomena that might have caused such incidents. Where it is established that the negligence attributable to State officials or bodies on that account goes beyond an error of judgment or carelessness, in that the authorities in question, fully realising the likely consequences and disregarding the powers vested in them, failed to take measures that were necessary and sufficient to avert the risks inherent in a dangerous activity […], the fact that those responsible for endangering life have not been charged with a criminal offence may amount to a violation of Article 2, irrespective of any other types of remedy which individuals may exercise on their own initiative. (para. 93)

We should note, even though for some this may seem derisory, that the Court does not state that the absence of criminal charges and criminal proceeding amounts to a violation of Article 2 but simply holds that it 'may' amount to such a violation. In my opinion, this nuance is fundamental.

In addition to exceptional circumstances and the seriousness of the offence come other necessities, such as *combating impunity* and *avoiding abuse of power*. It is significant to note that almost all the cases in which the Court finds that a criminal investigation is necessary to that end concern cases of police violence during custody or detention.

For example, in the *Krastanov* v. *Bulgaria* judgment of 30 September 2004, the Court held that if the authorities could confine their reactions to incidents of intentional police ill-treatment to the mere payment of compensation, while remaining passive in the prosecution of those responsible, it would be possible in some cases for agents of the State to abuse the rights of those within their control with virtual impunity. Accordingly, the payment of compensation in the framework of a civil procedure founded on the state's liability does not suffice to deprive the applicant of the status of victim within the meaning of Article 34 of the Convention (paras 48–60).

The *Bekos and Koutropoulos* v. *Greece* judgment of 13 December 2005 concerns police brutality against persons in detention. In this case, the Court held that, in spite of the fact that it was recognized that the applicants were particularly brutalized while in police custody, no police officer was ever punished, either through criminal proceedings or disciplinary procedure. The Court observed that the fine of less than 59 euros imposed on the police officer was ordered not on the grounds of ill-treatment but for his failure to prevent the occurrence of ill-treatment by his subordinates. In addition, neither the head nor the subordinate were at any time suspended from service, in spite of the recommendation of the report on the findings of the administrative inquiry. It is in this context that the Court points out that the investigation must be capable of leading to the identification and punishment of those responsible: 'Otherwise, the general legal prohibition of torture and inhuman and degrading treatment and punishment would, despite its fundamental importance, be ineffective in practice and it would be possible in some cases for agents of the State to abuse the rights of those within their control with virtual impunity' (para. 53). In fact, the Court uses the criterion of proportionality but inversely, not to restrict the sentence, but to expand it.

The *Okkali v. Turkey* judgment of 17 October 2006 may be even more significant. The applicant was 12 years old at the material time. Suspected of theft by his employer, he was taken to the police station where he was interrogated particularly forcefully and beaten violently by his interrogators. Applying the notion of a 'qualified' confession – when the person confessing to the offence simultaneously invokes circumstances that may be considered to exonerate or mitigate his guilt – the policemen were given minimum sentences and the administrative channel of compensation was rejected due to *prescription*. The Court notes, as a general principle, that 'the domestic judicial authorities must on no account be prepared to let the physical or psychological suffering inflicted go unpunished. This is essential for maintaining the public's confidence in, and support for, the rule of law and for preventing any appearance of the authorities' tolerance of or collusion in unlawful acts' (para. 65). There is obviously something very Durkheimian in this position. In the sociologist's opinion, the function of sentences is not directly utilitarian: 'They do not serve or only very secondarily to correct the guilty party or to intimidate possible imitators; from this dual point of view, their effectiveness is doubtful and, in any case, mediocre.' On the other hand, the function of sentences is essentially symbolic in nature, namely to 'maintain social cohesion intact by maintaining the vitality of the common conscience' (Durkheim 1973: 76).[2] It must 'be affirmed vigorously at the time it is contradicted … This is the sign attesting that collective feelings are still collective, that the communion of spirits in the same faith remains intact and that it consequently repairs the evil that the crime has done to society' (Durkheim 1973: 77).[3]

In addition, following the *Okkali* v. *Turkey* judgment of 17 October 2006:

> in the light of the Court's case-law according to which children, who are particularly vulnerable to various forms of violence, are entitled to State protection, in the form of effective deterrence, against such serious breaches of personal integrity, the authorities could have been expected to lend a certain weight to the question of the applicant's vulnerability. The Court observes, however, that not only was concern to give extra protection to the minor in question sorely lacking throughout the proceedings, but

the impunity which ensued was enough to shed doubt on the ability of the judicial machinery set in motion in this case to produce a sufficiently deterrent effect to protect anybody, minor or otherwise, from breaches of the absolute prohibition enshrined in Article 3. (para. 70).

Lastly, the 'Court reaffirms that when an agent of the State is accused of crimes that violate Article 3, the criminal proceedings and sentencing must not be *time-barred* and the granting of an *amnesty* or a *pardon* should not be permissible' (para. 76).

In this case, as in others (*Abdulsamet Yaman* v. *Turkey* judgment of 2 November 2004 and *Yazici* v. *Turkey* judgment of 5 December 2006), the Court identifies *obstacles to prosecution and sentencing* as particularly preoccupying. The grant of amnesty or pardon appears unacceptable in the case of the absolute prohibition of torture and inhuman or degrading treatment, which in all countries comes under *jus cogens* (*peremptory norms*), which are imperative norms of general international law, respect for which is more imperious than respect for mandatory norms.[4]

Lastly, in the *Giuliani* v. *Italy* admissibility decision of 12 March 2007[5], we see a similar reasoning but in another procedural context, that of *exhaustion of domestic remedies*. The recognition of positive procedural obligations requiring states to commence criminal prosecution, in response to the requirements of Articles 2 and 3 of the Convention, therefore produces certain *effects*. The Giuliani application concerned the death of the son of the applicants, Carlo Giuliani, age 23, during his participation in an anti-globalization demonstration at the G8 Summit held in Genoa in 2001. The applicants maintained that their son was killed by law enforcement officials and that the authorities neither protected his life nor conducted a real investigation into his death. The government pleaded an exception of non-exhaustion of domestic remedies on the ground that the applicants did not bring a civil action.

> Even supposing the existence of such a remedy, permitting the applicants to prove the State's responsibility in the death of Carlo Giuliani, the Court finds that, in the particular circumstances of the instant case, it would be unreasonable to ask the applicants to avail themselves of the said remedy and to await its outcome before examining the substance of the case. Concerning the procedural aspect, the Court points out that the State's obligations under Article 35.1 of the Convention may not be met by mere payment of compensation when death was inflicted by the State's security forces. The investigation required by Articles 2 and 13 of the Convention must be such as to lead to the identification and punishment of those responsible. By virtue of that fact, the civil procedures aimed at obtaining compensation and, if need be, vindictive damages, may not be taken into account in the review of the State's compliance with procedural obligations under Article 2 of the Convention. (para. 43).

The *Çamdereli* v. *Turkey* judgment of 17 July 2008 concerns the applicant's status as *victim*. The applicant maintained that she had been beaten by gendarmes. The government argued that the applicant had lost her status as victim, within the meaning of Article 35 of the Convention, because she had obtained compensation from a civil court. The Court rejected that argument after developing the following reasoning (paras 26–30):

26. As regards the Government's objection regarding the victim status of the applicant, the Court reiterates that an applicant is deprived of his or her status as a victim if the national authorities have acknowledged, either expressly or in substance, and then afforded appropriate and sufficient redress for, a breach of the Convention (see, for example, *Scordino* v. *Italy (no. 1)* [GC], no. 36813/97, §§ 178–193, ECHR 2006–...).

27. As regards the first condition, namely the acknowledgment of a violation of the Convention, the Court considers that the civil court's decision to order Mr T.Ü. to pay compensation to the applicant for having beaten her at the gendarmerie station [...] does amount to an acknowledgment in substance that there had been a breach of Article 3 of the Convention.

28. With regard to the second condition, namely appropriate and sufficient redress, the Court will have to consider whether the compensation awarded to the applicant remedied her complaints under Article 3 of the Convention. In this connection, the Court takes note that, even assuming that the modest compensation awarded to the applicant by the domestic court, after the Court of Cassation had already twice remitted the case back to it due to the low amount decided, could be deemed sufficient, the focal point of applicant's complaints, as laid down in the application form, concerns the inadequacy of the criminal proceedings, resulting in impunity for the person responsible for her ill-treatment. Consequently, the applicant's complaints, as laid down in the application form, concern matters which must be addressed from the angle of the adequacy of the mechanisms in place in order to maintain the deterrent power of the judicial system and the important role it plays in upholding the prohibition of torture [...].

29. In such cases, the Court considers that the breach of Article 3 cannot be remedied exclusively by an award of compensation to the victim. This is so because, if the authorities could confine their reaction to incidents of wilful police ill-treatment to the mere payment of compensation, while not doing enough in the prosecution and punishment of those responsible, it would be possible in some cases for agents of the State to abuse the rights of those within their control with virtual impunity and the general legal prohibitions of torture and inhuman and degrading treatment, despite their fundamental importance, would be ineffective in practice. Therefore, the possibility of seeking and receiving

compensation represents, in these cases, only one part of the measures necessary to provide redress for wilful ill-treatment by State agents (see, *mutatis mutantis, Nikolova and Velichkova* v. *Bulgaria*, no. 7888/03, §§ 55–56, 20 December 2007).

30. Consequently, the Court must ascertain whether the measures taken by the authorities, in the particular circumstances of the instant case, afforded the applicant appropriate redress in order to determine whether she can still claim to be a victim. As the Government's objection under this head is closely linked to the merits of the applicant's complaints, the Court decides to join them.

8.2.4 How to maintain a critical position?

In this set of problems, how can we assert a critical and legitimately critical position with regard to the use of criminal proceedings? Max Weber's famous distinction between the ethics of conviction and the ethics of responsibility applies here. On the one hand, the Court's rulings must respond to strong concerns and ceaselessly ensure the development of the rights and freedoms guaranteed by the Convention. This is the 'ethics of conviction' side. On the other, our rulings must also be enforced not only in the country in question (authority of *res judicata*) but also in the other Council of Europe member countries as guiding principles (interpretative authority). With our judgments we must make the States progress and ensure that the rights under the Convention have meaning for them. This is the 'ethics of responsibility' side.

Personally, my strategy is first of all not to deny blindly the reality of the tragic or even revolting nature of the situations submitted to us. It is important to remain credible, otherwise evolution is completely blocked. At the same time, however, it is necessary to point out as clearly as possible the limits of criminal law, to try to make clear the weakness of the use of criminal law and deconstruct the idealized image of criminal law held by some of the Court's judges, coming from other horizons, who often attach a great deal of importance to the symbolic aspect of criminal law. A passage from the partially dissenting opinion of Judge Rozakis *et al.* joined to the *Calvelli and Ciglio* v. *Italy* judgment of 17 January 2002 seems highly significant in this respect:

> Indeed, it is difficult to accept that respect for the right to life, as provided for by Article 2, can, in principle, be satisfied by proceedings, which by their nature, are not designed to protect the fundamental values of society, to show public disapproval of the taking of life or – on the other side of the coin – to establish any liability through a thorough examination of the circumstances which led to the death. Criminal proceedings contain exactly these safeguards. While, in contrast, civil proceedings are basically intended to satisfy private interests, material aspects of human transactions, they do not satisfy the requirement of expressing public disapproval of a serious offence, such as the taking of life, and do not usually guarantee a complete

and exhaustive investigation into the cause of death, and the full factual background. Under these circumstances, considering civil proceedings as a satisfactory means of recourse satisfying the requirements of Article 2 amounts to a debasement of the protection of the right to life provided for by this Article; it amounts to a 'privatization' of the protection of the right to life.

It is also important to show – but without offending – the contradiction or even the incoherence that obviously exists between the confidence expressed in criminal law in certain cases and the mistrust of the Court – sometimes the same judges – in criminal law in other cases. It is indeed sometimes discouraging to see how little impact theoretical analyses have on practices. How can the gulf between them be bridged?

Furthermore, it is essential in my opinion that this type of movement does not develop and spread to other situations that are less straightforward, which implies the need for constant vigilance. As things stand at present, this attempt of restriction may occur in two directions.

The first is based on the distinction made by the Court between criminal-law and civil-law remedies depending on whether homicide is intentional or the result of negligence or lack of caution. Is this distinction relevant? Is it sufficient? We will certainly have to discuss it. The Court has applied this distinction in the area of medical negligence.

For example, in *Calvelli and Ciglio* v. *Italy*, of 17 January 2002, the Court held:

> If the infringement of the right to life or to personal integrity is not caused intentionally, the positive obligation imposed by Article 2 to set up an effective judicial system does not necessarily require the provision of a criminal-law remedy. In the specific sphere of medical negligence, the obligation may for instance also be satisfied if the legal system affords victims a remedy in the civil courts, either alone or in conjunction with a remedy in the criminal courts, enabling any liability of the doctors concerned to be established and any appropriate civil redress, such as an order for damages and for the publication of the decision, to be obtained. Disciplinary measures may also be envisaged. (para. 51)

In the *Vo* v. *France* judgment of 8 July 2004 – where the confusion between two women resulted in the death of the child carried by one of them – the Court also held:

> In the circumstances of the case an action for damages in the administrative courts could be regarded as an effective remedy that was available to the applicant. Such an action, which she failed to use, would have enabled her to prove the medical negligence she alleged and to obtain full redress for

the damage resulting from the doctor's negligence, and there was therefore no need to institute criminal proceedings in the instant case. (para. 94)

The Court repeated this position in *Öneryıldız* v. *Turkey* of 30 November 2004 (paras 72–74): it has 'held that if the infringement of the right to life or to personal integrity is not caused intentionally, the positive obligation to set up an effective judicial system does not necessarily require criminal proceedings to be brought in every case and may be satisfied if civil, administrative or even disciplinary remedies were available to the victims'.

The judgment in *Byrzykowski* v. *Poland* of 27 September 2006 (paras 104–5) confirms the same principle with regard to the absence of an effective and swift inquiry into the death of the applicant's spouse and the serious injury caused to his son's health following a delivery by caesarean section.

> Although the right to have third parties prosecuted or sentenced for a criminal offence cannot be asserted independently (see *Perez* v. *France* [GC], judgment of 12 February 2004, para. 70), the Court has held on a number of occasions that an effective judicial system, as required by Article 2, may, and under certain circumstances must, include recourse to the criminal law. However, if the infringement of the right to life or to personal integrity is not caused intentionally, the positive obligation imposed by Article 2 to set up an effective judicial system does not necessarily require the provision of a criminal-law remedy in every case. In the specific sphere of medical negligence the obligation may for instance also be satisfied if the legal system affords victims a remedy in the civil courts, either alone or in conjunction with a remedy in the criminal courts, enabling any liability of the doctors concerned to be established and any appropriate civil redress, such as an order for damages and for the publication of the decision, to be obtained. Disciplinary measures may also be envisaged. However, the obligations of the State under Article 2 of the Convention will not be satisfied if the protection afforded by domestic law exists only in theory: above all, it must also operate effectively in practice within a time-span such that the courts can complete their examination of the merits of each individual case.

The other direction can be suggested by the problem of terrorism, which, as shown very clearly in the report by Dumortier *et al.* (see Chapter 6 this volume), has become a 'turbo' for criminalization. In a recent thesis on terrorism and the limitation of rights in the light of the European Convention on Human Rights and the Constitution of the United States, Stefan Sottiaux (2008) raises the question of the paradoxical relations between terrorism and human rights. On the one hand, terrorism is a threat to the enjoyment of fundamental rights and consequently represents a flagrant violation of such rights. On the other, however, the fight against terrorism can also erode an important number of guaranteed rights and freedoms. The States are therefore confronted with a dual responsibility.

On the one hand, they must protect human rights by combating terrorism effectively; on the other, they must respect human rights in their implementation of counter-terrorism measures. Are both obligations on the same footing? De Schutter (2002: 92–3) does not think so.

> The concept of 'balance' suggests equivalence between these notions. Legally, however, this equivalence does not occur […]. The obligation of *protection* does not apply to the point of compelling the State to infringe its obligation to *respect* the rights of these persons since, on the contrary, the first obligation finds its limit in the second. […]. It is precisely a presumption favourable to the obligation of respect that is introduced by the Convention: the State must *respect* the rights and freedoms recognised in the Convention, and it is only on a subsidiary basis, to the extent that doing so remains compatible with the obligation of respect, that it is also obliged to *protect* the persons under its jurisdiction from violations of their rights that other private persons could try to cause.[6]

The *Saadi* v. *Italy* judgment of 28 February 2008, which concerns the expulsion of a presumed terrorist to Tunisia where he risked torture or inhuman or degrading treatment, is a perfect illustration of this problem and also reflects, clearly and without hesitation, the absolute limit set by the Court on security requirements. The Court observes 'that States face immense difficulties in modern times in protecting their communities from terrorist violence. […] It cannot therefore underestimate the scale of the danger of terrorism today and the threat it presents to the community. That must not, however, call into question the absolute nature of Article 3' (para. 137). Accordingly

> Since protection against the treatment prohibited by Article 3 is absolute, that provision imposes an obligation not to extradite or expel any person who, in the receiving country, would run the real risk of being subjected to such treatment. As the Court has repeatedly held, there can be no derogation from that rule […]. In that connection, the conduct of the person concerned, however undesirable or dangerous, cannot be taken into account. (para. 138)

Lastly, another – more institutional – approach that some understandably suggest is to point out insistently that by imposing on states the obligation to criminalize certain infringements of fundamental rights, the Court risks pre-empting the role of the national legislator. Similarly, when it imposes prosecution, it can undermine the principle of discretionary prosecution that exists in many member states.

8.3 The defensive role of human rights

In spite of the offensive role that is developing, the defensive role of human rights continues to be exercised tirelessly, in different directions. In my opinion, it is also a response or a limit to the extension of the offensive role of human rights in the criminal sphere. It requires ceaseless vigilance.

8.3.1 Two sides

The *McBride* v. *United Kingdom* judgment of 9 May 2005 is a significant example to the extent that it represents the *reverse side* of the movement towards increased criminalization that I have just discussed. The applicant was the mother of a young man who was shot dead by two soldiers of the British army. The soldiers were prosecuted for murder and sentenced to life imprisonment. They spent six years in prison. Upon their release, the army commission, instead of discharging them, authorized them to rejoin their unit. There is no disputing the fact that an investigation meeting the requirements of the Convention took place with regard to the death of the applicant's son: the two soldiers who fired the fatal shots were prosecuted and found guilty of murder. The mere fact that the soldiers were authorized to rejoin their units after six years in prison cannot be considered a flagrant rejection of the criminal sentence against them or a cynical and retroactive approval of their conduct, which could be considered to be such as to jeopardize the effectiveness of an earlier criminal procedure intended to punish and be dissuasive. As for the applicant's argument of the future protection of citizens, the risk appears hypothetical and has no impact on the rights of the interested party.

8.3.2 Freedom of expression and the principle of proportionality

With regard to criminalization and recourse to criminal proceedings, I find particularly interesting the observations of Professor Lévay (Chapter 7 this volume), who discusses a significant debate within the Hungarian Constitutional Court on freedom of expression. Decision 30/1992 of the Constitutional Court concerning Article 269 of the Criminal Code appears to be extremely noteworthy in my opinion.[7] On the one hand, paragraph 1 of Article 269 of the Criminal Code punishes incitement to hatred on national, religious, racial or social grounds with imprisonment of up to three years. On the other, paragraph 2 of this same Article punishes speech that is insulting or humiliating to the Hungarian nation, a nationality, a people, a religion or a race with imprisonment of one year at most, corrective labour or a fine. While humiliation is the more moderate form of the crime of hatred, in both cases criminal liability can be incurred without taking account of the purpose of the act. After recalling Articles 18 and 19 of the International Covenant on Civil and Political Rights and Article 10 of the European Convention on Human Rights, the Constitutional Court of Hungary (1992, ABH, p. 176), while affirming that criminal law is an *ultima ratio*, states that Article 269, para. 1 of the Criminal Code 'provides an adequate and proportionate response to a harmful phenomenon, i.e. it is limited to what is strictly necessary to attain the objective sought, in conformity with the requirements set by the limits of constitutional fundamental rights'. It consequently rejects the proceedings aimed at establishing the unconstitutionality of this provision.[8]

In contrast, the same Decision 30/1992 of the Constitutional Court of Hungary (1992, ABH, p. 181) declares unconstitutional paragraph 2 of Article 269 of the Criminal Code. An abstract and possible threat to public security is not sufficient justification for limiting the fundamental right to freedom of expression, which is absolutely necessary for the functioning of the democratic rule of law. In addition, the use of criminal proceedings is not an adequate and proportionate measure for the objective sought. We find here an echo of what the Court held in *Cumpănă and Mazăre* v. *Romania* of 17 December 2004:

> Although sentencing is in principle a matter for the national courts, [it] considers that the imposition of a prison sentence for a press offence will be compatible with journalists' freedom of expression [...] only in exceptional circumstances, notably where other fundamental rights have been seriously impaired, as for example, in the case of hate speech or incitement to violence. (para. 115)

In *Yaşar Kaplan* v. *Turkey* of 24 January 2006, also concerning freedom of expression, the Court expresses the same concern for restraint in the use of criminal law. The Court points out that 'the government's dominant position demands that it show restraint in the use of criminal proceedings, especially if there are other ways of responding to unjustified attacks and criticisms against it or its institutions' (para. 44).

Of course, we are dealing here with the specific register of freedom of expression and Snacken (2006) raises a relevant question: why limit criminal law in matters of freedom of expression and not in matters of liberty? However, the principles that are developed here must hold for all criminal law and be capable of being established as guiding principles that underpin the interventions of all criminal stakeholders. In this connection, the principle of proportionality of penalties, as written into Article 49 of the Charter of Fundamental Rights of the European Union, appears essential and I am delighted that it is written into this text, especially in the light of recent developments in criminal law at the European level, which gradually is tending to cover the whole scope of criminal matters (Tulkens and van de Kerchove 2007: 169-205). Should it be written into an additional protocol to the European Convention on Human Rights? I do not think so but I will get to that in a moment. In any case, however, this principle of proportionality is and must remain a guiding principle of review by the European Court of Human Rights where recourse to criminal law is concerned.

8.3.3 'An increasingly high standard'

In the same vein of extension of the defensive function of human rights, it is also important to point out the many rulings where, particularly concerning Article 3, the Court puts in practice what it announced in *Selmouni* v. *France*: 'The increasingly high standard being required in the area of protection of human rights and fundamental liberties correspondingly and inevitably requires greater firmness in assessing breaches of the fundamental values of democratic societies' (para. 101). Accordingly, in many cases, it no longer hesitates to qualify as torture acts of brutality and violence that undermine the integrity of individuals (*Olmez* v. *Turkey* judgment of 20 February 2007, para. 60). Of course, I agree with Dumortier *et al.* (Chapter 6), when they state that the Court does not implement this principle in an entirely coherent way, as seen, for example, in the *T.* and *V.* v. *United Kingdom* judgments, where it held that the criminal trial imposed on minors aged 10 and 11 did not attain the threshold of gravity of Article 3 of the Convention (paras 77–78 and 79–80 respectively).

More generally, on the applicability of Article 3 of the Convention, the Court repeats a sentence that continues to leave me puzzled. It states, as is the case in the *Mouisel* v. *France* judgment of 14 November 2002, that ordinary detention does not as such come within the scope of this provision. On the contrary, as far as inmates are concerned, suffering must therefore go beyond the suffering inevitably caused by the legitimate requirements of the custodial sentence. The whole question, of course, is to know what concretely are the 'legitimate requirements of the custodial sentence', which necessarily raises the question of the purpose of the sentence and of the custodial sentence. The border is narrow because, conversely, it could be argued that imprisonment that endangers the very objectives of detention, namely prevention and reintegration, is likely itself to constitute inhuman and degrading treatment. In addition, can we continue to assert that suffering or even humiliation is an inherent part of the legitimate requirements of the sentence? I do not think so.

8.3.4 Towards law on enforcement of sentences

Lastly, a tendency that is slowly starting to take shape in the Court could also be included in this same movement. It can be interpreted as a will to put a brake on punitive action: the blurring of the traditional distinction between sentences and the enforcement of sentences. The Court's usual case law establishes that the Convention's guarantees apply to the determination of the sentence and not to the enforcement phase. Is it still tenable to exclude the latter entirely from the Convention's guarantees and in particular from the right to a fair trial (Article 6)? It would not seem so. There is a first sign to this effect concerning Article 13 in the *Schemkamper* v. *France* judgment of 18 October 2005, in which the applicant complained of not having access to any remedy, in conformity with Article 13, against the order of the judge responsible for the execution of sentences refusing to grant him a prison leave. The Court concluded that the provision had been breached. It held that it was for it to

> determine whether the applicant had [...] the means to lodge a complaint over the disputed refusal of leave [...] and whether these means were 'effective' in the sense that they could have prevented the occurrence or the continuation of the alleged infringement or could have provided the party concerned with an appropriate redress for all infringements having already occurred. (para. 42)

Will the Court expand this new approach? There may be the hint of an answer in the *Kafkaris* v. *Cyprus* judgment of 12 February 2008. The problem in this case concerned the meaning to be given to the expression 'life imprisonment' in terms of criminal code provisions and penitentiary rules. By virtue of general principles, the Court in its case law has drawn

> a distinction between a measure that constitutes in substance a 'penalty' and a measure that concerns the 'execution' or 'enforcement' of the 'penalty'. In consequence, where the nature and purpose of a measure relates to the remission of a sentence or a change in a regime for early release, this does not form part of the 'penalty' within the meaning of Article 7 [of the Convention]. *However, in practice, the distinction between the two may not always be clear-cut.* (para. 142) (author emphasis)

I would like to end with a few comments on *constitutional criminal law* as proposed in Chapter 6 of this volume. This proposal is very interesting and I subscribe to it fully. In many countries, and the situation in Hungary as described by Professor Lévay, who is himself now a judge at Hungary's Constitutional Court, confirms it very clearly, criminal law must develop within the framework and the limits of constitutional law. In addition, constitutional law is in many countries implemented and enforced by constitutional courts which can play a key role in this regard, especially when individuals may refer cases to it. Of course, the Court is not a constitutional court and the European Convention on Human Rights is not the Constitution of Europe. The Court, which exercises supranational control, functions with its own potentialities and limits, i.e. primarily, on the one hand, individual petition and, on the other, subsidiarity and as a corollary respect for states' discretion. In addition, the standards of the European Convention on Human Rights are minimum standards (Article 53).

In contrast, the strength of the control mechanism put in place by the European Court of Human Rights is that of individual petition and assessment *in concreto* of the facts of the case in point. This is where is developed what, in my opinion, is the miracle or the intelligence of the Convention: through an open, evolving and dynamic interpretation, it is capable of ensuring that the rights laid down in the Convention can adapt to present situations and be relevant to today's reality. As stated by Ricœur, the meaning of a text is not behind it but in front of it. When

Gutwirth discusses the substantial difference between the judgments in *Laskey, Jaggard and Brown* v. *United Kingdom* of 19 February 1997 and *K.A. and A.D.* v. *Belgium* of 17 February 2005, this is not so much a question of inconsistency, in my view, as the expression of the evolution that has occurred as to the role of criminal law over the last few years and the strong requirements of respect for privacy.

Of course, the Court's case law does not contain an explicit enumeration of the main principles that should govern criminal law. Many would like it to do so. However, might there be a need for additional protocols that would set out new rights and prohibitions capable of better encompassing a 'humanist criminal law'? For example, a protocol that would prohibit life imprisonment? At the level of principles, I could agree. At the level of reality, however, I am not sure. The risk involved with a protocol, as with any codification, is that further evolution can be frozen (Cartuyvels 1996). The question has been raised very often with regard to an additional protocol on the rights of prisoners, with some seeking a prisoners' charter that would be a sort of parallel to the European Convention on Human Rights and the European Social Charter. The convincing argument, in my view, is that a codification or an additional protocol would paradoxically risk being more restrictive. More flexible case law, more attached to individual situations, is perhaps capable of going further.

Notes

1. This reflects the author's personal view, and not that of the European Court of Human Rights.
2. Cf. also Tulkens and van de Kerchove (2007: 48 f.).
3. In a sense very close to Durkheim, certain of his followers, such as Erikson (1964: 14), also consider that the purpose of a sentence is to strengthen the authority of the norm that has been violated and to reiterate the social group's limits.
4. This concept is defined in Article 53 of the 1969 Vienna Convention on the Law of Treaties: 'For the purposes of the present Convention, a peremptory norm of general international law is a norm accepted and recognized by the international community of States as a whole as a norm from which no derogation is permitted and which can be modified only by a subsequent norm of general international law having the same character.'
5. As far as the decision on the merits of this case is concerned, see the judgment delivered by the Grand Chamber of the Court on 24 March 2011.
6. See also De Schutter and Tulkens (2008: 169ff., in particular 181–7).
7. See also Kovács (2007).
8. In parallel, it is interesting to note that the Council of Justice Ministers of the European Union reached political agreement, on 19 April 2007, on a framework decision concerning the fight against racism and xenophobia, which establishes minimum harmonization of relevant criminal provisions. Article 4 determines the behaviours considered to constitute the offences of racism and xenophobia (notably public incitement to violence or hatred with a racist or xenophobic intention, public insults or threats against individuals or groups for such a purpose, public condonement of crimes of genocide, crimes against humanity and war crimes, public denial or trivialization of such crimes, public dissemination or distribution of racist or xenophobic writings,

pictures or other media, heading a racist or xenophobic group, support for it and participation in its activities). Article 6 determines the penalties and sanctions, which must be 'effective, proportionate and dissuasive'. The most serious offences must be punishable by a deprivation of liberty, for a maximum of no less than two years.

References

Cartuyvels, Y. (1996) *D'où vient le Code pénal? Une approche généalogique des premiers codes pénaux absolutistes*. Brussels / Ottawa / Montreal: De Boeck Universités / Les Presses de l'Université d'Ottawa / Les Presses de l'Université de Montréal.

Cartuyvels, Y. (2007) 'Droits de l'homme et droit penal: un retournement?', *Les droits de l'homme, bouclier ou épée du droit pénal?* Brussels: Publications des FUSL.

Constitutional Court of Hungary (1992) *Az Alkotmánybíróság Határozatai (ABH)* (Collection of resolutions adopted by the Constitutional Court of Hungary).

De Schutter, O. (2002) 'La Convention européenne des droits de l'homme à l'épreuve de la lutte contre le terrorisme', in E. Bribosia and A. Weyembergh (eds), *Lutte contre le terrorisme et droits fondamentaux*. Brussels: Bruylant.

De Schutter, O. and Tulkens, F. (2008) 'Rights in conflict: the European Court of Human Rights as a pragmatic institution', in E. Brems (ed.), *Conflicts between Fundamental Rights*. Antwerp: Intersentia.

Durkheim, É. (1973) *De la division du travail social*, 9th edn. Paris: PUF.

Erikson, K. T. (1964) 'Notes on the sociology of deviance', in H. S. Becker (ed.), *The Other Side. Perspectives on Deviance*. New York and London: Free Press and Collier-Macmillan.

Kovács, P. (2007) *La Cour constitutionnelle, l'entente des civilisations et la paix interne. La jurisprudence de la Cour constitutionnelle hongroise en matière du discours de haine*. Paper for the conference on 'The Role of Constitutional Courts in Universal Peace and the Meeting of Civilisations', held in Ankara, 25–26 April, for the 45th anniversary of the Turkish Constitutional Court.

Snacken, S. (2006) 'A reductionist penal policy and European human rights standards', *European Journal of Criminal Policy and Research* (Springer), 12: 143–64.

Sottiaux, S. (2008) *Terrorism and the Limitation of Rights: The European Convention on Human Rights and the United States Constitution*. Oxford and Portland, OR: Hart.

Tulkens, F. and van de Kerchove, M. (2005) 'Les droits de l'homme: bonne ou mauvaise conscience du droit penal?', in F. Verbruggen, R. Verstraeten, D. Van Daele and B. Spriet (eds), *Strafrecht als roeping. Liber amicorum Lieven Dupont*. Louvain: Universitaire Pers Leuven, Coll. Samenleving, Criminaliteit en Strafrechtspleging.

Tulkens, F. and van de Kerchove, M. (2007) *Introduction au droit pénal. Aspects juridiques et criminologiques*, 8th edn. Brussels: Kluwer.

Tulkens, F. and Van Drooghenbroeck, S. (2003) 'La Cour européenne des droits de l'homme depuis 1980. Bilan et orientations', in W. Debeuckelaere and D. Voorhoof (eds), *En toch beweegt het recht*, Tegenspraak, Cahier 23. Bruges: Die Keure, 211 f.

Judgments of the European Court of Human Rights

(In alphabetical order)

ECtHR, *Abdulsamet Yaman* v. *Turkey*, judgment of 2 November 2004.

ECtHR, *Assenov and others* v. *Bulgaria*, judgment of 28 October 1998.

ECtHR, *Bekos and Koutropoulos* v. *Greece*, judgment of 13 December 2005.

ECtHR, *Byrzykowski* v. *Poland*, judgment of 27 September 2006.

ECtHR, *Calvelli and Ciglio* v. *Italy*, judgment of 17 January 2002.

ECtHR, *Çamdereli* v. *Turkey*, judgment of 17 July 2008.

ECtHR (GC), *Cumpănă and Mazăre* v. *Romania*, judgment of 17 December 2004.

ECtHR, *Giuliani* v. *Italy*, decision of 12 March 2007.

ECtHR, *Huylu* v. *Turkey*, judgment of 16 November 2006.

ECtHR, *Isayeva* v. *Russia*, judgment of 24 February 2005.

ECtHR (GC), *Kafkaris* v. *Cyprus*, judgment of 12 February 2008.

ECtHR, *Khashiyev* and *Akayeva* v. *Russia*, judgment of 24 February 2005.

ECtHR, *Krastanov* v. *Bulgaria*, judgment of 30 September 2004.

ECtHR, *M.C.* v. *Bulgaria*, judgment of 4 December 2003.

ECtHR, *McBride* v. *United Kingdom*, judgment of 9 May 2005.

ECtHR, *Mouisel* v. *France*, judgment of 14 November 2002.

ECtHR, *Okkali* v. *Turkey*, judgment of 17 October 2006.

ECtHR, *Olmez* v. *Turkey*, judgment of 20 February 2007.

ECtHR (GC), *Öneryıldız* v. *Turkey*, judgment of 30 November 2004.

ECtHR (GC), *Saadi* v. *Italy*, judgment of 28 February 2008.

ECtHR, *Schemkamper* v. *France*, judgment of 18 October 2005.

ECtHR (GC), *Selmouni* v. *France*, judgment of 28 July 1999.

ECtHR, *Siliadin* v. *France*, judgment of 26 July 2005.

ECtHR (GC), *T.* v. *United Kingdom* and *V.* v. *United Kingdom*, judgments of 16 December 1999.

ECtHR (GC), *Vo* v. *France*, judgment of 8 July 2004.

ECtHR, *Yaşar Kaplan* v. *Turkey*, judgment of 24 January 2006.

ECtHR, *Yazici* v. *Turkey*, judgment of 5 December 2006.

ECtHR, *X.* and *Y.* v. *Netherlands*, judgment of 26 March 1985.

PART 3

Punishment and Democracy – Which Role for Victims and Public Opinion?

9

VICTIMS AND THE PENAL PROCESS: ROLES, EXPECTATIONS AND DISAPPOINTMENTS

Noëlle Languin and Christian-Nils Robert with Milena Abbiati and Mina Rauschenbach

Victims can contribute to the dereliction of politics and the weakening of the State by throwing political debate off balance, leading it too far in the direction of emotions rather than that of rational analysis.[1] (Wieviorka 2005: 107)

9.1 Introduction

After what some called the Age of Aquarius out of esoteric passion, there can be no doubt that we are now living in the Age of Victims, out of victimophile passion. The forced individualism that characterizes our times gives a major role in the public realm to those who, in recounting their past, succeed in evoking real or imaginary suffering that can have no other cause but serious traumatisms experienced personally or vicariously, or even completely fantasized.

Numerous references can be found today to this western society that relives past events through never-ending commemorations. These commemorative exercises aim to unite us in a completely stereotyped memory that must be shared in a surge of compassion whose purpose often escapes us, for the very simple reason that not all have experienced the event being commemorated, or if they did experience it, subsequently took different, individualized paths.

The social realm is saturated by 'the competition of victims' (Chaumont 1997). We live in 'the society of victims' (Erner 2006) and our age is 'the age of victims' (Eliacheff and Soulez Larivière 2007). This finding in itself is distressing because it prompts legitimate doubts about whether we are living at present in a 'culture of traumatism' (Kaplan 2005), strangely blinded simultaneously by social relations, historic realities, political situations (Fassin and Rechtman 2007: 411) and individual destinies with their existential complexities.

An anthropological interpretation of traumatism requires, as Fassin and Rechtman demonstrate, epistemological subtleties, the return to a moral interpretation of a phenomenon that may apparently be objectivized, as some had suggested (Caruth 1996), or even the initiative of developing a sociology of victims.

Our society, which is no longer the risk society (Beck 2003) but the 'accident' society, gorges itself on the precautionary principle, which is daily and universally violated in all areas of human activity. In itself, this is the source of abundant traumatisms by providing input for the construction and justification of the widest range of disorders, up to the very widespread 'fear of crime', leading some to extreme states of social, intellectual and political paralysis that have been perfectly described in studies on this new theme in criminology, the 'fearful subject' (Robert 2002), already a potential or virtual crime victim.

In the face of this qualitative and quantitative amplification of the victim phenomenon, our society seems to offer only a very limited range of interventions, among which criminal justice holds a central and excellent position, at least in Western Europe. Thinking about the accident, through a commonplace shortcut, means thinking immediately about fault, guilt and criminal penalties, because 'how can one continue to feel that one chooses one's life, after suffering injury, other than by demanding that the guilty party be tracked down, which guarantees that one is not the toy of a capricious fate' (Eliacheff and Soulez Larivière 2007: 23)?[2]

What institution is best empowered, at least so it claims, to guarantee access to this now enviable status of victim? Criminal justice. It is the only institution that plays on words, that rules between the offender and the victim, that distinguishes between good and evil, that denatures what cannot be experienced as a fatality, the most effective means at our disposal for sanctifying the victim, sacrificing the offender and obtaining compensation for losses of all kinds supposedly suffered and above all carelessly seen as unquestionably caused by a past event. The scholasticism *post hoc ergo propter hoc*, with its simplicity and evidence, still gains ground to an impressive extent in the sad world of indulgence that takes delight in surrounding victims. The story is beyond doubt, the account gets the seal of approval and there follows the obvious and the normality of a painful pathology.

9.2 Criminal justice in a dominant position

The contemporary observer of criminal justice cannot help but detect its over-attentiveness or even its overzealousness given the mushrooming of cases referred to it. Together with others, we observe an intensification of complaints and denunciations in many areas of protection, ensured until then, in a purely declamatory way, by criminal provisions that existed only through rare domestic or economic cases or cases of honour. Today, the patchwork of society, with the multiplication of control bodies upstream from criminal justice, constitutes an effective pinpointing of situations suspected of resembling criminal liability. These situations are today quite systematically denounced, not only to ensure the protection of a supposed victim, but above all to free oneself of liability, which seems particularly to be the case in the area of ill-treatment of children (Eliacheff and Soulez Larivière 2007: 119). The same observation holds for new administrative controls in the area of finance and the economy, where new provisions, the legitimacy of which remains debatable, are also leading to an escalation of denunciations. The abundance of standards in numerous areas of industrial activity, construction, recreation and sport also finds a legal and judiciary field day in the concepts of negligence and serious misconduct.

The increasing number of victims during certain disasters or accidents is also an unquestionable factor of pressure on criminal justice, stimulating its zeal to elucidate, criminally speaking, multiple liabilities.

Expanding criminalization also affects the duration of punitive action. Asserted without real political reflection, the imprescriptibility of crimes under international criminal law is taken as a model in the area of crimes against children. Moral crusaders are today defending the extension of prescription or even imprescriptibility in this area (attempt in France and Switzerland). They go as far as to forget forgetfulness, the foundation of civic values (Loraux 1997), a necessity for any community, international or national.

There is a need to resist unfailing and 'incriminating memory' (Salas 2005: 92), which appears to be contrary to nature, since life is fortunately made up of great lapses of memory (Balzac), which are the essential condition of memory (A. Jarry).

Taking on insanity so as to judge it constitutes another imperialist desire of justice. Judging someone considered irresponsible appears to be its ultimate attempt to submit madness to punishment, to submit illness to guilt. We know the appalling result: prisons have to cope with serious pathologies that they are not in a position to keep under control. Why all this disorder and confusion? Because an absence of liability is unbearable for victims, as demonstrated in numerous recent trials.

Lastly, certain types of victims' organizations and associations are a factor in a new accommodating attitude that criminal justice shows in their regard, compelling it to perform in terms of explaining certain crimes. New forensic techniques (DNA, the statistical effectiveness of which nevertheless seems more obvious for proving the innocence of the accused rather than for unmasking them) and video-surveillance of public areas are said to contribute to these performances.

In addition, the media serve as a powerful publicizing vehicle for criminal justice. Without bringing out the subtler points, the media feed the popular conviction that this institution is capable of designating the guilty party, thus reinforcing the belief in the fundamental and salutary mechanisms of sacrifice. The victim demands an expiatory victim and the impressive cycle of the *pharmacon* unfolds as remedy and social poison at once (Robert 1986).

9.3 Criminal justice: swindle and lure

For individual victims, this justice cannot but be a lure (Eliacheff and Soulez Larivière 2007: 201). But is this point repeated enough? Certainly not, considering the virulent pseudoscientific discourse claiming that a criminal trial has therapeutic value for the victims. Nonsensical expressions stubbornly assert this conviction, often referring to the need to establish the longed-for recognition of the victim's suffering, without concern for the fact that recognition implies reliving and confronting once again the traumatizing events. Some sensibly see therein the risk of a secondary victimization.

Kaminer *et al.* (2001) denounce even reconciliation procedures as a forced recollection of tragic events that can further add to risks of psychiatric morbidity.

The truth that must be told is that 'criminal justice is credited with cognitive and reparatory expectations that far exceed its capacities' (Salas 2005: 79).[3] This is not simply a diagnosis of the insufficiency of its means alone. Clearly, the idea is to evoke the obvious antagonism between the emotional ethic of the therapeutic culture (Nolan 1998) and the ethic of law and the criminal penalties that can be ordered in its name. In the face of these two worlds, the victim seems to make a choice determined by disinformation that sets him on the difficult path of probable destruction. In the best of cases, 'justice will never be more than a mediocre secondary therapy' (Salas 2005: 91).[4] On this point at least, a certain entente should be denounced: 'Psychiatrists and judges engage in mirror discourse: the victim's therapy builds on justice that penalises the designated guilty party to help the therapy' (Eliacheff and Soulez Larivière 2007: 123).

9.4 Careless premises

The premises mentioned above concerning cathartic and therapeutic value are frequently mentioned in the vagueness of present-day knowledge of traumatic emotions and their lingering nature.

Most research on victims is dominated by empathic points of view (Fassin and Rechtman 2007: 411) or even obsessed with the enumeration of their supposedly obvious needs (Walklate S. 2007: 102ff.). Yet it is clear that there are different kinds of victims and that although the concept has taken on an almost unlimited scope, 'there is nothing to suggest that all victims necessarily consider themselves as such' (Fassin and Rechtman 2007: 409) or to allow us to take for granted that all self-proclaimed victims have suffered an event or events defined as objectively traumatizing. In the individual historical authenticity, suffering serves as proof of a past traumatism, which obviously biases all interrogation of victims and should render the 'victimologist' particularly cautious.

This incomplete state of knowledge prompted us to re-explore questions related to the emotions and expectations of victims in the face of what some present to them as the certain outcome of their suffering, the recognition of a legitimate status of victim–creditor to an unlikely debtor (state, individual or group responsible) and the establishment of a now comfortable social position nurtured by insatiable demands: the criminal trial (Eliacheff and Soulez Larivière 2007: 152 and 156).

As an introduction, we wish to reproduce three particularly relevant comments by Eliacheff and Soulez Larivière (2005: 203ff.).

1. There is a profound chronological conflict between the unchanging time of the judicial structuring of criminal liability and the profoundly adjustable and individual time of the duty of self-rebuilding.
2. The restoration of a moral order turned upside down by a tragic event implies putting the authors of the event back on stage. The play is re-enacted, each player then being bound by a script that is no longer individualized but stereotyped for the needs of the accusation. Suffering is aggravated by a stage that does not lend itself to emotions. Wounds are reopened as if by 'cruentation' (an ancient form of legal evidence where the accused was placed in the presence of his (dead) victim; if the corpse bled, the accused was found guilty of homicide).

   'The judicial handling of the criminal act […] abusively suspends the work of mourning' (Eliacheff and Soulez Larivière 2007), compromises it or when it has been completed, imposes itself again without regard for forgetfulness, as an incomplete or even impossible undertaking.
3. The final act of the trial, and the sentencing that brings it to conclusion, is almost always unrelated to the suffering experienced. 'The art of punishing' (Languin et al. 2006) is an alchemy whose secrets escape the victim's understanding. There is incommensurability between the two meanings of a single word,[5] the sentence ordered and the sorrow endured. The victim never obtains what he has been promised (Weitch 2007: 171) and the judicial treatment imposed on him is perceived as ineffective, of no help and unfair (Zedner 1997: 599).

Following on from the confusion between the sentence ordered and the sorrow endured, the word 'victim' is used by victims themselves to describe the fate of the condemned person. The confusion of genres, words and roles reaches a paroxysm here.

9.5 Victims' narratives

The victim's image vigorously asserts itself as a dominant figure in demands and conflicts in the public arena, and at levels as diverse as humanitarian ethics, lack of road safety, terrorism, occupational accidents and medical malpractice (Chaumont 1997; Cario 2000). For the last 20 years or so, the victims of acts of violence and criminal offences have taken on growing importance in the social and legal spheres. International[6] and national laws have made room for victims' rights and aid and support organizations have been created as a result. Today, *victim* means *empathy* and this movement implies the study of emotions, study that developed first in areas where the theme is anchored as a subject of study in itself – psychology, neurosciences or neuropsychology – and then gradually spread to other social science disciplines, including law. This phenomenon, which can be observed in Switzerland and in all Western nations, constitutes one of the ways whereby changes in law result from a growing consideration of the affect and of individual suffering. The evolution in the victim's 'status', through which the community demonstrates the latter's existence as such within the social structure (Fattah 1997; Bogalska-Martin 2004), attests perfectly to the importance of the question of emotions in regulating social life.

This problem is at the heart of the study conducted at the University of Geneva by CETEL (Law Faculty) in the framework of the Interfaculty Centre on the Science of Emotions (CISA), a study that aimed *inter alia* to check whether and how the recognized increase in importance of the victim in the social realm and in the criminal justice realm is a source of 'emotionalization' of law. Research into the role of emotions in legal phenomena has focused mainly on the progress of psychology in law (Bartol and Bartol 1994), which endeavours, for example, to unveil the psychological aspects of decision-making by players in the justice system (Ellsworth and Mauro 1998; Ellsworth and Sommers 2001; Richli 2000). On the other hand, the way emotions constitute one of the inner workings of legal regulation has been less studied. Yet as a link between the social sphere and the legal sphere, emotions can have an impact on the development of the rule of law (Lange 2002; Karstedt 2002).

The research was carried out in Geneva and the data collected by qualitative interviews (recorded and transcribed) of adult victims of violent crimes (physical assaults, sexual assaults and domestic violence,[7] N = 71) then explored by multivariate techniques of analysis of discourse and content. The partial results that are recounted in these pages sum up, with regard to the criminal justice system, the emotions expressed by victims and the effects of the judicial experience.

Two preliminary remarks are necessary.

1. The evaluation of the criminal justice system by the victims interviewed is sometimes positive, but the negative aspects are more numerous and the analysis concerns these negative aspects.
2. The victims interviewed were not all confronted with the criminal justice system, but those who were expressed greater demand for increased punitiveness for their assailant, precise expectations of how the procedure and the verdict will proceed, demand for recognition of their status and strong emotions. Fear, shame, guilt, humiliation, pain or even hatred were among the principal emotions expressed.

9.5.1 The verdict: a harsher sentence for the assailant

Apart from moral support and practical or institutional aid, victims' expectations concern the functioning of justice. Many expect respect, clear information, the possibility of active participation, speed and effectiveness against a backdrop of an ideal of Justice (with a capital 'J'). However, expectations also relate to the outcome of the trial and in particular the verdict, i.e. the punishment ordered against the offender.

Irrespective of the action taken on the complaint – a complaint having almost always been lodged – numerous victims are not tight-lipped when it comes to stating that the sentence they had hoped for is far harsher than the sentence actually ordered, in short that the 'suffering' demanded is not equal to the suffering experienced.

> 'Well, as far as the assailant is concerned, it's quite clear that he should be sent to prison, that he should serve a minimum sentence.' (Complaint lodged, no judicial action taken)

> 'I thought that after the hearing he was going to be punished and then that would be it. [...] At the time it's hard, you're expecting a punishment, you're expecting something.' (Complaint lodged, verdict: non-suit)

> 'I want them to suffer. I want them to pay. I don't want it to stop there [...] with a few years in prison [...]. Two or three years in prison would do them good, I think.' (Complaint lodged, case discontinued)

If the aim for victims is for the trial to make it impossible for the offender to do harm as well as to impose retribution on him (through sentencing), then this aim is apparently not being met, at least not in keeping with their expectations. There is a divergence between expectations and reality, a divergence that expresses disenchantment, disillusionment over the handling of the case. It is the expression of a discrepancy between the victim's situation, his emotional experience, the enduring traumatism of the assault suffered and the objective, factual and strict framework of the trial, which endeavours to respect the legality of prosecution of the offence. This discrepancy is expressed very well in the following comments:

> 'The system looks for legal fault, not just fault pure and simple!' (Complaint lodged then withdrawn)

> 'In fact, I'm a file, [...] and then this story was created and only the story was read, but no one tried to find out who I was at the start, who he is and who can be believed more easily.' (Two complaints lodged, two trials; verdict: one month with suspension in the first case; case discontinued and appeal in the second).

The result is that a wide variety of feelings are expressed but all are in a negative range with regard to justice.

In some cases, *discouragement* and *disappointment* dominate. The absence of clear explanations, the lack of follow-up or more in-depth handling of the case and the lack of consideration for the victim are reasons given for or that underpin this disillusionment.

In other cases, feelings of *helplessness* or even *failure* are clearly mentioned. The victim believes he has influence only to learn that he has none. A great deal of effort is made for very meagre results. The victim thinks that justice will fight for his cause and hopes that truth and good faith will be enough to be believed and to convince, but nothing of the sort happens. That leads to comments like 'a very hard experience', 'a traumatising experience' and 'the ineffectiveness of justice'.

A profound feeling of injustice, which in some cases goes as far as revolt, can even emerge and comments like 'there is nothing more unjust than justice' and 'there is no justice at the law courts' express this feeling very well.

9.5.2 The victim and his needs: making himself heard so as to be recognized

If a victim's expectations as to the fate of his assailant are clear and well accepted, the victim's own needs are also perfectly obvious and the main criticism of justice is that it fails to take them into account. These needs concern first and foremost a desire, or even a demand, for someone to listen attentively to his story. Many victims declare that no one listened to what they had to say, that they were unable to put across their message or simply that they were unable to present their version of the facts or that they weren't believed, which leads to frustration and incomprehension. 'I did not feel understood at all […]. Nothing, nothing at all was taken into account.' 'No one understands or listens to you.' 'I had the impression I was faced with a wall of incomprehension.'

With this widely expressed demand to be heard – literally and figuratively – victims express the need for their suffering to be recognized by the judicial institutions and society as a whole. If they choose criminal remedy it is for the sake of obtaining public assurance that what they suffered is evil, unfair, undeserved and that it will not happen again (Zehr 1998). This huge need for recognition is not new in itself: it is necessary to life in a community, already described by Jean-Jacques Rousseau in his *Discourse upon the Origin of Inequality*: 'Each began to look at the others and to want to be looked at himself.' What is new is its application to the 'status' of victim. There is a process of assigning meaning here that entails a symbolic and socio-political dimension (Bogalska-Martin 2004), as demonstrated excellently with regard to the Shoah by Jean-Michel Chaumont. He identifies three dimensions of recognition (Chaumont 1997, and before him Honneth 1992): (1) self-confidence that allows confidence in the world and in others – if this confidence is shattered by traumatism (assault, rape) the effects can be devastating; (2) self-respect, which is the demand for one's rights, one's dignity, the demand to be the equal of others and a fully-fledged member of the community. These two types of recognition reinforce the individual in apprehending himself and others as his fellows. They are recognitions of confirmation (Todorov 1995) addressed to the legal order; (3) self-esteem, which is a social esteem, related to the group and to the latter's positive valuation.

This need for recognition also leads to a request for symbolic and psychological reparation for victims, which is becoming increasingly insistent and sometimes exceeds the classic demand for reparation and punishment.

> 'What I want is to be recognized. [...] If I turned to them – *the judges* – it was to have the courts recognize that there was a crime. [...] You're not heard, you're not recognized. A victim is not out to have his assailant buried, all he wants is to be recognized.' (Complaint lodged, trial, verdict: acquittal)

> 'Even so, I found it very hard to hold out a year, to go to the hearings, to try to stay on my feet, not to give up, and the end the result was very little recognition. [...] I would have liked for there to be a trace, for it to be put down in black and white that he did those things, that he is recognized guilty. I don't care what he risks afterwards.' (Complaint lodged, trial, verdict: non-suit)

> 'I'll live the rest of my life without ever having been recognized [...] and every night I think about it, that no one knows the truth. I would like to shout it out to the whole world, to everyone: "look at what he did to me" ...' (Complaint lodged then withdrawn)

It is recognition of victim 'status' that is clearly being sought here. Its mark can also be seen clearly in the satisfaction sometimes expressed by victims who become parties claiming damages in criminal proceedings when they win compensation.

> 'It's something material, so it represented ... recognition. That is part of recognition.' (Complaint lodged, trial, verdict: acquittal)

> 'It's recognition, people believe me, [...] I'm a victim and even though we didn't go all the way through with a trial and the blokes were not accused, the judicial system believes me. [...] Yes, it's a certification that I was a victim, that my story is believed, that something happened to me and it wasn't my fault.' (Complaint lodged, case discontinued)

These comments attest, if need be, that the process is considered by the victims who expect social rehabilitation and seek to regain their dignity[8] as a system making it possible to restore symbolically the social order that has been knocked askew and their integrity.

The questions of whether the criminal trial – with its risks of secondary victimization related to the proceedings – is the most appropriate place for reconstruction of the victim as subject (Cesoni and Rechtman 2005) and of whether the trial really helps victims to surmount their suffering and rebuild their lives remain unresolved and subject to reflection (O'Connell 2005), but are clearly raised by the victims themselves.

> 'Listen, non-recognition, non-recognition is almost a crime!' (Complaint lodged, assailant discharged)

9.5.3 Victim and accused: who plays what role?

Another tendency is emerging which can be described as an inversion of roles. The victim, who presents himself with his truth, his expectations of seeing justice done through the punishment of his assailant and having his dignity restored through public recognition of his victim status, often feels or considers that the accused has stolen the limelight so to speak … This inversion of roles is clearly perceptible in victims' comments. Their discourse suggests that the criminal justice system gives more importance to the accused than to the victim, that they feel they do not exist, that they have been placed in a situation of weakness or even fault during the trial or have been denigrated. The lack of equal treatment is highlighted through the greater attention paid to the accused than to the victim, an inequality experienced as an injustice.[9] The professionalism of the judge is of course generally recognized, but while his human qualities are appreciated during the investigation they are in large measure considered lacking by victims during the trial itself.

> 'Once again, it's like an assault, […] you're transformed into nothing. You're transformed into an object. And that's exactly what was repeated in the judicial procedure. What counted was the young man. So I was just there to provide information about the young man. And then the young man is very well looked after but the person who is the so-called victim in the story, they couldn't care less about.' (Complaint lodged, trial in juvenile court, verdict: one year)

> 'I had the impression throughout the year when we had to appear before the judge, and during the hearings, that at some point I had become the guilty person … and he was the victim.' (domestic violence, complaint lodged, verdict: non-suit)

> 'But then, during the judgment, his lawyer said that … that he had suffered terribly, […] and at that moment I had the impression that he was the victim.' (rape, complaint lodged, trial, verdict: acquittal)

9.6 Conclusion

When addressing the question of the relevance of the intensification and extension of primary and secondary criminalization of individual (or even collective) behaviours, the increase in victimophily with 'its requirements [that] exacerbate exclusively punitive expectations' (Salas 2005: 18)[10] must be seen as an important factor. In terms of primary criminalization, this compassionate ideology results first in the multiplication of incriminations, which can be observed throughout Europe (zero tolerance already applied by the legislator), and the lengthening of prescription periods; secondary criminalization is feeling the full brunt of the entreaties of an unbridled search for guilty parties, following various private or collective events that have led to real or supposed traumatisms.

As put very succinctly by Eliacheff and Soulez Larivière, 'too much criminal law is the death of criminal law' (2007: 168).

However, victims do not deserve that, for meagre results, the criminal justice system ends up being saturated and paradoxically affected by what we described a decade ago as victimopathy, an illness that has become chronic and is widely recognized today (and already denounced: Robert 1997; Salas 2005; Meyran 2007).

Criminal justice suffers from its victims, who cause 'interference' with their noisy incursions into the courts and the media (Eliacheff and Soulez Larivière 2007: 174).

Notes

1. Translator's note: unofficial translation.
2. Translator's note: unofficial translation.
3. Translator's note: unofficial translation.
4. Translator's note: unofficial translation.
5. Translator's note: the single word 'peine' in French means both 'sentence' and 'sorrow'.
6. The two basic texts are: the Declaration of Basic Principles of Justice for Victims of Crime and Abuse of Power, adopted by the United Nations in 1985, and the Framework Decision on the standing of victims in criminal proceedings, adopted by the European Union in 2001.
7. The offences are those punished by Articles 122–126, 180–181, 183 and 189–190 of the Swiss Penal Code (physical integrity, sexual integrity and freedom).
8. Research has led to the development of a typology of victims. Apart from those seeking social rehabilitation, others take refuge in withdrawal and depression, others in detachment and indifference, and still others want their case to be brought to justice.
9. A presumption of victim could help make up for this injustice and provide a solution to this procedural formal inequality (Vandermeersch 2005).
10. Translator's note: unofficial translation.

References

Bartol, C. R. and Bartol, A. M. (1994) *Psychology and Law.* Pacific Grove, CA: Cole.
Beck, U. (2003) *La société du risque* (trans.). Paris: Flammarion.

Bogalska-Martin, E. (2004) *Entre mémoire et oubli – le destin croisé des héros et des victimes*. Paris: L'Harmattan.

Cahiers de l'Institut d'Etudes sur la Justice (2005) *La place de la victime dans le procès pénal*. Brussels: Bruylant.

Cario, R. (2000) *Victimologie – De l'effraction du lien intersubjectif à la restauration sociale*. Paris: L'Harmattan.

Caruth, C. (1996) *Unclaimed Experience. Trauma, Narrative, and History*. Baltimore, MD: Johns Hopkins University Press.

Cesoni, M. L. and Rechtman, R. (2005) 'La réparation psychologique de la victime: une nouvelle fonction de la peine?', *Revue de droit pénal et de criminologie*, 2: 158–78.

Chaumont, J.-M. (1997) *La concurrence des victimes. Génocide, identité, reconnaissance*. Paris: La Découverte.

Eliacheff, C. and Soulez Larivière, D. (2007) *Le temps des victimes*. Paris: Albin Michel.

Ellsworth, P. C. and Mauro, R. (1998) 'Psychology and law', in D. T. Gilbert, S. T. Fiske et al. (eds), *The Handbook of Social Psychology*, Vol. 2. New York: McGraw-Hill, pp. 684–732.

Ellsworth, P. C. and Sommers, S. R. (2001) 'White juror bias: an investigation of prejudice against black defendants in the American courtroom', *Psychology, Public Policy and Law*, 71(1): 210–29.

Erner, G. (2006) *La société des victimes*. Paris: La Découverte.

Fassin, D. and Rechtman, R. (2007) *L'empire du traumatisme*. Paris: Flammarion.

Fattah, E. A. (1997) 'Toward a victim policy aimed at healing, not suffering', in R. C. Davis, A. J. Lurigio and W. G. Skogan (eds), *Victims of Crime*. Thousand Oaks. CA: Sage, pp. 257–72.

Honneth, A. (2000) *La lutte pour la reconnaissance* (trans.). Paris: Le Cerf.

Kaminer, D. et al. (2001) 'The Truth and Reconciliation Commission in South Africa: relation to psychiatric status and forgiveness among survivors in human rights abuses', *British Journal of Psychiatry*, 178: 373–7.

Kaplan, E.-A. (2005) *Trauma Culture: The Politics of Terror and Loss in Media and Literature*. New Brunswick, NJ: Rutgers University Press.

Karstedt, S. (2002) 'Emotions and criminal justice', *Theoretical Criminology*, 6(3): 299–317.

Lange, B. (2002) 'The emotional dimension in legal regulation', *Journal of Law and Society*, 29(1): 197–225.

Languin, N., Kellerhals, J. and Robert, C.-N. (2006) *L'art de punir, Les représentations sociales d'une 'juste' peine*. Geneva, Zurich and Basle: Schulthess.

Loraux, N. (1997) *L'oubli dans la mémoire d'Athènes*. Paris: Payot.

Meyran, R. (2007) 'Les effets pervers de la victimisation', *Sciences humaines*, 178: 36.

Nolan, J.-L. (1998) *The Therapeutic State: Justifying Government at Century's End*. New York: New York University Press.

O'Connell, J. (2005) 'Gambling with the psyche: does prosecuting human rights violators console their victims?', *Harvard International Law Journal*, 46: 295–345.

Richli, P. (2000) *Interdisziplinäre Daumenregeln für eine Faire Rechtsetzung*. Basle: Helbing & Lichtenhahn.

Robert, C.-N. (1986) *L'impératif sacrificiel: justice pénale: au-delà de l'innocence et de la culpabilité*. Lausanne: Editions d'En-Bas.

Robert, C.-N. (1997) 'Autour des victimes, pensée unique, pensée critique', *Cahiers médico-sociaux*, 41: 323–9.

Robert, C.-N. (2002) 'Le 'sujet craignant', objet récent de la criminologie', in Etudes offertes au professeur Jean-François Perrin, *Pour un droit pluriel*. Basle: Helbing & Lichtenhahn, pp. 379–92.

Roche, D. (2004) *Accountability in Restorative Justice*. Oxford: Oxford University Press.

Salas, D. (2004–5) 'L'inquiétant avènement de la victime', Sciences humaines, 47: 90–3.

Salas, D. (2005) *La volonté de punir. Essai sur le populisme pénal*. Paris: Hachette.

Todorov, T. (1995) *La vie commune*. Paris: Seuil.

Vandermeersch, D. (2005) 'Les droit de la victime au stade de l'instruction', in Les Cahiers de l'Institut d'Études sur la Justice, *La place de la victime dans le procès pénal*. Brussels: Bruylant, pp. 123–43.

Walklate, S. (2007) *Imagining the Victim of Crime*. Maidenhead: Open University Press.

Weitch, S. (2007) *Law and the Politics of Reconciliation*. Aldershot: Ashgate.

Wieviorka, M. (2005) *La violence*. Paris: Balland.

Zedner, L. (1997) 'Victims', in M. Maguire, R. Morgan and R. Reiner (eds), *The Oxford Handbook of Criminology*. Oxford: Oxford University Press, pp. 577–608.

Zehr, H. (1998) 'Justice as restoration, justice as respect', *Justice Professional*, 11: 71–87.

10

VICTIMS AND THE CRIMINAL JUSTICE SYSTEM: THREAT OR PROMISE?

Dan Kaminski

> [...] the people
> Had forfeited the confidence of the government
> And could win it back only
> By redoubled efforts. Would it not be easier
> In that case for the government
> To dissolve the people
> And elect another?
> (Brecht, 1976)

10.1 Introduction

The answer is yes: victims are today's elected people, albeit with concern; they are the people cited if not elected by the governments of Europe. David Garland describes the principle of this election: the crime victim is no longer represented as an unfortunate citizen and his concerns are no longer subsumed within the public interest that guides penal decisions (Garland 2001: 144). Today, the victim is a representative character whose experience is taken to be common and collective rather than individual and atypical; moreover, it constitutes sufficient evidence, flying in the face of all statistics for example, of the existence, expansion or growing dangerousness of the experience in question. During a recent televised debate (RTBF, *Faire le point*, Sunday 4 May 2008), Alain Courtois, a Belgian Liberal Senator (an elected representative of the people), claimed, in the face of research statistics showing a decrease in juvenile delinquency, that the figures were simply inaccurate because people's experience proves the opposite. Compassion, a politically imperative attitude nowadays (Richard 2006; Revault d'Allonnes 2008), is on the rise. It encourages the emergence of and sustains a 'society of complainants' (Garapon 1996: 105). Reiner *et al.* (2003) confirm the public dimension of the election of victims (which can be described as stardom) in a study on the evolution of media coverage of crime in the English press from 1945 to the present: during the period under review, the victim and his close relations have acquired a pre-eminent position in the media. In the end, the victim has become the pole of attraction of the judicial system, 'as if the wandering complaint had at last found its home base' (Salas 2005: 75).[1]

This contribution is voluntarily radical and unilateral. It results from the author's indignation with the political treatment of the question of victims of crime and the contemporary victimological (com)passion. Two hypotheses come to the fore: first, that the recognition of victims fundamentally modifies the configuration of modern penality in the sense of contributing to more procedural, civilized and communicative justice; second, that it merely contributes to saving (at least rhetorically) a penality failing in its functioning and in its legitimacy. This paper argues that the second hypothesis is more close to reality.[2]

10.2 Grouped victims, threatening victims, rhetorical victims

The concept of victim is not univocal. I would like to point out three problematic collective versions that set themselves apart from the experience or suffering of individuals who have experienced the consequences of a crime.

Activist victims, represented in associations, unquestionably have an influence on primary criminalization and on institutions. Their impact is by no means insignificant: *grouped victims* put forward their demands and are transformed into political interlocutors with an influence on the development of penal norms. This is evidenced in the already lengthy experience of the impact of the feminist movement on criminalization and the increasing punitiveness in matters of domestic violence (Parent 2002). I shall not develop here the legal or organizational developments that have favoured the status and fate of crime victims. De Fraene *et al.* (2005) have done so very convincingly for Belgium (see also Aertsen 2003). These developments concern the strengthening of the victim's legal position in the penal system as a whole, as well as the creation of support and assistance systems in the psycho-social sector, the police and the judiciary.

The influence of victims in their 'spectral' form is probably also significant in the processes of secondary criminalization: it is hard to measure the impact – although it can be felt – of the symbolic escalating influence of threatening victims in daily decisions on prosecution, detention on remand or sentencing and implementing arrangements. The victim is not just an individual frustrated by the handling of his case. The victim is also the name given to a threat mounting against penal actors who take decisions every day in an 'independence' (judges) or 'dependence' (those carrying out decisions) that is merely statutory[3] (see Snacken 1997). Development of the logic of immunity (De Coninck *et al.* 2005) in the judicial sphere is a serious indicator of the phenomenon: it becomes more important for penal actors to stay immune from social critique than to implement the law.

Also of consequence is the role of the signifier 'victim' in recourse to law and the penalization of phenomena that used to be considered accidental. Victimism is spreading, paving the way to rhetorical victims, those Denis Salas (2005) refers to as 'cited victims' ('victimes invoquées'). Victimism consists of a representation of the human world in which the victim's point of view and the identity quarrel implied thereby replace representations of the common good, justice and solidarity (Erner 2006: 192). Victims take on a political, allegorical and instrumental role, sparking the sacralization of ideologies and institutions, e.g. the creation of the State Secretariat for Victims' Rights in the French Republic (see Cesoni and Rechtman 2005).

10.3 Compassion: a divisive policy

The victimist society is distinguished by compassion for some and lack of compassion for others. It is a penalizing society: compassion contains its reverse side of violence. Guillaume Erner (2006: 175)[4] is peremptory: 'by sympathising with victims' suffering, we help the executioners to carry out their task'. Compassion serves a mental configuration or ideological barrier (Sparks 2000) that identifies greater or diversified control and penality as the best response to the problem (Beckett 1997). Although the people's moral or emotional frame of mind is no longer focused solely on vengeance, but on the contrary on altruism and solidarity with victims, it must be acknowledged that compassionate altruism and selective solidarity present two components that make them as cruel as they are morally appreciable.

On the one hand, 'showing compassion for the victim is also a way of accusing a guilty party' (Erner 2006: 96)[5]. In other words, pity entails 'an aggressive dimension' (ibid.: 97). The empathic and identifying dimension of victimist narrative forces a polarization between offenders and victims to the point of leaving offenders outside of any possible comprehension (their point of view is negligible and any effort to take an interest in them is reprehensible). Victimism renews and reinforces the ideal–type image of the innocent and vulnerable victim as a counterpoint to the ideal–type image of the strong and evil offender (see Christie 1986).

On the other hand, and consequently, the victim must be irreproachable, 'a proper victim' (Erner 2006: 96), failing which he will lose the anticipated empathy. The victim must behave well and be perfectly innocent, in which case his dignity will be praised for its magnificent rarity. In short, the compassionate dualization of the world remains a carbon copy of social divisions. Pratt (2007: 85) states that the ideal victim is the victim who will be idealized, an indispensable condition for his experience to be accepted as the most authentic mode of knowledge (which ensures the at least temporary muzzling of other forms of knowledge). In other words, according to three Belgian researchers (De Fraene *et al.* 2005), policy in favour of victims is based first and foremost on a stereotyped image of a 'deserving' individual victim whose interests can be clearly distinguished from those of delinquents.

This divisive policy contributes to the segmentation of aid and assistance practices for victims and offenders:'Irrespective of their representation in mediation projects and other restorative justice initiatives [...], the two groups – aid for the victim and aid for the offender – are confined to an exclusive, segmenting or protective approach to their clientele' (Aertsen 2003: 112).[6] This policy also contributes to the reinforcement of a secondary division between good victims and others (bad delinquents and bad victims).

10.4 Does penality bend under the influence of victims?

Penality is a concept that identifies a threefold reality: (1) an apparatus, (2) its profane and professional uses (on which I shall not dwell here), and above all (3) a social institution, full of rationality (Kaminski 2010). An institution is a social convention stabilized to such a point that it has become transparent. According to Mary Douglas, penality can be said to structure a number of conventional arrangements related to the right to punish, so that, in the face of a potential challenge, the 'natural' reaction will refer to the adequacy of the penality 'to the nature of the universe' (Douglas 2004: 81). An institution is an entity to which we transfer the task of thinking for us (ibid.: 123) to the point of having no doubts about whether its thinking is legitimate.

Traditional penality nevertheless reveals a limited capacity to meet victims' needs or expectations. This being the case, and given the apparently compelling requirement of satisfying victims, some anticipate the threat represented by the emotionalization of trials, which legitimizes a 'more extensive and more intensive' (Languin *et al.*, Chapter 9 this volume) penalization; others see it as an innovative promise (Aertsen, Chapter 11 this volume). There is hence a wavering between two perspectives.

For the first, compassion legitimizes an increase in criminalization, ensuring the durability of modern penal rationality in its most problematical dimensions. This could be interpreted as a movement for the remoralization of penal law, served by victimist and compassionate ideology. To illustrate with a Belgian example, the recent promotion of the objective of reparation or restoration in the implementation of prison sentences is not unrelated to the sacralization of the victim in Belgian post-Dutroux penal policy. The remoralization of penality out of victimist concerns temporarily shields penality from its nudity, i.e. from its contemporary deficit of legitimacy. 'More than violence, it is suffering that has become the watchword today, the criterion by which sentencing is dispensed. In the name of an unprecedented recognition of the value of human life, suffering has become the evil and the modern subject a potential victim' (Le Goaziou 2004: 21).[7] A sort of competition is encouraged between social groups claiming to be victims (Salas 2005, 63ff.; Chaumont 1997). 'This may give rise to the emergence of masses of victims in the field of public policies and further downstream in the police and judicial spheres. This movement of sensibilities contributes to the demand for security and protection by the State, which has responded through a process of escalated criminalization' (Mucchielli 2008: 123).[8] In other words, penal populism stems from the consumerist concern to satisfy victims by doing more with the same.[9]

For the second perspective: if traditional penality is so structurally incapable of meeting victims' expectations, is the influence of victims capable of provoking its collapse? Consideration of the victim's point of view can then be perceived as a factor of procedural innovation in the handling of offences. This interpretation gives greater emphasis to the promise of reform that the attention to victims carries, through the promotion of alternative procedures, since 'the victim's perception of fairness and justice depends on the procedure that led to them rather than on the outcome of the procedure' (Aertsen, Chapter 11 this volume).

Predictive interpretations are pessimistic or optimistic – threat or promise – and are in direct opposition. They foresee either an 'identical reproduction' (see Cauchie and Kaminski 2007a and 2007b) of penal policy under the pressure of victims, or the innovative promise according to which recognition will be assured by new procedures, repairing the damages through their process rather than in the result of the penal action. Alongside local experiences with restorative justice, carried out with little public notice, which tend to give credit to the promise of innovation, it must be noted that the effects of penal populism (Pratt 2007; Salas 2005; Roberts *et al.* 2003), of which victimism is an intrinsic element, tend to confirm the critical perspective, condemning the tendency of a retrenchment of penality to the strict defence of society.

In fact, the social context of the emergence of victims is hardly favourable to the optimistic interpretation. The risk society is no longer that of emancipation but of Manichaean or exclusive recognition,[10] which the law must ensure by excluding the person responsible for an evil (to be repaired, although irreparable).

> The more we extend the sphere of risks, the more pressing and urgent is the search for someone responsible, that is, someone, whether a physical or a legal person, capable of indemnifying and making reparation. It is as though the multiplication of instances of victimization gives rise to a proportional increase in what we might well call a social resurgence of the accusation. (Ricœur 2003: 26)

This analysis by Paul Ricœur is summed up in one sentence by Zygmunt Bauman (2007): 'There's a bad guy in the story.'

The insurance-based welfare state relied on the value of solidarity. This value is dislodged by the very idea of risk that engendered it, 'insofar as protection against risk runs in the direction of security rather toward the affirmation of solidarity' (Ricoeur 2003: 26). Victimism is in this regard a stabilization or even a cancerization of this 'resurgence of accusation'. In the hierarchy of credibility of representations, first place is granted to the supposed emotional virginity of the legitimate sufferers of a situation defined as criminal. As much as the terminology of the *axis of evil* imposes its Manichaean conception in the new military world order, so does the compassionate perspective in 'ordinary' local crime impose a demonization of the other, distancing a perspective of solidarity.

On top of this, the victims' movement provides a hold for the managerial legitimation of penality (Kaminski 2002; Kaminski 2010). Indeed, the perceptible uptake of consumerist vocabulary and practice obviously grants partiality for the victim, the customer whose attitude corresponds best to a position of applicant on the penal services market. The general policy declaration of the then Belgian Minister for Justice (J.) contains, under the title 'A modern judiciary organization' (Vandeurzen 2008: 57), comments that are extremely significant for the inclusion of victims' expectations in a 'commercial' spirit, where satisfaction and credibility override justice and the value of penal action is measured by its acceptance. What is most important is to avoid disappointing, rather than to recognize that justice can give only what it has.

> The judiciary organization must follow the general trend of transparency, efficiency and effectiveness, like private sector enterprises and public institutions. The latter must provide products or services that respond to quality criteria. For judicial organizations, the aim is to associate the requirements of awareness of net costs, of efficiency and effectiveness, with the fundamental values of the judiciary's independence, the right to a fair trial, equality, a verdict within a reasonable period, accessible justice, etc. It is also essential to stress the importance not only of the back-office (everything related to improving the internal working of the judiciary but which is less important, at least on the face of it, for citizens and for society), but also of the front-office (what citizens and society see directly). Accordingly, it is necessary to produce 'facts and figures' on the basis of which effectiveness and the legitimacy of justice can be checked. The smooth working of justice can thus be measured by the yardstick of its effects on society, by checking confidence in the interventions of justice, the satisfaction it generates and its social acceptance.

10.5 Would you take your broken car to the pizzeria?

Apart from this macro-social interpretation of the effect of the victimist movement on penality there also arises the question of the relevance of penal consumerism that has just been mentioned: is the victim knocking on the right door by believing that penality can satisfy his singular requests or political demands? The irony of the story is that a (penal) system built on a monopolistic mode at the time of the development of large modern states to minimize the victim's role to at most that of the party claiming damages, seems today to need the victim to regain a certain morality! Or, inversely, the victim believes that he can actually achieve a satisfactory result by taking his broken car to the pizzeria. However, it is important to realize that the 'return of the victim' is not a fairy tale but a political struggle whose value is both indisputable, i.e. favouring the blackout of criticism — how can one not devote greater attention to individuals weakened by victimization? — and politically problematical.

10.5.1 Needs or expectations?

The question of vocabulary is quite revealing for the terms of this debate. Are victims considered to have expectations or needs? If we define the perseverance of grouped, threatening and rhetorical victims from the angle of expectations, we take the liberty of thinking that such expectations can be satisfied or disappointed. They belong to the semantics of the assessable and of political debate and are subject to a questioning of their legitimacy and possible recognition. On the other hand, defining the perseverance of these victims as needs takes us into the realm of non-negotiable demands: needs *must* be met; under this name, they can only be overriding. The choice of representing victims' demands as expectations or needs has considerable consequences. Apart from certain natural needs that it is hardly suitable to discuss here, there are three basic, dominant needs: eating, drinking and sleeping. The semantics of needs concerns the biological constitution of subjects and not their social inscription or their position as players.[11] In other words, the vocabulary of needs naturalizes the stakes, prevents debate – needs cannot be discussed – and condemns those with such needs to objectivization and a perennial elective status. A victims' bio-policy is emerging, denying that life is made up of situations of suffering, accidental or otherwise, that bring into play the desires and pleasures of victims, their subjective capacities, the different constraints they experience and the social inequalities that affect them, as subjects and as citizens, short of their election to the nobility of victims.

10.5.2 Punitiveness

The feeling that criminals have been favoured at the expense of victims and the public in general and that the working of the criminal justice system produces only bitterness, disenchantment and disillusion is the populist basis for complaint and demands. Languin *et al.*, argue in this volume (Chapter 9) that victims' expectations remain frustrated in the face of the concrete results obtained. However, Aertsen (Chapter 11, this volume) maintains that restorative justice systems can modify victims' punitive needs. These punitive needs must be tied in with the public opinion's expectations of punitiveness. Expectations are punitive for an obvious reason, namely that the promises on which a political and institutional premium is placed are punitive. We must accept, at least temporarily, the simple fact that the penal system is a pain delivery system (Christie 1981). The mediocre rationality of the penal system is that of the length of pain inflicted on the only subject of penal attention, namely the offender. What can it offer the victim other than the demonstration that it is delivering pain, and in sufficient quantity, in spite of the populist suspicion that the penal system is lax?

The singular experience of mediation or restorative justice – in which the procedure counts more than the result – is smothered under the massive demands of the victimist collective. The already well-established experience of the impact of the feminist movement on criminalization and the increase in punitiveness on domestic violence (Parent 2002) shows that the best pizzeria in the world only serves pizzas. Victims' demands are thus shaped in terms of the penal institutional offering (which is not addressed to them, however). For example, after clarifying that a traffic accident is always 'intentional' (that there is always a bad guy), the head of a Belgian association of victims of traffic accidents explains:

> Because when you've lost a child, when a child has been killed by someone else, even if he did not do so on purpose, even if there is only a wrongful action on the part of the driver, somewhere we expect reparation. And such reparation can only be penal. Money won't repair the damages, so there has to be a penalty, a punishment, recognition of the offender's fault. How can it be measured? Through the length of the sentence. And if the sentence is very limited compared with the pain we suffer because of our grief … Even if the offender goes to prison for 15 years, we know perfectly well that won't bring our child back, but there is nevertheless a public recognition of the act. So that is what we expect, but we aren't receiving it. Because if justice were fair there would not be so many outcries over injustice. […] Handing down justice, after all, is about trying somehow to comfort the victim by imposing a sanction that is suited to the loss suffered.[12]

The legal and symbolic concessions made to the victim by penality contribute to 'masking the difficulties of managing the penal crisis' (De Fraene *et al.* 2005: 85) and accentuating its retributive dimension – the degree zero of satisfaction in question in the interview excerpt above – and not transforming it within a civilizing or reparatory perspective. The pain delivery system formats expectations to the point of producing astounding statements such as: 'I want them to suffer; that will be good for them' (Languin *et al.*, Chapter 9 this volume). Victims' expectations are not a natural need but the transcription, in the penal rationality, of an expectation of justice which, if it had the opportunity of encountering other formatting or other rationalities, would be expressed differently. The penal system can therefore disadvantage criminals (a bit further), but how will that reduce the bitterness, disenchantment and disillusion of the victims? The pizza will be served but the car will still need to be repaired. A bit more cheese, more tomatoes, another ingredient? The car will still be broken.

10.5.3 Disappointment and rights

The punitive need is doomed to disappointment. Disappointment is part and parcel of the programme. The political world's enthusiasm for compassion with victims has produced, not only in the United States but also in some European countries, an increase in prison sentences and a limitation of mechanisms for their reduction (longer periods to be served before possibility of release, real life imprisonment, imprisonment without possibility of release). Raising the stakes quantitatively is the principal tool for the illusory satisfaction of victims' formatted expectations. Hatred of the other cannot be measured. Such hatred is encouraged by the focusing of penal rationality on the antagonism between the two victims of the action, the one known as the victim and the other known as the offender. The rivalry between the two positions – the agonistic[13] logic of the criminal trial – pushes demands to the sordid limits of stardom: 'the accused steals the limelight from the victim' (Languin *et al.*, Chapter 9 this volume).

If we understand this assertion, recognition owed to the victim should go as far as to deprive the criminal of the public trial. The trial for the crime should become the public receptacle of the victim's narrative. However, the ongoing transformation of expectations into rights can only maintain and overexcite disappointment. The recognition of victims' rights within the framework of criminal proceedings can only reinforce the feeling of not really being heard. Cesoni and Rechtman (2005) argue that 'control of the criminal proceedings by the victim' is based on the erroneous premise that the trial and the sentence contribute to subjective reparation to the victim (see also, from a clinical angle, Damiani 2002). Judging the accused, sentencing them and determining modalities for the implementation of the sentence are the tasks of criminal justice. Penal law and its application are far too narrow to take in and deal with the physical, material and symbolic suffering of victims (Salas 2005: 75). The law, the trial and the sentence, focused entirely on the offender, necessarily contribute to disappointment of the expectations of having a say, of obtaining consideration or recognition, all of which are extraneous to penal rationality. The formalization of new rights for victims in criminal proceedings cannot but exacerbate disappointment, increased by a belief in the value of these rights. The agonistic structure of the trial aims precisely to break the rivalry of the real protagonists of the crime. The sentence, measured by its length, will by this very fact always be qualitatively and thus quantitatively insufficient. The victims, whether grouped, threatening or rhetorical, and sometimes the singular victim – save in the case of noteworthy and instructive exceptions – demand the limelight in the trial, which is not their place. Disappointed, they fall back on the result, of which the nature of the measurement (three months, two years, 15 years, etc.) structurally induces punitive outbidding. A noteworthy and instructive exception was the recent trial in Belgium of four young people who violently assaulted a man to steal his cell phone and wallet, leaving him blinded by their blows. The victim recounted in a particularly courageous and sensitive way in an interview that he had pardoned his assailants, that they had apologised to him and that he intended to visit them again in prison. Surprisingly, in this victimist age, he also said the trial and the sentence were not his business but that of the judicial system. He simply voiced the hope that these two consequences of the crime, which were extraneous to his expectations, would be useful.

The reinclusion of the victim in the treatment of his victimization supposes new naming, semantics and pragmatics which remove it from those of penality. The transformation of victims' expectations into rights or the transformation of criminal proceedings into subjects of satisfaction are delusions that are harmful to the overall emancipation of society from complainants and to the singular reparation of life's hard blows. The re-inclusion of the victim happens elsewhere. Or it supposes nothing less – and nothing less likely today – than that the crime, the offender and the victim are subsumed in the conditions of a participatory justice, an alternative to penal justice.

Notes

1. Translator's note: unofficial translation.
2. I also try to construct theoretically the observation of 'innovation' in the criminal justice system, through either 'banal' or 'remarkable' reforms (see Cauchie and Kaminski, 2007c). Innovation is then conceptualized as a change of rationality, whose effects are the opposite of identical reproduction. This observation of innovation is demanding and distant from the beatific optimism of the reformers.
3. This means that the distinction is purely formal or juridical and doesn't tell anything about the real sensibilities of the penal actors towards a variety of influences.
4. Translator's note: unofficial translation.
5. Translator's note: unofficial translation.
6. Translator's note: unofficial translation.
7. Translator's note: unofficial translation.
8. Translator's note: unofficial translation.
9. We recently witnessed an extreme and sinister version of this movement, which technically results in reinstating solitary confinement for debt: the party claiming damages in a gruesome criminal case had the property of the offender, who was sentenced to life imprisonment, seized in his prison cell (and in the prison's internal bank account). The convicted person ended up, as it were, in a punishment (bare) cell through a civil decision aimed at providing reparation and taken in the interest of the victim. Ironically, the low value of the goods seized allowed for their restitution to the prisoner (Robert 2007).
10. The concept of recognition appears compromised, considering its philosophical significance as outlined by Ricœur (2005). Paul Ricœur insists, in his last book, on our capacity to recognize people, and on self-recognition in relation to the gift of mutual recognition.
11. I am conscious to reduce here the way in which Abraham Maslow (1943), the tireless reference of contemporary marketing, piles so called 'needs' for protection and security, love and belonging, self-esteem and self-fulfilment on top of those biological needs. I merely argue that these 'needs' do not represent the same vital necessity and are not equally experienced as needs by all. They are mainly social or cultural, fundamentally differentiated, not recognized or overvalued, depending on the 'needs' of the society which neglects or promotes them.
12. Private interview. Translator's note: unofficial translation.
13. A game is agonistic if one player must necessary lose (or be excluded) for the benefit of the victory of another player (e.g. tennis).

References

Aertsen, I. (2003) 'Le verticalisme dans la prise en charge des victimes', in D. Kaminski and P. Goris (eds), *Prévention et politique de sécurité arc-en-ciel, Actes de la journée du Réseau*

Interuniversitaire sur la Prévention. Brussels: RIP, pp. 221–30.

Bauman, Z. (2007) *Le présent liquide. Peurs sociales et obsession sécuritaire*. Paris: Seuil.

Beckett, C. (1997) *Making Crime Pay: Law and Order in Contemporary American Politics.* New York and Oxford: Oxford University Press.

Brecht, B. (1976) 'The Solution', in B. Brecht, *Poems 1913–1956*. London: Methuen, p. 440.

Cauchie, J.-F. and Kaminski, D. (2007a) 'Éléments pour une sociologie du changement pénal en Occident. Éclairage des concepts de *rationalité pénale moderne et d'innovation pénale*', *Champ Pénal/Penal Field*. On line at: http://champpenal.revues.org/document613. html.

Cauchie, J.-F. and Kaminski, D. (2007b) 'L'innovation pénale: oxymore indépassable ou passage théorique obligé?', in J.-F. Cauchie and D. Kaminski (eds), Enjeux autour de l'innovation pénale. Internet publication of the proceedings of the Ottawa – Louvain-la-Neuve seminar (March and May 2006) on penal innovation. *Champ pénal/Penal Field*. Online at: http://champpenal.revues.org/document1353.html.

Cauchie, J.-F. and Kaminski, D. (2007c) 'Theoretical problematization of penal innovation: the case of community service in Belgium', *Champ Pénal/Penal Field*. Online at: http://champpenal.revues.org/document4493.html.

Cesoni, M. L. and Rechtman, R. (2005) 'La réparation "psychologique" de la victime: une nouvelle fonction de la peine?', *Rev. dr. pén. crim.*, 85(2): 158–78.

Chaumont, J.-M. (1997) *La concurrence des victimes. Génocide, identité, reconnaissance*. Paris: La Découverte.

Christie, N. (1981) *Limits to Pain*. Oxford: Robertson.

Christie, N. (1986) 'The ideal victim', in E. Fattah (ed.), *From Crime Policy to Victim Policy. Reorienting the Justice System*. London: Macmillan, pp. 17–30.

Damiani, C. (2002) 'Comment concilier réalité psychique et réalité judiciaire', *Revue Francophone du Stress et du Trauma*, 3(1): 55–8.

De Coninck, F., Cartuyvels, Y., Franssen, A., Kaminski, D., Mary, P., Rea, A. and Van Campenhoudt, L. (2005) *Aux frontières de la justice, aux marges de la société. Une analyse en groupes d'acteurs et de chercheurs*. Ghent: Academia Press, Politique scientifique fédérale.

De Fraene, D., Lemonne, A. and Nagels, C. (2005) 'Débats autour de la victime: entre science et politique', *Revue de droit de l'ULB*, 31(1): 55–92.

Douglas, M. (2004) *Comment pensent les institutions*. Paris: La Découverte (first published: 1986).

Erner, G. (2006) *La société des victimes*. Paris: La Découverte.

Garapon, A. (1996) *Le gardien des promesses. Justice et démocratie*. Paris: Odile Jacob.

Garland, D. (2001) *The Culture of Control*. New York: Oxford University Press.

Kaminski, D. (2002) 'Troubles de la pénalité et ordre managérial', *Recherches Sociologiques*, 33(1): 87–107.

Kaminski, D. (2010) *Pénalité, management, innovation*. Namur: Presses Universitaires de Namur.

Le Goaziou, V. (2004) *La violence*. Paris: La Cavalier bleu.

Maslow, A. (1943) ' A theory of human motivation', *Psychological Review*, 50: 370–96.

Mucchielli, L. (2008) 'Penser la violence. Une analyse socio-historique des violences interpersonnelles en France, des années 1970 à nos jours', *Déviance et Société*, 32(2): 115–47.

Parent, C. (2002) 'Face à l'insoutenable de la violence contre les conjointes', in C. Debuyst *et al.* (eds), *Essais sur le tragique et la rationalité pénale*. Brussels: De Boeck, Coll. Perspectives criminologiques, pp. 83–103.

Pratt, J. (2007) *Penal Populism*. London/New York: Routledge.

Reiner, R., Livingstone, S. and Allen, J. (2003) 'From law and order to lynch mobs: crime news since the Second World War', in P. Mason (ed.), *Criminal Visions. Media Representations of Crime and Justice*. Cullompton: Willan, pp. 13–32.

Revaut d'Allonnes, M. (2008) *L'homme compassionnel*. Paris: Seuil.

Richard, M. (2006) *La République compassionnelle*. Paris: Grasset.

Ricœur, P. (2003) 'The concept of responsibility. An essay in semantic analysis', in P. Ricœur, *The Just*. Chicago: University of Chicago Press, pp. 11–35.

Ricœur, P. (2005) *The Course of Recognition*. Cambridge, MA: Harvard University Press.

Robert, L. (2007) 'Een deurwaarder in de gevangenis. Naar een cachot pour dettes', *Fatik*, December, 116: 16–20.

Roberts, J. V., Stalans, L. J., Indermaur, D. and Hough, M. (2003) *Penal Populism and Public Opinion. Lessons from Five Countries*. Oxford: Oxford University Press.

Salas, D. (2005) *La volonté de punir. Essai sur le populisme pénal*. Paris: Hachette.

Snacken, S. (1997) 'Surpopulation des prisons et sanctions alternatives', in P. Mary (ed.), *Travail d'intérêt général et médiation pénale. Socialisation du pénal ou pénalisation du social?* Brussels: Bruylant, pp. 367–401.

Sparks, R. (2000) 'The media and penal politics', *Punishment and Society*, 2(1): 98–105.

Vandeurzen, J. (2008) *Déclaration de politique générale* (Belgian Ministry of Justice). Online at: http://www.just.fgov.be/communiques/2008/04/doc/declaration.doc.

11

PUNITIVITY FROM A VICTIM'S PERPSECTIVE

Ivo Aertsen

11.1 Introduction

Developing a better understanding of evolutions in 'punitivity', and in particular the role of victims and the victims movement therein, is not a simple task. This chapter aims at contributing to this analysis. In this exercise, the concept of 'punitivity' will be used to refer to the interrelated levels of the individual, social and judicial opinions, attitudes and conducts (Kury *et al.* 2004). 'Punitivity' often has a negative connotation when being associated with the evolution towards a harsher penal climate in society or the uncritical, disproportionate and inadequate application of criminal justice (de Roos 1994: 45–6). This concern is justified. Many observers in western countries assume that during recent decades the criminal justice system 'has endured a substantial punitive intensification on many fronts' and that the spirit of the age is characterized by an 'expansive punitivity'. This punitivity also reveals itself in social language as well as in policies of local authorities, companies and other fields of society (Kelk 1994). This 'upward spiral movement' in penal policies appears to be at odds with commonly accepted (legal) conceptions regarding parsimony, subsidiarity and minimal intervention by criminal justice. The criminal justice's fundamental orientation on legal protection and power balances threatens to be pushed into the background, the offender decays into an object of judicial intervention and social reintegration – instead of being a right – becomes a condition. Until the early 1990s the punitive turn could be explained as a logical consequence of increasing crime rates, yet this way of legitimation has lost its credibility from the middle in the 1990s during which time a stagnation or even decrease in conventional types of violent and property crime has been observed in western countries (van Dijk *et al.* 2007). All this seems to confirm that criminal justice and punishment are not merely predetermined by unambiguous and rational processes. They are rather part of a broader societal and cultural phenomenon of 'penality' (Garland

1990), and we will investigate the victim's potential role in evolutions concerning punitivity from this approach.

This contribution hence focuses on the role of the victim. Since the 1970s ever more attention has been paid in many countries to the victim of criminal offences as well as to victimization in general. Initially the attention focused on particular victim categories but before long this was expanded to victims in general (Peters 1993). Criminal justice reformers, specific categories of 'vulnerable' victims, self-help groups, victim support workers, victim surveys, specific events, the media and academics have played a primary role in rendering the victim socially visible (Dignan 2005: 14–17). For example, in Belgium the 1990s in particular were characterized by an increased willingness within the fields of the police, criminal justice and social assistance to take the initiative and to set out policies that aimed at a stronger position of the victim in the criminal procedure as well as creating and improving social services for the target group (Aertsen *et al.* 2002; Nationaal Forum 2004; Lemonne *et al.* 2007). Comparative research indicates that Belgium was among the best of European pupils concerning victim-oriented legislative initiatives during the 1990s (Brienen and Hoegen 2000). In any case the manifold developments at practice and policy level – together with the catalyst effect of the Dutroux case – also brought with them the idea that in Belgium the victim is no longer a stranger and even has taken a central place in the practice and discourse on insecurity and the administration of criminal justice.

As social interest in the victim increased and in particular the victim's position in the consecutive stages of the administration of justice became stronger, there was also an increasing concern for a balanced assessment of the victim's interests compared with the offender's position and needs. More in general the question was raised as to the social and judicial impact of this interest in victims and more specifically whether or not this increased attention for victims has contributed substantially to a polarization of sentencing policies. This chapter consequently focuses on the central question whether, and to what extent, the interest in victims has resulted in an increased punitivity. Or else, in the absence of unambiguous links, the question remains as to the (changed) meaning of punitivity because of the victim's presence. In order to investigate these issues, we will focus on different levels of penal reactions (individually, socially and judicially). First, however, we will elaborate on the public perception of the victim.

11.2 Conceptions of victimhood

11.2.1 The virtual victim

Even early on in the development of the attention on victims of crime, criminologists and particularly victimologists referred to imbalances in the way victims are perceived in society. As a matter of fact the victim is mostly considered in its 'ideal' role. Christie (1986a) described this ideal-type victim as weak and subordinated to an (ideal-typical) strong and unknown offender and as someone who constantly evokes sympathy because of his/her innocent and legitimate appearance (cf. Kaminski, Chapter 10 this volume). This dominant image codetermines the social and judicial reaction characterized by a strong individualization of victimization in both assistance and criminal justice processes (Sebba 2000), where particular attention is paid to offences with an easily identifiable victim (Antilla 1974). The consequence will be selectivity in services to (entitled) victims as well as an approach to services from a consumer's perspective. Fattah (1997) and others, however, argued that there is no such thing as an unambiguous definition of the concept 'victim' and that this interpretation strongly depends on the frame of mind used. Meanwhile victimology has shown an image of victimization that is more based on the empirical reality. Demographic as well as other characteristics of victims indicate that it is not the ideal-typically vulnerable groups of victims that are most exposed to actual victimization (most victims of violent crime are young and active men, not old or vulnerable women). Furthermore, it has been shown that members of particular social groups and neighbourhoods run a disproportionately high risk of victimization (and offending), that there are significant concentrations of recurrent victimization among people, that there is a substantial overlap of groups of victims and offenders, and that the roles of victim and offender often are interchangeable to some extent (Dignan 2005: 18–20; Fattah 1991, 1994).

The 'virtual' victim is based on the ideal-typical conception. This is codetermined to a large extent by social opinions and images of insecurity, crime and victimization. The media play a crucial, almost determining role in creating this victim image. News reports and press coverage mainly emphasize the individually suffering victim while the concept 'victimization' is being applied to a wide variety of human misfortunes. As opposed to, say, ten, years ago, the victim's position is currently much more emphasized in the (audio-visual) press. In talk shows the victim of flesh and blood offers ample 'victim entertainment'.

Apparently the tendency to constantly broaden victim categories seems to be adopted by professional services as well. Apart from focusing on victims of crime, victim assistance programmes now also deal with victims of road traffic accidents, victims of disasters, relatives in cases of suicide, etc. … The expansion of victim groups is blurring the boundaries of victimhood. The multitude of groups can be contoured and dealt with less easily in the framework of the criminal procedure. At the same time, non-criminally defined victims also express clear expectations towards the police and the justice system (Dignan 2005: 20–3; Lemonne et al. 2007: 346). In this regard, decision-makers are given a certain room for interpretation to decide which victims have for example 'a legitimate and direct interest' to participate in a specific procedure, or who can be considered to be a surviving relative or a 'vulnerable victim'.

This broadening and spread of the concept of 'victimhood' within social services and criminal justice reflect larger and deeper social changes. Several authors have indicated the changing, more demanding attitude of citizens, the lament culture and 'victimism' (Pollefeyt 2000), and the way in which identification with a metaphorical victim gives meaning to our moral thinking (Boutellier 1993). Confronted with the fragmentation of traditional social bonds, a growing sense of anxiety and a fading sense of belonging, the experience of victimhood assists many citizens in constructing a new social identity. In this context Furedi (1997) refers to the 'culture of victimhood' that pervades contemporary western society (cf. Languin *et al.*, Chapter 9 this volume).

At the same time, the debate on victimhood, victim services and criminal justice reveals a stream of thought that deliberately disassociates itself from the stereotypical image of the passive and submissive victim, and that rather approaches victimhood from an emancipatory perspective at both the personal and social level (van Dijk 2008: 153–75). Victims are then becoming 'survivors'. Against the background of 'the relatively mild sentencing climate in Western societies' Boutellier (1994) discriminates between four prototypical conceptions of victimhood which are mainly 'social forms' to deal with concrete victimization: the calculating victim (who as a continuous complainant is out for his own profit), the revenging victim (driven by excessive vengeance), the merciful victim (dominantly present in the Christian culture) and the emancipated victim (carrying elements of all of the three aforementioned types, and whose vengeance is not excessive but sometimes accommodating and sometimes calculating – on the one hand this victim is out for recognition of his victimization yet on the other hand he will extricate himself from his status of subordinate victim).

The aforementioned may have made clear that the concept of 'victimhood' is contingent, liable to various interpretations and susceptible to continuous evolution. Apart from the actual victim in society there is also the virtual victim who can take on several potential social roles of victimhood. This virtual victim will influence who actually will get the status of victim. Prototypical concepts of victimization mainly concern personal victims of conventional crime (such as theft, fraud, assault and battery, rape, manslaughter …) and other damaging events. Almost automatically connected to this is the tendency to look for personal offenders, individual responsibilities and penalties.

11.2.2 *Political rhetoric*

Against the background of the aforementioned developments and social expectations a distinct political discourse can be observed that on the one hand reacts to these expectations of the virtual victim and on the other hand will further determine these expectations.

However, this political discourse varies between countries. In Belgium, for example, it is impossible to imagine policy declarations of the consecutive Ministers of Justice since the early 1990s without mentioning the interests of the victims. What strikes most are the literally recurrent issues on victims and victim policies through the years. Sometimes new accents are stressed but often the victim issue is used to support or legitimize more general reform plans or priorities. Sometimes even the victim issue offers a thankful way out of the political deadlock. An example of this was the agreement within the Belgian federal government in September 2006 following the turmoil resulting from the provisional release of a detained foreigner: henceforth the provisional release scheme would also be advised upon by the victim. Following this agreement the government could again turn to the order of the day.[1]

With regard to the political 'use' of victims Belgium is still a very moderate student. Countries such as the United Kingdom and the United States pursue in a much more extreme way politics of severe punishment (and even the death penalty) in the name of the victim. This might be accompanied by a striking black-and-white thinking regarding the offenders' acceptance (or not) of responsibility 'to make amends' and the demagogic use by politicians of a victim-related discourse to discredit the efforts of prison reformers.[2] Even more striking is the barely concealed concerted action between politics and media to present victims in support of repressive sentencing policies with regard to specific groups within society. The English story of John Tulloch (2006) is a striking example of this.[3] The victim rhetoric (which is also expressed visually) drastically influences common conceptions of crime and is able to specifically support the hardening of penal policies. Authors such as Garland (2001) have pointed out the way in which the 'ideal victim' forms a mechanism for politicians (at least in some countries) to advocate the implementation of more severe sentences based on a renewed 'law and order' thinking. When making official statements politicians are accompanied by victims and particular laws are named after a victim (for example the 'Megan's laws' in the US that enable neighbourhood watch regarding sexual offenders). Politicians deliberately use victims' stories and stress the uncertainties and fears of citizens in the sphere of insecurity in order to popularize and impose a personal agenda.

11.3 The actual victim: needs and expectations for punishment

The common picture of victimhood does not necessarily correspond with the situation and experiences of actual victimhood. Here we focus on the question of the presence and nature of punitive attitudes with individual victims as well as any possible evolutions. The fact that punitive needs with regard to the offender in the sense of individual feelings of revenge and retaliation are inherent in the victim experience need not be confirmed here. We are more interested in getting a more differentiated picture of the punitive expectations and needs of individual victims within the context of criminal justice and the way the system deals with it.

11.3.1 Some research findings

In victimological literature attempts have been made to summarize research findings on victims' expectations with regard to the criminal justice process (Strang 2002; Goodey 2005; Walklate 2007). When taking the necessary caution into account with regard to the possible generalization of these findings in different legal systems (most findings stem from countries with a *common law* legal system), the victims' expectations mainly seem to be with regard to receiving adequate information concerning the judicial procedure, a respectful and correct treatment, a settlement beyond the bureaucratic, an involvement that is personal to a larger extent and the ability to participate in the personal case, access to financial or material compensation and finally the supply of psychological redress through the offender's attitude. Otherwise, when questioned thoroughly, victims say it is not revenge or vengeance or the demand for a severe punishment that takes precedence with regard to the functioning of criminal justice. The expectations appear to be in the procedural sphere rather than in the (punitive) outcome. It is understood that individual experiences with, and expectations with regard to, the criminal justice system only make up a part of the victims' coping process. If we want to understand the punishment needs of individual victims, they need to be placed in a broader framework of dealing with and processing the criminal offence. The psychological coping following the experience of a criminal offence boils down to a large extent to a cognitive process of attributing a meaning in which an interpretation has to be given to the abrupt violation of basic assumptions while using specific mental scenarios (see, among others, Janoff-Bulman and Frieze 1983; Greenberg and Ruback 1992). In this process of cognitive restructuring there is a permanent interaction between the victim and both his informal and institutional environments. Otherwise the attitudes and opinions expressed about punishment are not established in a personal or social vacuum.

Research into the punitive needs and actual expectations of punishment has repeatedly indicated that *generally* punitive attitudes of victims do not assume extreme proportions (Shapland *et al.* 1985; Spalek 2006: 28). Yet individual differences and differences between types of crime seem to play an important part: in most European countries, imprisonment is not the preferred sanction for victims of, for example, burglary, while surviving relatives in the case of homicide really favour a 'severe' punishment in the sense that the punishment should be in line with the scope of the inflicted distress. However, there are also substantial differences within the group of, for example, burglary victims: victims who are really affected demand more severe punishments, and the same goes for victims who believe that the offenders are professionals as opposed to those who think of offenders as amateurs (Maguire 1982). Research in Flanders among a group of victims of serious crimes and burglary showed that a majority (56 per cent) advocated a rigorously punitive reaction while the remaining 44 per cent rather favoured an approach of reparation or a combination of punishment and reparation (Aertsen 1993). More recent research by the National Institute of Criminalistics and Criminology (NICC, Brussels) into the experiences and expectations of a group of victims of (usually severe) crimes regarding the criminal justice process indicated that the punishment, and imprisonment in particular, for a number of victims happens to offer a more significant recognition than the damages awarded would do (Lemonne *et al.* 2007). However, few victims think that they should pronounce judgment on the nature and extent of the punishment. Yet victims do want to be informed about the punishment imposed. Victims consider severe punishment to be a sign of social recognition of the seriousness of the facts and the distress inflicted. Other victims mainly see imprisonment as the protection of society, while another group does not regard a custodial sentence as a solution for their grieving process or quest for the truth. As far as thinking about punishment is concerned, two groups of victims can be distinguished in the NICC research: on the one hand there are victims who generally think of punishments as being *too soft* and who argue for making punishments more dissuasive or deterrent; on the other hand there are victims who consider current sentences to be *maladjusted* and who think there should be more meaningful alternatives (Lemonne *et al.* 2007).

A recurrent research finding is that people who suffer or have suffered the experience of being a victim because of a crime do not appear to be more punitively oriented than citizens in general (Wright 1989; Gelb 2008; Costelloe *et al.* 2009). With regard to their judgment on advisable sentences victims appear to vary to the same extent as people from the public in general (Williams 2005: 90). With regard to the punitive needs of the public (whether or not members have become victims themselves) reference is often made to the large-scale empirical survey of Sessar in Hamburg in the 1980s (Sessar 1992, 1999). Being faced with a choice between punishment and/or compensation for the damage, a vast majority of victims of both petty crimes against property and violent offences favoured compensation, whether or not this was to be achieved through mediation. When it came to the more severe nature of these types of crime this approach was advocated by only a minority. The large proportion of acceptance of restitutive types of settlement in the former case found its origin in a general disbelief with regard to the significance of conventional punishment. However, if need be, imprisonment was considered to be preventive and protective rather than retaliatory. Sessar's survey also showed that judicial authorities (public prosecutors, civil judges and criminal judges) generally assume a more punitive attitude than do members of the broad public. Beyens (2000) came to the same conclusion in her empirical survey covering two judicial districts in Belgium. In the German enquiry punitive attitudes among legal professionals appeared to be established mainly through socialization processes during their education at Faculties of Law and their additional education on the job.

Subsequent studies of the International Crime Victim Survey (ICVS) among representative groups of the population in a wide variety of countries also result in indications of the existence of rather moderate punitive attitudes (Nieuwbeerta 2002; van Dijk *et al.* 2007). When confronted with the question of the most appropriate sentence for a 21-year-old recidivist burglar – the choice between actually serving a prison sentence or performing community service – the latter is preferred by far in most western industrialized countries. Exceptions to this are the US and the United Kingdom. Periodical ICVS sweeps (approximately every four years) also allow an examination of the evolution of punitive attitudes. Although the fluctuations are rather limited, the general public's attitude appeared to have hardened during the years 1996–2000, followed by a period of moderation (2000–4). Conclusively for the US and the United Kingdom a distinct relationship could be shown between the general preference for imprisonment (as measured in the ICVS) and the actual imprisonment rates.

The fact that a final conclusion cannot yet be taken on individual punishment expectations and needs, and that there are at least significant differences between surveys, is confirmed by a survey from 2004–5 in Austria (Sautner and Hirtenlehner 2007). This research indicated that, with regard to the type of punishment, victims of severe crimes to a large extent preferred a prison sentence, while 60 per cent rejected the possibility that reparation should be taken into account when establishing the sentence. One of the comments of the researchers was the question whether victims are inclined to adopt specific penal views from the court.

11.3.2 Affecting factors

Several methodological factors can be considered co-responsible for victims' diverging punishment expectations and needs, as found in research. In the first place there is the possible effect of the different types of questions used in surveys (neutral or suggestive questions, open and abstract questions rather than offering a choice between different actual and identifiable alternatives). Another influencing factor appears to be the availability of background information about the offence and the offender. From Sessar's (1999) survey it appeared that the disposition of information on the respective consequences of the different alternatives to a large extent is codetermining in the formation of opinions. It is understood that results might vary quite considerably with regard to punishment expectations as the respondents are being well informed about the offence and the personal background of the offender and the potential consequences of particular sanctions, as opposed to whether this concerns an open question for the general public which is mainly or exclusively familiar with conventional sanctions. In this respect reference can be made to the frequent public opinion surveys that indicate that *in abstracto* the public deems sentencing too permissive, that this general judgment mainly refers to violent crimes and repeated offenders, that punitive attitudes sharply decline when concrete information is given to people, that persons with a high level of anxiety are more inclined to punitivity, that the public – notwithstanding a certain punitivity – shows a distinct preference for non-judicial interventions and non-custodial sentences, and finally that this public takes less interest in a prison sentence when the offender comes with gestures of compensation (Gelb 2008). Notwithstanding these and other qualifying findings Roberts and Hough (2006: 150–1), in their review of research on public attitudes regarding criminal justice, conclude that nevertheless the public often reacts 'in a punitive fashion' – especially where violent crime is concerned. Reactions tend to be punitive when certain prerequisites are being met, such as: the criminal offence has a violent nature (in particular acts of sexual aggression), a vulnerable victim is involved (for example children), the respondent's attention is on the criminal offence rather than the offender, the respondent is not offered a summary of all possible reactions on the offence, and the respondent is given a short time to fill out the questionnaire.

More than once a discrepancy has been pointed out between on the one hand the conception of punitive needs based on surveys or other enquiry forms, and on the other hand the conception of punitive needs when the respondent is confronted with an actual concrete situation within his personal environment or when the respondent himself is involved in the decision-making process for the most appropriate reaction. In the case of personal involvement most people would be inclined to take rather moderate and thoughtful decisions arising from their sense of responsibility (Christie 1986b).

11.4 The victim movements and punitivity

11.4.1 The rise of victim movements

Questions could be asked concerning the role of 'the victim movement' on the subject of the − be it intentional or not − encouragement of a more punitive climate and severe penal policy. The concept of 'victim movement' indicates the many types of actions, projects, organizations, networks and institutions on a local, national and international level that aim at a better protection of crime victims' interests (Peters 1993: 48). In fact a distinction should be made between the different types of victim movements, namely the official victim movement that is recognized by the government and that tends to assume a system-preserving attitude, and the unofficial victim movement that targets the problem of subordinated groups or minorities and emphasizes socio-structural differences as the major cause of victimization processes (Elias 1993). For that matter the question could be raised as to the extent to which the official victim movement still has all characteristics of a 'social movement' (Spalek 2006: 20). Anyway, partly due to the feminist victim movement, victimology adopted a more practice and policy oriented approach in the 1970s and 1980s. This development was first seen in North America and the United Kingdom and later also on the European continent. Van Dijk (1988) described within this early victim movement several 'victimagogic' ideologies: a care ideology, an instrumental ideology, a retributive ideology and an abolitionist ideology. This ideological diversity happened to provide support for the victim movement in the various countries on account of a wide diversity of political groups. Initially in the US the victim movement presented itself mainly through communities of interests and lobbies, while in Western Europe victim assistance services took the lead: in countries such as the UK, the Netherlands, Belgium, Germany and France these groups established networks of victim support programmes that operated to a large extent based on (soon officially acknowledged and supported) volunteer work (Williams and Goodman 2007). In North America attention was initially paid to a large extent to vesting victims in various social fields with rights (Victims' Bills of Rights) as well as to reinforcing their legal position in the criminal justice process. In Europe emphasis was put rather on starting and improving assistance and services to victims, which possibly has contributed to a certain moderation concerning the reforms advocated in Western Europe for quite some time (Goodey 2005: 101–9; Groenhuijsen 1999). Later, from the second half of the 1990s on and also due to the work of 'Victim Support Europe' (the European network of national victim support organizations, formerly called the 'European Forum for Victim Services') and new EU regulations concerning the victim's position in the criminal procedure, the rights' approach also gained ground in Western Europe.[4]

The focus of the European victim movement on assistance and services as well as the choice to aim at gradual reforms has possibly restrained circles of victim support workers from developing a punitive discourse. The fact that in countries such as the UK, the Netherlands and Belgium assistance programmes for victims initially were started in *probation* circles and offender-oriented work (Rock 1990; De Beer 1989; Meyvis 1993) has possibly influenced a balanced attitude. Apart from this, in a number of countries, for example, in Belgium, the influence from academics and other experts (see, for example, Jung 2003) could be observed. It would be far from correct to pretend that services for victims – for example in Belgium and the Netherlands – explicitly waged war *against* offenders or advocated more repressive sentencing policies. Victim organizations' opinion texts and statements of principles, for example, read: 'Victim support also adequately takes into account the offender dimension in its assistance and services. It contributes to a restorative oriented approach.'[5] In this respect Victim Support Europe also has assumed a moderate attitude and in its consecutive public statements has given account of the offender's position, the importance of assistance programmes to offenders and the possible role of mediation between victim and offenders. The pursuit of a better position for the victim was part of a broader humanization tendency within the administration of criminal justice (Groenhuijsen 1996: 175). This thoughtful attitude is fully in line with the approach advocated in international victim-oriented regulations since the 1980s from the United Nations, the Council of Europe and the European Union.[6]

Services for victim assistance in Europe are, however, not a homogeneous group and it cannot be denied that national organizations, for example in Germany or Austria, actually did express a repressive undertone during specific time periods. The same goes for some 'single-issue' victim groups that arose (and still arise) in a number of countries and that – more in agreement with the image of the ideal-typical victim – aim at one specific category of victims (victims of incest, stalking, paedophiles, …). The punitive impact of self-help groups or groups of fellow-sufferers, which in several countries exerted a strong influence on policy making during specific periods, is less obvious to assess. Also in these groups a punitive attitude is not completely overruled – for obvious reasons. Professional support for these groups has possibly had a restraining and steering impact (Guffens and Aertsen 2006). Anyway, it is striking to see that at times the representatives of these self-help groups speak thoughtfully and to some extent with a certain understanding of those who caused distress to them.

11.4.2 The victim movement and penal policies

In several European countries victim support organizations have pioneered more global victim policies. Victim services from the field of psychosocial assistance often took the lead and have forced reforms in the police and justice fields. As a consequence they are to a large extent representative of or have set the tone for 'the victim movement'. The relatively moderate attitude of the European victim movement cannot always be seen in other continents and consequently the balance between the victims' and offenders' interests in criminal justice reforms may no longer be preserved. In countries such as the US or Japan a strong victims lobby acts as a significant *agenda setter* of criminal justice policies in general. In the US right from the start the victim movement strongly leaned on conservative political groups while in Europe this movement happened to be less politically bound (Mawby and Walklate 1994: 69–94; Young 2006). It is striking to see the discourse, initially developed mainly in the US, that presents the interests of victims and the interests of offenders in a comparable or competitive way (Young 1999).

Japan happens to be a remarkable example of the way in which the victim movement within a short time could become the 'overseer' of the field of official criminal justice policies (Miyazawa 2008). The establishment, on the initiative of relatives of murdered people in Japan in 2000, of the National Association of Crime Victims and Surviving Families (NAVS) actually heralded a shift from 'victim support' to 'victims' rights', resulting in radical legislative actions and lobbying in the highest political circles. According to adherents of this Japanese organization the confirmed position of the victim in the criminal justice procedure and the possibility of adopting an active participation in it (even including expressing an opinion concerning the advisable punishment) did not result in a more retributive criminal justice system (Hayashi 2007). Yet according to some people it appears that among members of this influential organization there is an indisputable tendency to support the Japanese discourse on more severe punishments (genbatsuka) (Miyazawa 2008).

For the time being it is difficult to say whether the Japanese example of victim-oriented lobbying is an isolated fact in the international context or rather serves as a pattern for the developments that can be expected in other countries. On the one hand several Western European countries have already suffered critical periods in which – as has already been mentioned – victim groups obtained an influential position *without* the immediate outcome of a more repressive sentencing policy. On the other hand a parallel can be drawn with recent evolutions in the UK where new groups of 'activist victims' – 'homicide survivors' and other fellow-sufferers – appear to have established a new generation in the victim movement that, as was the case in Japan, can get to the very heart of national politics and on the legislative level extract new victim rights that among other things relate to sentencing severity (Rock 2008). It remains to be seen whether and in what way this new victim movement's profiling will exert any influence on punitivity in general.

From an international viewpoint it cannot be denied that a number of victim groups – in particular *single-issue* victim groups – have openly conducted a campaign for more severe punishments or a more restrictive sentencing policy. The implementation of this has had a specific impact. Furthermore, in some countries in particular, extreme victims' stories were politically used in campaigns for more severe punishments (the 'horror story syndrome' – Walker (1985), quoted in Fattah 1992: 401) where the impression was given that these extreme examples are representative of 'the' victims (Reeves and Mulley 2000: 142). As opposed to the situation in the US and Japan, the European victim movement openly claims a more strict sentencing policy only to a lesser extent. This does not necessarily imply that an indirect impact could not be noticed. Anyhow the victim movement – whether moderate or not – indeed has its role and meaning in a bigger social and political entity. Hence an increased punitivity because of the victim movement will only be seen within *specific* social contexts. In times of social transition or when the citizens' confidence in the authorities dwindles, or when an expert culture is pushed back to increasingly make room for the individual story of citizens, penal policies become more mechanical-punitive (less individualization, more fixed punishments) and sentencing goals tend to be more expressive and victim-oriented (Zimring and Johnson 2006). Also due to the victim issue (presented as extreme) and the identification of many people with victimization processes, crime can achieve the status of a substantial social problem. Citizens – through their identification with victims and victim groups – can ventilate their lack of confidence in the authorities by respectively demanding, supporting or tacitly adopting more severe penal policies. For example, the Brussels 'White March' shortly after the Dutroux facts became known in 1996 has made clear the possibly massive nature of this group identification.

11.5 The victim in the criminal justice system

11.5.1 Toward participatory rights in the stage of sentencing

In the third section of this chapter on the actual victim, we examined the individual needs and expectations of victims regarding punishment. The various research results could hardly be compared, among other things because of substantial differences in the survey methodology and the different contexts in which the questioning took place. However, it gradually became clear that it is not wise to look at individual and social punishment needs and expectations as isolated entities or to link sound conclusions to them. A hindering factor is the representation of the punitive needs of the 'virtual' victim in society and their possible manipulation, as we have explained in the second section on conceptions of victimhood. Finally, in the fourth section on victim movements and punitivity, we have elucidated the possible influence of the 'victim movement' – in other words, the various types of victim movements. In this respect we have observed an evolution – even in Europe – in dealing with the victim issue, and where, apart from the recognition of a number of *basic needs* regarding assistance and services, focus now is on victim *rights*. Although this also concerns the rights regarding the various social services (Victim Support Europe 1998) it is mainly the discussion on the legal position of the victim in criminal justice proceedings that tops the agenda.

Meanwhile there is – also based on international developments – a clear catalogue of 'fundamental rights' that the victim should have at his disposal in the consecutive stages of the criminal justice process (reporting to the police, criminal investigation, trial, sentencing and administration of the sentence) (Goodey 2005: 130). In Belgium, for example, these victim rights can be summarized as the right to respectful and correct treatment, the right to get information, the right to provide information, the right to legal aid and legal advice, the right to financial reparation, the right to assistance and the right to protection of privacy (Nationaal Forum voor Slachtofferbeleid 1998, 2005). This happens to be an inventory of rights that were first collected in the English Victim's Charter (Home Office 1990); this was subsequently further elaborated and promoted by Victim Support Europe (1996) and eventually found its way to the European Union policy level in the form of the Framework Decision of 15 March 2001 on the standing of victims in criminal proceedings. This catalogue of victim rights as formulated in the European Framework Decision is imperatively the rule in all EU member states.

The question is now whether this interpretation of victims' needs in terms of victim rights and the moving legal discourse of the victim's position contribute to an increase in punitivity, be it on the level of the individual victim or of the functioning of criminal justice. In this respect we focus on the increased opportunities for the victim to participate in the criminal procedure. Within an inquisitorial criminal procedure, as it is commonly known in Belgium and neighbouring countries, from time immemorial victims have had a number of possibilities in terms of participation, for example within the legal framework of the procedure of civil party at the level of the investigating judge to commence criminal proceedings and the direct summons (Tulkens and van de Kerchove 1996). However, since the late 1990s participatory procedures have been substantially expanded, both at the investigation stage and in the stage of the implementation of the sentence.

The various modalities of victim participation in the criminal procedure can be classified in dispositive and non-dispositive types (De Mesmaecker 2006). In the former case the victim supervises a specific aspect of the judicial decision process in which the judicial decision-maker is compelled to implement the victim's preference or choice. In the latter case the victim's contribution is one of advice, dissemination of information or expression, where the judicial system should consider the victim's expressed preference or his information, or else should give the victim the possibility to express himself (Edwards 2004). It is a fact that – in several countries – recent developments have had a far-reaching and more substantial impact than the aforementioned rights. While the rights already acquired mainly relate to types of passive participation or engagement (the right to be treated in a correct and adequate way, to receive information, …), new rights let the victim participate in the criminal justice process to a more active extent, in particular in the decision-making process. This becomes especially clear, and also is most debated, when the (active) participation rights relate to the stage of sentencing. Here, experiences with regard to various types of 'victim impact statements' (or 'victim personal statements') in mainly common law countries become important. In countries such as the USA, Canada, Australia, New Zealand, the UK and Ireland – within an adversarial criminal justice system that has relatively few possibilities for the victim to participate – several legal modalities have been implemented that enable the victim to give a written explanation on the (various) consequences of the criminal offence on him and/ or his environment. This document is written – whether or not by or with the assistance of the police or another body – on behalf of the judicial decision-making authorities (public prosecutor, judge, sometimes also the authorities that have to decide upon parole applications). A variation of the written victim statement is the oral statement during the trial. In most countries these victim statements give the victim (or his relatives) the right to tell the judge about the crime's impact at a financial, physical, psychological, social or family level. In some jurisdictions the victim (of a severe criminal offence) also has the legal possibility to give his opinion on the advisable sentence (the so-called 'victim statement of opinion'). The victim statements (whatever their form) have primarily been enabled to offset the alienating nature of the criminal justice system and to offer the victim better recognition and respect. Advocates argue that 'victim statements' help the victim to acquire (in a *common law* legal system, that is) a lawful position within the criminal procedure, enable the victim to actually illustrate the damage suffered and to provide better information to the criminal justice authorities on the consequences of the criminal offence in order to achieve a better decision process, and finally encourage victims to expand their collaboration with the justice system. Opponents fear that the subjective and emotional stories of victims will inappropriately influence the criminal decision process and more particularly sentencing decisions, that the rights of the defence will be affected and that unrealistically high expectations will be raised for victims (Goodey 2005: 166). The legal introduction of the victim statement sometimes appears to be based on unclear or competing rationalities, which could then result in confusion or wrong expectations for victims: on the one hand the expressive function of the victim statement is emphasized in the hope of improving the coping process for victims by offering catharsis; on the other hand it is considered possible the victim actually had an impact on the criminal decision process (Spalek 2006: 105).

11.5.2 The impact of participatory rights

Empirical research, both quantitative and qualitative, has mapped the effects of *victim statements* for a number of countries. By and large these results can be categorized in two main findings (Erez 2000; Dignan 2005: 76–80; Sanders and Jones 2007; Walklate 2007: 114–21). In the first place the victim statements have only a small or no impact on the criminal procedure and no significant impact at all on the final sentence. It so happens that the dreaded punishment-aggravating effect is not to the point. For one thing, it is emphasized that the effect did not follow because of an inefficient implementation of this new provision. On the other hand, when asked, prosecutors and judges had ambivalent feelings with regard to the victim statement, considering this statement's implementation in a restricted way due to specific assumptions of what could be considered to be 'normal' consequences for victims. Secondly, from a number of enquiries there seems to be a positive impact of the victim statement on the victim's general well-being, with a possible foundation within the socio-psychological theory of procedural justice (Lind and Tyler 1988; see also Wemmers 1996). Further satisfaction with the criminal justice system, however, does not appear to be positively influenced. Although the victim's initial experience when making a victim statement is often positive (in the sense of experiencing this as a recognition), after some time this satisfaction appears to decline (Wemmers and Cyr 2006) or even becomes a disappointment following the observation that the victim statement does not contribute to the decision process by the judge. In other words, the expectations created remain unanswered. According to some the limited or disappointing results from the system of victim statements can be reduced to the fundamental issue of having tried to implement a new victim-oriented provision in a hostile, polarizing environment. Hence victim statements do not encourage the communication or actual involvement of victims (and offenders) and offer only small guarantees that the information given will be handled adequately in the decision process (Sanders and Jones 2007; see also Henham and Mannozzi 2003). Reforms like these cannot be successful if at the same time one does not appeal to the legal and professional culture, the organizational structures and the underlying group dynamics in the court (Erez 2000; Dignan 2005: 85).

Until recently the implementation of victim statements was restricted to jurisdictions with a common law legal tradition; however, two types of victim statement have been implemented in the Netherlands today[7]: since May 2004 victims of relatively severe criminal offences can make a written victim statement, and since January 2005 a verbal statement can also be given at the trial. Drawing up statements like these is done through the services of victim support. The statement is seen by the public prosecutor, the judge and possibly the accused. In his statement the victim gives information on the consequences of the criminal offence; however, he is not allowed to pronounce an opinion on the facts, the offender, the evidence or the advisable punishment. Evaluative research during the preceding pilot phase indicated general satisfaction among victims: they feel they are being taken seriously, they appreciate the opportunity to provide a statement and to express their emotions, and confidence in the criminal procedure is encouraged (Kool *et al.* 2002). As a small-scale qualitative survey by Victim Support Netherlands has shown, it appears that a vast majority of victims prefer the written victim statement to the oral declaration because the latter would be too much of a burden for many victims, or because the oral type of statement is found not to be needed (Leferink and Vos 2007). Although there are national guidelines, the actual procedural settlements of the victim statements in the Netherlands appear to be different depending on the judicial district. In this respect the culture of the public prosecutors' office and the existence of priorities in investigation and prosecution combined with a high work pressure appear to play an important role. This brings to mind the 'Solomon model' of criminal proceedings (Shapland 2000) characterized by a high case load and the demands of rational decision processes, where there is no (mental) place for the victim. Moreover, in the survey by Victim Support Netherlands a number of positive psychological effects on the victim are being reported, as far as both the written victim statement and its verbal equivalent are concerned: there is a more pronounced personal involvement in the criminal process although a therapeutic effect has not been observed. Members of the public prosecutor's office and judges most certainly appreciate the informative function of the victim statements; according to them they pay attention to this information which should play a particular role in balancing the facts. This is confirmed by the evaluative research of Kool *et al.* (2006) into the implementation of the new legal provisions in the Netherlands, and furthermore it shows that judges assess the use of the right to speak during the session – provided that it has been well prepared – to be a surplus value. According to judges the use of the right to speak does not imply any impact whatsoever on the sentence; yet among other things they hope that for the offender this will be a meaningful confrontation with the consequences of his deeds. Finally, in the Netherlands there seems to be only a small basis of acceptance for the victim *statement of opinion* type. For victims the right to have a say in the sentencing decision is not considered vital (Leferink and Vos 2007).

Based on the foregoing, the actual question should be: to what extent do victims really want to be able to participate in the criminal justice process? Several studies appear to indicate – and this is also constantly emphasized by victim support workers – that victims are not looking for the power to decide the sentence of the offender (Doak 2008: 116–17); rather they would prefer to get clear information and a restricted form of (passive or active) participation. Anyway a general finding is that satisfaction with the criminal justice system increases when victims have a sense of *empowerment* and experience an official (albeit mainly symbolic) recognition. In short, the development of a 'communicative model' of victim participation would be much more significant than implementing an 'impact model'. This communicative model for criminal justice proceedings would be beneficial for both the victim and the offender provided that there is good advice on the limited objective and scope of their participation (Roberts and Erez 2004).

The victim statement as a form of participation in the sentencing stage as previously described should actually be distinguished from similar legal provisions for victims in the execution stage of the prison sentence. Not that much research has yet been done on the needs, expectations, (legal) position and experiences of victims when confronted with the administration of a community sanction or measure in which they are not directly involved as a formal party (such as probation, community service or electronic monitoring). More attention has been paid to the position of the victim vis-à-vis the execution of the prison sentence. Several countries have adopted legal provisions which grant the victim – or at least some categories of victims – specific rights mainly in relation to the decision--making process regarding parole. In Belgium, for example, the judge is bound to notify the civil party of the possibility of being informed about particular modalities concerning the execution of the punishment. Victims who are not a civil party also have the possibility to make a victim statement provided that the judge on the execution of the sentence recognizes their 'direct and legitimate interest'. The victim statement, furthermore, enables the victim to be heard by the court responsible for the execution of sentences and for conditions to be formulated for the victim's sake that possibly may have to be implied when particular modalities concerning the execution of the sentence are decided upon. Research on the experiences of victims in Belgium when involved in similar parole decisions revealed that, generally speaking, they welcomed this possibility as positive; however, their expectations on this matter can widely differ: from accepting the possible release of the prisoner to it being completely inconceivable (Lemonne *et al.* 2007: 281–7). Here also the main (positive) effect had to do with the feeling of recognition and participation in the procedure. With respect to the actual opportunity to be heard by the authority that decides upon parole, the expectations again were quite divergent: the ability to put a face to the offender, trying to prevent a release, the expectation that the offender should still reveal a part of the truth or should apologise. Also at the execution stage of the sentence the judge appears to consider the input of the victim and other victim-oriented information as a useful part of the framework of a balanced decision-making process (Aertsen and Lauwaert 2009).

11.6 Conclusion

In the last section of his book *Slachtoffers als zondebokken* (*Victims as Scapegoats*), van Dijk (2008: 135–40) deals with 'the phantom of the revengeful victim'. Referring to Groenhuijsen he draws attention to 'the remarkable thinness of arguments against victim rights pleaded by criminal justice lawyers' and he cuts across the presupposition that granting more rights should pave the way for excessive revenge and the undermining of modern criminal justice's human nature. Van Dijk argues that there is no causal relation between the chronologically parallel movement for more victim rights on the one hand and the rise of more repressive criminal justice proceedings on the other. He acknowledges the attempts to legitimize more severe sentencing by appealing to the metaphorical victim. But many actual victims cannot identify with the extreme punitive demands of specific victim groups. There are victim groups, even in the USA, that work hard for constructive penalties, reconciliation and restoration. Victims' punitive needs and expectations generally keep a moderate voice, and with a sense of differentiation and responsibility. In short, van Dijk (2008: 139) concludes that 'there is no empirical evidence whatsoever for the assumption that the hardening of the penal climate in many Western countries is caused by the movement for victim rights' (our translation).

In this chapter we have dealt with the various elements of van Dijk's argument: the punitive turn, the virtual victim and his political manipulation, the punitive needs and expectations of the actual victim based on empirical research, the influence of the victim movement that in Europe also aimed at reinforcing the legal position during the past decade, and finally the rise of participatory rights during the sentencing phase. All these developments indeed result in quite comforting arrangements. However, we do not feel completely at ease. It is understood that we recognize the rather laborious integration of the victim's perspective in formal criminal proceedings (Aertsen 2003) and the necessity to strengthen the legal position of victims and the quality of their assistance in a mutual balance. This is accompanied by a sufficient amount of empirical evidence, based on scientific research and practical experience, that more rights for the victim – even at the level of the sentencing process – do not automatically result in more and/or more severe punishments.

Our concern has mainly to do with the determining importance of the *context* in which new victim provisions are being implemented. Recent developments, as described above, indicate that the victim rights and victim movement are open to interpretation. Since 'victimization' has several meanings and since the increased attention to victims possibly influences the different layers of punitivity (individually, socially and judicially) it is extremely hard to descry unambiguous developments within these complex dynamics, let alone take unambiguous directions. Within the different layers there are different ways to handle, for example, the exercising of individual rights or respond to feelings of social insecurity by referring to the victim. We have sufficiently indicated that more victim rights do not automatically cause more severe punishment, yet a number of indirect unintentional influences can play a part and eventually result in a longer or more severe punishment. Examples of this are taking the victim's interest into account when legal proceedings are decided upon in order to enable claims for damages; an increased influence of the attention on victims when deciding upon the criminal offence's seriousness and the degree of guilt; or imposing victim-oriented conditions when executing specific penalty modalities. Victim-oriented conditions can be out of all proportion to the offence's seriousness or the length of punishment, and these conditions can have an actual freedom-depriving or punitive impact. Procedures (for release on parole) can be extended due to the potential recording of the victim needs or expectations. Finally, at the different stages of criminal justice proceedings general-preventive considerations appear to play a part, as a consequence of which – for the sake of the victim's interest or because of possible risks for potential victims – more caution and reserve are shown when deciding upon the fate of the accused. Developments like these cannot be settled while adopting a 'so what?' attitude. They form a part of the eventual social punitivity and should be carefully observed.

A sound and balanced development of victim rights is only possible in the framework of a body of coherent criminal and social policies in which finally all the different actors participate, including the political elite, judicial authorities and the media. All three of these actors are often not quite rational in the way in which they interact. On an implementation level solid guidance for victims is needed, within both social assistance programmes and criminal proceedings. A suitable infrastructure should be created for different types of victim participation in court and during the execution of the sentence. The professional and the organizational cultures within the criminal justice system need to further develop through information, sensitization, training and cooperation with external agencies. Within these chalk lines and hence, provided that an adjusted context can be created, it is fully possible to argue strongly in favour of a more emancipatory approach to victims of crime. An active and safe participation of both the victim and the offender should facilitate another quality of criminal proceedings, in which punitivity and punishment would not necessarily disappear but could adopt another function that is less harmful and more integrative towards society.

Notes

1. 'All parties expressed their satisfaction on the agreement following the assembly of the federal government and the chairpersons of the purple majority parties. Support has been restored. Now the budget talks can start, could be heard.' (*Gazet van Antwerpen*, September 27, 2006).
2. 'I think that semantics are very important for victims of crime. We can all do more to support them: indeed, this morning I challenge those of you who work so effectively to keep pressure on government over standards in prison, to tell me how you think the victim could be put more at the heart of your work' (Jack Straw, then Lord Chancellor and Secretary of State for Justice, Royal Society of Arts, London, 27 October 2008).
3. Tulloch was a victim of the London Underground bomb attack in July 2005. The use of the photograph showing his mutilated face on the front page of a number of English newspapers was seen as an example of manipulation by the media to support the government's terrorism policy ('Tell Tony he is right'), a manipulation with which the victim himself could not agree. Tulloch, being a professor in media studies, wrote on this: 'This is using my image to push through draconian and utterly unnecessary terrorism legislation. […] If you want to use my image, the words coming out of my mouth would be "Not in my name, Tony"' (*Guardian,* 10 November 2005).
4. See, for example, EU Council Framework Decision of 15 March 2001 on the standing of victims in criminal proceedings (*Official Journal* L 82 of 22 March 2001).
5. This example comes from the Flemish services for victim support (Steunpunt Algemeen Welzijnswerk, *Visie en werkingprincipes Diensten Slachtofferhulp*, online at: http://www.steunpunt.be/).
6. For a compilation of these regulations, I refer to Groenhuijsen and Letschert (2006).
7. It should be noted that the Netherlands, compared to many other Western European countries, do not have the same legal procedure of civil party.

References

Aertsen, I. (1993) 'Slachtoffers van crimineel geweld. Een kwalitatief-fenomenologische analyse', in T. Peters and J. Goethals (eds), *De achterkant van de criminaliteit. Over victimologie, slachtofferhulp en strafrechtsbedeling.* Antwerpen: Kluwer Rechtswetenschappen België, pp. 177–21.

Aertsen, I. (2003) 'Het verticalisme in de slachtofferzorg', in P. Goris and D. Kaminski (eds), *Preventie en het paars-groene veiligheidsbeleid.* S.l., Interuniversitair Netwerk Criminaliteitspreventie, pp. 222–31.

Aertsen, I. and Lauwaert, K. (2009) 'De rol van de magistratuur in herstelgerichte praktijken', *Tijdschrift voor herstelrecht*, 9(2): 38–51.

Aertsen, I., Christiaensen, S., Hougardy, L. and Martin, D. (2002) *Vademecum politiële slachtofferbejegening* (tweede herwerkte uitgave). Ghent: Academia Press.

Antilla, L. (1974) 'Victimology – a new territory in criminology', *Scandinavian Studies in Criminology*, 5: 7–10.

Beyens, K. (2000) *Straffen als sociale praktijk. Een penologisch onderzoek naar straftoemeting.* Brussels: VUB Press.

Boutellier, H. (1993) *Solidariteit en slachtofferschap. De morele betekenis van criminaliteit in een postmoderne cultuur.* Nijmegen: SUN.

Boutellier, J. C. J. (1994) 'Het geëmancipeerde slachtoffer. Een nadere beschouwing over solidariteit en slachtofferschap', in M. Moerings (ed.), *Hoe punitief is Nederland?* Arnhem: Gouda Quint, pp. 195–201.

Brienen, M. E. I. and Hoegen, E. H. (2000) *Victims of Crime in 22 European Criminal Justice Systems. The Implementation of Recommendation (85)11 of the Council of Europe on the Position of the Victim in the Framework of Criminal Law and Procedure.* Nijmegen: Wolf Legal Publishers.

Christie, N. (1986a) 'The ideal victim', in E. Fattah (ed.), *From Crime Policy to Victim Policy. Reorienting the Justice System.* London: Macmillan, pp. 17–30.

Christie, N. (1986b) 'Images of man in modern penal law', *Contemporary Crises*, 10(1): 95–106.

Costelloe, M. T., Chiricos, T. and Gertz, M. (2009) 'Punitive attitudes toward criminals: Exploring the relevance of crime salience and economic insecurity', *Punishment and Society*, 11(1): 25–49.

De Beer, A. (1989) 'Tussen dader en slachtoffer', in J. Soetenhorst-De Savornin Lohman (ed.), *Slachtoffers van misdrijven. Ontwikkelingen in hulpverlening, recht en beleid.* Arnhem: Gouda Quint, pp. 181–94.

De Mesmaecker, V. (2006) *De participatie van het slachtoffer aan het straftoemetingsproces, Licentiaatsverhandeling Criminologische Wetenschappen.* Leuven: Katholieke Universiteit Leuven.

De Roos, T. A. (1994) 'Beheerste reactie of overkill? Hedendaagse punitiviteit in de strafrechtspolitiek', in M. Moerings (ed.), *Hoe punitief is Nederland?* Arnhem: Gouda Quint, pp. 45–58.

Dignan, J. (2005) *Understanding Victims and Restorative Justice.* Maidenhead: Open University Press.

Doak, J. (2008) *Victims' Rights, Human Rights and Criminal Justice. Reconceiving the Role of Third Parties.* Oxford: Hart.

Edwards, I. (2004) 'An ambiguous participant: the crime victim and criminal justice decision-making', *British Journal of Criminology*, 44(6): 967–82.

Elias, R. (1993) *Victims Still: The Political Manipulation of Crime Victims.* London: Sage.

Erez, E. (2000) 'Integrating a victim perspective in criminal justice through victim impact statements', in A. Crawford and J. Goodey (eds), *Integrating a Victim Perspective within Criminal Justice.* Aldershot: Ashgate, pp. 165–84.

Fattah, E. (1991) *Understanding Criminal Victimization. An Introduction to Theoretical Victimology.* Scarborough, Ont.: Prentice-Hall Canada.

Fattah, E. (1992) 'The United Nations Declaration of Basic Principles of Justice for Victims of Crime and Abuse of Power: a constructive critique', in E. Fattah (ed.), *Towards a Critical Victimology*. New York: St. Martin's Press, pp. 401–24.

Fattah, E. (1994) *The Interchangeable Roles of Victim and Victimizer*. Helsinki: Heuni.

Fattah, E. (1997) 'Toward a victim policy aimed at healing not suffering', in R. C. Davis, A. J. Lurigio and W. G. Skogan (eds), *Victims of Crime: Problems, Policies, and Programs*. Thousand Oaks, CA: Sage, pp. 257–72.

Furedi, F. (1997) *Culture of Fear: Risk-taking and the Morality of Low Expectation*. London: Cassell.

Garland, D. (1990) *Punishment and Modern Society: A Study in Social Theory*. Oxford: Oxford University Press.

Garland, D. (2001) *The Culture of Control: Crime and Social Order in Contemporary Society*. Oxford: Oxford University Press.

Gelb, K. (2008) 'Myths and misconceptions: public opinion versus public judgement about sentencing', in A. Freiberg and K. Gelb (eds), *Penal Populism, Sentencing Councils and Sentencing Policy*. Cullompton: Willan, pp. 68–82.

Goodey, J. (2005) *Victims and Victimology: Research, Policy and Practice*. Harlow: Pearson Education.

Greenberg, M. S. and Ruback, R. B. (1992) *After the Crime: Victim Decision Making*. New York: Plenum Press.

Groenhuijsen, M. (1996) 'Conflicts of victims' interests and offenders' rights in the criminal justice system', in S. Summer, M. Israel, M. O'Connell and R. Sarre (eds), *International Victimology: Selected Papers from the 8th International Symposium*. Canberra: Australian Institute of Criminology, pp. 163–76.

Groenhuijsen, M. (1999) *Trends in Victimology in Europe with Special Reference to the European Forum for Victim Services*. Tilburg: Tilburg University.

Groenhuijsen, M. and Letschert, R. (eds) (2006) *Compilation of International Victims' Rights Instruments*. Nijmegen: Wolf Legal Publishers.

Guffens, H. and Aertsen, I. (2006) 'Avenues to redress within a parents of murdered children mutual support group: respect for autonomy versus need of guidance', *Bulletin InfoPV – Association québécoise Plaidoyer-Victimes* (June), pp. 53–9.

Hayashi, R. (2007) 'Crime victims' movement towards the establishment of victim rights', in J. P. J. Dussich, H. Morosawa and N. Tomita (eds), *Voices of Crime Victims Change our Society*. Tokyo: Seibundo, pp. 22–9.

Henham, R. and Mannozzi, G. (2003) 'Victim participation and sentencing in England and Italy: a legal and policy analysis', *European Journal of Crime, Criminal Law and Criminal Justice*, 11(3): 278–317.

Home Office (1990) *Victim's Charter. A Statement of the Rights of Victims of Crime*. London: Home Office.

Janoff-Bulman, R. and Frieze, I. (1983) 'A theoretical perspective for understanding reactions to victimisation', *Journal of Social Issues*, 39: 1–18.

Jung, H. (2003) 'The renaissance of the victim in criminal policy: a reconstruction of the German campaign', in L. Zedner and A. Ashworth (eds), *The Criminological Foundations of Penal Policy*. Oxford: Oxford University Press, pp. 443–62.

Kelk, C. (1994) 'Verbreding van het punitieve spectrum', in M. Moerings (ed.), *Hoe punitief is Nederland?* Arnhem: Gouda Quint, pp. 13–29.

Kool, R., Moerings, M. and Zandbergen, W. (2002) *Recht op schrift. Evaluatie projecten schriftelijke slachtofferverklaring*. Utrecht/Deventer: Willem Pompe Instituut/Kluwer.

Kool, R., Passier, R. and Beijer, A. (2006) *Evaluatie implementatie schriftelijke slachtofferverklaring*. Utrecht: Willem Pompe Instituut.

Kury, H., Kania, H. and Obergfell-Fuchs, J. (2004) 'Worüber sprechen wir, wenn wir über Punitivität sprechen? Versuch einer konzeptionellen und empirischen Begriffsbestimmung', in R. Lautmann, D. Klimke and F. Sack (eds), *Punitivität (Kriminologisches Journal 8. Beiheft)*: 51–88.

Leferink, S. and Vos, K. (2007) *Spreekrecht en schriftelijke slachtofferverklaring: recht of kans? Een onderzoek naar het Victim Impact Statement in de praktijk van het Nederlandse strafrecht.* Utrecht: Slachtofferhulp Nederland.

Lemonne, A., Van Camp, T. and Vanfraechem, I. (2007) *Onderzoek met betrekking tot de evaluatie van de voorzieningen ten behoeve van slachtoffers van inbreuken.* Brussels: Nationaal Instituut voor Criminalistiek en Criminologie.

Lind, E. A. and Tyler, T. R. (1988) *The Social Psychology of Procedural Justice.* New York: Plenum Press.

Maguire, M. (1982) *Burglary in a Dwelling.* London: Heinemann.

Mawby, R. I. and Walkalte, S. (1994) *Critical Victimology.* London: Sage.

Meyvis, W. (1993) 'Slachtofferhulp in beweging', in T. Peters and J. Goethals (eds), *De achterkant van de criminaliteit. Over victimologie, slachtofferhulp en strafrechtsbedeling.* Antwerpen: Kluwer Rechtswetenschappen België, pp. 231–66.

Miyazawa, S. (2008) 'The politics of increasing punitiveness and the rising populism in Japanese criminal justice policy', *Punishment and Society*, 10(1): 47–77.

Nationaal Forum voor Slachtofferbeleid (1998) *Handvest voor het slachtoffer van een misdrijf.* Brussels: FOD Justitie.

Nationaal Forum voor Slachtofferbeleid (2004) *Aanbevelingen van het Nationaal Forum voor Slachtofferbeleid. Stand van zaken.* Brussels: FOD Justitie.

Nationaal Forum voor Slachtofferbeleid (2005) *Uw rechten als slachtoffer van een misdrijf.* Brussels: FOD Justitie.

Nieuwbeerta, P. (ed.) (2002) *Crime Victimization in Comparative Perspective: Results from the International Crime Victims Survey, 1989–2000.* The Hague: Boom Juridische Uitgevers.

Peters, T. (1993) 'Slachtofferschap: probleemanalyse, sociale en penale reacties', in T. Peters and J. Goethals (eds), *De achterkant van de criminaliteit. Over victimologie, slachtofferhulp en strafrechtsbedeling.* Antwerp: Kluwer Rechtswetenschappen België, pp. 5–90.

Pollefeyt, D. (2000) 'Vergeving: valkuil of springplank naar een betere samenleving? Op zoek naar een nieuw begin voor dader en slachtoffer', in R. Burggraeve, D. Pollefeyt and J. De Tavernier (eds), *Zand erover? Vereffenen, vergeven, verzoenen.* Leuven: Davidsfonds, pp. 143–72.

Reeves, H. and Mulley, K. (2000) 'The new status of victims in the UK: opportunities and threats', in A. Crawford and J. Goodey (eds), *Integrating a Victim Perspective within Criminal Justice.* Aldershot: Ashgate, pp. 125–45.

Roberts, J. and Erez, E. (2004) 'Communication in sentencing: exploring the expressive function of victim impact statements', *International Review of Victimology*, 10: 223–4.

Roberts, J. V. and Hough, M. (2006) *Understanding Public Attitudes to Criminal Justice.* Maidenhead: Open University Press.

Rock, P. (1990) *Helping Victims of Crime: The Home Office and the Rise of Victim Support in England and Wales.* Oxford: Oxford University Press.

Rock, P. (2008) 'The treatment of victims in England and Wales', *Policing*, 2(1): 110–19.

Sanders, A. and Jones, I. (2007) 'The victim in court', in S. Walklate (ed.), *Handbook of Victims and Victimology.* Cullompton: Willan, pp. 282–308.

Sautner, L. and Hirtenlehner, H. (2007) *Opfererwartungen im System der Strafjustiz. Eine empirische Analyse der Ansprüche von Kriminalitätsopfern an Strafrecht und Strafprozess. Forschungsbe-richt.* Linz: Zentrum für Rechtspsychologie und Kriminologie.

Sebba, L. (2000) 'The individualization of the victim: from positivism to post-modernism', in A. Crawford and J. Goodey (eds), *Integrating a Victim Perspective within Criminal Justice.* Aldershot: Ashgate, pp. 55–76.

Sessar, K. (1992) *Wiedergutmachen oder Strafen. Einstellungen in der Bevölkerung und der Justiz.* Pfaffenweiler: Cantaurus-Verlagsgeschellschaft.

Sessar, K. (1999) 'Punitive attitudes of the public: reality and myth', in G. Bazemore and L. Walgrave (eds), *Restorative Juvenile Justice: Repairing the Harm of Youth Crime.* Monsey, NY: Criminal Justice Press, pp. 287–304.

Shapland, J. (2000) 'Victims and criminal justice: creating responsible criminal justice agencies', in A. Crawford and J. Goodey (eds), *Integrating a Victim Perspective within Criminal Justice*. Aldershot: Ashgate, pp. 147–64.

Shapland, J., Willmore, J. and Duff, P. (1985) *Victims in the Criminal Justice System*. Aldershot: Gower.

Spalek, B. (2006) *Crime Victims. Theory, Policy and Practice*. New York: Palgrave Macmillan.

Strang, H. (2002) *Repair or Revenge: Victims and Restorative Justice*. Oxford: Oxford University Press.

Tulkens, F. and van de Kerchove, M. (1996) 'La justice pénale: justice imposée, justice participative, justice consensuelle ou justice négociée?', in P. Gérard, F. Ost and M. van de Kerchove (eds), *Droit négocié, droit imposé?* Brussels: Publications des Facultés Universitaires Saint-Louis, pp. 529–79.

Tulloch, J. (2006) *One Day in July: Experiencing 7/7*. London: Little, Brown.

Van Dijk, J. (1988) 'Ideological trends within the victims movement: an international perspective', in M. Maguire and J. Pointing (eds), *Victims of Crime: A New Deal?* Milton Keynes: Open University Press, pp. 115–26.

Van Dijk, J. (2008) *Slachtoffers als zondebokken*. Antwerpen: Maklu.

Van Dijk, J., van Kesteren, J. and Smit, P. (2007) *Criminal Victimisation in International Perspective. Key Findings from the 2004–2005 ICVS and EU ICS*. The Hague: Boom Juridische Uitgevers.

Victim Support Europe (1996) *Statement of Victims' Rights in the Process of Criminal Justice*. London: European Forum for Victim Services.

Victim Support Europe (1998) *The Social Rights of Victims or Crime*. London: European Forum for Victim Services.

Walklate, S. (2007) *Imagining the Victim of Crime*. Maidenhead: Open University Press.

Wemmers, J. M. (1996) *Victims in the Criminal Justice System: A Study into the Treatment of Victims and Its Effects on Their Attitudes and Behaviour*. Amsterdam: Kugler.

Wemmers, J. and Cyr, K. (2006) *Victims' Needs within the Context of the Criminal Justice System*. Montreal: International Centre for Comparative Criminology.

Williams, B. (2005) *Victims of Crime and Community Justice*. London: Jessica Kingsley.

Williams, B. and Goodman, H. (2007) 'The role of the voluntary sector', in S. Walklate (ed.), *Handbook of Victims and Victimology*. Cullompton: Willan, pp. 240–54.

Wright, M. (1989) 'What the public wants', in M. Wright and B. Galaway (eds), *Mediation and Criminal Justice: Victims, Offenders and Community*. London: Sage, pp. 264–9.

Young, M. A. (1999) 'Justice for all – even the victims', in J. J. M. van Dijk, R. G. H. van Kaam and J. Wemmers (eds), *Caring for Crime Victims*. Monsey, NY: Criminal Justice Press, pp. 179–86.

Young, M. A. (2006) 'A history of the victims movement in the United States', in S. Cornell (ed.), *The Use and Application of the United Nations Declaration of Basic Principles of Justice for Victims of Crime and Abuse of Power – Twenty Years after Its Adoption*. Tokyo: UNAFEI, pp. 69–80.

Zimring, F. E. and Johnson, D. T. (2006) 'Public opinion and the governance of punishment in democratic political systems', *Annals of the American Academy of Political and Social Science*, 605: 266–80.

12

PUNITIVE NEEDS, SOCIETY AND PUBLIC OPINION: AN EXPLORATIVE STUDY OF AMBIVALENT ATTITUDES TO PUNISHMENT AND CRIMINAL JUSTICE

Kristof Verfaillie

12.1 Introduction

In the fall of 2004, shortly after the release of a report about the number of Belgians held captive in foreign prisons, a journalist asks Rudi Veestraeten, Director-General of Consular Affairs of the Belgian Ministry of Foreign Affairs: 'Isn't it ambiguous that the public demands harsher punishment for criminals in Belgium, but sympathizes with imprisoned Belgians abroad?' (*De Standaard*, 16 October 2004). The question highlights two important issues in the public debate about crime control policies. On the one hand, that debate is characterized by references to the opinions, desires and expectations of 'the public', and most often those references are negative: politicians, magistrates, police and media assume that the public wants harsher punishment. On the other hand, the journalist suggests that the public is ambivalent about these issues. Apparently, the public isn't that clear about what the right punishment is or should be.

In this chapter[1] I will focus on the popular assertion that 'the public wants harsher punishment'. I will do so in light of the debate about penal populism. Penal populism is seen as one of the driving forces behind more punitive penal policies. Populist politicians are punitive, they develop policies aimed at punishment, precisely because they believe that such policies can bring political success. However, is 'the public' 'punitive'? Is a more severe penal policy a popular penal policy? Can we refer to the desires and expectations of the public in such (general) terms?

12.2 Punitiveness and penal populism

12.2.1 Punitiveness as attitude

Before I can address these complex questions, let me first examine in brief what it means to be 'punitive'. Punitiveness is an attitude, a particular kind of decision-making or judgment. When people make decisions or render judgment, they interpret the world they live in. They evaluate practices, and they inevitably do so from a particular position in that world (e.g. Kress and Van Leeuwen 1996; Blommaert *et al.* 2005). As such, the practices people evaluate don't convey fixed meanings, but they become meaningful throughout multiple and various interactions (e.g. Fairclough 1992; Silverstein and Urban 1996; Weiss and Wodak 2002; Blommaert and Verfaillie 2009). When social scientists suggest that practices don't convey fixed meanings, they don't suggest that these practices do not exist or do not have concrete effects. It simply means that 'meaning' is not dictated by the practices under study (e.g. Sellars 1997). Practices are 'criminal' or they are 'uncivil' because people find it useful to talk about these practices in that particular way. When we refer to practices as 'criminal' or 'uncivil', we categorize these phenomena, they are made intelligible, or we frame them in a particular way (see also Verfaillie *et al.* 2007; Blommaert and Verfaillie 2009).

People render judgment about the world they live in, they evaluate concrete practices and events, and this process is often captured by scientists in terms of attitudes. Someone is 'conservative' or 'progressive' because they express particular points of view, have a particular perspective on things or evaluate practices a certain way. These points of view, evaluations, or perspectives correspond to what scientists have defined as 'conservative' or 'progressive'. 'Punitiveness' can be understood in a similar way. Punitiveness is an attitude, a particular perspective or decision-making aimed at inflicting punishment. This means that people (citizens, police, magistrates, politicians, journalists, but also scientists) evaluate, categorize, define and make practices intelligible in a way that might evoke or favour punishment.[2]

This process of categorizing human practices is a dynamic one in which remarkable transformations can occur. When criminologists suggest that western societies have become more punitive societies, this refers to much more than the mere observation that more and harsher punishment is being delivered regarding traditional categorizations of crime and criminal behaviour. The evolution toward more punitive societies also entails an important qualitative transformation or a widening of crime- or security-related categorizations. Mary (1997), Young (1999), Garland (2001) and Wacquant (2004), among many others, have reported remarkable transformations in this regard. Whereas practices were once defined as a social problem, a problem of exclusion, poverty, unemployment, housing and so forth, these problems are now increasingly defined as 'uncivil', 'criminal' or as sources of feelings of insecurity. Mary (1997; see also Mary and Nagels this volume) has defined this process, and the transformation it entails, as *la pénalization du social:* an increasing number of social issues are redefined in terms of security issues. Criminologists and sociologists of punishment are critical about these categorizations, because they conflict with normative ideals (e.g. human rights) or because they seem less useful from a perspective of reintegration, structural problem-solving, constructive conflict resolution or other, restorative, arguments.

In sum: 'punitiveness' is an attitude, a set of evaluative practices, categorizations or decision-making processes. Those processes or practices give rise to (more) punishment but cannot be attributed to one single actor. The increased use of prisons and the rise in prison populations are, among other things, the outcome of decision-making processes that occur throughout society and can be situated on different levels and fields, which influence each other significantly (Beyens *et al.* 1993; Snacken *et al.* 1995, 2002; Garland 2001). In this chapter I will focus on one of these decision-making processes, i.e. the political decision-making process or, more specifically, a policy format that criminologists find important in explaining punitiveness and they have come to refer to as 'penal populism'.

12.2.2 Penal populism

A growing number of analyses suggest that punitive trends in western societies can be attributed to populist currents in the policy process (e.g. Bottoms 1995; Newburn 1997; Garland and Sparks 2000; Garland 2001; Roberts *et al.* 2003; Pratt *et. al.* 2005; Roberts and Hough 2005; Salas 2005; Downes and van Swaaningen 2007; Pratt 2007; Freiberg and Gelb 2008). Garland (2001: 13) suggests that:

> Somehow the relation between politicians, the public and professionals has been transformed, with major consequences for policy and practice … there is now a distinctly populist current in penal politics that denigrates expert and professional elites and claims the authority of 'the people', of common sense, of 'getting back to basics'. (Garland 2001: 13)

Let us explore this issue of penal populism based on a well known example in Belgium. In 2003, the former president of the Flemish social-democratic party, Steve Stevaert, suggested the revision of the legal framework on early release in the wake of a popular television show *Doe de Stem Test*, near the end of the 2003 federal electoral campaign. In this TV show, celebrities (as well as the viewers) are asked to respond to a series of propositions. Based on the responses that are given, a political profile is drawn, in first instance of the participating celebrities, but the show intends to help viewers assess their position in the political landscape as well. In the 2003 show, one of the propositions was: 'under certain conditions, offenders of serious crimes can be eligible for early release'. Of the viewers 88.9 per cent disagreed, and Steve Stevaert suggested that the legal framework on early release needed to be revised accordingly.

The political intervention of Stevaert is 'populist', and Abts (2004: 6–7; see also Corijn 2004; Blommaert 2004) identifies four features of a populist policy rhetoric. First, populism redefines the foundations of 'legitimacy' and 'legitimate politics'.

Legitimate policies are those policies which are based on what the 'public wants', and this public is perceived as a homogeneous body. Second, populism creates a 'politics of simplicity': it suggests that policy-making is easy and that policy choices are a matter of common sense. Politics should be as straightforward and unmediated as possible. The typical features of a representative democracy, with its complex and technical procedures and its various institutions, should therefore be distrusted. The voice of the people is filtered throughout these institutions and procedures, which is seen as less democratic. Third, populism redefines the conditions and restrictions which are imposed on the public debate and the policy-making process, precisely because it favours a politics of simplicity. What can be said about political issues, and the way political opinions may be expressed, is thus very much bound by formats which favour common sense, simplicity and straightforwardness. Fourth, populism reduces the public debate to dualisms and political essentialism. The public debate is polarized and every issue is perceived in uncompromising and unequivocal terms.

As a policy format, populism thus inevitably implies a significant reduction of the complexity of social and political issues. Policy-making is no longer the outcome of a transparent, evidence-based debate among representatives of different political perspectives, nor is it a carefully balanced appraisal of rational arguments. Quite the contrary. Policy choices are inspired by what is popular in the eye of the public or what is electorally attractive (Blommaert *et al.* 2004; Beyens 2006; Reynaert *et al.* 2006). In the field of crime control, populism thus implies that the electoral advantage of a policy takes precedence over its penal effectiveness (Roberts *et al.* 2003: 5). The electoral advantage of a policy is primarily assessed based on opinion polls, and is dependent on communication formats and strategies that support a 'politics of simplicity'. What can be said about crime, insecurity, punishment and crime control, and the way political opinions about these topics may be expressed, is thus very much bound by communication formats and strategies which emphasize and favour simplicity, straightforwardness and common sense ideas ('what everyone knows') about crime and punishment.[3]

12.2.3 Political responsiveness and punitiveness

Penal populism leads to punitive policy choices because populists believe that promoting harsh and severe punishment is popular and will provide electoral advantages (Bottoms 1995). This belief in the popularity of severe punishment is based on specific assumptions about the desires, expectations and opinions of people. The question is where these assumptions come from and how they emerge. What we know about people's attitudes and opinions,[4] and what policy-makers and politicians want to know about 'the public', depends on the ways in which knowledge about the public is made and can be acquired. Politicians and policy-makers can acquire knowledge about people's opinions in various ways. They can turn to opinion poll results, but at the same time they engage in everyday conversations and are confronted with various media or the outcome of elections. All these information sources provide information about people's opinions. When politicians and policy-makers refer to 'the people', 'the public' or 'public opinion', they inevitably do so in light of specific information sources (and this is true for scientists, media or other actors as well). The image of 'the public' is thus very much shaped by particular information sources and the uptake of these sources in the policy rhetoric.

A public can be constructed in a variety of ways, but today notions like 'the people', 'the public' or 'public opinion' quite often seem to refer to the results of opinion polls. At best these polls meet scientific criteria and make statements based on the principle of random sampling (Glynn *et al.* 1999).[5] Such polls are often depicted as neutral, objective (scientific) and democratic ways of representing people's opinions about social issues or political preferences. Polls, however, are methodological tools that, like any other methodology for that matter, produce a specific kind of knowledge about people's attitudes and opinions (see also Bourdieu 1979). Poll results are the outcome of a process of methodological choices or technical procedures that measure and inevitably shape opinions and attitudes.[6] Quantitative polls, based on a random sample of respondents, will first and foremost produce knowledge about how opinions are distributed within a social group or across a society: they do not provide information about why respondents express opinions in a particular way (Shiraev and Sobel 2006: 3).

People's opinions can thus be measured and represented in various ways, but the kinds of information resources or methodologies that are selected and used in the policy process are just as much dependent on the kinds of knowledge policy-makers and politicians want to gather. A penal populist will mobilize methodologies to assess what policy choices are popular and what initiatives will provide electoral advantage. Populists do not find much use for complexity and ambivalence. They claim to express what everyone knows, the straightforward truth about punishment and criminal justice. As such, populists prefer polls that present unambiguous arguments or they will rephrase more complex and nuanced results in terms of a politics of simplicity. Elitist politicians, on the other hand, might use polling techniques to assess how the policies they want to pursue can best be communicated or 'sold' to the public (see Jacobs and Shapiro 2000). Based on a detailed case-study of the debates that occurred within the Clinton administration and Congress over healthcare reform in 1993 and 1994, Jacobs and Shapiro (2000) found that 'when not facing election, contemporary presidents and members of Congress routinely ignore the public's policy preferences and follow their own political philosophies, as well as those of their party's activists, their contributors, and their interest group allies'. Jacobs and Shapiro (2000: xv) thus warn about 'crafted talk' and 'simulated responsiveness': politicians and policy-makers study public opinion, not so much to find inspiration for the development of their policies, but 'to find the most effective means to move public opinion closer to their own desired policies'.

In sum: when politicians and policy-makers use words like 'the public' or 'public opinion', they refer to information about people's opinions. Such information can be derived from different sources or methods that are used to acquire information about people's opinions (e.g. polls, everyday conversations, …). At the same time, however, references to 'the public' may not relate to any information about people's opinions whatsoever. 'The public' is then a rhetorical tool, an expression of political ideas and ideologies, mobilized to serve political strategies and purposes. With reference to the work of Latour (1990), 'the public' and 'public opinion' can perhaps best be described as a 'knowledge assembly'. 'Public opinion' is then the result of drawing things together, a process in which all kinds of materials (research strategies, ideas, (political) motives, desires, observations …) are drawn together or assembled (Lippens 2006, 2007). The debate about penal populism then requires a critical empirical analysis of how public opinion is assembled and what the effects are of particular assemblages. In addition we will need a normative appraisal of the knowledge that is and should be used in the criminal policy process. Does knowledge about people's opinions need to be used in the policy process? What knowledge about these opinions – what 'public opinion' – should inspire policy choices?

I have suggested that contemporary constructions of the public seem to be shaped more and more by the results of opinion polls. However, there are important reasons to question the value of that knowledge. To question the value of opinion polls is not so much inspired by the important qualitative differences that exist among the different polling tools. Owing to quantitative research that meets high quality standards, we know a lot about people's opinions about punishment and criminal justice (e.g. Roberts and Hough 2005). But when one considers the key findings of this line of research, there seem to be quite a lot of research findings that are rather troubling or confusing. For instance, people seem to be convinced that judges aren't severe enough. At the same time, we know that people don't know how severe judges are, or what judges do altogether (Roberts and Hough 2005: 85). In other words, it is unclear how people evaluate 'punishment' and 'criminal justice', a problem which surfaces quite often in analyses of people's punishment preferences. Several authors have argued that people seem to be ambivalent about how we should punish (Doble 1987; Flanagan 1996; Longmire 1996; Kaukinen and Colaveccia 1999; Tonry 1999; Garland 2001; Stalans 2002; Roberts *et al.* 2003; Roberts and Hough 2005; Hutton 2005).

12.3 Public ambivalence about punishment and criminal justice

People seem to be ambivalent about crime and punishment, and this finding raises important questions about the value of general statements about 'what the public wants'. Public ambivalence about crime and punishment is not a recent or a new find. One of the key findings from American public opinion research of the past 25 years is that Americans' opinions about crime, punishment and criminal justice is characterized by paradoxes. Flanagan (1996, 2003: 20, 22) argues that one of the themes that has characterized American public opinion about crime and criminal justice over the past 25 years is the apparent logical inconsistencies between views on related issues. Flanagan wonders how we should make sense of a public that supports punishment as the main goal of sentencing criminals, but also favours treatment, education, counselling and training programmes for inmates? How to make sense of an American public that favours capital punishment for murder because they believe it acts as a deterrent, but when informed that capital punishment is not a deterrent for murder, the support for capital punishment remains all the same. Shiraev and Sobel (2006: 73) point to the paradoxes in a 2003 ABC News survey in which 64 per cent of the respondents supported the death penalty for persons convicted of murder. In that same survey, however, 'only' 49 per cent of the respondents were in favour of the death penalty when asked whether they preferred the death penalty or life in prison with no chance of parole as punishment for people convicted of murder.[7] Stalans (2002: 15–16) suggests that research findings about public attitudes to punishment in the United States support both the existence of a 'punitive public', which favours long prison terms, and a 'merciful public', in support of rehabilitation, community-based sentences and less severe sentences than the law allows.

Ambivalence is quite often explained in terms of (diverging) theoretical perspectives and methodological choices (e.g. Stalans 2002). Researchers find that, depending on the methodology that is used, a different notion of 'the public' and 'public opinion' will appear (Asher 2007). People tend to show more punitive attitudes when they are asked to respond instantaneously to abstract questions in single-item surveys, and they tend to be far less punitive when given the chance to deliberate and render judgment based on detailed information about a case (Freiberg and Gelb 2008: 4–5). Longmire (1996: 107) found that people were not simply in favour of or opposed to the death penalty, their attitudes about the death penalty 'vary with information about the biases associated with its administration'. The inconsistencies found by researchers should therefore not be attributed to the capriciousness of the respondents. Page and Shapiro (1992) analysed and reviewed 50 years of trends in Americans' policy preferences and concluded that the American public is a rational public and that the 'myth of capricious change' about opinion formation should be refuted. Page and Shapiro (1992: 384) recognized that *individuals* are often not that well informed about public issues, and 'their expression of policy preferences varies markedly and somewhat randomly from one survey to the next'. They do find, however, that collective policy preferences have very different properties, in the sense that 'collective policy preferences are generally stable … they change in understandable and predictable ways, and they are differentiated, patterned, and coherent' (Page and Shapiro 1992: 383–4).

The effect that Page and Shapiro find is obviously a methodological one: the result of differences between analyses conducted on the individual level or on the collective level. But there is more. Even on the collective level, the inconsistencies are apparent: respondents can have conflicting or apparently inconsistent opinions about issues within one policy field. In the field of welfare for instance, Page and Shapiro found that Americans' policy preferences were very much shaped by the way these measures are represented (Page and Shapiro 1992: 126). For instance, there seems to be a lot more public support for policy measures that aim to support people in need, i.e. people who are believed not to be responsible for the ordeal they are in (old age, certain diseases, certain crime victims or victims of natural disaster, …). Policy measures that are not presented in these terms receive much less public support. Opinions about the redistribution of wealth, about solidarity, are in other words connected to specific themes, identities and topics, and it is precisely these connections that can explain why people might express contradictory points of view about issues such as the redistribution of wealth.

These findings remind us how important theoretical perspectives and methodologies are for the production of knowledge about public opinion to punishment and criminal justice. According to Stalans (2002: 16–17), the image of an ambivalent, complex and ambiguous public stems from the various methodologies researchers have mobilized to measure attitudes to punishment. Despite these efforts, Stalans (2002: 20) finds that researchers have barely scratched the surface of public attitudes to punishment, and she suggests that we need to come to a more thorough understanding of information processing and attitude structures. Stalans' argument thus implies that a lot of the research strategies and tools we have used thus far to measure public attitudes to punishment and criminal justice may not be useful to understand how and why these opinions and attitudes come about.

12.3.1 Opinion formation and the importance of authority

Herbert Blumer developed insightful arguments on the issue of opinion formation in his influential paper 'Public Opinion and Public Opinion Polling' (1948). Blumer argued that opinion polls provide rather limited insight into the opinion formation process because they are based on un-sociological notions and conceptions of 'the public' and 'society'. Opinion polls tend to reduce 'public opinion' to the sum or aggregation of individual opinions on a particular issue. As such, every individual is seen as equally important to the opinion formation process, and this is never the case in our societies, which are essentially structured or organized hierarchically. According to Blumer (1948: 546–7), public opinion should rather be conceived as 'a function of a structured society, differentiated into a network of different kinds of groups and individuals having differential weight and influence and occupying different strategic positions'. Accordingly, Blumer (1948: 549) discards the idea that public opinion polls represent the vox populi. Such a claim is a normative statement: public opinion should be the sum or aggregation of individual opinions. From an empirical point of view, however, this perspective is untenable. If we want to *understand* public opinion, we need methodologies and perspectives which are not based on assumptions of what public opinion should be like. Scientists need to develop tools that enable them to analyse public opinion as an empirical reality:

> If one seeks to justify polling as a method of studying public opinion on the ground that the composition of public *opinion ought* to be different than what it is, he is not establishing the validity of the method for the study of the empirical world as it is. Instead, he is hanging on the coat-tails of a dubious proposal for social reform. (Blumer 1948: 549–50)

In other words, if we want to understand how 'public opinion' or collective policy preferences come about, we should explore perspectives and methodologies that allow us to grasp the complexity of opinion formation. Blumer's work suggests that this requires, first and foremost, a better understanding of 'authority'. 'The public' is not a homogenous group, but is highly differentiated. Not every individual is equally important to the opinion formation process. If we are to come to a better understanding of 'authority', i.e. the observation that some actors are more important than others in shaping people's opinions about punishment and criminal justice, we need to explore how people are informed about punishment and criminal justice. What are important information sources? Who are the opinion leaders and why?

The importance of 'authority' to opinion formation and the concept of opinion leadership obviously isn't new nor is it limited to the work and comments of Herbert Blumer. In fact, decades of scientific research suggest that 'there is a group of people in any community to whom others look to help them to form opinions on various issues and matters' (Weimann 1994; Weimann *et al.* 2007: 173). A classic study in the field of opinion leadership theory is the People's Choice study of Paul Lazarsfeld *et al.* (1944), who laid the groundwork for the seminal 'two-step flow of communication' hypothesis (see also Katz and Lazarsfeld 1955; Katz 1957). The People's Choice study explored the influence of the media on voting intentions in Erie County, Ohio during the 1940 American presidential campaign. The study revealed that informal conversations with politically engaged friends and family were far more important and influential on people's voting intentions than the mass media (campaign messages). The 'two-step flow of communication' hypothesis thus suggests that the influence of the media on people's opinions and behaviour is mediated by a small minority of opinion leaders or influentials, who pass on their reading of the media content to opinion followers. This highly influential hypothesis has given rise to numerous studies, criticism and revisions (see Watts and Dodds 2007). Contemporary studies seem to suggest that media influence and opinion leadership are best understood as a multi-step flow process rather than a two-step flow process: opinion leaders in one particular topic area are found to be involved in a process of exchange with the people they influence, making them both disseminators and recipients of influence (Weimann 1982; Weimann *et al.* 2007).

Opinion leadership theories thus imply that a thorough understanding of 'authority' and its importance to people's opinions about punishment and criminal justice requires a conceptualization of attitudes and opinions which is very different from the predominant quantitative research designs that primarily intend to produce knowledge about the distribution of opinions within a social group or across a society. To explore this issue further, I will turn to the work of Blommaert, Meert and others who have suggested that it might be more useful for social scientists to study opinions and attitudes in terms of logically structured paradoxes.

12.3.2 Attitudes as logically constructed paradoxes

Meert *et al.* (2004; see also Blommaert *et al.* 2003; Blommaert *et al.* 2005; Blommaert 2005) have argued, based on the work of Foucault, Goffman and Bourdieu, that opinions cannot be understood in terms of answers to survey questions, but should be analysed in terms of situated discourses and behaviour.[8] Opinions are shaped relative to concrete events and occurrences in space and time. People interpret or evaluate these events and occurrences, they categorize the information they receive and structure it hierarchically. Opinions are thus situated, dynamic and complex, they are organized thematically, i.e. related to specific issues, themes and fields. Precisely because opinions are organized thematically, people often seem to be ambivalent or inconsistent from an ideological point of view. Someone might hold 'progressive' views regarding ecological issues, but he/she might be 'conservative' when it comes to education. The same is true, however, for the issues themselves. People might express conflicting opinions regarding 'ecology', they might vote for an ecological political party but drive a highly polluting car. In the field of education, people might be Muslim but send their children to a Catholic school. From an ideological point of view, people may thus appear to be confused or inconsistent. According to Meert *et al.* (2004), however, there is a logic to these 'inconsistencies' or paradoxes. Their research findings show that people do not seem to act based on one clear and consistent ideological attitude towards society. Individuals do not assess every event or issue in terms of one clear-cut (ideological) standard or perspective. Meert *et al.* (2004) thus find it more useful to describe people's attitudes and opinions as 'logically structured paradoxes': people's statements are consistent with almost microscopically and thematically organized hegemonies (see also Blommaert 2005).

An insightful example of this perspective on opinion formation is the analysis by Meert *et al.* (2004) of the socio-spatial and discursive dimension of attitudes towards asylum-seekers, refugees and refugee centres. The researchers found that people do not articulate one coherent 'opinion' or 'attitude' about a topic such as the presence of a refugee centre in their neighbourhood. This issue consists of many different sub-themes and issues, each of them evoking specific answers and reactions. Meert *et al.* (2004) found that people could be positive towards refugee centres *in general* and express faith in the public authorities with respect to their general approach to the matter. At the same time, however, the researchers found that people articulated more negative attitudes towards the presence of a refugee centre *in their neighbourhood*, or they expressed fear of falling victim to burglary and demonstrated a lack of faith in the public authorities with respect to their capacity to protect property. So even though the issue of the presence of an asylum centre in a neighbourhood might appear to be a unified topic, in reality it is a highly fragmented and heterogeneous collection of topics and orientations. Meert *et al.* (2004; see also Blommaert *et al.* 2003) furthermore found that the quality of opinions (e.g. content, complexity) is highly dependent on 'place'. Distance and proximity proved to be important to explain qualitative differences in people's attitudes. The people that lived close to the asylum centre developed complex and highly dynamic attitudes, whereas people that did not live in the proximity of an asylum centre developed significantly less complex attitudes and these attitudes were mainly constructed based on translocal information (e.g. media reports).

12.3.3 Ambivalence and the importance of authority: an ethnographic approach

The question of ambivalence prompts criminologists to develop a more thorough understanding of people's opinions about punishment and criminal justice. I turned to the work of Blumer, who identified 'authority' as a highly important notion in the opinion formation process. The issue of 'authority' and its importance to opinion formation raises questions about the way people are informed about punishment and criminal justice. How are their opinions and attitudes constructed? What are important information sources? Who are the opinion leaders and why? The work of Meert and Blommaert provided important analytical clues for me to explore these questions. Their work provides compelling arguments for an *ethnographic* approach to attitudes and opinions. In order to understand people's opinions about a topic, researchers should analyse people's narratives and conversations and the interactions people engage in. Researchers should context- ualize these discourses and interactions, i.e. analyse them in concrete settings or in terms of people's spatial, temporal and socio-economic positions and trajectories. As such, these kinds of analyses can reveal how people are informed about particular issues and why certain information sources are more important to them than others.

In the remainder of this chapter, I will explore the issue of ambivalence based on the narratives of one of the participants, a woman named Judy, in an ethnographic study I conducted in 2007–08.[9] The analysis I will present here is an exploratory one, not a final research report. It should also be clear that I do not intend to make statements which are representative of 'the Belgian population'. My sole intention here is to come to a preliminary exploration of ambivalent attitudes to punishment and to deepen my understanding about *how* and *why* authority and opinion leadership shape the paradoxes and inconsistencies that are found in people's discourse about these issues. The argument that I will develop can be summarized as follows: people's discourse about crime, punishment and criminal justice is polycentric,[10] it contains multiple normative points of orientation which can be contradictory when considered as a whole. In the narratives I analysed, I found these contradictions to be inevitable. Precisely because inconsistencies in people's discourse about crime and punishment proved to be inevitable, general or abstract statements about 'the right punishment', 'people's expectations about criminal justice' and so forth should be approached or interpreted with care.

12.4 Ambivalent opinions about punishment and criminal justice: an exploratory analysis

Judy is a middle-aged woman with a higher education and no outspoken political preferences who works part-time as a high-school teacher in Mechelen, a city between Brussels and Antwerp. Judy fell victim to a burglary at the time of the study, an issue which has proven to be important throughout my analysis. I conducted one interview with Judy. The first part of the interview I asked her to explain, justify and elaborate on the answers to the items in the *Justice Barometer* survey. In the second part of the interview I asked her additional questions about her daily life and the experiences she has with crime, punishment and criminal justice in particular.

The first issue I need to address is whether Judy is in fact ambivalent about punishment and criminal justice. Analysis of Judy's narratives reveals the following inconsistencies.

Judy is in favour of youth prisons but she opposes harsh punishment for juveniles. She believes that the vast majority of cases that are brought before the courts receive fair punishment but she is convinced that judges are often too lenient. Judy favours rehabilitation but she opposes conditional release. She perceives herself as someone who has progressive political views but she is convinced that foreigners, and Moroccans in particular, are more involved in crime than 'native' Belgians. She furthermore believes that police are too lenient towards these cases. Finally, Judy believes due process to be very important but she could never agree with an acquittal due to a violation of criminal procedure.

In sum: the results of the survey contain numerous inconsistencies and these inconsistencies cannot be understood in terms of the answers to the survey questions. I therefore asked Judy to elaborate on her answers and this process generated various narratives about crime, insecurity, punishment, police, criminal justice, offending and victimization. These narratives are important because they clarify how Judy experiences and informs herself about these issues and how she categorizes them. Filling out a survey evokes narratives that function as a frame of reference, a context, for the answers that are given. This has several important consequences.

12.4.1 The importance of the issue

Judy evaluates each survey question based on references to concrete cases and events. Questions about 'trust in the criminal justice system' evoke stories she has picked up in the media and those media narratives have induced the idea that criminal trials are often long and nebulous procedural battles. The stories Judy uses to justify her mistrust in the criminal justice system are selections and interpretations of information, and in this case this information was obtained from visual media (news reports). The narratives contain storylines with specific constructions or images of judicial actors ('the lawyer who plays games' or 'lawyers who hide behind procedures') and refer to concrete cases or settings ('big media trials' or 'the Dutroux case'). The storylines and constructions of actors and settings are important because they provide a contextual framework: Judy's answers become meaningful and intelligible in light of these stories. Each question evokes a particular story, and this is why issues or propositions in the survey that seem connected or closely related (e.g. 'all decisions are just' and the questions about the right punishment of various crimes) might receive conflicting answers. In such cases, similar questions evoked different stories.

Answers to survey questions cannot be understood apart from the context in which they are produced. Yet surveys inevitably involve a process of decontextualization. People's narratives are reduced in terms of the categories provided in the survey. When the results from the survey are released, a second recontextualization occurs: these results are taken up in new contextual frameworks (e.g. policy discourses) where they are given new meaning. Such processes of recontextualization[11] are deeply problematic. Policy-makers might interpret (or mobilize) the given answers in ways that are very different from what the respondent intended. For instance, Judy agrees with the proposition that prisoners should serve the full length of their sentence. Most criminologists would define this point of view as a punitive one. However, Judy cannot agree with the early release of prisoners because she believes this infringes upon a judge's expert assessment of a case. In other words, she does not understand why a judge's ruling should not be respected: 'if you render a judgment, stick to it' and 'why is everything so complicated?', 'you have to provide a fixed term'. Her opposition to early release furthermore stems from a conviction that systems of early release lead to uncertainty. She believes prisoners are entitled to hope and transparency: 'you should not give someone life without parole'; 'if you give someone a sentence of ten years, but he will only have to serve four years, give him four years right from the start'; 'you should give someone hope – in the end that is what matters'; 'you have to be clear and straightforward'; 'they should know exactly what is coming to them'. Judy is convinced that prisoners should be given a fixed sentence and that this term should be used to prepare their return to society.

12.4.2 Normative judgments are situated

Each survey question is interpreted in light of specific narratives and convictions. As such, Judy never speaks in abstract, absolute or neutral terms about crime, insecurity, punishment and justice. These topics are inevitably bound by a context, a frame of reference, i.e. they imply references to concrete situations, people and events. This contextual framework is important since it inevitably implies a normative or ethical stance or judgment about the issue at hand. A lawyer or any other judicial actor 'who hides behind procedures' or 'who plays games' is someone 'who disregards the truth' or 'discards what is legally correct', and is thus someone who should be mistrusted. When Judy answers that she mistrusts the criminal justice system, she thus refers to concrete situations and people (identities) who are to be mistrusted. She makes a particular normative categorization of judicial practices and this categorization clarifies what 'trust' means and in what circumstances or contexts criminal justice should be mistrusted.

Another example can be found in Judy's judgments about procedural errors. She disagrees with the proposition that someone can be acquitted if the procedure wasn't respected or followed. That proposition evokes stories in which the guilt of the offender has been established beyond any reasonable doubt and the issue of guilt or innocence is thus not dependent on whether the criminal procedure was breached. In other words, no link is assumed between respecting criminal procedures on the one hand, and the question of guilt or innocence on the other hand. In those specific situations where someone's guilt is established, and that person's guilt or innocence cannot be linked to whether the criminal procedure was breached, an acquittal is perceived as highly unjust or unfair.

Despite this stance, Judy still argues that respecting criminal procedure is important. She emphasizes that the 'rules of the game should be abided[by]', and that 'a retrial should always be possible'. However, these stances are linked to different contextual frames than the ones in which an acquittal on procedural grounds was argued for. In sum: statements about 'the right punishment', 'a good criminal justice system', 'a righteous judgment' are situated, they imply references to concrete situations, people (identities) and occurrences that clarify in which circumstances something is 'good', 'right' or 'just'.

12.4.3 Important qualitative differences exist among judgments

Important differences exist among the answers that are given to the survey questions. Some questions evoke highly complex narratives that imply a clear evaluation of a certain topic. For instance, the negative evaluation of police should be situated or explained in terms of an elaborate and complex narrative about the police performance of a burglary that took place in Judy's home. Other questions, however, evoke little or no stories. Judy claims she does not have an opinion about how the criminal justice system functions since she has no concrete experiences with that system.

Questions for which there does not seem to be any frame of reference quite often lead to additional questions for the interviewer ('what do you mean exactly?'; 'in what situation?'), or to additional specifications and explanations ('that depends ...'; 'in this situation ...'), or result in reflections based on specific assumptions ('in every field there are people who perform well and people who don't'). Those questions, specifications and clarifications are attempts to find or provide a context which is felt as a precondition to provide sensible answers to survey questions. The question about the support for a sentence reduction for offenders who helped in the prosecution of criminal offences required a concrete example. When Judy was asked whether traffic offences received adequate punishment, the survey response categories were perceived as a problem since, in Judy's mind, the category 'traffic offences' covered a range of highly diverse practices ('to kill someone in traffic' or 'not using your blinker when leaving a roundabout'). Because Judy connects each of these practices to quite different normative responses and stances, she could not come to a general judgment about the 'appropriate' punishment for 'traffic offences'.

When evaluating the performance of judges, lawyers and prosecutors similar mechanisms came into play. Here the need for context was felt as well ('in pro-deo cases they probably won't try as hard' or 'their performance is dependent on the client or offender'). When no information about judges, lawyers and prosecutors is available, Judy expresses assumptions about how they function in analogy with other professions ('... as there are good and bad doctors' or 'in every field there are people who perform well and people who don't'). In other words, in such cases a contextual appraisal of people's performance is assumed, on the one hand because Judy cannot refer to concrete information that allows her to express an opinion about these 'identities', while on the other hand she constantly experiences the importance of context throughout her own daily interactions. Despite the lack of information about the performance of judges and prosecutors, Judy evaluates them in a positive way based on particular expectations: 'I hope they know their cases' or 'I hope they treat every citizen in an equal manner'.

In other words, there are important qualitative differences (content, complexity) in Judy's evaluations (narratives) of the topics in the survey. Analysis of those different narratives suggests that there is a wide variety of information resources Judy can use to evaluate topics (personal experiences, experiences of significant others, media, etc., ...). However, the content, structure and complexity of the narratives suggests that not every source of information is equally important when evaluating issues. But at the same time, not every issue is equally important to Judy.

12.4.4 The importance of emotions, involvement and identification

The questions and propositions in the survey evoke all kinds of stories and assumptions that can be quite different from one another. Not every assumption or story is equally important and those differences in authority seem to cohere with emotions, processes of involvement or identification. This can be illustrated based on the sources of information that emerge in Judy's narratives. Judy indicates that she watches the news on a daily basis and that she often watches newsmagazines that deal with criminal justice related issues. She reads the newspaper on a nearly daily basis and when there are articles about criminal justice she sometimes reads them. However, the information from those information resources (media) is used in a rather limited and selective way, especially when compared with the information she can draw from her own experience. For instance, Judy's judgments about the performance of the police contain, almost exclusively, references to various personal experiences with police performance (in traffic, in the context of the school where she teaches or in dealing with the burglary she fell victim to). However, the information that is dispersed throughout the media about police performance is hardly referred to. When Judy needs to evaluate the performance of the criminal justice system, she has no personal experience to draw from. In those cases the information obtained from media sources seems to become more important. However, in these cases references to the media seem to be a lot more shallow, the narratives are a lot less elaborate and complex compared with the stories that are based on personal experiences. In sum: the importance of the authority of information resources (personal experiences, experiences of significant others, media, etc. ...) is situated and contextual: information from media sources seems to become more important when personal experience is missing.

The selection of information is not only dependent on processes of identification and involvement but seems to be bound by emotions. The stories that emerge as a response to the survey questions, whether they refer to personal experiences or to information from media sources, are often negative and are connected to feelings of injustice. Judy does not refer to the positive news that is dispersed about police and criminal justice. She refers to situations that evoke strong emotions and that she feels are highly unjust. Often, but not exclusively, these are situations that are connected to Judy's personal world. Stories that evoke strong emotions and are connected to Judy's personal world seem to have more authority, they seem to matter more to Judy's judgments and evaluations. The authority of certain stories over others can be observed in the stories Judy disseminates herself. She does not discuss the media reports on a daily basis with her neighbours or peers. The moment she became a victim, however, she did engage in various conversations with neighbours, family members and other peers about this issue. Throughout these interactions Judy continuously re-evaluated her experiences and perceptions about 'victimization', 'criminal justice', 'police', 'punishment', and so forth. She shares her experiences with other people, and this process evokes stories with the people she interacts with. Often people seem to connect Judy's stories to their own experiences with theft or burglary, and police performance, or they refer to the experiences of others who fell victim to such crimes.

12.5 Conclusion

In this chapter, I have scrutinized the popular assertion that 'the public wants more and harsher punishment', and I have done so in light of the debates about penal populism. Penal populism is seen as one of the driving forces behind punitive criminal policies. Populist politicians are punitive: they make choices aimed at inflicting punishment or they develop a rhetoric aimed at promoting punishment. They do so because they believe such discourses can help obtain electoral success. Penal populists assume that 'people want harsher punishment', and I have suggested that such generalizing references to the desires, expectations and opinions of people might not be useful. On the one hand, a populist discourse implies a significant reduction of the complexity of issues such as crime, uncivil behaviour and feelings of insecurity. Politicians who make a general plea for more and more severe punishment are oblivious to the complexity of the practices and behaviour that we have come to define as 'criminal', 'uncivil' or 'deviant'. As such, they disregard the need to develop nuanced and differentiated problem-solving approaches for these issues. A general plea for more, and more severe, punishment hinders a meaningful reintegration of offenders in society and disregards durable solutions to social problems and constructive kinds of conflict resolution. Many criminologists will furthermore add that a general plea for harsher punishment is in violation of normative ideals (see Part 2 on 'Punishment and Human Rights' in this volume). Those ideals imply that punishment, regardless of its effects, should be used as a last resort.

The assumptions of penal populists are not very useful, not only because they suggest that complex social issues can be dealt with in simplistic ways, but also because of how they refer to people's expectations and opinions about punishment and criminal justice. 'People want more and harsher punishment', and this is a matter of common sense, what everyone knows about crime control and what everyone wants and expects. With Roberts and Hough, we found that there is a lot we know about people's opinions about punishment and criminal justice. At the same time, however, Stalans suggested that there is a lot we do not understand about people's opinions and that we need a more profound understanding of how these opinions are formed or emerge. Key findings of public opinion research suggest that people are ambivalent about punishment and criminal justice. This ambivalence is a problem for policy-makers, and for populists in particular, because it suggests that simple and straightforward conclusions about people's opinions cannot easily be drawn.

This chapter illustrates how an ethnographic research design might help us deal with people's ambivalence and can help us deepen our understanding of how people's opinions are shaped. This preliminary analysis of the interview data of one of the participants of the study, Judy, tries to make sense of the various contradictions and inconsistencies that characterized her discourse about punishment and criminal justice. This discourse appears to be polycentric, it contains multiple normative points of orientation. When considered as a whole, Judy's statements and assumptions seem ambivalent and contradictory. Those contradictions seem inevitable, precisely because each answer to a survey question is shaped in light of specific narratives and convictions. Because ambivalence about punishment and criminal justice seems inevitable, generalizations or global statements about 'the right punishment', 'the criminal justice system' and 'public opinion' should be treated with care. The exploratory analysis I developed in this chapter suggests that further and more in-depth analysis about opinion formation might focus on: (1) the importance of concrete issues and topics to opinion formation; (2) the situated nature of normative judgments, or the idea that normative judgments should be connected to concrete contexts and settings; (3) the important qualitative differences that exist among judgments, which point to important differences in authority of the various information sources that are available to people; (4) the importance of emotions, involvement and identification to (collective) opinion formation and the diffusion of ideas within communities. To explore these issues further is to embrace complexity and accept that opinions cannot be fully understood in terms of answer categories in survey questions. The debates about penal populism point to the possible negative consequences of a reduction of the complexities of 'public opinion' for the development of crime control policies. In light of these debates it seems sensible to explore knowledge assemblages that might do more justice to the complexities inherent to opinion formation. If we think about new ways to produce knowledge about people's opinions, if we rethink 'public opinion', we will have to go beyond scrutinizing the opinion polls politicians and policy-makers have grown accustomed to. Inevitably such an endeavour will challenge us to rethink public involvement in policy formation altogether.

Notes

1. This chapter is a revised version of the chapter K.Verfaillie (2009) 'Punitieve behoeften, samenleving en publieke opinie', in I. Aertsen, K. Beyens, T. Daems and E. Maes (eds), *Hoe punitief is België?* Ghent: Maklu, pp. 85–106.
2. Criminologists define 'punitiveness' (and thus the aim to punish) as a negative indicator, attitude or process. As such, the debate about punitiveness is in essence a debate about how societies should categorize deviant human behaviour as well as what constitutes meaningful or useful ways of dealing with such behaviour. There is no consensus among criminologists about the answers that should be given to these questions. In other words, the kind of behaviour that should be punished, how we should punish, the very nature of punishment or if we should punish at all together are much debated issues (see, for example, Matthews 2005) Yet, the answers to these questions matter a great deal to the ways in which 'punitiveness' will be defined. Some criminologists might argue that the use of a prison system as such is an indication of punitiveness, which would mean that most societies are punitive. Consequently these criminologists will focus on varying degrees of punitiveness. Other criminologists will argue that the notion of 'excess' is a prerequisite to speak of punitiveness (see Matthews 2005) As such, only those countries that punish beyond certain limits will be referred to as punitive (see similar discussions about the nature and use of community sanctions, therapy, treatment, etc. …).
3. Despite a growing body of literature on the topic, much can be said about the validity of the claims made about the nature and the importance of penal populist policy formats (see Matthews 2005) I will, however, not address those issues here. Clearly, not every development in punishment and crime control is the outcome of populist policy-making, even within a particular country (see Pratt 2007) The policy process, and even the ideological nature of contemporary policy choices, seems highly fragmented or ambivalent (e.g. Garland 2001). Some punishment policies have come about after thorough debate and reflection and with the involvement of expertise aimed at rehabilitative or restorative effectiveness. Other developments are the direct result of highly mediatized criminal cases and do subscribe to the logic of penal populism (Snacken 2007; Snacken and Verfaillie 2009).

4. In this chapter the notions 'attitude' and 'opinion' will be used interchangeably.
5. Obviously polls and survey methodologies come in different shapes and sizes, and the quality of these tools is a much debated issue. The issue of the scientific standards of opinion polls is a very important one, but the point here is that polls and survey methodologies inevitably produce knowledge, regardless of the quality of that knowledge. The debate about the quality of polls and surveys is in essence a debate about the conditions or criteria that determine if the knowledge which is produced is useful or not.
6. Scientists have long documented the ways in which the selection, phrasing, framing and order of survey questions influence the responses of respondents (e.g. Billiet 1996; Asher 2007).
7. Similar and more recent results can be found at: http://www.pollingreport.com/crime.htm.
8. The theoretical and methodological perspective that Meert and Blommaert have developed can be described as a 'Critical Discourse Analysis' (see Fairclough 1995; Jaworski and Coupland 1999; Blommaert 2005). This qualitative research format suggests that if one intends to understand notions such as 'punitiveness', a classic text study or concept analysis will not suffice. Analyses of concepts and discourses require a profound historic, socio-cultural and political contextualization.
9. Each of the participants (20) in this study were asked to talk about their experiences with crime and criminal justice based on the questionnaire of the *Justitiebarometer* (a Belgian survey: see Parmentier *et al.* 2004). The participants were asked to fill out the questionnaire and explain and elaborate on their answers. This process provided me with extensive narratives about punishment preferences, trust in the police and criminal justice, as well as the origins and contexts of such perceptions.
10. This concept is borrowed from the work of Blommaert (2005), who argues that a system is polycentric when it contains different centres to which people can (or have to) orient. The notion of polycentrism is a very important one, for analytical purposes, and requires a more in-depth discussion than I can offer here. However, in the context of this chapter a brief introduction of this notion will suffice.
11. These processes might be referred to as 'entextualization' (Bauman and Briggs 1990; Silverstein and Urban 1996; Blommaert 2005; Blommaert and Verfaillie 2009). Entextualization refers to a process where discourses are decontextualized and then recontextualized, they become part of a different context so that they become a 'new' or different discourse, i.e. they are given new meaning. Entextualization is part of what Silverstein and Urban have defined as the 'natural history of discourse'. Original pieces of discourse, i.e. socially, culturally and historically situated unique occurrences, are lifted from a particular context and are introduced in a new discourse (Blommaert 2005: 251–2; Blommaert and Verfaillie 2009: 332).

References

Abts, K. (2004) 'Het populistisch appel: voorbij de populaire communicatiestijl en ordinaire democratiekritiek', *Tijdschrift voor Sociologie*, 25(4): 451–76.

Asher, H. (2007) *Polling and the Public. What Every Citizen Should Know.* Washington, D.C. CQ Press.

Bauman, R. and Briggs, C. (1990) 'Poetics and Performance as Critical Perspectives on Language and Social Life', *Annual Review of Anthropology*, 19: 59–88.

Beyens, K. (2006) 'Publieke opinie, democratie en beleid', *Orde van de Dag*, 29: 3–5.

Beyens, K., Snacken, S. and Eliaerts, E. (1993) Barstende muren. Overbevolkte *gevangenissen: omvang, oorzaken en mogelijke oplossingen. Antwerpen*: Kluwer-Rechtswetenschappen.

Billiet, J. (1996) *Methoden van sociaal-wetenschappelijk onderzoek: ontwerp en dataverzameling.* Leuven: Acco.

Blommaert, J. (2004) 'Populisme als spreekregime', in J. Blommaert, E. Corijn, M. Holthof and D. Lesage, *Populisme*. Berchem: EPO, pp. 123–50.

Blommaert, J. (2005) *Discourse: A Critical Introduction*. Cambridge: Cambridge University Press.

Blommaert, J. and Verfaillie, K. (2009) 'Discoursanalyse', in T. Decorte and D. Zaitch (eds), *Kwalitatieve methoden en technieken in de criminologie*. Leuven and The Hague: Acco, pp. 311–38.

Blommaert, J., Corijn, E., Holthof, M. and Lesage, D. (2004) *Populisme*. Berchem: EPO.

Blommaert, J., Dewilde, A., Stuyck, K., Peleman, K. and Meert, H. (2003) 'Space, experience and authority: exploring attitudes towards refugee centers in Belgium', *Journal of Language and Politics*, 2(2): 311–31.

Blommaert, J., Beyens, K., Meert, H., Hillewaert, S., Verfaillie, K., Stuyck, K. and Dewilde, A. (2005) *Grenzen aan de solidariteit. Formele en informele patronen van solidariteit in het domein van migratie, huisvesting en veiligheid*. Ghent: Academia Press.

Blumer, H. (1948) 'Public opinion and public opinion polling', *American Sociological Review*, 13: 542–54.

Bottoms, A. (1995) 'The philosophy and politics of punishment and sentencing', in C. Clarkson and R. Morgan (eds), *The Politics of Sentencing Reform*. Oxford: Clarendon Press, pp. 17–49.

Bourdieu, P. (1979) 'Public opinion does not exist', in A. Mattelart and S. Siegelaub (eds), *Communication and Class Struggle. Vol. I: Capitalism, Imperialism*. New York: International General, pp. 124–30.

Corijn, E. (2004) 'Het populisme en de autoritaire verleiding', in J. Blommaert, E. Corijn, M. Holthof and D. Lesage, *Populisme*. Berchem: EPO, pp. 23–60.

Doble, J. (1987) 'Interpreting public opinion: five common fallacies', *Kettering Review*, 7–17.

Downes, D. and van Swaaningen, R. (2007) 'The road to dystopia? Changes in the penal climate in the Netherlands', in M. Tonry (ed.), *Crime and Justice: A Review of Research*, No. 35. Chicago: University of Chicago Press, pp. 31–71.

Fairclough, N. (1992) *Discourse and Social Change*. Cambridge: Polity Press.

Fairclough, N. (1995) *Critical Discourse Analysis: The Critical Study of Language*. New York: Longman.

Flanagan, T. J. (1996) 'Public opinion on crime and justice: history, development, and trends', in T. J. Flanagan and D. R. Longmire (eds), *Americans View Crime and Justice: A National Public Opinion Survey*. Thousand Oaks, CA: Sage, pp. 1–15.

Flanagan, T. J. (2003) *Public opinion, crime and justice: an American perspective'*, in S. Parmentier, G. Vervaeke, R. Doutrelepont and G. Kellens (eds), *Public Opinion and the Administration of Justice: Popular Perceptions and Their Implications for Policy-making in Western Countries*. Brussel: Politeia, pp. 15–32.

Freiberg, A. and Gelb, K. (eds) (2008) *Penal Populism, Sentencing Councils and Sentencing Policy*. Cullompton: Willan.

Garland, D. (2001) *The Culture of Control. Crime and Social Order in Contemporary Society*. Oxford: Oxford University Press.

Garland, D. and Sparks, R. (2000) 'Criminology, social theory and the challenge of our times', in D. Garland and R. Sparks (eds), *Criminology and Social Theory*. Oxford: Oxford University Press, pp. 1–22.

Glynn, C. J., Herbst, S., O'Keefe, G. J. and Shapiro, R. Y. (1999) *Public Opinion*. Oxford: Westview Press.

Hutton, N. (2005) 'Beyond populist punitiveness', *Punishment and Society*, 7(3): 243–58.

Jacobs, L. and Shapiro, R. (2000) *Politicians Don't Pander. Political Manipulation and the Loss of Democratic Responsiveness*. Chicago: University of Chicago Press.

Jaworski, A. and Coupland, N. (eds) (1999) *The Discourse Reader*. London: Routledge.

Katz, E. (1957) 'The two-step flow of communication: an up-to-date report on an hypothesis', *Public Opinion Quarterly*, 21: 61–78.

Katz, E. and Lazarsfeld, P. (1955) *Personal Influence: The Part Played by People in the Flow of Mass Communications.* Glencoe, IL: Free Press.

Kaukinen, C. and Colavecchia, S. (1999) 'Public perceptions of the courts: an examination of attitudes toward the treatment of victims and accused', *Canadian Journal of Criminology*, 41: 365–84.

Kress, G. and van Leeuwen, T. (1996) *Reading Images: The Grammar of Visual Design.* London: Routledge.

Latour, B. (1990) 'Drawing things together', in M. Lynch and S. Woolgar (eds), *Representation in Scientific Practice.* Cambridge, MA: MIT Press, pp. 19–68.

Lazarsfeld, P., Berelson, B. and Gaudet, H. (1944) *The People's Choice: How the Voter Makes Up His Mind in a Presidential Campaign.* New York: Duell, Sloan & Pearce.

Lippens, R. (2006) 'Crime, criminology, and epistemology: tribal considerations', in B. Arrigo and C. Williams (eds), *Philosophy, Crime, and Criminology.* Chicago: University of Illinois Press, pp. 138–80.

Lippens, R. (2007) 'Zwerven en assembleren. Eclecticisme en tribale identiteit onder criminologen', in T. Daems and L. Robert (eds), *Zygmunt Bauman. De schaduwzijde van de vloeibare moderniteit.* The Hague: Boom Juridische Uitgevers, pp. 175–90.

Longmire, D. R. (1996) 'Americans' attitudes about the ultimate weapon: capital punishment', in T. J. Flanagan and D. R. Longmire (eds), *Americans View Crime and Justice: A National Public Opinion Survey.* Thousand Oaks, CA: Sage, pp. 94–108.

Mary, P. (1997) 'Le travail d'intérêt général et la médiation pénale face à la crise de l'état social: dépolitisation du la question criminelle et pénalisation du social', in P. Mary (ed.), *Travail d'intérêt général et médiation pénale. Socialisation du pénal ou pénalisation du social?* Brussel: Bruylant, pp. 325–47.

Matthews, R. (2005) 'The myth of punitiveness', *Theoretical Criminology*, 9(2): 175–201.

Meert, H., Blommaert, J., Stuyck, K., Peleman, K. and Dewilde, A. (2004) *Van Balen tot Onthalen: De geografische en discursieve dimensies van attitudes tegenover asielzoekers.* Ghent: Academia Press.

Newburn, T. (1997) 'Youth, crime, and justice', in M. Maguire, R. Morgan and R. Reiner (eds), *The Oxford Handbook of Criminology.* Oxford: Oxford University Press, pp. 613–38.

Page, B. and Shapiro, R. (1992) *The Rational Public.* Chicago: University of Chicago Press.

Parmentier, S., Vervaeke, G., Goethals, J., Doutrelepont, R., Kellens, G., Lemaître, A., Cloet, B., Schoffelen, J., Vanderhallen, M., Biren, P., Sintobin, M., van Win, T. and Vandekeere, M. (2004) *Justitie doorgelicht. De resultaten van de eerste Belgische justitiebarometer.* Reeks: Actuele problemen met betrekking tot de sociale cohesie. Ghent: Academia Press.

Ponsaers, P. (2006) 'Weerstanden tegen de Veiligheidsmonitor of de mythe dat het beleid zich laat ondersteunen', *Orde van de Dag*, 29: 27–34.

Pratt, J. (2007) *Penal Populism.* Londen: Routledge.

Pratt, J., Brown, D., Brown, M., Hallsworth, S. and Morrison, W. (eds) (2005) *The New Punitiveness: Trends, Theories, Perspectives.* Cullompton: Willan.

Reynaert, H., Van de Walle, S. and Verlet, D. (2006) *Naar een DJ-Overheid? Burgers en hun overheid.* Brugge: Vanden Broele.

Roberts, J. V. and Hough, M. (eds) (2002) *Changing Attitudes to Punishment: Public Opinion, Crime and Justice.* Cullompton: Willan.

Roberts, J. V. and Hough, M. (2005) *Understanding Public Attitudes to Criminal Justice.* Maidenhead: Open University Press.

Roberts, J. V., Stalans, L. J., Indermauer, D. and Hough, M. (2003) *Penal Populism and Public Opinion.* Oxford: Oxford University Press.

Salas, D. (2005) *La volonté de punir. Essai sur le populisme pénal.* Parijs: Hachette.

Sellars, W. (1997) *Empiricism and the Philosophy of Mind.* Cambridge, MA: Harvard University Press.

Shiraev, E. and Sobel, R. (2006) *People and Their Opinions. Thinking Critically About Public Opinion.* New York: Pearson Longman.

Silverstein, M. and Urban, G. (eds) (1996) *Natural Histories of Discourse*. Chicago: University of Chicago Press.

Snacken, S. (2007) 'Penal policy and practice in Belgium', in M. Tonry (ed.), *Crime, Punishment and Politics in Comparative Perspective, Crime and Justice: A Review of Research*, No. 36. Chicago: University of Chicago Press, pp. 127–216.

Snacken, S. and Verfaillie, K. (2009) 'Media, "public opinion" and (criminological) research', in H. Eisendrath and J. P. Van Bendegem (eds), *It Takes Two to Do Science. The Puzzling Interactions Between Science and Society*. Brussels: VUB Press, pp. 159–82.

Snacken, S., Beyens, K. and Tubex, H. (1995) 'Changing prison populations in Western Countries: fate or policy?', *European Journal of Crime, Criminal Law and Criminal Justice*, 1: 18–53.

Snacken, S., Beyens, K., Tubex, H., Raes, A. and De Pauw, W. (2002) 'Bestraffing als maatschappelijke constructie', in M. Bouverne-De Bie, K. Kloeck, W. Meyvis, R. Roose and J. Vanacker (eds), *Handboek Forensisch Welzijnswerk*. Ghent: Academia Press, pp. 381–416.

Stalans, L. (2002) 'Measuring attitudes to sentencing', in J. V. Roberts and M. Hough (eds), *Changing Attitudes to Punishment: Public Opinion, Crime and Justice*. Cullompton: Willan, pp. 15–32.

Tonry, M. (1999) 'Rethinking unthinkable punishment policies in America', *UCLA Law Review*, 46: 1781–91.

Verfaillie, K. (2009) 'Punitieve behoeften, samenleving en publieke opinie', in I. Aertsen, K. Beyens, T. Daems and E. Maes (eds), *Hoe punitief is België?* Ghent: Maklu, pp. 85–106.

Verfaillie, K., Beyens, K., Blommaert, J., Meert, H. and Stuyck, K. (2007) 'De overlastmythe. Het geïnstitutionaliseerd onvermogen om constructief om te gaan met samenlevingsproblemen?', *Panopticon. Tijdschrift voor strafrecht, criminologie en forensisch welzijnswerk*, 28(3): 6–20.

Wacquant, L. (2004) *Punir les pauvres. Le nouveau gouvernement de l'insécurité sociale*. Marseille: Agone.

Watts, D. and Dodds, P. (2007) 'Influentials, networks, and public opinion formation', *Journal of Consumer Research*, 34: 441–58.

Weimann, G. (1982) 'On the importance of marginality: one more step into the two-step flow of communication', *American Sociological Review*, 47(6): 764–73.

Weimann, G. (1994) *The Influentials: People Who Influence People*. Albany, NY: State University of New York Press.

Weimann, G., Tustin, D. H., van Vuuren, D. and Joubert, J. P. R. (2007) 'Looking for opinion leaders: traditional vs. modern measures in traditional societies', *International Journal of Public Opinion Research*, 19(2): 173–90.

Weiss, G. and Wodak, W. (eds) (2002) *Critical Discourse Analysis Theory and Interdisciplinarity*. New York: Palgrave Macmillan.

Young, J. (1999) *The Exclusive Society: Social Exclusion, Crime and Difference in Late Modernity*. London: Sage Publications.

13

CONCLUSION: WHY AND HOW TO RESIST PUNITIVENESS IN EUROPE

Sonja Snacken

Punishment is a tragic institution (Garland 1990: 80)

We should always punish with a bad conscience. (Hudson 1996: 151)

This book has looked into the relations between levels of punitiveness and social policies, human rights and the influence of victims and public opinion in a democracy. Lower levels of punitiveness appear to be related to more social equality, a better protection of human rights for offenders and prisoners, a balanced approach to defending the rights and interests of victims and a correct understanding of the complexities and contextualization of opinions about crime and punishment formed by members of the public. I now want to turn these empirical findings into *normative arguments* for resisting and reducing punitiveness on the basis that each of these factors refers to fundamental values that are considered important in Europe (see also Snacken 2010).

We have argued in the Introduction to this book, together with other authors, that penal policies and their ensuing levels of punitiveness result from a complex interaction of different factors, are not determined by crime rates but are at least partly influenced by political decision-making (Rutherford 1984; Zimring and Hawkins 1991; Snacken *et al.* 1995; Snacken 2007; Goldson 2010). We also referred to the debate following David Garland's analysis of the relative importance of politicians in determining penal developments and policies and his contention that political decision-making must resonate with the political, public and professional cultures emerging in the same period (Garland 2001, 2004). This raises fundamental questions about the nature of that relationship, more particularly where practices of punishment in a democracy are concerned. I therefore want to turn to the specific characteristics of punishment in a democracy and to the importance of the distinction between 'constitutional' and 'populist' interpretations of democracy.

I will argue that the very nature of punishment requires specific guarantees that can only be offered by a 'constitutional' interpretation of democracy, which aims at the general interest and protects the rights of unpopular minorities against the 'tyranny of the majority' (de Toqueville 1835). I will also argue that social equality, human rights and a constitutional rather than a populist interpretation of democracy are part of the public, judicial and political cultures in Europe, which should enable policy-makers to foster moderate penal policies without losing legitimacy.

13.1. Punishment in a democratic constitutional state

Punishment imposed under the criminal law has often been defined as 'the conscious inflicting of pain' (Christie 1982: 4), 'the organized infliction of pain by the state upon an individual in response to that individual's criminal wrong-doing' (Loader 2010: 353) or 'the authorized imposition of deprivations – of freedom or privacy or other goods to which the person otherwise has a right, or the imposition of special burdens — because the person has been found guilty of some criminal violation, typically (though not invariably) involving harm to the innocent' (Bedau and Kelly 2010). Punishment hence is a *human* institution, in which a political authority has the *power* to impose certain pains, deprivations of rights or burdens on persons believed to have acted wrongly.

The emphasis on 'human' institution and on 'power' is important here. 'Democratic constitutional states' such as the European countries fundamentally aim to control and limit the power of humans over their fellow human beings. In order to achieve that aim, 'democratic constitutional states' are characterized by three core elements: the protection of human rights, respect for the rule of law and democracy. The protection of *human rights* is at the very core of the political construct of a democratic constitutional state. Human rights express the recognition of the power of the individual, drawing the limits and frontiers of the power of the state and of state intervention. In principle, the state is not allowed to encroach upon or to interfere with these rights. They work as a shield or a bulwark, protect individuals against excessive steering of their lives and entitle individuals to determine freely and autonomously their lives and choices and to participate in the political system (de Hert and Gutwirth 2004). The *rule of law* ('constitutionalism') guarantees that a democracy is also a *Rechtsstaat*. It expresses the idea that our societies are governed by rational and impersonal laws and not by arbitrary and/or emotional commands of humans. It limits the power of government through a system of imposed weighing, checking and balancing powers and subjects government and other state powers to a set of restricting constitutional rules and mechanisms. The rule of law hence provides for the principle of legality of government: public authorities are bound by their own rules and can only exercise their powers in accordance with the law. It implies that government is *accountable* and that its actions must be controllable and thus transparent. *Democracy* recognizes the people's sovereignty or self-determination and the principles of democratic representation. The only valid justification of power must be sought in the citizens' consent or will. This crucial link is expressed through the different variations upon the theme of the social contract (Beccaria, Locke, Rousseau). It is important to note that social contract theories can be invoked as legitimating very different forms of government: from a minimal liberal state (along the lines of Locke and Beccaria) to a more republican nation (along the lines of Rousseau and Kant). This might help us to understand differences not only between, respectively, Anglo-Saxon and continental European legal systems (Damaska 1986; Garapon and Papadopoulos 2003) but also between more 'populist' or more 'constitutional' interpretations of 'democracy', which can then be related to a differential approach to (populist) punitiveness.

While all western democratic constitutional states recognize these three principles, the balance between these varies over time and place. A democratic constitutional state aims at guaranteeing both and simultaneously a high level of individual freedom *and* a social order in which such freedom is made possible and guaranteed (Gutwirth 1998; De Hert and Gutwirth 2004). Criminality infringes the social order and the individual rights or 'dominion' of victims (Braithwaite and Pettit 1990; see Chapters 9–11 this volume) but punishment is probably the most interfering intervention by state authorities into the lives, fundamental rights and freedoms of suspects or convicted offenders (see Chapters 6–8 this volume). Penal policies and their levels of quantitative and qualitative punitiveness are therefore developed and decided within these tensions. While 'constitutional' democracies are characterized by the protection of the human rights of all citizens, including unpopular minorities such as offenders or immigrants, populist democracies seem to emphasize the importance of the will of the majority over the rights and interests of unpopular minorities. I have argued elsewhere (Snacken 2010) that this latter approach endangers the very concept of democracy. If a majority were to decide to exterminate an unpopular minority, that genocide would still be a crime against humanity, it would not become legitimate because it was decided by a majority. For illustration, the Third Reich was not a democracy because Hitler was elected in a democratic election; it was a totalitarian state because it flouted the most fundamental human rights of some (unpopular) minorities such as Jews, Freemasons, homosexuals and gypsies. Democracies therefore do not aim at the protection of the interests of a majority, but pursue the *general interest*. The rule of law or *Rechtstaat* is not limited to the majority but is applicable to all persons subjected to state power. And that includes offenders and prisoners and (legal or illegal) immigrants, who remain what Kelk (2000) called *rechtsburgers*. The concept of *rechtsburgerschap* literally means legal citizenship. However, it does not refer to citizenship of a national state in the narrow sense but to participation in the legal process. Kelk defines the essence of *rechtsburgerschap* as the ability to participate in legal matters and the possibility of claiming that legal principles and values must be applied to them in a discursive process where belief in the rationality of the arguments prevails. Such process must allow claims and counter-claims to be made before an independent decision-making authority

(Kelk 2000: 15). Moreover, a democratic constitutional state is characterized by pluralism and diversity, aptly described by Gutwirth (1998) as 'the polyphony of the democratic constitutional state'. There is no democratic constitutional state without a multitude of (individual) viewpoints, opinions, projects, behaviours, lifestyles and so on. Decision-making therefore requires a debate in which these diverging interests are openly discussed and where the policies resulting from these debates are framed in the general interest. Hence, systems of representation and accountability are of crucial importance, which again calls for transparency of public decision-making and policies. Expert opinion can be a factor of this accountability and legitimacy, as it can help to determine what the public or general interest entails and how effective policies are in achieving this general interest. In contrast, 'populism' refers to a 'not mediated, direct link between politicians and the public' (Blommaert *et al.* 2004: 10). Some of its core features are hostility to representative politics, authoritarianism, anti-elitism and mistrust of expert opinion (Taggart 2000). Populism is characterized by the negation of pluralism and the absence of democratic debate. Populist policies are pursued for purely electoral aims independent of their real effects on the general interest. 'Populist' penal policies are generally more punitive because politicians assume that this is what 'the public' wants, despite evidence that public attitudes towards punishment are ambivalent and dependent on the information received (Roberts *et al.* 2003; Verfaillie in Chapter 12 this volume). The danger of 'populist democracies' is therefore that the fundamental guarantees offered by the protection of human rights and the rule of law are made dependent of the will of a (real or supposed) majority.

13.2 'Constitutional democracy' and (moderate) penal policies in Europe

In principle, both the Council of Europe and the European Union stand for a 'constitutional' interpretation of democracy based on fundamental human rights and the rule of law. This is illustrated by their most recent basic texts, the Warsaw Declaration of 2005 for the Council of Europe and the Treaty of Lisbon which came into force on 1 December 2009 for the European Union.

Warsaw Declaration (2005):

> We, Heads of State and Government of the Member States of the Council of Europe, gathered in Warsaw on 16–17 May 2005 for our Third Summit, bear witness to unprecedented pan-European unity. Further progress in building a Europe without dividing lines must continue to be based on the common values embodied in the Statute of the Council of Europe: democracy, human rights, the rule of law.

> (In the Statute of the Council of Europe of 5 May 1949 the founding member states were 'Reaffirming their devotion to the spiritual and moral

values which are the common heritage of their peoples and the true source of individual freedom, political liberty and the rule of law, principles which form the basis of all genuine democracy.')

Treaty of Lisbon, Preamble (2009):

Drawing inspiration from the cultural, religious and humanist inheritance of Europe, from which have developed the universal values of the inviolable and inalienable rights of the human person, freedom, democracy, equality and the rule of law.

This 'constitutional' interpretation of the fundamental importance of human rights and the rule of law in a democracy is referred to as a core value that is part of the common heritage of the European peoples. This is confirmed at the judicial, political and public levels.

At the *judicial level*, the examples discussed in Chapters 6 to 8 (this volume) of the abolition of the death penalty and the strengthening of prisoners' civil and political rights by the ECtHR, but also by national Constitutional Courts in former communist countries such as Hungary, illustrate this concept of 'constitutional' democracy in which the human rights of offenders and the application of the rule of law are not left dependent on the whims of a temporary 'public opinion'.

At the *political level*, this emphasis on universal human rights was also made clear when central and eastern European countries wanted to join the Council of Europe (and eventually the EU) in the 1990s. Conditions for joining were the ratification of the European Convention of Human Rights (ECHR) and the acceptance of the individual complaint procedure before the ECtHR, the ratification of the European Convention for the Prevention of Torture and Inhuman and Degrading Treatment or Punishment (ECPT), an immediate moratorium on executions and the obligation to abolish the death penalty within two years. This indicates that at the political level, allegiance to human rights protection and the abolition of the death penalty were seen as essential values in a 'European identity' and preconditions for acquiring 'European' membership (Snacken 2006). All European states (except Belarus) have ratified the ECHR and are bound in international law to apply it. The jurisprudence of the Court has considerable prestige. Most European countries (though not the UK) have a monistic legal system, in which international binding conventions, such as the ECHR, have direct effect before the national courts (Snacken 2006). And although there are legal variations in the extent to which the national law is directly determined by the decisions of the ECtHR, in practice these decisions have a significant impact in all jurisdictions and not only in those countries whose laws or policies have been challenged in an individual case (van Zyl Smit and Snacken 2009: 365).

Europe's institutional stance towards the rights and interests of victims, analysed in Chapter 11 (this volume), also seems in line with such a constitutional approach, in which a better protection of these rights and interests is not pursued to the detriment of the rights and interests of offenders. Both the European Union (FD 15 March 2001 on the standing of victims in criminal proceedings) and the Council of Europe (e.g. European Convention on Compensation of Victims of Violent Crime, 1983; Rec(2006)8 on assistance to crime victims) have opted for a balanced approach, promoting mediation where possible and emphasizing the rights of victims to be treated with respect for their dignity, to provide and receive information, to receive medical, psychological and social assistance and support, to understand and be understood, to be protected at the various stages of the procedure and to receive compensation by the offender or by the state. While I agree with the dangers described in Chapters 9 and 10 (this volume) of a 'victimist society', the risks of secondary and tertiary victimization of crime victims by creating unrealistic expectations of the criminal justice system and of a resulting punitive outbidding, the European institutional response seems more in line with Ivo Aertsen's arguments in Chapter 11 (this volume) for a (non-punitive) participatory model rather than a (potentially more punitive) impact model.

But the picture of 'Europe' emerging from this book is more complex. The European Union has also been criticized for placing crime control over civil liberties in its elaboration of the Third Pillar on 'An Area of Freedom, Justice and Security' (Amsterdam Treaty, 1 May 1999), though not in a manner fitting into the 'new punitiveness' mould (Baker and Roberts 2005: 128). EU policies on immigration have resulted in a vast overrepresentation of foreigners and ethnic minorities in European prisons (Wacquant 2006), while counter-terrorism measures described as 'turbo-penalization' have been imposed on member states without much debate (Hosein 2005; see Chapter 6 this volume). The increased emphasis on the principle of mutual recognition of decisions as the cornerstone of judicial cooperation in civil and criminal matters (Tampere conclusions 1999) has led to several recent Council Framework Decisions aiming at facilitating the implementation of custodial and non-custodial sanctions in the country of origin of an offender: FD 2008/909/JHA of 27 November 2008 on custodial sanctions; FD 2008/947/JHA of 27 November 2008 on supervision of probation measures and alternative sanctions; FD 2009/829/JHA of 23 October 2009 on supervision measures as alternatives to provisional detention. These Framework Decisions send a mixed message as far as 'resisting punitiveness' is concerned. On the positive side, they claim 'to enhance the social rehabilitation of sentenced persons' (Article 9 of FD 2008/909), to 'enhance the right to liberty and the presumption of innocence' and 'to promote where appropriate the use of non-custodial measures' (Articles 3–4 of FD 2009/829). On the negative side, they refer to 'the overriding objective of protecting the general public' (FD 2009/829), they subordinate human rights concerns arising from unequal and often demeaning prison conditions throughout EU member states (see Chapter 6 this volume) to the principle of mutual recognition, they do not consistently foster the principle of subsidiarity of the prison sentence, they abolish the requirement of consent to the transfer by the offender[1] (FD 2008/909/JHA of 27 November 2008 on custodial sanctions) and they generally leave little room for sentenced persons to initiate transfers or to evaluate their prospects of reintegration (de Wree *et al.* 2009). Similarly, although the ECtHR has emphasized the importance of aiming at reintegration of offenders and has consistently recognized that punishment (and imprisonment in particular) entails inherent elements of humiliation, it has up to now failed to impose a strict principle of proportionality to national sentencing and parole policies and practices in Europe and to systematically foster inclusive rather than exclusionary penal sanctions and measures (Snacken 2006; van Zyl Smit and Snacken 2009; Chapter 6 this volume).

The fact that protection of human rights is also an important aspect of *public culture* in Europe is illustrated by the Special Eurobarometer 290 on the role of the European Union in Justice, Freedom and Security policy areas (2008). Seventy-two per cent of respondents support greater EU influence in the protection of fundamental rights. According to respondents, the promotion and protection of fundamental rights, including children's rights, should be among the three EU priorities (35 per cent) in the area of 'justice, freedom and security', just behind the fight against terrorism (50 per cent) and against organized crime (48 per cent). Although the question in the Eurobarometer relates to human rights in general and not to human rights for offenders or prisoners, the constitutional interpretation of democracy described above should result in the application of human rights to all *rechtsburgers*.

Returning to Garland's arguments concerning the necessary links between political decision-making and public, political and professional cultures, I would conclude that human rights are sufficiently part of these cultures in Europe to be used as a basis for moderate penal policies. European political and judicial institutions could and should go even further in that direction than is currently the case.

13.3 Social equality and (moderate) penal policies in Europe

In line with their earlier publications, David Downes (Chapter 2 this volume) and Tapio Lappi-Seppälä (Chapter 3 this volume) demonstrate the inverse correlations between prison rates and welfare investments/social equality in different European countries. The specific characteristics of the Scandinavian welfare model and its interactions with relatively moderate penal policies are further elaborated upon by Tapio Lappi-Seppälä (Chapter 3 this volume) and Stein Kuhnle (Chapter 4 this volume). David Downes' conclusion that 'a substantial welfare state is increasingly a principal, if not the main, protection against the resort to mass imprisonment in the era of globalization' raises the question whether other European countries and 'Europe' at the institutional level (Council of Europe, European Union) can learn from the Scandinavian experiences.

Investing more in social policies than in punitive measures seems at first sight a politically interesting option. Lappi-Seppälä shows in Chapter 3 that the Scandinavian countries, who have the lowest prison rates and highest welfare expenditures in Europe, enjoy the highest levels of public trust and political legitimacy and the lowest levels of fear of crime, contrary to the countries with the highest prison rates and lowest welfare expenditures, the UK and most Eastern European countries, who have the lowest levels of public trust and legitimacy and the highest level of fear. The high levels of trust and legitimacy are hence positively correlated with welfare investments and social equality but not with more punitive penal policies.

However, some authors have argued that the Scandinavian model is intrinsically linked to the typical characteristics and histories of the Scandinavian societies (Pratt 2008). Stein Kuhnle, on the contrary, argues in Chapter 4 (this volume) that the Scandinavian welfare states can and actually sometimes do serve as a positive model for other countries because they are successful in terms of values and objectives highly regarded by many: limited poverty, a relatively high degree of income equality and social stability.

13.3.1 What do we know about the importance of these values in Europe?

Fighting unemployment and social exclusion are apparently important concerns not only of Scandinavian but of most *European citizens*. The Standard Eurobarometer 71 of September 2009 shows that the three most important personal concerns of respondents in the EU were inflation (39 per cent), the economic situation (26 per cent) and unemployment (21 per cent). Crime ranked only eighth with 8 per cent and terrorism 13th out of 14 with 2 per cent (Eurobarometer 71: 22). Unemployment ranked first as the most important issue faced by their country (49 per cent), followed by the economic situation (42 per cent) and inflation (21 per cent) (Eurobarometer 71: 49). The most important measures to be taken by the EU in fighting the financial and economic crisis are support for small businesses (37 per cent), support for the unemployed (27 per cent), investment in education/research (26 per cent) and support for the poorest (20 per cent) (Eurobarometer 71: 209). Unemployment is seen as the most important social factor explaining poverty (Eurobarometer Survey 321 on Poverty and Social Exclusion, October 2009).

At the *European institutional* level, the importance of social rights, social inclusion and social equality is recognized – at least in legal texts and discourse – both by the Council of Europe through its European Social Charter (1961, revised 1996) and by the European Union through its Charter of Fundamental Human Rights (2000: Chapter IV on 'Solidarity', article 34: 'entitlement to social security benefits and social services providing protection in cases such as maternity, illness, industrial accidents, dependency or old age, and in the case of loss of employment, in accordance with the rules laid down by Community law and national laws and practices'). At the EU political level, 2010 was declared 'European Year for Combating Poverty and Social Exclusion' by joint decision of the European Parliament and the Council (European Parliament 2008) and a 'Renewed social agenda' for the EU was set out in 2008 by the European Commission. In this 'Renewed Social Agenda', *welfare, solidarity, social cohesion and social inclusion* are described as being an intrinsic part of the European identity (European Commission 2008: 3–4). However, compared with the European Convention on Human Rights, the protection offered by the European Social Charter seems much weaker: the monitoring is performed not by a court but by the European Committee for Social Rights and is based upon national reports by the member states. A collective complaint procedure was established in 1998, through which certain organizations of employers and employees may lodge a complaint with the European Committee for Social Rights, but this leads only to a report and to recommendations. At the level of the European Union, while both social and penal policy remain primarily the responsibility of the member states, the penal Europe seems to be developing much more swiftly than the social Europe. Despite the EU's rhetoric about fighting unemployment it is precisely the area in which it is perceived by European citizens as performing very poorly (3.9/10 average, Eurobarometer 71: 156), while its protection of social rights and ensuring economic growth score hardly better (4.8 and 4.6 respectively; Eurobarometer 71: 156). The European Social Fund (ESF), established in 1957 in order to help people find (better) jobs by improving their skills, will distribute some 75 billion euros to EU member states over the period 2007–13. But this represents only 10 per cent of the EU budget and two-thirds of respondents have never heard of the ESF (Special Eurobarometer 316, 'European employment and social policy', July 2009). Following Lappi-Seppälä's analysis on the correlation between social expenditures, political legitimacy and penal policies, one could argue that focusing more on social policy could foster penal moderation while at the same time reinforcing the legitimacy of both national and European (EU) institutions. On 17 December 2010, the date of the closing of the 'Year for Combating Poverty', the European Council (pressed by the Belgian Presidency) adopted the 'Final Declaration concerning the Year for Combating Poverty' and this was included in the fundamental strategic objectives of the European Union for the coming decade. However, it was acknowledged that 'much work remains to be done to translate these goals in tangible results' and that 'the coming years will not be easy, especially with the budget decisions to be made by the Member States' (EU Trio Belgium 2010).

The European Values Study (1999) equally describes solidarity as a 'typical European value', although the concern of respondents is higher with elderly, sick and disabled people and the unemployed than with immigrants. This may indicate a form of 'welfare state chauvinism' of Europeans (Coffé *et al.* 2007), eager to protect 'their' welfare against sharing with 'others' (cf. 'fortress Europe'). It reminds us of Mary and Nagels' demonstration in Chapter 5 that welfare investments in continental European countries increasingly go to healthcare and pensions, resulting in a higher risk of poverty for the unemployed (and for elderly women) and in the highest poverty and unemployment rates for the immigrant population (and primarily for non-EU nationals).

13.3.2 How do we then relate this (qualified) support for basic values such as social inclusion, social equality and solidarity to normative arguments for more moderate penal policies?

Empirical research consistently shows that punishment is divided unequally over social and ethnic lines. Prison populations in Europe are typically made up of young males coming from the lower socio-economic strata in society, and increasingly from an ethnic minority background (Dünkel and Snacken 2005; van Kalmthout *et al.* 2007). Research on sentencing and parole has shown over the last 30 years that, while ethnicity or unemployment in themselves may have only a marginal effect on decision-making compared with the seriousness of the offence and the criminal record, the combination of both characteristics is a much stronger predictor for the application of remand custody or sentencing to imprisonment (Jongman *et al.* 1978; Hood 1992; Beyens 2000; de Pauw 2000, 2010; for an overview, see Vanhamme and Beyens 2007). This results from a more negative prognosis by penal actors of socially vulnerable groups, who are seen as less well integrated and hence more at risk of delinquency or recidivism. Higher welfare investments should normally reduce social inequality and social vulnerability, hence reducing the number of people being sent to prison not because of the seriousness of their offence, but because they are seen as less well integrated. This would increase the 'fairness' of the criminal justice system (Hudson 1987; von Hirsch 1993). At the same time, higher welfare investments increase the possibilities of developing workable alternatives to imprisonment, as non-custodial sanctions and measures often require guidance and assistance from a range of social services in society.

Applying the same logic of constitutional democracies protecting unpopular minorities against the tyranny of the majority to the relationship between social equality and moderate penal policies would mean that politicians in Europe could and should build on the public support for fundamental values such as social inclusion, social equality and solidarity to legitimize moderate penal policies. They should apply these values not in the interest of a majority only, who may have increasing feelings of 'welfare chauvinism', but in the general interest which includes the interests of unpopular minorities such as immigrants or offenders.

13.4 To conclude

Criminality is a human act that infringes the social order and (often) the rights and well-being of victims. Punishment is a human institution through which humans have the power to impose deprivation or pain on offenders. Different forms and levels of punishment have a different impact on the social inclusion and the human rights of offenders. Penal policies are not directly related to crime rates, but are social constructions resulting from the interaction of many factors, including decision-making by policy-makers and practitioners. Penal moderation is related to higher levels of social equality, a stronger emphasis on human rights, a balanced approach to the interests of victims, offenders and society at large and a 'constitutional' rather than a 'populist' interpretation of democracy. In a 'constitutional democracy', the government must foster the general interest and protect the fundamental rights of unpopular minorities such as offenders, prisoners or immigrants from the 'tyranny of the majority'. In Europe, the abolition of the death penalty and the increased protection of prisoners' rights illustrate this approach. In a democracy, governments are accountable for their policies and must engage with the public in order to explain the reasons for their choices and to defend the values on which these policies are based. I have tried to demonstrate in this conclusion that penal moderation based on human rights and social inclusion is in accordance with some of those fundamental values cherished by many Europeans. In line with the abolition of the death penalty, 'Europe' therefore should and could do more to foster moderate penal policies.

Note

1. This consent was required under the Council of Europe's European Convention on the Transfer of Sentenced Persons of 1983, but had already been abandoned by the Additional Protocol of 1997 to this Convention in cases of sentenced persons subject to an expulsion or deportation order or who had fled from the sentencing state. In addition to these, consent is not required under the FD 2008/909/JHA of 27 November 2008 on custodial sanctions if an offender is transferred to a country where he 'lives', meaning 'the place to which that person is attached based on habitual residence and on elements such as family, social or professional ties'.

References

Baker, E. and Roberts, J. (2005) 'Globalization and the new punitiveness', in J. Pratt, D. Brown, M. Brown, S. Hallsworth and W. Morrison (eds), *The New Punitiveness: Trends, Theories, Perspectives*. Cullompton: Willan, pp. 121–38.

Bedau, H. A. and Kelly, E. (2010) 'Punishment', *The Stanford Encyclopedia of Philosophy*, Spring 2010 Edition, ed. Edward N. Zalta. Online at: http://plato.stanford.edu/archives/spr2010/entries/punishment/.

Beyens, K. (2000) *Straffen als sociale praktijk: Een penologisch onderzoek naar straftoemeting*. Brussels: VUB Press.

Blommaert, J., Corijn, E., Holthof, M. and Lesage, D. (2004) 'Wat goed is voor de pensen: de nieuwe recepten van het populisme', in J. Blommaert, E. Corijn, M. Holthof and D. Lesage (eds), *Populisme*. Berchem: EPO, pp. 7–22.

Braithwaite, J. and Pettit, P. (1990) *Not Just Deserts: A Republican Theory of Criminal Justice*. Oxford: Oxford University Press.

Christie, N. (1981) *Limits to Pain*. Oslo: Universitetsforlaget and New York: Columbia University Press.

Coffé, H., Heyndels, B. and Vermeir, J. (2007) 'Fertile grounds for extreme right-wing parties: explaining the Vlaams Blok's electoral success in Flemish municipal elections', *Electoral Studies*, 26: 142–55.

Damaska, M. R. (1986) *The Faces of Justice and State Authority: A Comparative Approach to the Legal Process*. New Haven, CT: Yale University Press.

De Hert, P. and Gutwirth, S. (2004) 'Rawls' political conception of rights and liberties: an unliberal but pragmatic approach to the problems of harmonisation and globalisation', in M. van Hoecke (ed.), *Epistemology and Methodology of Comparative Law*. Oxford and

Portland, OR: Hart, pp. 317–57.

De Pauw, W. (2000) *Migranten in de balans*. Brussels: VUB Press.

De Pauw, W. (2010) *Justitie onder invloed. Belgen en vreemdelingen voor de correctionele rechtbank in Brussel*. Brussels: VUB Press.

De Toqueville, A. (1956 [1835]) *Democracy in America*, ed. Richard D. Heffner. New York: Mentor Books.

De Wree, E., Vander Beken, T. and Vermeulen, G. (2009) 'The transfer of sentenced persons in Europe: much ado about reintegration', *Punishment and Society*, 11: 111–28.

Dünkel, F. and Snacken, S. (2005) *Prisons en Europe*. Paris: L'Harmattan.

EU Trio Belgium (2010) *Closing Session of the European Year of Combating Poverty*. Online at: http://www.eutrio.be/pressrelease/closing-session-european-year-combating-poverty (27 December 2010).

European Commission (2008) *Renewed Social Agenda: Opportunities, Access and Solidarity in 21st Century Europe*. Communication from the Commission to the European Parliament, the Council, the European Economic and Social Committee and the Committee of the Regions, 2 July, COM(2008)412 final.

European Parliament (2008) 'Decision No. 1098/2008/EC of the European Parliament and of the Council of 22 October 2008', *Official Journal of the European Union*, 7 November.

Garapon, A. and Papadopoulos, I. (2003) *Juger en Amérique et en France: Culture juridique et common law*. Paris: Odile Jacob.

Garland, D. (1990) *Punishment and Modern Society: A Study in Social Theory*. Oxford: Oxford University Press.

Garland, D. (2001) *The Culture of Control: Crime and Social Order in Contemporary Society*. Oxford: Oxford University Press.

Garland, D. (2004) 'Beyond the culture of control', *Critical Review of International Social and Political Philosophy*, 7(2) (Special issue on Garland's *The Culture of Control*): 160–89.

Goldson, B. (2010) 'The sleep of (criminological) reason: knowledge-policy rupture and New Labour's youth justice legacy', *Criminology and Criminal Justice*, 10: 137–54.

Gutwirth, S. (1998) 'De polyfonie van de democratische rechtsstaat', in M. Elchardus (ed.), *Wantrouwen en onbehagen*, Balans 14. Brussels: VUB Press, pp. 137–93.

Hood, R. (1992) *Race and Sentencing*. Oxford: Clarendon Press.

Hosein, G. (2005) *Threatening the Open Society: Comparing Anti-Terror Policies in the US and Europe*. London: Privacy International. Online at: http://www.privacyinternational.org/issues/terrorism/rpt/comparativeterrorreportdec2005.pdf.

Hudson, B. (1987) *Justice through Punishment? A Critique of the 'Justice' Model of Corrections*. London: Macmillan.

Hudson, B. (1996) *Understanding Justice. An Introduction to Ideas, Perspectives and Controversies in Modern Penal Theory*. Buckingham and Philadelphia: Open University Press.

Jongman, R. W., de Jong, J., Schilt, T., Smale, G. and Veendrink, L. (1978) *Klasse-elementen in de rechtsgang*. Groningen: Kriminologisch Instituut Groningen.

Kelk, C. (2008 [2000]) *Nederlands detentierecht*, 3rd edn. Deventer: Gouda Quint.

Loader, I. (2010) 'For penal moderation: notes towards a public philosophy of punishment', *Theoretical Criminology*, 14: 349–67.

Pratt, J. (2008) 'Scandinavian exceptionalism in an era of penal excess, Part I: The nature and roots of Scandinavian exceptionalism', 'Part II: Does Scandinavian exceptionalism have a future?", *British Journal of Criminology*, 48: 119–37; 275–92.

Roberts, J.V., Stalans, L. J., Indermauer, D. and Hough, M. (2003) *Penal Populism and Public Opinion: Lessons from Five Countries*. New York: Oxford University Press.

Rutherford, A. (1984) *Prisons and the Process of Justice: The Reductionist Challenge*. London: Heinemann.

Snacken, S. (2006) 'A reductionist penal policy and European human rights standards', *European Journal of Criminal Policy and Research*, 12: 143–64.

Snacken, S. (2007) 'Penal policy and practice in Belgium', in M. Tonry (ed.), Crime, Punishment and Politics in Comparative Perspective, in *Crime and Justice: A Review of Research*, Vol. 36. Chicago: University of Chicago Press, pp. 127–216.

Snacken, S. (2010) 'Resisting punitiveness in Europe?', *Theoretical Criminology*, 14: 273–92.

Snacken, S., Beyens, K. and Tubex, H. (1995) 'Changing prison populations in Western Countries: fate or policy?', *European Journal of Crime, Criminal Law and Criminal Justice*, 1: 18–53.

Taggart, P. (2000) *Populism*. Buckingham: Open University Press.

van Kalmthout, A. M., Hofstee-van der Meulen, F. B. A. M. and Dünkel, F. (eds) (2007) *Foreigners in European Prisons*. Nijmegen: Wolf Legal Publishers.

van Zyl Smit, D. and Snacken, S. (2009) *Principles of European Prison Law and Policy: Penology and Human Rights*. Oxford: Oxford University Press.

Vanhamme, F. and Beyens, K. (2007) 'La recherche en sentencing: un survol contextualisé. Actualités bibliographiques', *Déviance et Société*, 31(2): 199–228.

von Hirsch, A. (1993) *Censure and Sanctions*. Oxford: Oxford University Press.

Wacquant, L. (2006) 'Penalization, depolitization and racialization: on the overincarceration of immigrants in the European Union', in S. Armstrong and L. McAra (eds), *Perspectives on Punishment: The Contours of Control*. Oxford: Oxford University Press, pp. 83–100.

Zimring, F. E. and Hawkins, G. (1991) *The Scale of Imprisonment*, Studies in Crime and Justice. Chicago: University of Chicago Press.

INDEX

Added to a page number 'f' denotes a figure, 't' denotes a table and 'n' denotes a note.